The Second World War
Ambitions to Nemesis

Bradley Lightbody

Routledge
Taylor & Francis Group

LONDON AND NEW YORK

First published 2004
by Routledge
11 New Fetter Lane, London EC4P 4EE

Simultaneously published in the USA and Canada
by Routledge
29 West 35th Street, New York, NY 10001

Routledge is an imprint of the Taylor & Francis Group

Typeset in Galliard by
Florence Production Ltd, Stoodleigh, Devon
Printed and bound in Great Britain by
TJ International Ltd, Padstow, Cornwall

British Library Cataloguing in Publication Data
A catalogue record for this book is available from the British Library

Library of Congress Cataloging in Publication Data
Lightbody, Bradley.
   The Second World War : ambitions to nemesis/Bradley Lightbody. –
   1st ed.
       p. cm.
   Includes bibliographical references.
   1. World War, 1939–1945. I. Title: 2nd World War. II. Title.
   D743.L54 2004
   940.53 – dc22   2003025507

ISBN 0–415–22404–7 (hbk)
ISBN 0–415–22405–5 (pbk)

My immense thanks to Carol, Emma and Stuart for their patience, understanding, and the regular supply of coffee, during weekends taken up with research and writing.

Contents

Maps

Introduction

The Second World War was a war of ambitions and denials. The ambitions belonged to Germany, Japan and Italy. All three nations were determined to expand their national frontiers at the expense of neighbouring states. Hitler and Germany wished to dominate central Europe and to reduce Poland and the USSR to the status of vassal states. Hirohito and Japan sought dominion over China and South East Asia. Mussolini and Italy coveted the Balkans and the Mediterranean region in a planned revival of the glories of ancient Rome.

At first the League of Nations, primarily represented by Britain and France, attempted to moderate and to appease the different national ambitions. However, as the demands for expansion escalated appeasement was gradually replaced by denial. The result was a series of wars as Japan, Italy and Germany resorted to military force to secure their national ambitions.

Japan was the first nation to move beyond diplomacy to war with the annexation of Manchuria in September 1931, followed by the invasion of China in July 1937. Italy also defied world opinion with the invasion of Abyssinia in October 1935. Both wars were major acts of aggression, but they remained isolated regional conflicts. However, the German invasion of Poland in September 1939 triggered a chain of actions and alliances that ultimately engulfed six of the world's seven continents in war. In particular, in October 1940 Germany, Japan and Italy signed the Tripartite Pact and united as the 'Axis' powers with the shared ambition of a new world order. The result was global warfare.

The Second World War began at 4.45 a.m. on 1 September 1939 with the German invasion of Poland. Franz Honiok was the first recorded victim of the war. Honiok was a Polish prisoner who was murdered by the SS and dumped at the scene of a fake Polish attack on the German radio station at Gleiwitz on the Polish border. Several other border incidents were also staged by the SS, and a further twelve Polish prisoners, all unidentified, were murdered to create the pretext for invasion.

The Second World War finally ended at 11 p.m. on 14 September 1945 with the surrender of Japan. Italy had capitulated in 1943 and Germany was fought to a standstill in the ruins of Berlin in April 1945. The war cost the lives of approximately 55 million people, and many died in the most horrific of circumstances. It is impossible to name the last victim of the war because long after the war had ended many ex-prisoners and Holocaust survivors died from malnutrition and the injuries sustained during captivity. In Hiroshima and Nagasaki the radiation dose absorbed by the population from the detonation of two atomic bombs in August 1945 also continued to claim lives for decades after the end of the war.

The first theme of this book, 'Ambition', seeks to explain the aims of Japan, Italy and Germany and the different responses of the USSR, Britain, France and the USA as each nation manoeuvred for advantage.

The expansion of the war from a European war into a world war is the focus of the themes, 'Outbreak' and 'Advance' as Germany, Italy and Japan united to form the 'Axis' powers and launched a determined bid to establish a new world order. The involvement of the USSR in the dismemberment of Poland and later war against Finland is also examined in terms of Soviet policy before the Nazi invasion of June 1941 forced the USSR into alliance with the western powers.

The theme, 'Expansion' charts the success of the Axis powers as they significantly extended their territorial control and forced the Allied powers into retreat. There was not one war but a series of very different, overlapping wars fought in the Atlantic, the deserts of North Africa, the mountains of Scandinavia, the ice and snow of the Eastern Front, the jungles of the Far East, the islands of the Pacific, and the beaches, hedgerows and cities of western Europe. The expansion of the war was not only conventional but racial. In 1941 the Nazi war against the Jews of occupied Europe escalated into the Final Solution. The immediate opposition to the Axis expansion was from the resistance movements of the occupied territories and the intelligence services, and in particular the 'code-breakers'. Both groups made a significant contribution to the diversion of Axis military resources and the identification of enemy intentions to the benefit of the Allied cause throughout the war.

The gradual over-extension of the Axis powers is detailed in the theme, 'Containment' when the further expansion of the Axis powers was decisively curtailed at Midway, El Alamein and Stalingrad.

The failure of the Axis powers to achieve outright victory is the subject of the themes 'Contraction' and 'Rout' and details how military successes gave way to military reversals and, ultimately, retreat and defeat.

Finally, the theme 'Nemesis' examines the collapse of the Axis powers. Mussolini was captured by Italian partisans and summarily executed on 28 April 1945. Hitler committed suicide on 30 April 1945. Hirohito was controversially absolved of any responsibility for the war, and Prime Minister Tojo was blamed for leading Japan into war. Tojo attempted suicide but his life was saved by US army surgeons. However, it was only a temporary lease on life as he was found guilty of war crimes and hanged on 23 November 1948.

In the immediate post-war period, and with the onset of the Cold War, Hitler, Mussolini and Tojo were blamed for imposing personal dictatorships and personal ambitions upon reluctant nations.

The concluding section, 'Reconstruction', considers the cost of the war and the attempt to forge a new world of equal, democratic nations before the onset of the Cold War and the emergence of communism became the new battleground for liberalism.

Overall, this book provides a comprehensive overview of the global ambitions and the global warfare that was the Second World War. The nine themes identify the separate phases of the war and collectively chart the chronology of the war.

Read and reflect upon the immense social, economic and political impact of the Second World War. Finally, bear witness to the human cost of the most destructive war in world history.

Bradley Lightbody
October 2003

Ambition

1 Rising sun

Japan is ambitious, she is already a world power;
she aspires to be master of the Pacific.[1]
    William C Calhoun, US Attache in China

On 14 July 1919 a contingent of Japanese troops joined the victory parade down the Champs Élysées in celebration of the end of the Great War and the conclusion of the Treaty of Versailles. Japan signed the Treaty as a 'Principal Allied' nation in recognition of her status as a Great Power and acknowledged rank as the third naval power in the world after the USA and Great Britain. The display of international unity masked disagreement. Japan had defeated Germany in the Pacific and in return the Japanese army and nationalist opinion had expected to gain all Germany's colonial possessions in the Pacific and China. Instead, Japan encountered disquiet at Versailles at the scale of Japanese empire ambitions. Japan's contribution to the war had been relatively minor and amounted to the policing of the Pacific and the escort of troop convoys between Australia and the Mediterranean. Japan was also regarded as having taken advantage of the distraction of the Great War to extend her authority over China, marked by the presentation of the 21 Demands ultimatum to the Chinese government in January 1915. The demands collectively meant the subjugation of China's vast resources to Japanese economic interests. The 21 Demands were imposed without reference to western economic interests and provoked opposition to Japan's empire ambitions. The new climate of international co-operation arising from President Wilson's fourteen-point peace proposals of January 1918, and the formation of the League of Nations, also conflicted with Japan's empire aspirations. The League renounced empire and affirmed the principle of self-determination and free unfettered trade between all nations. The future envisaged was a world community of equal nations and an end to empire and the Great Power rivalry that many blamed for the outbreak of the Great War.

Japan had no choice but to be satisfied with mandate authority over all Germany's colonies in the Pacific, north of the equator. Germany's colonies south of the equator were allocated as mandates to Australia and New Zealand after both nations objected to the advance of Japan into the South Seas. Similarly, a long-term lease, rather than empire acquisition, answered the Japanese claim to Shantung province in China. The Japanese army protested at the denial of territory won in war. Shantung province was occupied following the defeat of the German garrison in the port of Tsing Tau (Kiao-Chow) on 6 November 1914 in Japan's only significant military engagement of the war. The Chinese people were equally outraged, but in their case by the denial of complete independence. Riots and a boycott of Japanese goods greeted the decision in China's major cities on 4 May 1919. The European powers also firmly invited Japan to withdraw from Siberia, occupied by Japan in the aftermath of the Russian Revolution, and to relax the 21 Demands imposed upon China in 1915. The Japanese Army reluctantly withdrew from Siberia in 1922 and from northern Sakhalin in 1925.

Mochizuki Kotaro, a journalist and member of the Japanese Diet, declared 'Our empire has lost everything and gained nothing'.[2] Versailles produced a deep sense of injustice, and this was compounded by the refusal of the League of Nations to accept a Japanese amendment to the Charter of the League of Nations outlawing racial discrimination. Australia in particular vehemently opposed racial equality and maintained a 'whites only' immigration policy. Many Japanese were stung by the rejection and identified with the nationalist sentiment that despite matching the West in economic and military strength, and conforming to western mores, they would never be accepted as equals. The renewal of the pre-war British and French empires in the Pacific also exhibited a double standard, to the anger of Japanese nationalists.

However, the immediate post-war prosperity promoted public confidence in the government and deprived the nationalists of any significant constituency. Prime Minister Hara Takashi and Foreign Minister Shidehara Kijuro were also in a position to dismiss the nationalist focus on empire, given the substantial tilt in the balance of world power to Japan's advantage. The Great War had devastated European trade and industry leaving the USA and Japan as the dominant world industrial powers. Japan's pre-war rivals in the Pacific, Germany and Russia, had not survived the war. Germany was defeated and disarmed and Russia had collapsed into revolution and civil war. Britain was a victor, but the cost of the war had saddled Britain with a national debt of £6.6 billion compared to £400 million in 1914 and, coupled with the loss of international trade, an economy in sharp decline. Japan had no need to pursue military conquest with all of its attendant risks when economic hegemony and co-operation with the West promised to deliver primacy in the Pacific.

The seal on the new 'internationalism' was set at the Washington conference in November 1921, with the Nine Power Agreement of February 1922. In Washington the four Pacific powers – the USA, Britain, France and Japan – negotiated a settlement of their respective interests in the Pacific. A related naval agreement established a ratio for capital ships of USA: five, Great Britain: five, and Japan: three. The Japanese Navy presented a counter proposal of 'ten–ten–seven' but finally accepted the lower ratio after a commitment from USA and Great Britain that neither would build any further naval bases closer to Japan than Hawaii and Singapore respectively. In operational terms this amounted to a declaration of the western Pacific as Japanese waters. The only lamented part of the agreement was the end of the Anglo-Japanese Naval Agreement and the end of a naval partnership dating back to 1902. The Nine Power Treaty of 1922 proposed co-operation between all of the nations with economic interests in China – namely, the USA, Japan, Great Britain, France, Italy, Belgium, the Netherlands, Portugal and China. The outcome was a commitment to equal trading rights and the goal of full independence for China. In effect this repealed Japan's 21 Demands imposed in 1915 and, acting in the spirit of the agreement, Japan offered an immediate withdrawal from Shantung province.

To Japanese nationalists it all amounted to a loss of prestige, submission to American and British demands and acceptance of a secondary position in the Pacific. The depth of nationalist anger was dramatically expressed. First, in November 1921, Prime Minister Hara Takashi was killed at Shimbashi railway station, Tokyo, by an assassin who condemned the betrayal of Japan. Second, in March 1922, a member of the Black Dragon nationalist movement committed suicide in front of the imperial palace, Tokyo, in protest at the liberal and western habits of the 21-year-old Crown Prince Hirohito. The Crown Prince was a disappointment to nationalists because he was a noted anglophile who reputedly enjoyed a full English breakfast, played golf and spent all of his spare time in the academic pursuit of marine biology. He also offended Shinto beliefs by questioning his divinity and the Shinto spiritualism of *Kokutai* that upheld the Japanese people as the descendants of Gods. Hirohito was not the martial leader that nationalists craved and despite the legendary obedience to the emperor, inculcated at every level of Japanese society, he later became the target of assassination plots.

The nationalists were a minority but they were strongly represented in the junior officer ranks of the army and their common demand was empire. The enchantment with the West that had dominated pre-war Japan, expressed as *datsu-A nyu-O* (meaning 'leaving Asia' and 'entering Europe'), was increasingly reversed to *nyu-A datsu-O* (the 're-entry to Asia' and the 'abandonment of Europe'). Traditional Japanese culture was revived and the government and education system was urged to reflect and uphold Japanese values. Leaders who offended were deemed to be unworthy. A total of six Japanese prime ministers were assassinated between 1912 and 1941 for 'failing' Japan. Political opinion polarised in the late 1920s between those who endorsed the extension of western-style democracy and the new internationalism, and those who endorsed *Kodo-Ha* – literally the imperial way and interpreted as a revival of Japan's martial past and the fulfilment of a divine destiny to assume leadership over Asia. Kita Ikki, the nationalist writer, actively promoted the vision of a Japanese empire in Asia in his book, *Reconstruction of Japan*, published in 1919. It was the closest Japanese nationalists came to articulating a vision of the future, but ultimately Japanese nationalism failed to produce a single charismatic leader like Mussolini or Hitler. There was no coherent challenge to the government but rather spasmodic outbreaks of defiance from the army and, by selective assassination, a progressive usurpation of power.

The chief exponent of the new internationalism was Foreign Minister Shidehara Kijuro, and at first under his influence and that of the dominant liberal Minseito Party Japan subscribed to the Washington system. President Roosevelt felt able to remark in 1923 that the USA and Japan, 'have not a single valid reason and won't have as far as we can look ahead for fighting each other'.[3] This confidence reflected a Japan that had reduced its military budget by 25 per cent and in 1925 enacted universal male suffrage for those over 25 years old, increasing the electorate from 3 million to 13 million. Confidence was further increased with the accession to the throne of Emperor Hirohito, following the death of Emperor Taisho on 25 December 1925. Hirohito announced a new imperial era of *Showa*, interpreted as a time of enlightenment and peace, and declared, 'friendship to all nations of the Earth'.[4]

China, however, continued to be the focus of Japanese hostility rather than friendship. The Guomindang government of China under the leadership of Jiang Jieshi was increasingly stamping its authority on China by suppressing local warlords and winning a civil war against Mao Zedong's communist forces. His success created tension because the existence of disorder rather than order legitimised the need for the Japanese Army in Manchuria to protect Japanese industry. The Kwantung Army (the Japanese Army based in Kwantung, Manchuria) pressed for the immediate annexation of the province of Manchuria, but Foreign Minister Shidehara refused. Instead, in January 1927, he restated the Nine Power Agreement on China and upheld the goal of eventual Chinese sovereignty. This goal was bitterly questioned by the Kwantung Army and produced an acrimonious challenge that contributed to the collapse of Prime Minister Wakatsuki's government and the removal from office of Foreign Minister Shidehara, who upheld the Washington system. The new government under Prime Minister Tanaka Giichi (1927–29) subsequently authorised three military interventions in Manchuria to challenge and contain the advances of the Guomindang Army. Giichi also colluded in a cover-up of the the assassination of the Chinese warlord Chang Tso Lin by the Kwantung Army on 4 June 1928 – but it was a step too far. The emperor, in a rare exercise of imperial authority, censured the Kwantung Army and invited Giichi to resign. A new liberal government under Prime Minister Yuko Hamaguchi was appointed, but his administration ended abruptly when Hamaguchi was shot at Tokyo railway station on 14 November 1930. Hamaguchi later died of his wounds, while the assassin was praised in the national press as a patriot acting in the best interests of Japan. It illustrated the growing public ambition for empire expansion in China and ultimately constrained the emperor in later years. The mounting public disillusionment with politicians increased sharply after the Wall Street Crash of 24 October 1929 and further boosted support for military leadership. The world-wide slump in trade hit Japanese exports and resulted in high unemployment and widespread financial hardship. There was intense poverty in the Japanese countryside when the silk industry that most peasants relied upon to boost their basic incomes collapsed. The Wall Street Crash highlighted Japan's vulnerability to international trade and gave credence to the military demand for empire expansion and self-sufficiency in natural resources.

The Kwantung Army became increasingly mutinous at the lack of any government action to secure Manchuria for the nation. Dissatisfaction, and the desire for a military coup, was expressed through the formation of the *Sakurakai* (Cherry Blossom) society in 1930. The short-lived beauty of the Cherry Blossom is still a revered symbol of life and death in modern-day Japan – and particularly the sacrifice of life for a noble cause. During the Second World War it was consequently adopted as the badge of the Kamikaze. The army believed that the civilian government had failed Japan, and in March 1931 army officers in Tokyo plotted to seize the Diet and declare a military government under the leadership of General Ugaki. The plot was called off when the General Staff vetoed the plan and instead secretly endorsed a plan for an 'incident' in Manchuria to force the government's hand. On 18 September 1931 a bomb attack on the Japanese-controlled Manchurian railway line destroyed a section of the track five miles north of Mukden. The attack was attributed to Chinese saboteurs and in response the Kwantung Army attacked and occupied Mukden and launched an all-out attack on the Chinese Army in Manchuria. By November 1931 the whole of Manchuria was under direct military occupation. Ostensibly it was a spontaneous act, but the Kwantung Army acted with the connivance of the General Staff in Tokyo to the point that direct orders from Prime Minister Wakatsuki and Emperor Hirohito forbidding any further military action were suppressed. Wakatsuki and Hirohito subsequently failed to enforce their authority over the army due to popular demonstrations, press reports and cinema newsreels, all of which celebrated the bravery of the Japanese Army. The fear of assassination was also very real. Wakatsuki resigned as prime minister in December 1931, but his successor, Prime Minister Inukai Tsuyoshi, was murdered by army officers in his own office on 15 May 1932 when he promised to restrict military authority and strengthen parliamentary democracy. The assassins defended their actions as patriots and received minor prison sentences. Leading members of the Shempeitai, Japan's secret police, were later arrested in July 1933 following evidence of a plot to assassinate the emperor.

The Kwantung Army posed a challenge, not just to democracy in Japan but to the League of Nations and the Nine Power Agreement of 1922. The attitude of Washington was important to this first breach of the post-war accords and the Kellogg–Briand Pact of 1928 which outlawed war. China was a member of the League and invoked the League Charter, but the European powers were reluctant to act. A.J.P Taylor noted that 'the Japanese had a good case'.[5] There was a reservoir of support for Japan in recognition of Japan's investments in Manchuria, dating back to 1905, and the lawless nature of China. A strong Japan was also welcomed by the West as a block to Soviet expansion in the north Pacific. However, the opportunity to resolve the matter as a limited 'police action' was removed by the clumsy brutality of the Kwantung Army. In March 1932 the army and navy launched a sustained attack on Shanghai, including indiscriminate aerial bombing in full view of the western diplomatic community and press. The fighting also intensified across Manchuria in contradiction of the government's claim that the army was returning to barracks. The League was forced to act, but after a lengthy enquiry by Lord Lytton, Japan, much to China's disappointment, was merely censured in March 1933. Japan nevertheless withdrew from the League in protest and placed itself at odds with the western powers. The USA, France and Britain eschewed military or economic sanctions because of the weakness of their naval forces in the Pacific and the domestic pre-occupation with high unemployment. In March 1932, in an attempt to legitimise its actions, Japan declared Manchuria to be a new independent state under Japanese protection. The last emperor of China, 26-year-old Pu Yi, was installed as a puppet ruler and Manchuria was renamed Manchuko. The major casualty was the new post-war internationalism, and, without decisive action to uphold international law, the world slipped back to the familiar territory of national interest and *realpolitik*. The lesson was not lost on Mussolini and Hitler in later years.

After 1931 the army increasingly exerted its influence over government. Admiral Saito was appointed prime minister in May 1932, but the real authority in the self-proclaimed government of 'national unity' lay with War Minister General Araki Sadao. The cult of *bushido,* the 'way of the warrior', was encouraged and in a further link with Japan's martial past all army officers were issued with a Samurai sword. However, there was no consensus on future aims or policy beyond a general emotional desire for expansion and empire. The nationalists were riven by factions.

On 26 February 1936 tensions within the military between the *Kodo-ha* faction and the *Toeis-ha* group sprang into the open. The latter favoured war with the USSR and expansion into Siberia to regain the territory lost at Versailles, whereas the former saw the future as expansion in China and the South. The *Kodo-ha* rebels seized and occupied government buildings in central Tokyo and murdered leading liberal enemies. The coup was ended on 29 February when Emperor Hirohito issued a direct order to the General Staff to use military force to end the rebellion. In contrast to the lenient treatment of the rebels in May 1932, thirteen officers were executed by firing squad and 25 per cent of senior officers were demoted. Four civilians linked to the plot were also executed, including the author Kita Ikki. Hirohito imposed his authority, but his action did not herald an end to the empire ambitions of the military; rather, it handed direction to the *Toeis-ha* group. Hirohito remained a prisoner of the army that murdered every liberal prime minister he appointed.

Attempts were made in August 1936 to define the national foreign policy as an expansion to the south and the containment of the USSR in the north. To this end the government signed the Anti-Comintern Pact with Germany and Italy in November 1936, and expressed a desire for an alliance with Jiang Jieshi to further intimidate the USSR. But the actions of the Kwantung Army once again dictated policy. On 7 July 1937, following a brief skirmish at the Marco Polo bridge near Peking, the Kwantung Army opened fire on the Chinese Army. Orders for a cease-fire were ignored and the government, in crisis session, attempted to negotiate a solution. The reluctance to escalate the conflict was evident when the government refused four requests for rein-forcements before three divisions were finally despatched to China on 27 July 1937. There was no declaration of war by either side, but by mid-August a full-scale war engulfed China. The Kwantung Army was confident of victory within three months. But after fifteen months of intense warfare only the major cities and seaboard had been secured. The Chinese countryside remained a continuous battleground of guerrilla warfare. Jiang Jieshi rejected all offers of negotiation from Japan and formed a 'united front' with Mao Zedong's communist forces to resist the Japanese invasion.

He was aided by the brutality of the Japanese Army in China, which ultimately ended any possibility of a diplomatic settlement to the war. Japanese atrocities in China breached every ethical code of warfare and branded the Japanese as brutal oppressors rather than the propaganda image of liberators from western imperialism. The descent into barbarism was marked most of all by the 'Rape of Nanking' after the occupation of the capital city of Nanking on 12 December 1937. The scale of the atrocities is still denied in modern-day Japan and there was nationalist protest in 1993 when Prime Minister Morihiro Hosokawa issued a statement regretting a 'war of aggression'. The reality of the 'aggression' for the citizens of Nanking was six weeks of mass murder. The official death toll published by the War Crimes Commission in 1948 was 260,000 killed, but more recent studies estimate that 340,000 unarmed civilians were shot, bayoneted or bludgeoned to death. One of the most disturbing aspects was the system-atic gang rape of virtually every woman encountered by the Kwantung Army from young child to pensioner. The details are so frequently refuted as fabrication that it is perhaps necessary to quote at length the words of one remorseful Japanese veteran, Nagatomi Kakudo:

> Few know that soldiers impaled babies on bayonets and tossed them alive into pots of boiling water, they gang raped women from the ages of twelve to eighty and then killed them when they could no longer satisfy sexual requirements. I beheaded people, starved them to death, burned them, and buried them alive, over two hundred in all. It is terrible that I could turn into an animal and do these things.[6]

The atrocities were also confirmed at the time by eye-witness testimonies, photographs and newsreel pictures smuggled out of China and published in the western press during 1938 to 1939. The deliberate strafing and sinking of the US gunboat *Panay* by the Japanese Air Force during the battle for Nanking further harmed relations with the

United States. President Roosevelt demanded and received a prompt apology and compensation, but in private he condemned Japan as a 'bandit' nation.

The invasion of China left Japan without a clear policy, or allies, and barely in control of its own army. The behaviour of the Kwantung Army prevented any consideration of an appeasement dialogue with a nation that was clearly guilty of war crimes. The only advantage was the absence of an intervention by the western powers. The USA remained locked into 'isolationism'. In 1937 the US Senate extended the 1936 Neutrality Act into a comprehensive ban on any intervention in foreign disputes or wars. The US public regarded European politics as rooted in endless squabbles over empire expansion and they had no wish to become embroiled in wars for territory by one side or the other. Britain's investments in China were ten times greater than those of the United States; consequently the United States was wary of finding herself at war to defend Britain's trade and empire interests in the Pacific. Japan, however, had little to fear from Britain and France because they were fully occupied by the possibility of war with Germany and Italy. The USSR was the power best placed to curb Japan, and at first border skirmishes in Mongolia between Japanese forces and the Soviet Army at Changkufeng in July 1938 raised the possibility of a major war. Prime Minister Konoye (1937–39) attempted to salvage Japan's foreign policy and to identify a way forward for Japan. In a speech on 3 November 1938 he proclaimed a 'new order' in the East and endorsed the nationalist vision of a Japanese empire, but his speech promoted division rather than unity. Konoye resigned on 4 January 1939, leaving Japan's foreign policy in disarray. Confusion was the hallmark of Japan's foreign policy, and in the ten years from 1931 to 1941 twelve prime ministers had tried and failed to find a formula to satiate the nationalist ambition for empire.

The apparent weakness of Britain and France in the face of Hitler's demands from 1938 to 1939 encouraged Japanese nationalists to press for expansion, confident that neither power had the military capacity to intervene. Japan observed the weakness of Britain at first hand in June 1939 when the Kwantung Army blockaded the British Legation at Tientsin in northern China. The Japanese insisted on the right to enter the Legation to arrest Chinese citizens suspected of guerrilla activity, and ultimately Britain was forced to yield. For Japanese nationalists the only question was whether to expand into the south Pacific at the expense of Britain and France or whether to expand north across the Manchurian border into Siberia at the expense of the USSR. In both cases Germany's future actions were the key, and Japan watched and waited for opportunities to exploit as Hitler accelerated the Polish crisis towards war.

References

1. Richard Overy and Andrew Wheatcroft, *The Road to War*, Macmillan, 1989, p. 228.
2. Peter Duus (ed.), *The Cambridge History of Japan, Volume Six: The Twentieth Century*, Cambridge University Press, 1988, p. 283.
3. William Carr, *Poland to Pearl Harbor: The Making of the Second World War*, Edward Arnold, 1985, p. 27.
4. Edwin P. Hoyt, *Hirohito: The Emperor and the Man*, Praeger, 1992, p. 54.
5. A.J.P. Taylor, *The Origins of the Second World War*, Penguin, 1961, p. 90.
6. Iris Chang, *The Rape of Nanking*, Penguin, 1998, p. 59.

2   Weimar revision

The first task of German policy . . . is the liberation
of German soil from any occupying force.
We must get the stranglehold off our neck.[1]
                Chancellor Stresemann, 7 September 1925

On 28 April 1919, a chartered train left Berlin for Paris carrying a 160-member government delegation to the Paris peace talks led by the foreign minister of Germany, Count
Ulrich von Brockdorff-Rantzau. The delegation was accommodated in the Hotel des
Reservoirs, the same hotel that Bismarck had allocated to the representatives of France
after their defeat in the Franco-Prussian war of 1870–71. The reversal of fortunes
did not end there. On 7 May 1919 the German delegation was received in the
Hall of Mirrors, Palace of Versailles, to be presented with the Treaty of Versailles: the
earlier triumphant scene of the proclamation of the German empire in 1871. Count
Brockdorff-Rantzau was highly nervous, and in a hesitant speech he declared Germany's
objection to the 200-page, 440-article, 75,000-word Treaty of Versailles. The Germans
had travelled to Paris expecting to participate in the negotiation of a peace treaty based
on President Wilson's fourteen-point peace plan of January 1918, but instead they
were directed to sign and accept a treaty of punishment. Article 231 of the treaty held
Germany solely responsible for the outbreak of the Great War, and from this premise
Germany was the 'prisoner in the dock' rather than an equal in a conference chamber.
The Speaker of the Reichstag referred to the treaty as, 'the continuation of the war
by other means',[2] and the chancellor, Philipp Scheidemann, resigned from office rather
than sign it. Versailles was condemned in Germany as a diktat and finally signed, under
protest and threat of occupation, in the Hall of Mirrors at 2.45 p.m. on 28 June
1919. As the ink dried, the boom of cannon-fire from the nearby Mont Saint-Cyr
battery signalled both victory and revanchism over Germany. It was also the starting
pistol for the challenge that led directly to the outbreak of the Second World War.
    The Treaty of Versailles was a palpable shock to all Germans because neither the
government nor the military had shared with the general public the reality of Germany's
military collapse, let alone raised any question marks over Germany's war aims. Most
Germans believed that they had fought a defensive war and assumed that the armistice
was not surrender but a military stalemate to be followed by a negotiated peace
settlement between equal nations. Within governing circles there was a more realistic
assessment of Germany's position, but there was an assumption that the abdication of
the kaiser and the movement to democracy would soften the Allied attitude. It was a
forlorn hope. Prime Minister Clemenceau of France, embittered by the devastation of
northern France, demanded retribution and proposed to weaken Germany permanently
by creating a separate Rhineland State. In contrast, Prime Minister Lloyd-George of
Great Britain argued against a punitive treaty and was alert to the dangers of stirring
future German hostility. In the Fontainbleau memorandum, written on 25 March 1919,
he warned against the imposition of territorial changes on Germany with the words,
'I cannot conceive of any greater cause of future war.'[3] President Wilson of the USA
equally urged moderation and for a firm but fair settlement based on his fourteen-

point peace plan, but his efforts were derided by Clemenceau who complained that even God only had Ten Commandments. Public opinion in France and Great Britain was virulently anti-German. Ultimately this and the defiant manner and the apparent lack of contrition displayed by the German military delegation persuaded Wilson and Lloyd-George to side with retribution rather than simple restitution. Germany was ultimately given no choice and only 24 hours to accept a range of controversial sanctions in relation to territory, disarmament and reparations.

The territorial changes were perhaps the most emotive for Germany and formed the core of Hitler's later challenge. The return of Alsace-Lorraine to France, annexed by Germany in 1871, was expected – but not the redrawing of all Germany's principal borders. Germany lost territory to Belgium, Denmark, Poland, Czechoslovakia and Lithuania. Resented most of all was the award of Posen and West Prussia to Poland and the creation of the Polish Corridor across German territory to the Baltic Sea, thereby dividing Danzig and East Prussia from the rest of Germany. A potential territorial gain, union with Austria, was barred by Article 80 of the Treaty to avoid strengthening Germany. Overall, Germany lost approximately 13 per cent of her national territory and some 6 million citizens to the border revisions. All overseas empire was also removed. Germany's loss of sovereignty was underscored by the appearance of Allied military checkpoints on the Rhine bridges following the declaration of the Rhineland as a demilitarised zone. This was a measure insisted upon by Clemenceau to act as a tripwire against any future German hostility.

The disarmament clauses of Versailles were designed to dismantle the Imperial Army and to remove Germany's war-making capacity. The Allies forced the closure of the General Staff headquarters and the cadet schools that trained the elite Prussian officer corps, and restricted the new German army, the Reichswehr, to an 'internal policing' role. Commensurate with this domestic peacekeeping function the army was restricted to 96,000 soldiers and 4,000 officers, with a ban on heavy weapons or tanks. No air force was permitted and the navy was beset with tight restrictions on the size, armament and number of ships, along with a total ban on submarines. The future of the kaiser's powerful navy was settled when in a final act of defiance on 21 June 1919, Vice-Admiral Ludwig von Reuter ordered the German fleet, interned in Scapa Flow, to be scuttled. Within an hour, all seventy-four ships, the powerful symbol of Germany's pre-war *Weltpolitik,* went to the bottom.

The economic sanctions were far-reaching, taking into account all direct and indirect costs of the war including lost livestock and the cost of widows' and disability pensions. The calculation of reparations was devolved to the Allied Control Commission, and in April 1921 Germany was presented with a demand for 132 billion gold marks or approximately £6.6 billion. Not only Germany protested. The economist Maynard Keynes resigned from the Allied commission and in an influential treatise, *The Economic Consequences of the Peace*, published in 1920, he warned that the reparations were short-sighted because a healthy German economy was central to a healthy European economy. The burden of reparations later became a popular explanation for all Germany's economic ills – but in effect the reparations were never fully applied. The main burden on the recovery of the German economy was the unlimited wartime spending that had raised the national debt from 5,000 million marks in 1913 to 144,000 million marks by 1919.

The significance of Versailles was the impasse it created between Germany and Europe. It also provoked considerable opposition in the USA and a Senate veto on US involvement in the League of Nations for fear of the subordination of US forces and policy to the League. The result was the withdrawal of the USA from European affairs into neutrality and 'isolationism' and the loss of a powerful arbitrator. However, the US did intervene during the period 1924–29 to ease Germany's reparation payments and to underwrite the recovery of the European economy with cheap loans. How far Versailles was too harsh remains a matter of historical debate, but into the scales must go Germany's treatment of defeated France in the Treaty of Frankfurt, 1871, the plans of Chancellor Bethman-Hollwegg for the subjugation of Europe in the September Programme of 1914, and the Treaty of Brest-Litovsk imposed on defeated Russia in March 1918. In 1919 the Allies, in defending the Treaty of Versailles, were in no doubt that a German victory would have resulted in a German continent.

The years 1919–23 marked a violent transition from *Kaiserreich* to democratic state. The declaration of democratic republic by the majority Social Democratic party in the Reichstag (Sozialdemokratische Partei Deutschlands or SDP) was bitterly opposed by both left-wing and right-wing forces. The first priority of the leader of the SDP, Friedrich Ebert, was survival. Berlin was in the grip of bands of revolutionary soldiers and sailors and the communist Spartakist League was openly threatening revolution with the aim of a workers' state on the Bolshevik model. Ebert entered into a Faustian pact with the Reichswehr and gained the promise of military support in return for a commitment to respect the independence of the Reichswehr. The deal subsequently allowed the army High Command to escape any critical assessment of its strategy and responsibility for the outbreak of the Great War. The kaiser's aristocracy, industrialists, judiciary and civil service also remained behind their desks, unchallenged and unreformed. To Fischer, the shared aim of this political and social elite was 'the restoration of the German Great Power position in Europe and ultimately in the world'.[4] With the support of the Reichswehr, and in particular the recruitment of nationalist ex-soldiers to form the Freikorps (Free Corps), order was restored. A *putsch* by the Spartakist League in January 1919 (renamed the German Communist Party: Kommunistische Partei Deutschlands or KPD) was ruthlessly suppressed by the Freikorps. Karl Liebknecht and Rosa Luxemburg, the leaders of the *putsch*, were both captured and summarily executed.

To restore stability to the shattered state a National Assembly was elected in January 1919 and charged with creating a constitution for the new republic. The delegates, guarded by some 6,000 *Freikorps*, formulated the new constitution in the small, southern town of Weimar between February and July 1919 because Berlin was considered to be too dangerous. The Weimar Constitution specified a model democracy, but there were flaws. The commitment to a proportional representation (PR) voting system allowed the extremists of the right and left to gain seats in the Reichstag and promoted a succession of unstable, coalition governments that over time weakened faith in democracy. Prior to Hitler in January 1933, Germany had fifteen chancellors, an average term in office of only eleven months. A further significant flaw was Article 48 of the constitution which gave the president the right to appoint a chancellor and the power to rule by decree. It was a constitutional safeguard for times of national emergency, but in practice it offered a backdoor to dictatorship. It was a door later exploited by Hitler.

The right wing bitterly opposed the democratic constitution and favoured the restoration of the monarchy or an authoritarian, military government. Most blamed Ebert and the SDP for the abdication of the kaiser in 1918 and promoted the stabbed-in-the-back myth (*Dolchstosselegende*) of an undefeated German army. Corporal Adolf Hitler, stationed in Munich with his regiment, was fiercely anti-Weimar and in his role as education officer (*Bildungsoffizer*) for new army recruits he regularly condemned Jews and socialists for betraying Germany. In September 1919, Hitler began his political career when he decided to join the tiny right-wing German Workers' Party (Deutsche ArbeiterPartei) based in Munich. He was member 555 on a membership list that started from 500. Within a year Hitler had made his mark as an effective orator and displaced Anton Drexler as the leader of the party. He renamed the party as the National Socialist German Workers' Party (Nationalsozialistische Partei Deutschlands or NAZI) and adopted the common emblem of the right wing, the swastika, as the party insignia. The first four points of the Nazi party 25-point programme,[5] published in February 1920, signposted the challenge to come. Point 1 demanded the 'union of all Germans'. Point 2 the 'abolition of Versailles'. Point 3, 'land . . . for our population surplus', and Point 4, 'no Jew can be considered to be a fellow German'. Hitler's extreme nationalist and racist ideas were developed during his years of transient employment and poverty in Vienna from 1908–13. Hitler wrote in *Mein Kampf*, 'there took shape within me a world picture and a philosophy which became the granite foundation of all my acts'.[6] In Vienna, Hitler indiscriminately absorbed a whole range of pseudo-scientific race theories and notions of Social Darwinism propagated by the writers Gobineau and Houston Stewart Chamberlain. The result was a fixation with anti-Semitism, the supremacy of the Aryan race, warrior culture, eugenics, xenophobia, the repudiation of Christian passivity, euthanasia and the *volkisch* state – an idealistic vision of the 'purity' of peasant life. All of these base theories were later elevated into 'higher learning' by the Nazi state. A branch of the SS, the Ahnenerbe, was later devoted to archaeology and a search for evidence, including an expedition as far as Tibet, to support the thesis that all civilisation originated from the Aryan race. The end result was a racial state and ultimately a racial war.

Right-wing protest against the Weimar state was triggered in March 1921 by a decision to disband the 250,000 Freikorps in order to comply with the military restrictions of the Treaty of Versailles. The Erhardt brigade of the Freikorps led by Wolfgang Kapp, a founder member of the Fatherland Party in 1917, stormed central Berlin. The Reichswehr refused to intervene after General Seeckt, its Chief of Staff between 1920 to 1926, observed, '*Reichswehr* does not fire on *Reichswehr*'.[7] The kaiser, in exile, opened champagne and expected a return to the throne, but Ebert called a General Strike and successfully isolated and ended the *putsch*.

Economic rather than political turmoil dominated 1923. In January 1923, French and Belgium troops occupied the Ruhr to enforce reparation payments after Germany defaulted on a scheduled delivery of timber. The French eagerness to enforce the Versailles Treaty inflamed all Germans and also raised some disquiet in Great Britain. In response Chancellor Cuno (1922–23) ordered strikes and passive resistance, and resorted to printing money to pay the striking workers. The result was hyperinflation. In January 1923 there were 10,000 marks to the dollar, but by September 1923 the mark plummeted to 98 million marks to the dollar; by November 1923 it was measured in trillions of marks to the dollar and rendered worthless.

Hitler, in the belief that the Republic was teetering on the edge of collapse, attempted to seize power in a *putsch* on the night of 8–9 November 1923. Supported by General Ludendorff, the retired commander-in-chief of the Imperial Army in the Great War, Hitler hoped to emulate the success of Mussolini's 'March on Rome' with a march on Berlin. In the event the march failed to reach the centre of Munich and Hitler was arrested and placed on trial for treason. The Nazi Party made headline news across Germany and Hitler seized the opportunity for publicity. He defended his attempted *putsch*, and in lengthy speeches from the dock he condemned Versailles and proclaimed his wish to be, 'a destroyer of marxism'.[8] The sympathetic judge acquitted Ludendorff and sentenced Hitler to a minimum term of five years in the Landsberg fortress prison, fifty miles west of Munich. Here he was feted as a nationalist hero and released a few days before Christmas 1924 after having served only nine months of his sentence. Hitler used his time in prison to commit to paper his political views in a two-part diatribe entitled *Mein Kampf* (My Struggle). In later years *Mein Kampf* became required reading and the sales made Hitler a millionaire.

Hitler re-entered a very different Weimar Republic. Chancellor Stresemann, in power for only 103 days from August to November 1923, had successfully stabilised the economy and defeated hyperinflation by the issue of a new currency the *Rentenmark*. As foreign minister between 1924 and 1929, Stresemann also stabilised foreign relations by reviving the policies of 'fulfilment' towards Versailles first pursued by Chancellor Wirth (1921–22) and endorsed by Chancellor Marx in the periods 1923–25 and 1926–28. Stresemann was determined to remove or at least ease the 'stranglehold' of Versailles and in 1926 he was awarded the Nobel Peace Prize for his negotiation of a series of agreements that collectively relaxed the Versailles diktat. He gained a rescheduling of the reparation debt against Germany's ability to pay and a generous US loan of 800 million marks in the Dawes Plan of 1924. The reparations were further reduced by the Young Plan of 1929 to a quarter of the original Versailles demand. Stresemann also accepted Germany's western borders as defined by Versailles in the Locarno Treaty of 1925, took Weimar into the League of Nations in 1926 and signed the Kellogg–Briand Pact of 1928 which outlawed war.

The result was Weimar's 'Golden Years' (1924–29) when the diplomatic advances and rising employment produced an era of political and economic stability. The restoration of political calm was aided by the election of retired Field Marshal Hindenburg, the hero of the Great War, as president in 1925. He was a substitute emperor (*Ersatzkaiser)* for the right wing and embodied the revival of traditional authority and a rejection of the limitations imposed by Versailles. Whereas Stresemann had endorsed Germany's western borders he refused to accept Germany's eastern borders. In a letter to the Crown Prince in September 1925, Stresemann declared his aim of restoring to Germany all of those Germans living, 'under a foreign yoke in foreign lands'.[9] In 1925 Brigadier-General Morgan of the Allied Disarmament Commission observed that the Reichswehr maintained all its pre-war facilities and barracks despite the reduction in manpower and concluded that 'the army is, and is destined to be a cadre for expansion'.[10] Morgan's suspicions were justified because in secret in March 1926 Chief of Reichswehr Operations Joachim von Stulpnagel specified Germany's immediate goals as rearmament and the revision of Germany's borders and, in the longer term, 'the regaining of her world position'.[11] The Reichswehr also developed links with the USSR, these being first established in the Treaty of Rapallo 1922 to evade the military restrictions imposed by Versailles. The unlikely partnership was born out of mutual isolation as pariah nations, and in particular the shared detestation of Poland, as noted by General Seeckt: 'Poland's existence is intolerable, incompatible with the survival of Germany. It must disappear . . . For Russia, Poland is even more intolerable'.[12] The Treaty of Berlin (1926) deepened the relationship and provided the Reichswehr with additional military training facilities out of sight from western observers. Tank warfare was practised at Koma and pilots were trained at Lipetsk. The mutual co-operation during the period 1922–33 laid the foundations of the Nazi–Soviet Pact of August

1939, when Hitler and Stalin set their ideological differences to one side in favour of national interest and the common grievance of Poland. Overall, this right-wing challenge to the 'stranglehold' of Versailles provided a reservoir of clandestine support for the fledgling Nazi Party.

The industrialists Thyssen, Kirdorf and the Reichswehr provided generous financial aid to the Nazi Party. The Nazi Party expanded and opened offices nation-wide in the five years from 1924 to 1929, and party membership climbed from 27,000 in 1925 to 178,000 by 1929. The SA (Sturmabteilung or Stormtroopers) founded in 1921 to police meetings of the Nazi Party also expanded rapidly, and after 1925 they adopted a brown uniform. The uniform was surplus military stock originally intended for the German Army in Africa during the Great War and gave the SA the appellation, 'brownshirts'. However, the expansion of the party was not matched by votes and electoral support remained elusive. In the 1928 elections, Hitler and the Nazi Party polled a mere 2.6 per cent of the vote and gained only twelve seats in the Reichstag. The communists in comparison were significantly more successful with 10.6 per cent of the vote and fifty-four seats in the Reichstag.

The Wall Street crash of 24 October 1929 dramatically altered Nazi Party electoral fortunes. Germany was plunged into a severe economic depression measured by a sharp rise in unemployment from 6.3 per cent in 1928 to 14 per cent in 1930 and finally a peak of 29.9 per cent in 1932. Stresemann died from a heart attack only three weeks before the Wall Street crash, but, just before his death, he achieved a further notable success with an agreement for the withdrawal of the Allied forces from the Rhineland. This took effect in 1930, and, in addition, pressure from Chancellor Bruning to end reparations came to fruition in Lausanne in July 1932 when the Versailles reparations were reduced to a token demand of 3,000 marks. The Nazi challenge erupted just as the 'stranglehold' of Versailles was substantially relaxed.

An estimated 55 per cent of the unemployed, along with the financially ruined middle classes and significant numbers of disenchanted first-time voters, voted Nazi in the election of September 1930. The scale of the electoral breakthrough was startling. The Nazis gained 107 seats or 18.3 per cent of the vote and became the second biggest party in the Reichstag. The Communist Party (KPD) were also beneficiaries of the public distress and increased their seats to 77, representing 13.1 per cent of the vote. However, the communist success inadvertently assisted the Nazis by stoking the fear of a communist *putsch*.

Chancellors Muller (1928–30) and Bruning (1930–32) tried and failed to find a formula to restore the economy. Both were forced to rely upon Article 48 of the constitution and to govern by presidential decree because neither could secure a working majority in the Reichstag. The state was paralysed, and democracy was in effect suspended between 1930 and 1932 when Article 48 was invoked 109 times to secure the passage of legislation in the Reichstag. To assist political stability all political parties were requested not to contest the presidential elections in March 1932, thereby allowing 84-year-old Hindenburg to continue in office unopposed. Hitler rejected the request. It was an opportunity for power that he could not ignore and, although he failed to unseat Hindenburg, the scale of Nazi propaganda further boosted support for the Nazi Party. Hitler's next opportunity for power was presented by the resignations of Minister of Defence Groener and Chancellor Bruning in May 1932. Both had been discredited by the pro-Nazi Deputy Minister of Defence General von Schleicher as part of his ambitious plan for personal power. Schleicher took Groener's place as minister of defence and used his new position to ingratiate himself with the Nazi Party by lifting a ban on the SA imposed by Chancellor Bruning. Hindenburg appointed a trusted aristocrat Franz von Papen as the chancellor of a 'caretaker' government in June 1932, pending elections. In doing so he set a precedent by granting Papen and his 'barons' cabinet' of conservative aristocrats full presidential powers to govern the state without reference to the Reichstag. It was power both Schleicher and Hitler coveted. The subsequent elections of July 1932 confirmed the collapse of the democratic centre and the rise of the extremes of right and left. The Nazi Party gained 37.1 per cent of the vote and 230 seats in the Reichstag and the status of the biggest single party in the Reichstag. The Communist Party (KPD) climbed more slowly but increased its support to 14.3 per cent of the vote and 89 seats in the Reichstag. Hitler emphasised his popular mandate and demanded the position of chancellor with full presidential authority like Papen. There was a difference. Whereas Hindenburg trusted Papen not to abuse his power he deplored the violence of the SA and entirely distrusted Hitler. Although Hindenburg could not ignore Hitler's political mandate he successfully blocked Hitler's appointment as chancellor on the grounds that he lacked an overall majority in the Reichstag. His preference was for Hitler to serve a political apprenticeship as a vice-chancellor under Papen or to find a political partner to form a coalition government. In a stormy meeting with Hindenburg on 13 August 1932, Hitler refused to accept anything less than the chancellorship. After he left the room Hindenburg contemptuously remarked to a colleague, 'that man for a Chancellor? I'll make him a postmaster and he can lick stamps with my head on them'.[13] Papen was once again returned to office as the 'caretaker' chancellor, and in a search for stability fresh elections were held in November 1932. Nazi support stumbled, but to the alarm of many Germans the support for the KPD maintained an upward trend and reached a new high of 100 seats and 16.9 per cent of the vote. However, the Nazis retained their position as the biggest single party in the Reichstag with 196 seats and 33.1 per cent of the vote. The battle of wills between Hindenburg and Hitler was renewed. To the dismay of the wider Nazi Party and the SA, who urged a *putsch*, Hitler maintained his insistence upon the position of chancellor or nothing. He gained 'nothing' and with the downturn in Nazi electoral support the democratic press happily wrote Hitler's political obituary.

At 12 noon on 30 January 1933 Hitler was appointed chancellor of Germany. Hitler's success was not the result of a surge of new electoral support but the result of a political deal, described by A.J.P. Taylor as 'political intrigue' and by Bullock in similar terms as 'backstairs intrigue'. After the failure to reach an agreement with Hitler, Hindenburg intended to re-appoint Papen as chancellor but Minister of Defence General von Schleicher intervened to discredit Papen. Schleicher convinced Hindenburg that an accommodation with the Nazi Party was essential to avoid civil war and assured Hindenburg that he enjoyed the support of Gregor Strasser and other senior Nazis and was in a position to split the Nazi Party and depose Hitler. It was the culmination of Schleicher's plan for personal power. He envisaged an authoritarian government using elements of the Nazi Party and the army to underpin his personal rule. Schleicher was appointed chancellor on 2 December 1932, but his plan failed when Gregor Strasser refused to lead a revolt within the Nazi Party against Hitler's leadership. Within weeks, Schleicher was essentially reduced to operating as a one-man government and his position became untenable.

The chancellorship was secured for Hitler by Papen after he discovered Schleicher's treachery. In a deal that bridged the gulf between Hindenburg and Hitler he proposed a return of his trusted 'barons' cabinet' of 1932, but with two important compromises. First, Hindenburg agreed to accept Hitler as the Chancellor; second, Hitler agreed to accept only a token Nazi presence of two Nazi ministers in the eleven-member cabinet. Papen, as the vice-chancellor, supported by the majority in the cabinet, expected to wield real power and to use Nazi popular support to underpin an authoritarian government of the military and aristocratic elite in a reworking of Schleicher's plan. Papen was so confident of his ability to tame Hitler that in a letter to a friend he remarked, 'in two months' time we will have squeezed Hitler into a corner until he squeaks'.[14] Two months later Hitler was on the threshold of total power and under his leadership the diplomatic revisionism of the Weimar governments was replaced by a military challenge.

References

1. J.C.G. Rohl, *From Bismarck to Hitler*, Longman, 1970, p. 113.
2. Charles L. Mee Jr., *The End of Order: Versailles 1919*, Secker and Warburg, 1980, p. 216.
3. Martin Gilbert, *A History of the Twentieth Century, Volume One 1900–1933*, HarperCollins, 1997, p. 554.
4. Fritz Fischer, *From Kaiserreich to Third Reich: Elements of Continuity in German History 1871–1945*, Allen and Unwin, 1986, p. 83.
5. William Simpson, *Hitler and Germany*, Cambridge University Press, 1991, p. 34.
6. D.C. Watt, 'Introduction', in Adolf Hitler, *Mein Kampf*, Hutchinson, 1990, p. 21.
7. J.W. Hiden, *The Weimar Republic*, Longman, 1982, p. 52.
8. Alan Bullock, *Hitler: A Study in Tyranny*, Penguin, 1962, p. 117.
9. J.C.G. Rohl, *From Bismarck to Hitler*, Longman, 1970, p. 112.
10. Ibid., p. 109.
11. Ibid., p. 111.
12. J.W. Hiden, *The Weimar Republic*, Longman, 1982, p. 95.
13. Martin Gilbert, *A History of the Twentieth Century, Volume One 1900–1933*, HarperCollins, 1997, p. 816.
14. William Simpson, *Hitler and Germany*, Cambridge University Press, 1991, p. 69.

3   Fascist Italy

Fascism does not believe in either the possibility or the desirability of permanent peace. It therefore rejects pacifism which hides an unwillingness to fight and refusal to accept sacrifice . . . The Fascist state is a will to power and empire . . . Peoples who rise or rise again are imperialistic, peoples who die are weak peoples.[1]

Definition of Fascism in the *Enciclopedia Italiana* XIV, 1932

The tears shed by Prime Minister Vittorio Emanuele Orlando at the Palace of Versailles on 19 April 1919 were the first major indication of Italy's dissatisfaction with the Treaty of Versailles settlement and of the challenge to come. Orlando burst into tears, to the embarrassment of the Italian delegation, when the USA, France and Britain denied Italy the right to annex the Adriatic port of Fiume. Orlando pressed his case for Fiume on the grounds that it had a population of some 30,000 Italians, but an exasperated President Wilson of the United States prompted Orlando's tears with the brusque dismissal: 'there are at least one million Italians in New York but I trust that you will not on this score claim our empire city as Italian territory'.[2]

The public clash between President Wilson and Orlando highlighted a significant ideological gap between Italy and the United States of America. Italy had purposely entered the Great War in 1915 to win an extension of her European borders and overseas empire, whereas the USA was firmly opposed to empire and anxious to uphold the principle of national self-determination. Wilson was not a party to, or in sympathy with, the Treaty of London (1915) that was negotiated between Italy and the Entente powers – namely, Great Britain, France and Russia. The treaty had promised Italy substantial territorial expansion in return for joining the war against Germany and Austro-Hungary. This was the old world of secret alliances, rivalries and empire that Wilson in his fourteen-point peace plan of January 1918 wanted to replace with a new world of co-operation and equality between independent nations. Wilson's disenchantment was not just with Italy but also with Great Britain and France for their reluctance to abandon their empires. Wilson prophetically warned Europe that the failure to embrace the concept of the equality of nations would result in 'another break up of the world, and [that] when such a break up came it would not be a war but a cataclysm'.[3] However, Wilson's idealism of a League of Nations to police the world was eventually defeated – not in Europe but by the US Senate in 1920. By a slim majority of seven votes the anti-League 'irreconcilables' in the US Senate vetoed the participation of the USA in the League of Nations for fear of involvement in future European wars.

Italy was prepared to compromise but expected most of the territorial commitments made in the Treaty of London to be honoured. Article Five of the Treaty of London promised Italy an extension of her frontiers into Dalmatia in the Balkans, following the defeat of the Austro-Hungarian empire. Article Nine offered Italy expansion into Asia Minor at the expense of the Ottoman empire, and Article Thirteen promised a share of colonial territory in Africa following the defeat of Germany. The first disappointment for Italy was the creation of the new state of Yugoslavia because it blocked expansion into the Balkans and particularly the acquisition of the Dalamatia coastline. There was deep frustration in Italy that despite the sacrifice of 650,000 Italians in the war the rights of a new nation were being upheld while Italy's rights as a victor nation were being denied. Italian anger increased sharply when the promised share of German and Turkish colonial territory was also denied. Great Britain and France justified their actions on the grounds that Italy, like Japan, had made a minor contribution to victory. Italy had not declared war on Germany until December 1916, and in 1917 the Italian Army had needed the intervention of Britain, France and the USA to stave off defeat.

The disagreements over Italy's war effort marred the victory celebrations in Italy. Not only were 650,000 Italians killed in the war but 1 million were injured and 450,000 of those were permanently disabled. Consequently Fiume was important to Prime Minister Orlando as a popular prize to take back to Italy to deflect the rising criticism of his leadership. The denial of Fiume caused an immediate rift in relations. Orlando stormed out of the Versailles conference in protest on 20 April 1919, and refused to sign the Treaty of Versailles. President Wilson attempted to appeal directly to the Italian people but his words were lost in a welter of anti-US street protests across Italy. The thrice-decorated war hero Grabiele d'Annunzio gave emotional expression to the mood of national resentment with the phrase *La vittoria mutilata* (the mutilated victory).

The nationalist cry of *La vittoria mutilata* overlooked the fact that Italy was awarded substantial gains along the disputed border with Austro-Hungary. The Italian border was pushed north to the Brenner Pass to encompass Alto Adige, the long-disputed *terre irredente* or 'unredeemed lands', at the expense of the new independent state of Austria. Orlando reluctantly signed the Treaty of Versailles on 9 May 1919 under the threat of losing Alto Adige, but this gain did little to assuage the bitter disappointment in Italy. The recriminations of Italian nationalists forced Orlando out of office in June 1919, and against a background of rising unemployment and inflation Italy was plunged into political instability. Four further prime ministers – Nitti (1919), Giolitti (1920), Bonomi (1921) and Facta (1922) – all attempted to quell the rising tide of protest in Italy without success before Mussolini and Fascism overwhelmed the state in October 1922.

Benito Mussolini founded the Fascio di Combattimentio (League of Returned Soldiers) on 23 March 1919, and championed the grievances of unemployed ex-servicemen. His first political programme reflected his socialist background and was strongly anti-establishment and anti-Church. The term *fascio* was derived from the Latin *fasces* which described the bundle of rods carried in procession before the magistrates of ancient Rome as a symbol of their authority. It was a common term used in Italy to describe any radical political group, but in later years Mussolini made it his own and promoted 'Fascism' as a new political doctrine.

At first it appeared that the flamboyant nationalist hero of the Great War, Gabriele d'Annunzio, might make a future leader of Italy rather than Mussolini. With a flare for publicity, d'Annunzio marched a force of 1,000 ex-servicemen across the Italian border into Fiume on 12 September 1919 and claimed it for Italy in defiance of the Treaty of Versailles. The *sacra entrata* or sacred entry into the city eventually attracted some 9,000 supporters but did not produce the national rising that d'Annunzio had hoped for. The nationalist cry of *La vittoria mutilata*, although very emotive, was too narrow a political platform to attract mass political support. Poverty was the main issue in 1919 and it was socialism that attracted the masses as Italy wrestled with record unemployment of 2 million and an inflation rate of 60 per cent. Membership of the Italian Socialist Party (PSI) had quadrupled from 50,000 in 1914 to 200,000 by 1919, and in the elections of November 1919 the PSI was returned as Italy's biggest political party. In contrast Mussolini's Fascists failed to win a single parliamentary seat and Fascist support was eclipsed by a socialist vote forty times greater than the votes for the Fascio di Combattimentio. The fear of a future dictatorship was from the left wing not the right wing, as the success of Bolshevism in Russia encouraged support for a general strike and radical workers' demands for social and political reform. The Red Flag flew in twenty-six out of Italy's sixy-nine provinces during Italy's *biennio rosso*, or two 'red years', 1919 and 1920. It was this fear of socialist revolution that propelled Mussolini into power. The anti-socialist forces in Italian society including the fragmented Liberal movement coalesced around Mussolini to combat socialism. Hitler was later to enjoy a similar advancement into power.

In November 1920 Fiume faded as an issue after Prime Minister Giovanni Giolitti negotiated the Treaty of Rapallo with Yugoslavia, and to the satisfaction of most Italians

Fiume was designated a free city. Few subsequently reacted when in December 1920 the Italian Army and Navy entered Fiume and drove d'Annunzio and his band of legionnaires out of the city and into political oblivion.

Regular street battles in the cities of northern Italy, between Mussolini's supporters and socialists from 1919 to 1922, raised the profile of the Fascio di Combattimentio and generated political and financial support. Mussolini dropped the socialist policies that had dominated his early manifestos and adopted a strident nationalist posture that copied much of d'Annunzio's style, including the blackshirt uniform, the Roman salute and the Fascist battle cry of *eia, eia, alala*. In the elections of May 1921, Mussolini's Fascists gained 35 out of 535 seats and a foothold on power when the new liberal prime minister, Ivanoe Bonomi, invited their support in parliament to keep the socialists out of government. Bonomi resigned in February 1922 in favour of Luigi Facta as Italy lurched into a revolutionary atmosphere. By September 1922 Mussolini controlled most of northern and central Italy and threatened a march on Rome to seize power. Facta was determined to resist Mussolini, but his efforts were undermined by widespread support for Mussolini within parliament, the Royal Court, the army, the police and from leading industrialists. All shared a horror of socialism and were attracted by Mussolini's supreme self-confidence and vision of a future great Italy. The Fascist leadership of Mussolini, Balbo, Bianchi, de Vecchi and de Bono held a major Fascist rally in Naples on 24 October 1922 and declared 28 October for a march on Rome and a seizure of power. The threat was given credence by a force of 20,000 Fascists assembled around Mussolini's headquarters in Milan and in tented encampments on the outskirts of Rome. Facta was resolute in his opposition and promised to declare martial law and to arrest Mussolini for insurrection should the Fascists attempt to march on Rome. The government met in crisis session and at 2.30 a.m. on 28 October 1922 King Victor Emmanuel authorised Facta to, 'defend the state at all costs, by all means and against all who violate its laws'.[4] Facta was in a strong position to fulfil the king's command because Rome was protected by a regular army detachment of 28,000 troops. The Fascists were unarmed, apart from cudgels, and were no match for the well-equipped army. Most expected a swift end to the Fascist insurrection.

At approximately 9 a.m. the king unexpectedly reversed his decision and refused to sign the order declaring martial law. The refusal resulted in the victory of Fascism. Conflicting explanations surround the king's failure to defend the state. After the Second World War the king blamed misinformation. He claimed to have received reports that Rome was under siege from 100,000 Fascists against a Rome garrison of only 8,000 troops. However, it is more likely that the appeal of a strong Fascist government to protect Italy from socialism was irresistible to many in the royal court and industry. A more personal reason for the sudden volte-face may have been the threat of a palace revolution in favour of the king's cousin the Duke of Aosta, a prominent Fascist supporter.

Prime Minister Facta resigned at 11 a.m., but Mussolini refused to serve in a new government led by ex-P.M. Salandra and after a brief hesitation the king invited Mussolini to Rome to form a government. At first Mussolini feared that it was a trick to arrest him, but once assured that the offer was genuine he travelled to Rome on 29 October 1922 by train. The much-vaunted March on Rome and the seizure of power was a myth propagated by Mussolini once he was safely in power. Mussolini ruled Italy by consent. He was appointed prime minister by the king and later, in July 1943, following the successful Allied invasion of Italy, he meekly accepted his dismissal from power by the king.

Fascist Italy was inaugurated in a victorious march-past of the Fascist Blackshirt *Squadristi* through Rome on 30 October 1922, while the salute was taken by Mussolini and the king. This was state ceremony rather than revolution, but it did not stop Mussolini from claiming, in later years, that 3,000 Fascists had lost their lives in the battle for Rome.

Mussolini's drive for greatness began immediately after his appointment as prime minister. He took personal charge of foreign policy and predicted a 'century of Italian power', declaring 'I want to make Italy great, respected and feared'.[5]

A week after taking office Mussolini insisted on joining the international conference at Lausanne to personally represent Italy in negotiations over the delineation of Turkey's borders. His unexpected arrival raised merriment rather than respect or fear. Mussolini, to the amusement of the world's press and the embarrassment of the Italian foreign office, adopted a grand imperial manner. He was ostentatiously accompanied to all meetings by an escort of Blackshirts and invariably arrived late. His only contribution to the detailed deliberations were the words 'I agree', uttered with a studied air of sagacity. The international press dismissed Mussolini as a buffoon, but the censorship of the press in Italy ensured that the Italian public only read reports of his decisive intervention.

Mussolini's first challenge to international order was a heavily orchestrated clash with Greece following the murder of an Italian border commission on Greek soil on 27 August 1923. Four days later the Italian navy bombarded Corfu and landed marines, forcing the intervention of the League of Nations. Whereas Corfu was restored to Greek rule on 27 September 1923, Mussolini was awarded compensation and gained a reputation for decisive leadership.

The image of a powerful Italy was reinforced by the transfer of the disputed seaport of Fiume to Italy under the Pact of Rome signed with Yugoslavia in 1924.

Both successes demonstrated Mussolini's flare for self-publicity and the ultimately the triumph of style over substance. Fascist rallies fanned the illusion of power and authority, and Mussolini, in stage-managed appearances, excited the nation with a vision of future empire and prosperity. After decades of endless coalition governments, political corruption and deference to Britain and France at Versailles, many Italians welcomed a leader who by word and deed promised a powerful Italy. Opposition voices, whether in parliament, newspapers or the street, were silenced by the violence of the *Squadristi* and by December 1925 Mussolini styled himself the *Duce* ('Leader') and assumed dictatorial powers.

Mussolini's obsessive goal was the establishment of an Italian empire in North Africa and the domination of the Mediterranean region. The power-brokers were Britain and France. At first Mussolini assiduously courted both powers in attempts to win empire advances for Italy. Mussolini also courted the smaller nations of Eastern Europe and assumed the mantle of a Great Power in the Balkan region. Treaties of Friendship were established with Albania in 1926, Hungary in 1927 and Austria in 1930. The treaties acted as a counterbalance to France's 'Little Entente' treaties with Romania, Czechoslovakia and Yugoslavia. Mussolini also stirred separatism in Yugoslavia by giving military support to the Croat nationalist movement, *'Ustasha'*, to further challenge French influence in the region.

Mussolini gained warm expressions of friendship from Britain but few tangible gains for the Italian empire. British foreign secretary Austen Chamberlain (1924–29) was an admirer of Fascism and his wife openly wore a Fascist pin on their regular visits to Rome. In a gesture of friendship Britain transferred the minor border strips of Jubaland in Kenya to Italian Somaliland and Jarabub in Egypt to Italian Libya. Foreign Secretary Briand of France also declared warm support for Italy but baulked at Mussolini's blunt demand for the transfer of Tunisia and the Cameroons to the Italian empire. Tunisia was home to approximately 100,000 Italian settlers and was a long-desired extension to neighbouring Italian Libya.

In one of his first foreign policy pronouncements Mussolini had stated '*do ut des*', or 'nothing for nothing', but by 1932, after ten years of Fascism, Italy had made no empire gains.

The rise to power of Hitler in Germany in January 1933 presented Mussolini with a potent lever to prise concessions from Britain and France. Hitler's foreign policy was avowedly revisionist and represented a threat to the Versailles settlement and to France in particular. However, support for Germany was a two-edged sword. Nazi agitators in Austria and the northern Italian province of Alto Adige (South Tyrol to Germans) were clamouring for *Anschluss* or union with Germany. The campaign for *Anschluss* was a threat to Italy's power and influence in Eastern Europe. Mussolini also enjoyed a personal friendship with Chancellor Dollfuss of Austria and had personally guaranteed the independence of Austria. In June 1933, Mussolini proposed a Four Power Pact, composed of Italy, Germany, Britain and France, to police Europe. The proposal was rejected by Britain and France because it would undermine the authority of the League of Nations and return Europe to the discredited pre-war politics of the Great Powers.

A year after Hitler's appointment as German chancellor in June 1934 Mussolini invited him to Vienna. Mussolini deliberately upstaged Hitler by welcoming him with full state ceremonial when Hitler, incongruously dressed in a long brown raincoat, had requested an informal meeting. The display of Italian military might was meant to impress Hitler and to demonstrate that Italy was not to be intimidated by Germany. This point was dramatically reinforced on 25 July 1934 when Mussolini ordered twenty divisions of the Italian Army to the Brenner Pass following the murder of Chancellor Dollfuss by Austrian Nazis in pursuit of an *Anschluss* with Germany. At the time Dollfuss's wife and children were in Italy as Mussolini's house guests. Hitler disowned the murder and to Mussolini's satisfaction made no attempt to annex Austria.

Both France and Britain took comfort in Mussolini's stern opposition to Hitler and to his open dismissal of Nazi Germany as a 'racialist lunatic asylum'.[6] Mussolini entered into an unspoken anti-Nazi alliance with Britain and France and in return expected tacit support for empire expansion in Africa.

A clash between Italian and Abyssinian forces at the oasis of Wal-Wal eighty miles inside Abyssinia in December 1934 provided a convenient *casus belli*. Mussolini ordered the build-up of an army of 500,000 troops in the neighbouring Italian colonies of Eritrea and Somaliland, complete with stockpiles of illegal mustard gas to promote a rapid victory. Mussolini's intentions were clear, but as a member of the League of Nations, Abyssinia was entitled to British and French support in the event of war. Hitler's decision in February 1935 to walk out of the international disarmament talks significantly strengthened Mussolini's position by presenting France and Britain with the spectre of a powerful, rearmed Germany. The result was the Stresa Front agreement of April 1935 whereby Italy, France and Britain entered into alliance to contain Nazi Germany. Abyssinia was not directly discussed during the talks, but Mussolini regarded their silence as tacit acceptance of his empire ambition.

On 2 October 1935 Italy launched a full-scale invasion of Abyssinia. One of the first air raids was against the town of Adowa where the Italian Army had been decisively defeated by the Abyssinian Army in 1896. Despite overwhelming numerical superiority and command of the air, a swift victory still eluded Italy. Britain and France condemned the invasion but failed to close the Suez Canal to Italian ships and cut Italy's supply line. It reflected the desire of Britain and France to keep Mussolini in alliance at a time when their forces were facing a rising challenge from Japan and Germany. In January 1936, the foreign ministers of Britain and France, Samuel Hoare and Pierre Laval, attempted to find a compromise solution by encouraging Abyssinia to strike a deal with Italy that would permit Italy to annex approximately two-thirds of Abyssinia. It was not in keeping with the public face of the League of Nations or public opinion, but it was the blunt reality of wider national interest and a desire to keep the Stesa Front intact. The plan was leaked to the press and both Hoare and Laval were forced to resign. To end the war swiftly, Mussolini authorised gas attacks by the Italian Air Force, and finally declared victory with the occupation of the capital Addis Abba in May 1936. The fact that the war continued for a further three years before Abyssinia was finally subdued was carefully concealed from the world, along with the mass execution of Abyssinia's intellectual elite. The war significantly harmed the reputation of France and Britain, weakened faith in the League of Nations and left Hitler as the true victor. On 7 March 1936, Hitler took advantage of the distraction provided by the war in Abyssinia to re-occupy the demilitarised Rhineland in defiance of the Treaty of Versailles restrictions.

With victory Mussolini became a prisoner of his own propaganda and believed that under his leadership Italy had created 'an army of five million men with a forest of bayonets, an airforce so large that it would blot out the sun over Italy'.[7] By 1938 he boasted of an army of 8 million 'bayonets', whereas in reality the Italian Army was at best 1.5 million strong. Similar exaggeration surrounded Italy's much-publicised drive for autarky with statistics for industrial and agricultural production that were far in excess of Italy's limited resources.

The successful defiance of the League of Nations convinced Mussolini that Fascism was in the ascendancy and that Italy's future lay with Germany and Japan. Mussolini appointed his son-in-law Galeazzo Ciano as Italy's foreign minister in June 1936, and directed him and the Italian press to flatter and cultivate Germany as a future alliance partner. Italy's commitment to defending the independence of Austria and to the Stresa Front was subsequently downplayed.

The ascendancy of Fascism was confirmed for Mussolini by the outbreak of the Spanish Civil War in July 1936 between the Fascist Falange movement and the left-wing Republican 'Popular Front' government. Mussolini enthusiastically ordered the Italian Army to assist the Fascist alliance led by General Franco. A Fascist Spain, under General Franco, was an attractive goal for Mussolini because it would complete the Fascist encirclement of France, pose a threat to British Gibraltar and offer Italy naval bases in the Balearic Islands. General Franco happily accepted Italy's offer of help, and the assistance of the German Luftwaffe, but there was no quick victory and the longer-than-expected war (1936–39) exhausted Italy's limited financial and military resources. It also provided the embarrassment of the defeat of the Italian Army at Guadaljara, in March 1937, by a force of irregulars from the International Brigade including Italian anti-Fascist volunteers. After achieving victory in March 1939, Franco disappointed Mussolini by refusing to enter into an alliance, and during the Second World War Spain remained militarily neutral. The only gain was the propaganda triumph of a further advance for Fascism.

Mussolini openly courted Hitler to the discomfort of Britain and France. The block to an alliance was the future of Austria. Hitler had resolved to annex Austria at the first opportunity, but he was wary of a repeat of 1934 when Italy had upheld the independence of Austria. Mussolini, however, indicated to Hitler that he was prepared to abandon Austria in return for an alliance with Germany, and in consequence negotiations moved forward rapidly. On 1 November 1936, in Milan, Mussolini revealed the conclusion of an accord with Hitler. He boasted of 'a Rome–Berlin Axis around which all European states that desire peace can revolve'.[8]

To cement the new relationship Hitler visited Rome in May 1937, and, to ensure a positive impression, Mussolini personally inspected the procession route and ordered some buildings to be demolished, the erection of false façades, the placing of artificial trees and the full repainting of all buildings. He created the illusion of a mighty, military state. In return Mussolini visited Berlin in September 1937 and was openly bewitched by the reality of Germany's military power and the industrial might of the Ruhr valley. The prolonged applause for his speech in Berlin from an estimated audience of 900,000 assembled in uniformed ranks, in the midst of a thunderstorm, was a Wagnerian spectacle that left an indelible imprint. Mussolini's conversion to Nazism was apparent on his return to Rome when he personally demonstrated the goose step to the Italian Army and insisted on its adoption, despite protests from the king, who was nominally the commander-in-chief of the army. Mussolini renamed it the *passo romano*, the Roman Step, and claimed it was originally the march of the Roman legionaries. He also enforced the raised straight-arm salute in place of the handshake, and ordered all Italians to be less passive and more commanding by replacing the polite form of you *(Lei)* with the more direct form *(Voil)*. A more unpleasant import in September 1938 was Germany's race laws. Mussolini later admitted that the introduction of anti-Semitism was purely for political reasons. The race laws were unpopular and rarely enforced, not least because the Aryan race theories held little welcome for dark Italians. Italy also had no history of anti-Semitism and the tiny Jewish population of 45,000 was well integrated. More personally, one of Mussolini's favourite mistresses, Marghvita Sarfatti, was Jewish and in 1939 he arranged for her safe passage to Argentina.

In December 1937, in a further tilt against Britain and France, Italy joined Germany and Japan in the Anti-Comintern Pact and finally withdrew from the League of Nations. However, Japan and Italy both refused to enter into a formal military alliance with Germany. National interest rather than Fascist solidarity governed the triangular relationship.

Mussolini's expectation of controlling and directing Hitler evaporated after 1937. It was Hitler and his foreign policy rather than Mussolini's that dictated the course of events from 1937–39 and took Europe into war. The *Anschluss* between Germany and Austria arose unexpectedly on 11 March 1938, when Hitler accused the chancellor of Austria, Schuschnigg, of implementing anti-Nazi policies. Hitler was determined to use the dispute to force the *Anschluss* and despite only twelve hours' notice, Mussolini promised not to oppose the entry of German troops into Austria. Hitler was ecstatic and personally promised Mussolini, *'ich werde ihnen dieses nie vergessen'* ('I shall never forget this'). It was a promise Hitler maintained to the bitter end. After the successful annexation of Austria on 12 March 1938, Hitler claimed the right to occupy the Sudetenland in Czechoslovakia in May 1938, and thrust Mussolini centre stage. At Munich, during 28–30 September 1938, Mussolini offered to act as an impartial arbitrator between Germany, Britain and France over the future of the Sudetenland. The Four Power Pact originally rejected by Britain and France in 1933 was enacted in all but name. League principle was abandoned in favour of appeasement to avoid war. The compromise solution accepted by the four powers was in theory Mussolini's proposal, but in reality it was Hitler's plan dictated to Mussolini prior to the start of the conference. Mussolini basked in the adulation of the international statesman, who at the eleventh hour had rescued Europe from war. He returned to Rome to a rapturous reception but expressed his discomfort at returning as a peacemaker rather than as a warlord. Peace was distinctly non-Fascist and a negation of his desire to convert Italy into a nation of warriors.

Britain and France expressed renewed hope of separating Mussolini from Hitler, but a visit by Prime Minister Chamberlain to Rome in January 1939 failed to break the Axis. Two months later, Hitler took direct military action in defiance of the Munich Settlement when German troops occupied the whole of Czechoslovakia. Mussolini was privately enraged because Hitler had not informed him in advance, but in public he saluted the boldness of Fascism. In an attempt to regain the initiative he ordered the invasion of Albania in April 1939. The invasion was uncontested, but the flight of King Zog into exile allowed Mussolini to declare a further victory for Italian Fascism. Mussolini dismissed the rising counter-challenge and threat of war from Britain and France as a strategy of bluff, and he expected a grand European peace conference and the offer of significant territorial concessions.

References

1. *Enciclopedia Italiana XIV*, 1932, pp. 847–8.
2. Charles L. Mee Jr., *The End of Order: Versailles 1919*, Secker and Warburg, 1980, p. 184.
3. Ibid., p. 16.
4. Robert Wolfson, *Years of Change: European History 1890–1945*, Edward Arnold, 1978, p. 262.
5. Ibid., p. 274
6. Denis Mack Smith, *Mussolini*, Weidenfeld and Nicolson, 1982, p. 186.
7. Ibid., p. 152.
8. Christopher Hibbert, *Benito Mussolini: The Rise and Fall of Il Duce*, Penguin, 1986, p. 102.

4 Nazi challenge

We National Socialists must hold unflinchingly to our aim in foreign policy namely, to secure for the German people the land and soil to which they are entitled on this earth.[1]

Adolf Hitler, *Mein Kampf*

Throughout the evening of 30 January 1933, and into the early hours of the next morning, a continuous procession of SA (Sturmabteilung) troopers, accompanied by Nationalist Party Stahlhelm troopers, marched through central Berlin in celebration of the appointment of Adolf Hitler as the Chancellor of Germany. The procession passed the golden Victory Angel commemorating Bismarck's defeat of France 1871, through the Brandenburg Gate topped by the eastward-facing Quadriga of Victory and down Wilhelmstrasse past the Chancellery. Standing at separate windows of the Chancellery, Hitler and President Hindenburg watched the victorious march-past. The marchers sang the anthem of the Nazi Party, the *Horst Wessel*, and alternatively chanted, 'Heil Hitler', 'Down with the Jews' and 'Germany Awake'. The latter was a call shared by Goebbels, who recorded in his diary: 'thousands march past our window in never ending uniform rhythm. The rising of a nation. Germany has awakened.'[2]

Hitler was appointed chancellor earlier in the day at 12 noon, but with the strict limitation of a cabinet containing only two other Nazis to guard against extremism. Hitler's immediate aim was to circumvent this limitation and to wield total power. The destruction of the Reichstag by fire on the night of 27 February 1933 provided Hitler with his opportunity. A young ex-communist Marinus van der Lubbe was captured by the police at the scene and Göring hailed the fire as the signal fire of a communist *putsch*. Within twenty-four hours all leading communists were arrested under State of Emergency legislation, 'For the Protection of the People and the State'. On 23 March 1933, with the absence of the Communist Party and the overt intimidation of the SA, Hitler secured the passage of the Enabling Act in the Reichstag by 441 votes to 94. It was a 'legal revolution' because the Enabling Act conferred the right to rule by decree for four years. Armed with this authority Hitler embarked on a process of *Gleichschaltung* (co-ordination), or the step-by-step imposition of a Nazi dictatorship. The first concentration camp for political enemies was opened at Dachau, on the outskirts of Munich, on 22 March 1933, and by September 1933 it was full to its capacity of 5,000 inmates – and all independent institutions, including alternative political parties, were either banned or Nazified. A new state secret police, the Gestapo, was founded on 26 April 1933, and charged with rooting out enemies of the state. To guard against the enemies 'within' Hitler secured his leadership by authorising the murder of an estimated 400 to 1,000 suspected political opponents during the Night of the Long Knives (30 June 1934). One prominent victim was Ernst Rohm, the leader of the SA, and with his death the SA was disbanded and the security of the state was entrusted to the SS (Schutzstaffel or protection squads) under the leadership of Heinrich Himmler. General von Schleicher, the previous chancellor, who had attempted to split the Nazi Party and depose Hitler, was also murdered along with his wife. Gregor Strasser, who had remained loyal to Hitler despite Schleicher's blandishments, was also executed to remove a potential leadership rival.

The death of President Hindenburg on 2 August 1934 permitted Hitler to attain supreme power. The necessary documentation was all prepared in advance and within an hour of Hindenburg's death Hitler merged the office of president with the office of chancellor and adopted the title 'Führer' (leader). It was a major disappointment to Kaiser Wilhelm II, living in exile in Doorn in Holland, because he had hoped for a return to the throne; but Hitler was not prepared to share power. The only independent institutions capable of challenging Hitler were the Roman Catholic Church and the Reichswehr. The Catholic bishops at first withdrew the sacrament from Nazi Party members and opposed the Nazi Party, but they were overruled by Pope Pius X1 who encouraged the Roman Catholic Centre Party to vote for the Enabling Act. He also entered into a controversial Concordat with the Nazi Party in July 1933. The pro-Nazi policy was directed by Cardinal Pacelli, later Pope Pius XII (1939–58). He was described by the author John Cornwell as 'Hitler's Pope' for his failure to unequivocally condemn the Nazi Party and the later Holocaust. The Reichswehr welcomed a leader who promised rearmament and to revise the territorial restrictions placed on Germany by the Treaty of Versailles in 1919. Consequently, on 2 August 1934, the Reichswehr, regiment by regiment, swore an oath of allegiance not to the state but to Adolf Hitler. It was an oath Hitler later used against his doubting generals to demand their total obedience to his orders. Hitler's revolution was complete and at Nuremburg, in September 1934, Hitler triumphantly declared: 'In the next thousand years there will be no other revolution in Germany.'[3] In the event the Third Reich lasted a mere twelve years as Hitler embarked on a disastrous foreign policy that ended in the destructive Second World War.

There were three discernible strands to Hitler's challenge to Europe. First, rearmament in defiance of the Treaty of Versailles restrictions. Second, the union of all German-speaking people into a 'greater Germany' (*grossdeutschland*). Third, the expansion of Germany territory to the east expressed as *lebensraum* (living space). Hitler found support for his policies among the ranks of the Reichswehr and the professionals in the Foreign Office and the wider German establishment. The policies were reminiscent of Germany's aims in the Great War and similar to the territorial demands of the Treaty of Brest-Litovsk, imposed on defeated Russia in March 1918. However, there were differences. Hitler criticised the kaiser's policy of *Weltpolitik* as a mistake because it led to war with Great Britain and misdirected the German nation away from expansion within Europe. Hitler stated in *Mein Kampf* in 1925: 'We stop the endless German movement to the south and west, and turn our gaze towards land in the east. At long last we break off the colonial and commercial policy of the pre-war period and shift to the soil policy of the future.'[4] Hitler also firmly believed that Jews were engaged in a world conspiracy to destroy western civilisation, and in *Mein Kampf* he directed a challenge not just to Versailles but to the entire Jewish race: 'the National Socialist movement has the mightiest task to fulfil . . . it must call eternal wrath upon the head of the foul enemy of mankind [Jews] as the real originator of our sufferings'.[5] There were early signs that this was not mere rhetoric. On 1 April 1933, a one-day, nation-wide boycott of Jewish shops and businesses publicly declared the Jews as *persona non gratae*. This was later made official by the Nuremberg Laws of September 1935 (Law for Protection of German Blood and Honour) which forbade marriage or sexual relations between Jews and gentiles.

Hitler's aims could only be achieved from a position of military strength. In April 1933 the Foreign Office advised Hitler of the need for caution: 'the main goal of the territorial revision remains the transformation of the eastern frontier . . . it is necessary to avoid diplomatic conflicts for as long as possible until we have become stronger'.[6] Hitler embarked on a peace offensive, and in a series of speeches between 1934 and 1936 he declared his desire for peace but also justice for Germany. He successfully courted international public opinion and gained a positive press for his condemnation of the many injustices of Versailles. He was aided by the rising public opinion in Europe that no single country had been responsible for the outbreak of the Great War and, by extension, a general acceptance that Versailles had been too harsh. Britain was effectively in appeasement mode long before Prime Minister Neville Chamberlain took office.

Rearmament was Hitler's first open breach of the Treaty of Versailles. Hitler wrong-footed Britain and France by insisting that both powers fulfil a commitment to universal disarmament contained in the Treaty of Versailles and the Charter of the League of Nations or permit Germany to rearm. At the Disarmament Conference in Geneva, Britain and France refused to give an immediate commitment in view of empire defence needs. Their caution was a propaganda triumph for Hitler. After accusations of unfair treatment and double standards Germany withdrew in protest from the Disarmament Conference on 14 October 1933, and a week later from the League of Nations. In a hastily arranged plebiscite Hitler gained a 95 per cent vote of approval for his actions and in essence gave notice of his intention to rearm in defiance of Versailles. But in an astute act of reassurance he announced a non-aggression pact with Poland in January 1934. The apparent acceptance of Poland as a legitimate state significantly enhanced Hitler's peace credentials but, his masterstroke was his statement that a rearmed Germany would 'create a bulwark against Bolshevism in Eastern Europe'.[7] A strong, anti-communist Germany was attractive to the western powers. In consequence, the attempts by the Soviet foreign minister, Litvinov, to sign a 'Collective Security' treaty with Britain and France against Hitler between 1934 and 1939 were consistently rebuffed. The western powers were satisfied that Hitler's challenge pointed east not west.

Hitler's confidence increased and in March 1935 he openly acknowledged the existence of an air force – the Luftwaffe – and announced conscription and the creation of an army of thirty-six divisions, or approximately 550,000 men, in open defiance of Versailles. The tiny Weimar Reichswehr was recast as the Wehrmacht, a vastly expanded and modernised force. The *Daily Mail* correspondent Ward Price accompanied Hitler on a review of the new German army on 18 March 1935 and concluded that Hitler had, 'no trace of any desire to do more than assert and maintain German independence and self-determination'.[8] However, the unilateral nature of Hitler's action was of concern to the western powers, and at Stresa in April 1935 Britain, France and Italy issued a formal protest. Stresa was intended as a check to Hitler, but the unity of the 'Stresa Front' was short-lived. In *Mein Kampf* (1924) and his 'secret book' (*Zweites Buch*, written in 1928), Hitler had expressed his admiration of the British empire and his desire for an alliance, 'one will control the sea, the other will be the strongest power on land'.[9] In June 1935, Hitler sent Ribbentrop as his personal emissary to London to discuss a naval agreement. The result was a deal that restricted the Germany Navy to 35 per cent of the tonnage of the Royal Navy and effectively guaranteed the security of Britain; but it undermined the Stresa Front. Neither France nor Italy, both naval powers, were consulted, and France in particular felt abandoned. The Italian invasion of Abyssinia in October 1935 was the final blow to the unity of the Stresa Front. In private both Britain and France were prepared to accept the Italian occupation of Abyssinia as the price of Italian support against Hitler. With world attention focused on the war in Abysinnia, Hitler ordered the Wehrmacht to reoccupy the demilitarised Rhineland on 7 March 1936. It was a significant gamble because Germany's forces were too weak to oppose the French Army and Hitler acknowledged that if France had acted 'we would have had to withdraw with our tails between our legs'.[10] France refused to act alone, without a British guarantee of military support, but public opinion in Britain was relaxed. Lord Lothian, commenting on the issue, stated: 'After all, they are only going into their own back-garden',[11] and inadvertently spoke for the nation. Hitler's offence seemed minor in comparison to the Japanese annexation of Manchuria (1931) and Italy's war in Abyssinia (1935–36), and few voices were raised in protest. Winston Churchill Member of Parliament did protest and warned of the danger of Hitler fortifying the Rhineland and creating a 'barrier across Germany's front door'.[12] He urged Prime Minister Stanley Baldwin not to trust Hitler. In contrast ex-Prime Minister David Lloyd-George toured Germany in 1936 and endorsed Hitler's leadership, although he later recanted his support in 1938. The Duke of Windsor, briefly King Edward VIII before his abdication in December 1936, also toured Germany and was an open admirer of Hitler. The wider world too endorsed Hitler's leadership by attending the Olympic Games in Berlin 1936: although the theory of the supremacy of the Aryan race was dealt a blow when the black American athlete Jesse Owens won four gold medals and broke two world records.

After the Rhineland, Hitler offered a more explicit challenge to European peace. The involvement of German forces in the Spanish Civil War (1936–39) was the first indication of an aggressive edge to Hitler's 'peace army'. In particular the destruction of Guernica by the Condor Legion of the Luftwaffe displayed, for the first time, the full horrors of modern, indiscriminate aerial warfare, as commemorated in Picasso's famous painting. It was a potent reminder of Prime Minister Baldwin's words in 1932: 'the bomber will always get through',[13] and, coupled with fears of gas bombs, produced a fear of future war that underpinned Prime Minister Chamberlain's policy of appeasement (1937–39). Hitler had no fear of war. In *Mein Kampf* he welcomed regular warfare as essential to the renewal of the nation. What Hitler feared was the wrong war. His territorial interests lay to the east, and his dominant interest in the years 1936–37 was to isolate the Soviet Union and to promote an anti-communist crusade. Hitler's first convert was Mussolini, who after the break with Britain and France over Abyssinia openly endorsed Hitler's policies and entered into the 'Axis' alliance with Germany on 1 November 1936. The term 'axis' was coined by Mussolini to describe Rome and Berlin as the future hub of world influence. On 6 November 1936, Italy, with the addition of Japan, signed the Anti-Comintern Pact with Germany which was directed against the Soviet Union. Following the success of the Naval Agreement with the Royal Navy, Hitler appointed Ribbentrop as ambassador to Great Britain in December 1936, with the instruction to 'get Britain to join the Anti-Comintern Pact'.[14] Ribbentrop's mission failed, not least because his vain, bombastic manner alienated any chance of success, and after a year of fruitless negotiation he advised Hitler in January 1938 that Great Britain would never permit Germany to dominate Europe. Hitler was prepared for this eventuality and had informed Ribbentrop that in the event of British opposition 'I am ready for war, I would regret it very much, but if it has to be, there it is.'[15]

In expectation of a future war, Hitler had directed Hermann Göring in August 1936 to oversee economic development with the command: 'the German economy must be fit for war within four years'.[16] Hitler's drive for autarky, or a defence-based economy (*Wehrwirtschaft*), was prompted by his memories of the crippling effect of the Royal Navy blockade during the Great War and the need for Germany to be self-sufficient in war materials. On 5 November 1937 Hitler convened a meeting attended by the commanders-in-chief of the army, navy and air force, and his military adjutant, Colonel Hossbach, to air his future strategy. A record of the meeting was made by Hossbach and discovered after the war. His notes recorded Hitler's directions to the armed forces to prepare for the future annexation of Austria and Czechoslovakia and military action to secure 'living space' for the German people. A variety of scenarios for immediate military action were discussed, but Hossbach noted Hitler's 'unalterable resolve to solve Germany's problem of space at the latest by 1943–5'.[17] Hossbach also recorded Hitler's stark assertion that 'Germany's problem could only be solved by means of force.'[18] Hitler's fear that he had cancer was also reflected in his direction to treat his words as his last will and testament in the event of his death. Within days of the meeting there was considerable unrest in the senior ranks of the army as they digested the possibility of imminent war. All advised caution because of the superior size of the

French Army, and all were relieved of their commands by Hitler between January and February 1938. The armed forces had escaped *Gleichshaltung*, or Nazi co-ordination, in 1934 but now Hitler appointed himself commander-in-chief of the Wehrmacht and established a new High Command (Oberkommando der Wehrmacht or OKH), with General Keitel as its first commander.

The Hossbach Memorandum provided a broad exposition of Hitler's commitment to the future achievement of *Grossdeutchsland* and *Lebensraum* rather than a master plan for war. It is significant that whereas Hitler believed that *Grossdeutchsland* might be achieved without war he accepted that *Lebensraum* would necessitate war. Above Hitler's fireplace, in his private study, was a large portrait of Bismarck who had gone to war on three occasions to secure the unification of Germany between 1864 and 1871. Hitler reminded his generals of Bismarck's achievements and directly praised this earlier example of war involving 'unheard-of-risk'.[19] Like Bismarck, Hitler was prepared to use war to achieve his aims. Events in 1938 and 1939 demonstrate that Hitler steered a zigzag course to attain his aims, including the surprising volte-face of an alliance with Stalin in August 1939, to the consternation of his Anti-Comintern allies. Bullock, in a widely endorsed view, summarised Hitler's actions as 'consistency of aim with complete opportunism in method and tactics'.[20]

The *Anschluss* with Austria in March 1938 arose from the misjudgements of Chancellor Schushnigg of Austria as he manoeuvred to maintain a close relationship with Germany yet preserve the independence of Austria. His complaints to Hitler, on 12 February 1938, of the violent activities of Austrian Nazis and evidence of plans for a *putsch* were met not with sympathy but with accusations that Schuschnigg's government was insufficiently pro-Nazi. Hitler demanded the inclusion of Austrian Nazis in the government, and after Schuschnigg hesitated and proposed a plebiscite Hitler demanded Schuschnigg's immediate resignation. It was annexation by telephone when in a succession of telephone threats made over the course of 11 March 1938 Göring secured Schuschnigg's resignation and his replacement as chancellor by the leader of the Austrian Nazis, Seyss-Inquart. Göring's final telephone call at 9.10 p.m. instructed Seyss-Inquart to request the 'German government to send troops as soon as possible'[21] to help restore law and order. It was an attempt to preserve an air of legality because the order directing the Wehrmacht to occupy Austria had been issued earlier at 8.45 p.m. To Hitler's delight, Mussolini gave the *Anschluss* his blessing and in doing so confirmed his own personal union with Germany. On 12 March, amid widespread scenes of public jubilation, Hitler visited his boyhood city of Linz and resolved to incorporate Austria fully into the Reich. The speed of the occupation, and the approval of the *Anschluss* by 99.8 per cent of the Austrian people in a plebiscite held on 10 April 1938, reduced Britain and France to the status of mere spectators.

It was a situation Prime Minister Chamberlain (1937–40) was uncomfortable with. Whereas he accepted that the Treaty of Versailles was flawed he wanted any further revisions of the treaty to be as a result of multilateral agreement rather than unilateral military action. His immediate point of concern was the future of Czechoslovakia. Vocal protests by the German population of the Sudetenland area of Czechoslovakia for union with Germany increased sharply after the *Anschluss*. Chamberlain was fully confident that the borders of Czechoslovakia could be resolved by direct negotiations. Consequently, he again rejected proposals from Foreign Minister Litvinov of the USSR for an anti-Hitler 'Collective Security' agreement, and pointedly refused to guarantee the borders of Czechoslovakia.

Chamberlain grossly underestimated the scale of Hitler's ambition. Hitler's interest was not just to incorporate the Sudetenland into the Reich but to occupy the whole of Czechoslovakia and to neutralise the well-equipped Czech army. Czech territory projected deep into Germany and the existence of alliances with USSR and France was a potent strategic threat to Germany. Czech airbases were within an hour's flying time of Berlin. Hitler's strategy was to stir a crisis and to seek a pretext for a lightning invasion of Czechoslovakia. On 28 March 1938 he instructed Konrad Henlein, the leader of the Sudetenland German Party, that 'we must always demand so much that we can never be satisfied'.[22] Twelve German divisions were stationed on the Czech frontier ready for instant action. The Czech government was alert to the danger, and in response to reports of German troop movements ordered mobilisation on 20 May 1938 to defend the state. Hitler was forced to deny any hostile intent when France, Britain and the USSR all gave pledges of support to Czechoslovakia. But in private, on 28 May, Hitler informed his High Command: 'it is my unalterable decision to smash Czechoslovakia by military action in the near future'.[23] He set a final deadline for military action as 1 October 1938.

Chamberlain resolved to solve the crisis by direct negotiations, and at the age of sixty-nine he undertook his first plane flight to meet Hitler at his alpine villa at Berchtesgaden on 15 September 1938. Chamberlain was treated to an anti-Czech tirade and the threat of imminent war. At face value Hitler's grievance was the Sudetenland, and it was a Versailles 'flaw' that Chamberlain was prepared to correct. Chamberlain returned to Germany for a second meeting with Hitler at Godesburg on 22 September with a solution. In the space of a week Chamberlain, with the support of France, had pressurised the Czech government to cede the Sudetenland to Germany. To Chamberlain's surprise Hitler rejected the settlement with the complaint that the proposed timescale was unacceptable, and he bluntly declared that the Wehrmacht would invade Czechoslovakia at 2 p.m. on 28 September. Hitler had no wish to be appeased. Chamberlain failed to realise that his prize was Czechoslovakia, not simply the Sudetenland.

In London the cabinet refused to consider any further concessions. Air raid sirens were tested and anti-aircraft guns were erected in the London parks, and the fleet was deployed to war stations. In France the forts of the Maginot Line were manned. Chamberlain addressed the British nation by radio on 27 September 1938, and paved the way for Munich with his description of the crisis as 'a quarrel in a far-away country between people of whom we know nothing'.[24] The lack of will to defend Czechoslovakia was evident, and at Chamberlain's suggestion Mussolini proposed a final conference at Munich on 29 September to resolve the dispute. The Munich Agreement was signed at 2 a.m. on 30 September 1938 by Hitler, Chamberlain and Prime Minister Daladier of France. The Czech government and the USSR were not invited to take part in the negotiations. The diktat of Versailles was effectively replaced with the diktat of Munich. Mussolini presented himself to the conference as a disinterested neutral but the compromise solution he suggested was specified in advance by Hitler. The final agreement was for the annexation of the Sudetenland in stages between 1 and 10 October, thus preserving the original date for action that Hitler had set his generals in May. Despite the success of Munich, the settlement was not to Hitler's liking because the Czech state still existed. Chamberlain, however, was euphoric and was personally convinced that Hitler was sincere and had no further territorial demands in Europe. It was this gross misjudgement that permanently destroyed his reputation and debased the policy of appeasement. The high point of appeasement was Chamberlain's triumphant return to England and his statement to the waiting crowds at Heston Airport, and later in Downing Street: 'I believe it is peace for our time.'[25] Chamberlain placed his faith in a personal declaration of peace signed by Hitler. The vast majority of people were relieved and congratulated Chamberlain, but Duff-Cooper, the First Lord of the Admiralty, resigned from government and expressed the opinion that Hitler only respected the 'language of the mailed fist'.[26] Churchill, too, condemned Munich and stated: 'we have sustained a defeat without a war . . . this is only the first sip, the first foretaste of a bitter cup'.[27] The challenge to Jews was also intensified with the burning of synagogues and the smashing of Jewish shop windows across Germany on the night of 9–10 November in the Reich *Kristallnacht* (crystal night). The outbreak of violence was in reprisal for the murder of a German diplomat in Paris by a young Jewish student and ended with the random arrest and deportation to concentration camps of approximately 30,000 Jews.

Churchill's judgement was accurate because on 21 October 1938, only a month after the Munich settlement, Hitler directed his armed forces to prepare for the invasion of Czechoslovakia. He encouraged Hungary and Poland to press claims to Czech territory, and encouraged the Slovaks to seek independence – all to stir a crisis. The end was sudden. President Hacha of Czechoslovakia, in an attempt to preserve his country, imposed martial law on 9 March 1939 and handed Hitler an opportunity to exploit. At Hitler's bidding, Slovakia protested and declared independence on 14 March 1939 and requested German protection. The following day Hitler held an interview with President Hacha of Czechoslovakia and threatened immediate invasion and the destruction of the capital, Prague, by the Luftwaffe, unless Hacha invited German troops to enter Czechoslovakia to restore law and order. It was a cynical reprise of the *Anschluss*. The occupation was implemented within hours, and before Britain and France could react Hitler also entered Slovakia on 16 March 1939. It had taken Hitler just two days to liquidate the entire state of Czechoslovakia. Within a week similar threats forced the tiny Baltic state of Lithuania to restore Memel to Germany.

Hitler was unconcerned by protests from Britain and France and he dismissed their counter-challenge of military action to curb any future Nazi expansion as bluff.

References

1. D.C. Watt, 'Introduction', in Adolf Hitler, *Mein Kampf*, Hutchinson, 1990, p. 596.
2. Victor Mallia-Milanes, *The Origins of the Second World War*, Macmillan, 1987, p. 81.
3. Alan Bullock, *Hitler: A Study in Tyranny*, Penguin, 1962, p. 311.
4. D.C. Watt, 'Introduction', in Adolf Hitler, *Mein Kampf*, Hutchinson, 1990, p. 598.
5. Ibid., p. 584.
6. John Laver, *Nazi Germany 1933–45*, Hodder and Stoughton, 1991, p. 83.
7. William Carr, *Hitler: A Study in Personality and Politics*, Edward Arnold, 1978, p. 49.
8. Ward Price, *The Daily Mail*, 18 March 1935.
9. William Simpson, *Hitler and Germany*, Cambridge University Press, 1991, p. 99.
10. Alan Bullock, *Hitler: A Study in Tyranny*, Penguin, 1962, p. 345.
11. Winston Churchill, *The Second World War: The Gathering Storm*, Cassell, 1950, p. 169.
12. Ibid., p. 175.
13. A.J.P. Taylor, *English History 1914–45*, Oxford University Press, 1988, p. 364.
14. William Simpson, *Hitler and Germany*, Cambridge University Press, 1991, p. 99.
15. Ibid.
16. Ibid., p. 86.
17. J.C.G. Rohl, *From Bismarck to Hitler*, Longman, 1970, p. 150.

18. Ibid.
19. Ibid.
20. Esmonde M. Robertson (ed.), *The Origins of the Second World War*, Macmillan Press, 1978, p. 193.
21. Alan Bullock, *Hitler: A Study in Tyranny*, Penguin, 1962, p. 430.
22. Ibid., p. 443.
23. Ibid., p. 447.
24. Winston Churchill, *The Second World War: The Gathering Storm*, Cassell, 1950, p. 261.
25. Ibid., p. 264.
26. Ibid., p. 269.
27. Ibid., p. 271.

5   Counter-challenge

In the event of any action which clearly threatens Polish independence and which the Polish Government accordingly consider it vital to resist with their national forces, H.M. Government would feel themselves bound at once to lend the Polish Government all support in their power.[1]

Chamberlain addressing the House of Commons 31 March 1939

Hitler's dismemberment and occupation of Czechoslovakia in March 1939, in defiance of the settlement reached at Munich six months earlier, left Chamberlain with little choice but to act. On 31 March 1939 he announced, to a crowded House of Commons, an unconditional guarantee of Poland's borders. It was a counter-challenge. But it was a counter-challenge that forced Britain to defend one of the most widely criticised territorial changes imposed upon Germany by the Treaty of Versailles in 1919 and ended any prospect of Poland considering territorial concessions to avoid war. Armed with the British guarantee, Poland steadfastly refused to countenance German demands for improved road and rail links to Danzig. Hitler responded to their intransigence with the words, 'I'll cook them a stew they'll choke on.'[2] On 3 April he issued orders to the Wehrmacht, codenamed 'Case White', to prepare for the invasion of Poland on 1 September 1939. He was set on war and signalled his hostile intent with the cancellation of the non-aggression pact with Poland, signed in 1934, and the Anglo-German Naval Agreement concluded in 1935. The latter had, in effect, been cancelled by Hitler in May 1938 when he had authorised a secret construction programme of new battleships (Z Plan) capable of confronting the Royal Navy. On 14 April President Roosevelt urged all European states to avoid war and invited Hitler to diffuse the crisis by reconfirming that he had no further territorial demands to make in Europe. Hitler rejected the appeal and Roosevelt's related proposal for an international peace conference. He insisted that Polish obstinacy was the block to peace and reminded Roosevelt of the vast territories gained by Americans through revolution and war rather than at the conference table. Chamberlain also rejected US mediation because of his distrust of Roosevelt and American liberalism. In February

1939, President Roosevelt had remarked: 'under no circumstances would the new world again be duped into doing the work of the old'.[3] His words reflected widespread criticism in the United States of the reluctance of Britain and France to withdraw from their empires and their qualified endorsement of the principles of equality between nations and national self-determination. Many Americans blamed European empire rivalry for the outbreak of the Great War in 1914 and criticised the Treaty of Versailles (1919) as a victors' charter rather than the new beginning for Europe espoused by President Wilson in his fourteen-point peace plan of 1918. The Neutrality Act of 1936 (and as amended in 1937) committed the United States to non-intervention in European affairs and reflected the determination of most Americans not to be 'duped' into war to preserve or extend European empires. A Gallup poll of American public opinion conducted in April 1939 revealed that 95 per cent of Americans polled opposed any involvement in a further European war. Later, in August 1939, when asked if US forces should go to war against Germany, 92 per cent of those polled rejected the proposal. Roosevelt, however, was instinctively drawn to the defence of democratic Great Britain against the dictatorship of Hitler, and he later used his influence to encourage all assistance to Great Britain short of war.

The possibility that Hitler might invade Romania to secure the Ploesti oilfields in order to gain self-sufficiency in oil, prompted Chamberlain to consider a wider anti-German coalition. Consequently, he offered defence guarantees to Romania, Greece, Turkey, Holland, Belgium, Switzerland, Norway, Sweden and Denmark. Chamberlain's strategy was to isolate Germany and to use the threat of trade sanctions to force Hitler to moderate his demands. In the event of an invasion of Poland, Chamberlain was confident that a Royal Navy blockade of the Baltic, combined with the threat of bombing German industry, would eventually force Hitler to withdraw. He expected any attempt by Hitler to launch a retaliatory attack in the west to be contained by the formidable barrier of the French Maginot Line, completed in 1938. Consequently Chamberlain firmly upheld the British guarantee of Poland's borders and expected deterrence rather than direct military intervention to defend Poland against Nazi aggression. The country best placed to lend Poland practical military assistance was the Soviet Union, but Poland refused Soviet offers of a military alliance. Colonel Beck, the Polish foreign minister, was concerned that once on its territory the Red Army would refuse to withdraw. Chamberlain shared this anxiety and was concerned that Stalin might also take advantage of an anti-Nazi alliance with the smaller states of the Baltic and Eastern Europe to expand Soviet influence. Prime Minister Daladier of France and members of the British cabinet pressed Chamberlain to reconsider his opposition to the Soviet Union. The re-establishment of the Triple Entente of the Great War was widely held to be the ultimate check to Hitler. In 1939 the Soviet Union could field 125 divisions, France 100 divisions, Poland 40 divisions and Britain 16 divisions (post-conscription). At best the Wehrmacht could field 130 divisions. On 17 April 1939, the foreign commissar of the Soviet Union, Maxim Litvinov, renewed his standing offer to Britain and France of a 'Collective Security' treaty, but Chamberlain hesitated. He preferred to await developments, confident that his counter-challenge would succeed in deterring Hitler without the need for the military assistance of the Soviet Union. After three weeks without a positive response from Chamberlain, Stalin lost patience. On 4 May he dismissed Litvinov from his post as foreign commissar and appointed Vyacheslav Molotov in his place. Litvinov had been associated with the promotion of the anti-Nazi policy of 'collective security' since 1934, and he was also a Jew. His dismissal was a clear signal to Berlin that Stalin was open to alternative proposals. Stalin had first signalled a more tolerant attitude towards Nazi Germany on 10 March 1939, when in a speech to the Eighteenth Congress of the Communist Party of the Soviet Party (CPSU) he declared a Soviet disinterest in the dispute between the western capitalist powers. The statement, and Litvinov's dismissal, reflected Stalin's mounting suspicions of the western powers. The Soviet Union had been excluded from the Munich talks, and Stalin feared a further settlement between France, Britain and Nazi Germany that would permit the German annexation of Poland and possibly give passive or even active support to a German invasion of the Soviet Union. Nazi propaganda regularly promoted the idea of a German-led crusade against communism, and this was known to be attractive to many in the west. In France, the pro-Fascist organisations Solidarite Française and Croix de Feu firmly rejected communism and urged greater ties with Germany, Italy and Spain; in Britain, Oswald Mosley's British Union of Fascists and the Link organisations also promoted a pro-German stance. The Roman Catholic Church was also strongly anti-communism but made no criticisms of Hitler. Stalin needed to avoid war because the Red Army had been significantly weakened by a major purge of the Soviet High Command between 1938 and 1939, and in addition a programme of modernisation and re-equipment was far from complete. The purge had resulted in the execution of three out of five marshals, thirteen out of fifteen army commanders, fifty-seven out of eighty-five corp commanders, 110 out of 195 divisional commanders and 220 out of 406 brigade commanders. In total Stalin had ordered the execution of approximately 30,000 army officers to enforce total subservience to his leadership. Stalin's primary interest was the survival of the Soviet Union, and if he could not deter Hitler in alliance with Britain and France he was willing to explore Hitler's price for future peace.

On 21 May 1939 Hitler's position was strengthened when Mussolini signed the 'Pact of Steel' military alliance with Germany. The original suggestion to call it the Pact of Blood was dropped as too melodramatic even for Mussolini. The Pact was opposed by King Victor Emmanuel, the Pope, Ciano, and many of the senior Fascists on the Fascist Grand Council owing to a general dislike of Nazi Germany and an increasing fear that Italy was serving Germany's interests. The alliance committed Italy to war and opened up the prospect of a Mediterranean front against Britain and France. Hitler also offered a military alliance to Japan to raise a threat to British and French possessions in the Far East. However, for the Japanese, Hitler had chosen the wrong enemy. Whereas Hitler was contemplating warmer relations with the Soviet Union, the Japanese Kwantung Army was contemplating the invasion of Siberia and was interested in an anti-Soviet alliance. The mismatch of interests prevented any agreement, but Hitler was convinced that neither Chamberlain nor Daladier would risk a war against Germany while facing threats to their empire possessions in the Mediterranean and the Pacific.

Mussolini assured Hitler of his commitment to the Pact of Steel and Italy's readiness for war, and with this assurance Hitler confirmed his plans for the invasion of Poland. He stated to a meeting of the German High Command, the OKW (Oberkommando de Wehrmacht), on 23 May: 'further successes can no longer be achieved without the shedding of blood . . . there is no question of sparing Poland'.[4] In preparation, two army groups were gradually massed on Poland's borders. The scale of the military build-up was successfully concealed by the top secret Welle Plan that mobilised the Wehrmacht in a series of insignificant 'waves'.

Chamberlain, under pressure from the British cabinet, finally acknowledged the military importance of the Soviet Union, and on 25 May he authorised the opening of exploratory talks with the Soviet Union. Five days later Hitler secretly gave Foreign Minister Joachim von Ribbentrop his permission to open informal contacts with Stalin to discuss trade relations and in particular the future of Poland. The possibility of a Nazi–Soviet pact was discounted in the west, given the volume and frequency of Nazi anti-communist propaganda. Stalin was generally considered to be so desperate for an anti-Nazi alliance that the only question was the terms. Thus Chamberlain's focus was not on wooing the Soviet Union but on setting safeguards to ensure that Stalin never took advantage of any negotiated defence treaty to 'protect' the smaller states of Eastern Europe and the Baltic. Chamberlain's dilemma was how best to avoid Europe being dominated by either Fascism or communism.

On 17 July, after slow and inconclusive negotiations with Britain and France, Stalin demanded evidence of a western military commitment to deter Hitler. The British and French military delegation took three weeks to arrive in Moscow, having travelled by ship and train. Whether they could have travelled faster is open to debate, but it added to Stalin's suspicion that Britain and France might choose to remain behind the security of the Maginot Line while the Soviet Union battled Germany on their behalf. Stalin's worst fears appeared to be confirmed during the first round of military talks on 12 August, when Admiral Drax, in command of the British delegation, admitted that he had not been given any plenipotentiary powers to sign a military agreement. When pressed on how many divisions Britain could immediately commit to war his answer was two and a half. It was an answer Stalin repeated to himself several times as though in disbelief. Drax was also forced to admit that Poland had refused transit rights for Soviet forces to cross Polish territory to engage the Wehrmacht. In contrast, parallel contacts with Ribbentrop offered Stalin trade agreements, a secret protocol to restore Russian territory awarded to Poland by the Treaty of Versailles in 1919, recognition of Soviet interests in the Baltic States and, of greatest importance, a peace treaty. The Nazi offer was, by far, the more attractive, and especially as Stalin detested the existence of Poland as much as Hitler. Stalin was also concerned by the possibility of a war with Japan. In July 1939, Georgi Zhukhov, who later organised the successful defences of Leningrad and Moscow in 1941, inflicted heavy losses on the Japanese Kwantung Army following an incursion on the Mongolian border. Stalin was ultimately keen to avoid a war on two fronts.

During a visit to Berlin from 9 to 13 August, Italian Foreign Minister Galeazzo Ciano was horrified to discover the extent of Germany's preparations for war. Before agreeing to the Pact of Steel, Ciano had emphasised that Italy could not be ready for military action until 1942 at the earliest, and in addition the Pact had specified joint agreement prior to a declaration of war. Ciano was alarmed by the lack of consultation and the apparent expectation, in Berlin, that Germany would lead and Italy would follow. It confirmed Ciano's worst fears: that for Hitler, Italy was only a convenient distraction to occupy France and Britain in the Mediterranean while Germany turned east. On his return to Rome, Ciano met with Mussolini, and bitterly declared: 'the Germans are traitors and we must not have any scruples in ditching them'.[5] Ciano's diary recorded that Mussolini collapsed into mental turmoil and changed his mind, on a daily basis, whether or not to end his alliance with Hitler.

On 19 August, Stalin made his decision and entered into a mutually beneficial trade agreement with Germany. The next day Stalin agreed to a request from Hitler to receive Ribbentrop to discuss a wider pact. On 22 August, while Ribbentrop was en route to Moscow, Hitler received his High Command at Berchtesgaden and sought to assuage their doubts as to the wisdom of going to war. They were concerned by the poor state of German defences in the west and the danger of a two-front war. Hitler detailed at length the military weaknesses of Britain and France and confidently declared that their leadership would never declare war: 'No masters. No men of action . . . Our enemies are small fry, I saw them in Munich.'[6] News of Stalin's acceptance of the non-aggression pact reached an impatient Hitler at Berchtesgaden in the early hours of 23 August. Champagne was opened, but eschewed by the teetotal Hitler. In ecstatic mood, Hitler declared to this entourage: 'Now Europe is mine. The others can have Asia.'[7] Hitler envisaged a short, victorious invasion of Poland and ordered it to commence on 26 August to take advantage of the disarray in Britain and France. There was also considerable disarray in Tokyo. The Japanese prime minister, Hiranuma, had expected to gain German support against the Soviet Union. He admitted his 'bafflement' at the unexpected news of the Nazi–Soviet Pact and resigned from office. However, after the fall of France in June 1940, Japan revived its ambition for an expansion into the southern Pacific at the expense of British and French colonial territories. By then only the powerful US Pacific Fleet based at Pearl Harbor was in a position to block Japanese expansion.

Hitler expected Great Britain and France to withdraw their support for Poland and to enter into a settlement, but on 25 August, Chamberlain offered Poland a formal military treaty. It was more gesture than substance. Britain and France could not directly reinforce Poland, and in response to Poland's request for a loan of £60 million in military aid Chamberlain promised £5 million if France would commit the same amount. However, Hitler was shaken by the news because he had counted upon Britain and France entering into a further Munich-style conference to recast European and colonial boundaries. Mussolini was also shaken by the news and on the eve of war he lost his nerve. With less than twelve hours to go before the invasion of Poland, the Italian ambassador in Berlin, Bernardo Attolico, delivered a telegram to Hitler from Mussolini with the news that Italy was unable to honour its treaty commitment to go to war. Coupled with Chamberlain's robust defence of Poland, Hitler hesitated and cancelled the invasion plan. Forward units of the SS in position for the dawn attack were hastily recalled. Mussolini blamed the Spanish Civil War from 1936 to 1939 for exhausting Italy's military supplies, but he promised to honour the Pact of Steel if Germany would supply Italy's minimum war needs. Mussolini's unspoken concern was an immediate attack on Italian shipping and the Italian empire in North Africa by the more powerful French and British navies. Hitler offered to make good Italy's deficiency in military supplies, but the shopping list advanced by Ciano was inflated to the point of absurdity and invited rejection. The list of munitions and equipment presented to Hitler was, in Ciano's words, 'enough to kill a bull – if a bull could read it'.[8] In all, Ciano requested 17,000 train loads of munitions – a clearly impossible quantity. When asked to clarify the timescale for the delivery of the munitions, the anti-Nazi Attolico added his own personal condition of delivery in advance of the commencement of hostilities with Poland.

Italy was off the hook but Hitler asked Mussolini to maintain the appearance of military solidarity to keep Britain and France under pressure. Within days, to Hitler's further irritation, the news of Italy's neutrality was leaked in Rome. Mussolini was hoping to renew his credentials as the independent statesman in expectation of a peace conference. The Italian people were delighted by the news of Italy's neutrality, but Mussolini was deeply uncomfortable with his decision. It was an embarrassing reminder of 1914 when Italy had also declared neutrality and failed to support Germany on the eve of war. More directly it was an embarrassing volte-face for a leader who openly boasted of the virtues of war. Mussolini's discomfort was apparent when he later side-stepped the word 'neutrality', and insisted upon describing Italy as a 'non-belligerent' nation. Thus Mussolini's bellicose challenge to Britain and France ended in burlesque semantics, but once France and Britain were on the verge of defeat, in June 1940, Mussolini, ever the opportunist, entered the war on Germany's side.

The involvement of Italy was not essential to Hitler's war plan and he rescheduled the invasion of Poland for dawn on 1 September. In the final days before the invasion Hitler remained confident that Britain and France would seek a peace settlement. He encouraged three lines of communication. First, he offered to enter into direct negotiations with Poland to reunite East Prussia and Danzig with Germany. Second, he authorised the Swedish businessman, Birger Dahlerus, to enter into informal negotiations with British Foreign Secretary Lord Halifax. Third, on 31 August 1939, he supported Mussolini's offers of a peace conference. However, all the contacts were ended when Hitler made it clear that he expected Britain to abandon Poland and that any conference would be held after the German occupation of Poland. Acceptance would have relegated Great Britain to a secondary position in Europe and promoted Hitler as the final arbiter of European affairs. In 1914, Emperor Wilhelm II had presented Britain with a similar choice. In 1939 Great Britain was equally determined not to yield its position as the leading Great Power to Germany. National interest rather than the defence of weaker nations or opposition to the evils of Nazism, as evidenced by the Munich settlement, governed the counter-challenge. Hitler pinned his hopes on delivering a knockout blow to Poland that would present Britain with a *fait accompli* and force Chamberlain to accept the reality of a German continent. At 12.30 p.m. on 31 August 1939, Hitler signed Directive No. 1 and ordered the invasion of Poland for dawn the next morning.

References

1. Alan Bullock, *Hitler: A Study in Tyranny*, Penguin, 1962, p. 498.
2. Ibid., p. 499.
3. Richard Overy and Andrew Wheatcroft, *The Road To War*, Macmillan, 1989, p. 276.
4. Alan Bullock, *Hitler: A Study in Tyranny*, Penguin, 1962, p. 509.
5. Christopher Hibbert, *Benito Mussolini: The Rise and Fall of Il Duce*, Penguin, 1986, p. 136.
6. J.C.G. Rohl, *From Bismarck to Hitler*, Longman, 1970, p. 154.
7. Donald Cameron Watt, *How War Came: The Immediate Origins of The Second World War 1938–39*, Heinemann, 1989, p. 462.
8. Ibid., p. 501.

Outbreak

6 Case White: Poland

> When starting a war it is not right that matters, but victory . . . The destruction of Poland has priority. Close your hearts to pity. Act brutally. Eighty million people must obtain what is their right.[1]
>
> Adolf Hitler, addressing his commanders-in-chief
> on 22 August 1939

At 4.45 a.m. on 1 September 1939 (Y Day), the German battleship *Schleswig-Holstein* opened fire, without warning, on the Polish garrison of the Westerplatte Fort, Danzig, in the first military engagement of the Second World War. Simultaneously sixty-two German divisions, supported by 1,300 aircraft, commenced the invasion of Poland. The invasion caught Poland by surprise with only seventeen divisions in the field, a further thirteen divisions in transit and nine still in barracks. Negotiations with Hitler over the future of Danzig were still in progress, and with the security of British and French military guarantees Poland was convinced that Hitler would not risk war.

To justify the invasion the SS staged 'Operation Himmler', a series of fake Polish attacks on German border positions on the evening of 31 August. The most notorious was the attack on the German radio station at Gleiwitz where, to add authenticity, concentration camp prisoners, codenamed 'canned goods', were murdered by lethal injection and left at the scene dressed in Polish army uniforms. The incident was over in minutes, but it provided the pretext for action. At 5.40 a.m. the next morning, Hitler addressed the German nation on the radio and, with the invasion already underway, he condemned the intolerable 'Polish aggression' at Gleiwitz and declared war. Earlier, Hitler had remarked to his generals: 'I shall give a propaganda reason for starting the war; whether it is plausible or not. The victor will not be asked whether he told the truth.'[2]

As the diplomats in Warsaw, Paris and London struggled to establish the facts the Luftwaffe, with the advantage of surprise, destroyed most of the Polish air force on the ground. Few of Poland's 842 aircraft escaped. Those that took to the air were no match for the superior German Messerschmitt, and by the end of the first day air supremacy was largely achieved. Warsaw, the capital, was bombed for the first time at 6 a.m. and thereafter suffered daily air attacks. Apart from a few sporadic counter-attacks the Polish air force ceased to exist as a fighting force. At 8 a.m. Poland requested military assistance from France and Great Britain, but Prime Ministers Daladier and Chamberlain recommended the intervention of Mussolini and a peace conference. The commencement of a slow round of discussions between London, Paris, Rome and Berlin was met with incredulity in Poland. The Polish foreign minister, Beck, telegraphed Paris in frustration: 'We are in the midst of war as a result of unprovoked aggression. It is no longer a question of a conference'.[3] The proposal for a peace conference floundered when Hitler refused to accept Daladier's and Chamberlain's precondition of ending the war.

On the ground two major army groups invaded Poland. Army Group North, under the command of Colonel-General von Block, crossed the border from Pomerania and East Prussia, and Army Group South, under the command of Colonel-General von Rundstedt, invaded from Silesia and Slovakia. The latter took advantage of the annexation of Czechoslovakia in March 1939 to push the invasion point further to the east. The strategy was to undercut the Polish front line and to attack in the rear of the Polish Army, which was largely deployed in a 'forward' defence along the border with Germany.

Map 1 Outbreak of war, 1939

To Chamberlain's undisguised annoyance, throughout 2 September the French government refused to join Britain in issuing an ultimatum for military action. Field Marshal Gamelin insisted that the French Army was not ready and, with any military action on the Western Front dependent on the French Army, Chamberlain was forced to delay. At 7.42 p.m. on Saturday, 2 September, there was a loud cheer when Prime Minister Chamberlain entered the House of Commons, sitting in emergency session. However, the cheers turned to jeers when instead of announcing an ultimatum for war Chamberlain spoke of his personal hopes for a peace conference. It was too much for the House. As Arthur Greenwood, the deputy leader of the Labour opposition, rose to speak, the backbench Conservative MP Leopold Amery shouted, 'Speak for England.'[4] Greenwood condemned the 36 hours of military inaction and stated: 'I wonder how long we are prepared to vacillate at the time when Britain and all that Britain stands for and human civilisation is in peril.'[5] Stung by the criticism, and faced with a backbench rebellion against his leadership, Chamberlain decided to act without waiting for France. At 11.30 p.m. the British cabinet approved the presentation of an ultimatum to Germany to withdraw from Poland with a deadline for acceptance of 11 a.m. on 3 September. There was little expectation of agreement and at 11.15 a.m. on Sunday, 3 September 1939, Chamberlain announced, on national radio, that Britain and Germany were at war. In France, Foreign Minister Bonnet and Gamelin were still keen to delay a declaration of war, but Daladier overruled their objections and declared war at 5 p.m. on 3 September. The open divisions in French politics that were to later produce collaboration and the partition of France in 1940 were already evident. The rest of Europe, including Italy, Germany's ally, declared neutrality. However, in support of Great Britain the Commonwealth nations – Australia, New Zealand and India – also declared war on Germany on 3 September followed by South Africa on 6 September and Canada on 10 September. The USA reaffirmed its neutrality on 5 September and placed an embargo on the export of all armaments to nations involved in the war. However, the sympathies of President Roosevelt were clearly evident when on 4 November he authorised an amendment to the Neutrality Act of 1937 to permit the export to Britain and France of arms on a cash-and-carry basis. It was as much help as President Roosevelt could offer at a time when the White House was flooded with over a million telegrams strongly against any US involvement in the war.

To mark the British declaration of war on 3 September ten RAF Whitley bombers dropped, not bombs, but 6 million propaganda leaflets on the Ruhr. The next day bombs were dropped on the German fleet in Wilhelmshaven, but the main RAF effort was restricted to further leaflet drops, disparagingly referred to as 'bumph drops' by the RAF crews. By the time the campaign ended in March 1940, an estimated 65 million propaganda leaflets had been dropped over Germany. It underlined Chamberlain's wish to deter Hitler and a fear of provoking retaliatory Luftwaffe air strikes on Britain's cities.

Hitler travelled to the front line on 3 September on board his armoured train, incongruously named *Americka*, to monitor the invasion. The rapid progress of the Wehrmacht exceeded his expectations. By 6 September the leading elements of both German army groups driving from north and south linked up at Lodz, in central Poland, and cleaved Poland in two. In less than a week the bulk of the Polish Army was encircled and trapped against the German border.

The danger had been foreseen. In pre-war military discussions the Chief of Staff of the French Army, Weygand, had warned the commander-in-chief of the Polish Army, Marshal Edward Smigly-Rydz, of the vulnerability of western Poland to encirclement.

Rather than trying to defend the long 1,250-mile border with Germany, Weygand had advised a shorter 420-mile defensive front, in central Poland, along the natural barriers of the broad Vistula and San rivers. Smigly-Rydz had rejected the advice, because western Poland contained Poland's most valuable industrial and agricultural regions of Upper Silesia: Lodz and Poznan. The control of resources was considered to be vital to national survival because Smigly-Rydz expected to fight a long war of attrition. Smigly-Rydz was confident that Poland could successfully resist a German attack, for at least three weeks, until France and Britain entered the war in the west and lifted the pressure. Like military planners in France and Britain, Smigly-Rydz was locked into a Great War mindset of fortified positions, probing attacks, artillery barrages, long frontal infantry assaults and, worse still, the cavalry charge. Twelve of Poland's divisions were cavalry armed with lance and sabre. Poland was totally unprepared for the mass deployment of the tank and the speed of the German advance.

The potential of a concentrated mass of tanks to break and overwhelm the enemy front line was promoted in Germany by Captain Heinz Guderian. He based his theories on the Experimental Armoured Force (EAF) established by Captain Liddell-Hart of the British Army in 1927. Guderian conducted his own experiments with tanks in 1928 using training grounds in Russia to evade the restrictions of the Treaty of Versailles. The German High Command, like their counterparts in Britain and France, were sceptical of the value of the tank, but this changed in 1935 when Hitler attended a demonstration of Germany's first experimental tank, the 'Panzer 1' and declared, 'that's what I need, that's what I want to have'.[6] In 1937, Guderian, promoted to colonel, published his ideas for tank warfare in *Achtung Panzer!* and recommended a strategy of 'concentrated surprise attack'.[7] In February 1938 Guderian was further promoted to general and placed in command of the world's first armoured corps, comprising six panzer divisions and four motorised infantry divisions.

In his early writings Liddell-Hart had referred to 'lightning war', but it was *Time* magazine in the issue of 25 September 1939 that popularised the term 'Blitzkrieg' to describe the new mobile warfare that unfolded in Poland.

Blitzkrieg changed the face of warfare. Poland was attacked from land and air in a carefully co-ordinated fast-moving assault. In a wide arc, in advance of the line of attack, the Luftwaffe bombed all major road and rail junctions, concentrations of troops and supply columns. The aim of the continuous air strikes was to disrupt and prevent the free movement of supplies and reinforcements to the front line. Towns and cities in the path of the advance were also bombed, with the deliberate aim of creating a fleeing mass of terror-stricken refugees to choke the roads and further hamper attempts by reinforcements to reach the battle front. Flying directly ahead of the armoured columns the Junkers Ju-87 dive-bomber (*Sturzkampfflugzeug*), more commonly known as the Stuka, fulfilled the role of artillery and destroyed any strong points in the immediate path of the advance. The Stukas also deliberately induced terror by generating a high-pitched wail from air sirens attached to the wheel spats when they dived. The firepower of the panzers destroyed any remaining opposition, and motorised infantry travelling close behind in trucks and half-tracks (for cross-country operations) engaged any surviving enemy forces. At all times the strategy depended upon movement to prevent the development of a static front line. Any major strong points or troop concentrations were bypassed and left to be engaged by the main infantry divisions of the Wehrmacht.

Poland urged Britain and France to invade Germany in the west to force the diversion of men and equipment. The commander-in-chief of the French Army, Maurice

Gamelin, in a gross distortion of the truth, reassured the Polish government that 'more than half of our active divisions on the North-east front are engaged in combat'.[8] In fact, Gamelin refused to authorise anything more than light, probing attacks to map the German defences. On 7 September, elements of the French 4th and 5th armies crossed the border into the Saarland, but after an advance of approximately eight miles they dug in half a mile from the defensive German 'West Wall'.

In contrast, by 8 September advance elements of panzers of the 10th Army reached the suburbs of Warsaw having covered 140 miles in eight days. The Polish Army in western Poland was forced into five isolated pockets centred around Pomerania, Poznan, Lodz, Krakow and Carpathia. Blitzkrieg corralled the Polish Army, but the victory was secured by the main force of traditional infantry on foot and reliant on railway and horse-drawn supplies. The only serious Polish challenge arose between 10 and 19 September when the Poznan Army attempted to break the encirclement and fall back on Warsaw. Pitched battles ensued around the Bzura river, but on 19 September General Bortnowski was forced to accept defeat and some 170,000 Polish troops were taken prisoner. Earlier, on 6 September, in a desperate act of defiance near Chelmno, Bortnowski's cavalry divisions had charged Guderian's panzers with drawn sabres. Poland had no answer to Blitzkrieg. In an attempt to rally the army, on 10 September Marshal Rydz-Smigly ordered the Polish Army to fall back and regroup in south-east Poland around Lvov for a final stand.

All hopes of national survival were pinned on a major invasion in the west by the British and French armies. However, on 13 September Gamelin ended the limited advance into the Saarland with the loss of twenty-seven French soldiers and twenty-two wounded. He remarked to General Ironside, the chief of staff of the British Army, that the offensive was only, 'A little test.'[9] The intervention of France and Britain was something the OKW feared. By 20 September, following the completion of initial mobilisation, France was able to field an estimated 57 divisions (full mobilisation would generate 110 divisions) to add to the four British divisions of the British Expeditionary Force (BEF) that had arrived in France on 19 September. It was a significant force at a time when the German opposition in the west was estimated at approximately 25 divisions. At the later Nuremberg War Crimes Trials in 1946, General Keitel expressed his surprise that the west had not invaded. The answer lay in outdated tactics. The Allied commanders had ruled out any significant attack until heavy artillery could be assembled and deployed to bombard the German lines. In his later memoirs, the French prime minister, Paul Reynaud, expressed his regret at Field Marshal Gamelin's tentative strategy. The tactics of the Great War dominated Allied thinking and significantly contributed to Poland's defeat.

By 15 September Warsaw was surrounded without hope of relief and the government and general staff were evacuated to Romania. The focus of German attention switched from Warsaw to intercepting the remnants of the Polish Army before it could establish a defensive line in south-east Poland. Guderian's panzers bypassed Warsaw and advanced directly south, reaching Brest-Litovsk on 17 September, linking up with the spearhead of Army Group South along the line of the Bug river. At dawn that morning, the Red Army unexpectedly crossed the eastern border of Poland and ended any hope of Poland's survival. There was minimal resistance and the Red Army rapidly occupied eastern Poland in fulfilment of the secret protocol to the Nazi–Soviet Pact signed on 23 August 1939. The secret was so well kept that the Wehrmacht chief of operations, General Jodl, on being informed that the Russians had entered the war, enquired: 'against whom?'[10]

There was no hope of further resistance and Poland's soldiers were ordered to retreat across the Romanian border. Approximately 100,000 did so, including Marshal Smigly-Rydz, the commander-in-chief, but most were subsequently interned following pressure from Germany. Those that reached the West formed the Free Polish Forces commanded by General Sikorski. Among them were many Polish pilots who were welcomed into the RAF and fought in the Battle of Britain in 1940. The tiny Polish Navy also escaped from the Baltic to British waters. Warsaw held out until 27 September, but after enduring eighteen days of continuous bombing, the city surrendered at 2 p.m. Poland was defeated.

The future of Poland was finalised by Ribbentrop and Molotov at 5 a.m on 29 September in Moscow, after an evening spent at the Bolshoi watching a performance of *Swan Lake*. Molotov, representing Stalin, drove a hard bargain and demanded the right to annex the Baltic states of Lithuania, Latvia and Estonia, as well as annexing the whole of eastern Poland. The Baltic States had been part of Tsarist Russia up to 1918 and Stalin, like Hitler, was keen to reclaim 'lost' territory. Hitler agreed to Stalin's demands without hesitation. He needed a passive USSR while he attended to the war in the west, and he was conscious of the importance of Soviet coal, oil, wheat and cotton to beat the Royal Navy blockade. Hitler paid for the resources with armaments at the expense of the Wehrmacht and even handed over the blueprints to the battleship *Bismarck*. It was a strategic decision. Hitler was determined to avoid a two-front war: a mistake which he believed had cost Germany the Great War.

With the end of the conventional war the racial war that was to culminate in the gas chambers of Auschwitz descended on Poland. Five SS Einsatzgruppen (action groups) of the SS security police (Sicherheitspolizei or SIPO) entered Poland on the heels of the Wehrmacht on 3 September. Each Einsatzgruppe was subdivided into four Einsatzcommandos (action commandos) of 100–150 men each. Their orders were to liquidate all Polish intelligentsia. It was a death sentence for doctors, priests, teachers, union leaders, members of political parties, journalists, writers, or anyone who could organise or rally opposition to the Nazi invasion. Colonel Wagner recorded in his personal diary a discussion with Hitler's chief of staff, General Halder, on 9 September: 'it is the Fuhrer's and Göring's intention to destroy and exterminate the Polish nation. More than that cannot even be hinted at in writing.'[11] In the hunt for the intelligentsia the Einsatzgruppen also murdered Jews in random massacres. The casual nature of the murders, openly conducted all across Poland, appalled many of the senior Wehrmacht commanders who protested and demanded the withdrawal of the SS from Poland. Admiral Canaris, the head of military intelligence, assuming that the SS were out of control, requested a meeting with Hitler to protest but was advised by General Keitel that 'this thing has been decided upon by the Fuhrer himself'.[12] The protests from the Wehrmacht intensified when ordinary soldiers refused to co-operate with the mass murder of civilians and, at the insistence of General von Rundstedt, the Einsatzgruppen were withdrawn from the operational area of the 14th Army. The tense situation between the Wehrmacht and the SS was finally resolved by Hitler on 5 October by the expedient of declaring the war over and handing control to the SS.

Western Poland was directly annexed and subdivided into three new *Reichsgau* (German regions) – Danzig West, Prussia and Posen (later renamed Warthengau) – under the command of trusted Nazi gauleiters (regional leaders). The remainder of German-occupied Poland was designated the General Government and placed under the administration of Hans Frank as governor-general. The intention of Himmler and the SS was to 'cleanse' the new *Reichsgau* of non-Aryan racial groups to make way for German settlers from across Europe – primarily the Baltic States, eastern Poland, Romania and Slovakia. In recognition of his new role, on 7 October Himmler was appointed by Hitler as the *Reichskommissar* for the Consolidation of German Nationhood, with responsibility for the resettlement policy. All Poles and Jews were to be dispossessed of farms, businesses and property and deported into the General Government as slave labourers. Himmler instructed his SS administrators: 'I propose that we be pitiless in the settlement [policy] because these new provinces must become Germanic, blond provinces of Germany . . . a Germanic blood-wall.'[13] Eventually some 47,000 Polish farms were transferred to German settlers. Himmler's obsession with race was reflected in the Procreation Order, issued in October 1939, which ordered the SS to father as many children as possible, in or out of wedlock, to increase the Aryan population of Germany and occupied territories. SS maternity homes (*Lebensborn*) were established to care for the 'racially pure' SS off-spring who were to populate the new expanded Germany. The Polish population, especially children, was combed for Aryan racial characteristics and as a result over a million Poles were awarded German nationality. Many Polish infants were also transferred to the *Lebensborn* to be raised as Germans. The future of the remainder of the Polish people was to be no more than an expendable labour force for their new German masters. Goebbels confided in his diary on 10 October: 'the Fuhrer's verdict on the Poles is damning. More like animals than human beings, completely primitive.'[14] Himmler's deputy, Heydrich, in overall command of the *Einsatzgruppen* in Poland, estimated on 27 September that only 3 per cent of the intelligentsia had escaped execution.

In line with Nazi race theories Jews were condemned as 'vermin' and 'disease carriers', and in order to limit contact with the wider population Heydrich issued an order on 21 September for all Jews to be confined to ghettos in the major cities.

Within Soviet-occupied eastern Poland a parallel programme of deportations and executions was conducted by the Red Army and the Soviet Secret police (NKVD) to cow the Polish population and enforce Soviet rule. An estimated 1.7 million Poles were uprooted from their homes and transported as slave labourers to the Gulag in Siberia. Approximately a million of those were worked to death, and at Katyn in April 1940 an estimated 15,000 Polish Army officers and 7,000 Polish 'intellectuals' were shot and buried in a mass grave by the NKVD. There was little to choose between the treatment of the Polish population by either Hitler or Stalin, but in 1941 Churchill welcomed Stalin as an ally and chose to ignore the Soviet invasion of Poland and the mass murder at Katyn because at the time the assistance of the USSR was vital to the defeat of Nazi Germany. It was a chapter of the war without honour for Great Britain and was compounded in 1945 by the acceptance of Soviet rule in Poland and the forcible return to the USSR of captured Russian Nazi collaborators for execution or slave labour in the Gulag.

The conquest of Poland was celebrated by Hitler with a victory parade by the Wehrmacht in Warsaw on 5 October, and the next day, in the Reichstag, he defended his actions and proclaimed that 'The Poland of the Versailles Treaty will never rise again.'[15] The victory had cost some 50,000 Polish dead and 10,572 Germans. On 6 October Hitler offered a peace settlement to France and Britain, but after a few days of deliberation his offer was rejected. Apart from the war at sea no further military action was taken and inaction or a 'phoney war' descended on Europe.

References

1. Alan Bullock, *Hitler and Stalin: Parallel Lives*, HarperCollins, 1991, p. 688.
2. Ibid.

3. William L. Shirer, *The Collapse of The Third Republic*, Pan, 1972, p. 560.
4. *Daily Telegraph*, 4 September 1939.
5. *Manchester Guardian*, 4 September 1939.
6. Len Deighton, *Blitzkrieg: From the Rise of Hitler to the Fall of Dunkirk*, Jonathan Cape, 1979, p. 144.
7. Heinz Guderian, *Achtung Panzer: The Development of Tank Warfare*, Cassell, 1992, p. 178.
8. William L. Shirer, *The Collapse of The Third Republic*, Pan, 1972, p. 586.
9. Ibid., p. 587.
10. Len Deighton, *Blitzkrieg: From the Rise of Hitler to the Fall of Dunkirk*, Jonathan Cape, 1979, p. 93.
11. Martin Gilbert, *Second World War*, Orion, 1989, p. 6.
12. Ibid., p. 8.
13. Peter Padfield, *Himmler: Reichsfuhrer SS*, Papermac, 1991, p. 293.
14. Fred Taylor (ed.), *The Goebbels Diaries 1939–41*, Sphere, 1983, p. 16.
15. Alan Bullock, *Hitler: A Study in Tyranny*, Penguin, 1962, p. 557.

7   The phoney war

Absolutely nothing is happening on the West Wall . . . The French have withdrawn to the border. It is impossible to say what they intend to do now. A crazy war.[1]

Goebbels, writing in his diary between 18 and 20 October

On 21 September 1939 with Poland all but defeated, Gamelin ordered the French Army to remain behind the security of the Maginot Line and not to take any offensive action. General Goutard later confirmed that French forces, 'were expressly forbidden to open fire on the Germans'.[2] It all served to confirm Goebbels' assessment of 'a crazy war'. Field Marshal Montgomery, in his memoirs published in 1958, recorded his personal frustration at the lack of military action: 'My soul revolted at what was happening. France and Britain stood still while Germany swallowed Poland . . . If this was war, I did not understand it.'[3]

The French termed the inactivity on the Western Front, *drole de guerre*, the British preferred 'twilight war' and the Germans spoke of *Sitzkrieg*. But it was the American press which coined the lasting popular term: 'phoney war'.

Only at sea was the war far from phoney as the Royal Navy hunted and engaged the German Kriegsmarine. In late August, a German raiding force comprising the battleships *Admiral Graf Spee*, *Deutschland*, *Scharnhost* and *Gneisenau*, and eighteen U-boats, dispersed unnoticed across the North Sea and the Atlantic. At 7.45 p.m. on 3 September their presence was dramatically revealed when U-30 sank the passenger liner SS *Athenia* with the loss of 112 lives. The raiding force was too weak to confront the Royal Navy directly and employed hit-and-run tactics, but it forced the introduction of convoys from 15 September and, to the discomfort of the Admiralty, achieved some notable successes. On 17 September the aircraft carrier HMS *Courageous* was the first Allied warship to be sunk, with the lost of 519 lives. More dramatically, on

14 October, in a daring raid, U-47 negotiated the defences of the Holm Sound and entered the 'safe' anchorage of Scapa Flow and sunk HMS *Royal Oak* riding at anchor. Rear-Admiral Blagrove perished, along with 832 of the crew. Hitler personally decorated the U-boat commander, Captain Prien, with the Knight's Cross in what was a major propaganda coup for the Kriegsmarine but a tragedy for the Royal Navy.

The Allied reluctance to invade Germany was born of a deep-seated fear of aerial attack and reliance on a defensive rather than an offensive military strategy. The security of France was vested in the Maginot Line and the security of Britain in the Royal Navy, but neither was a barrier to the Luftwaffe. The Luftwaffe possessed an estimated 2,000 bombers compared to a combined total for France and Britain of 950. It was estimated that in Britain alone 1,860 anti-aircraft guns were needed to defend key sites, but in 1939 only 108 were available. The British Expeditionary Force (BEF) requested 352 anti-aircraft guns to defend the front line in France but received only 152. The fear of air attack was very real. The Germans opened the war in Poland with the extensive bombing of Poland's major cities and both France and Britain feared thousands of civilian deaths from similar air attacks – in particular the dropping of gas bombs. Hitler stoked the fear by releasing photographs of bomb-damaged Warsaw to the international press and warned: 'That is how I can deal with any European city.'[4] The Committee for Imperial Defence calculated that within the first two months of war 600,000 people would be killed by air raids in Britain's heavily populated cities. Papier mâché coffins were stockpiled ready for the expected casualties, along with pre-signed, blank death certificates. Consequently both France and Britain wanted to avoid military action to give time to evacuate the major cities. Approximately 827,000 children and 535,000 women were evacuated from Britain's major cities between 1 and 3 September to the safety of homes in the countryside, and a further 2 million made their own private arrangements. However, by January 1940 the majority had returned home, following a combination of homesickness and the inaction of the phoney war. The only immediate casualties were the poisonous snakes of London Zoo. All were beheaded to settle a public fear of their escape during a bomb attack. Time was also needed for the bulk of the French Army to dig in along the Belgian border and to transfer the BEF across the English Channel. The headline in the *Manchester Guardian* on 4 September – 'Germans use Gas Bombs in Poland'[5] appeared to justify the caution in not rushing into war. The headline was mistaken, but the threat of a gas attack remained a potent fear throughout the war. To the delight of the British public the backbench MP Winston Churchill, who had consistently opposed Hitler throughout the 1930s, was appointed to the War Cabinet as First Lord of the Admiralty. It was a post he had first held in 1914 at the outbreak of the Great War.

With Poland defeated and occupied Hitler, in a speech to the Reichstag on 6 October, offered Britain and France a peace treaty. He described Poland as his final revision of the Treaty of Versailles and expressed his desire for lasting peace. There were some in France and Britain who recommended acceptance. They were encouraged by propaganda radio broadcasts from Radio Hamburg by the British defector William Joyce. He was nicknamed Lord Haw Haw by the *Daily Express* for his upper-class English accent and trademark pronunciation of Germany as 'Jairmany'. Joyce was captured at the end of the war and executed for high treason in 1946. His wife Margaret Joyce escaped a similar fate on 'compassionate grounds', despite an abundance of evidence of her involvement in treasonable activities. Hitler's offer of peace was rejected by France and Britain on the 10 and 12 of October respectively. However, neither was in a hurry to break the phoney war. Time was on the Allied side. Time would deplete Germany's resources and time would also allow the Allies to make good the deficiencies in men and equipment, and especially in air power. Chamberlain gave the priority in national resources to the Royal Air Force (RAF) in a strategy that envisaged a tight blockade of Germany by land and sea, and, by late 1940, the commencement of a bomber offensive to destroy German industry and force capitulation.

Hitler was well aware of the danger and he was not prepared to sit and wait to be attacked. As early as 27 September he had informed his High Command or OKW (Oberkommando de Wehrmacht) to prepare for the rapid transfer of the Wehrmacht from Poland to the Western Front ready for a lightning attack. He confirmed his orders in a memorandum on 9 October and set the date of 12 November for the attack. The order was resisted by the OKW and raised the strong possibility of a military *putsch* against Hitler. Hitler's orders were questioned by General Brauchitsch and the general staff because all firmly believed that Germany was too weak to win a general European war. Brauchitsch planned to dissuade Hitler from attacking in the west at a meeting on 10 October, but Hitler, alert to the discontent, struck first. Hitler berated Brauchitsch and the OKW for defeatism in a verbal attack that left him broken and speechless. Brauchitsch was also reminded of his oath of loyalty to the supreme commander of the Wehrmacht at a time of war. It was not until 1943 onwards, with the certainty of defeat, that elements of the OKW finally recovered their nerve and plotted Hitler's assassination.

On 19 October the OKW reluctantly fulfilled Hitler's bidding and prepared the attack plan for the west codenamed *Fall Gelb* or Case Yellow. It was a reprise of the 1914 Schliefflen Plan of a major sweep through Belgium into France involving 102 divisions. Hitler was not enthusiastic because it meant a frontal assault against the bulk of the French and British armies in prepared defensive positions, and he also feared slow movement through the towns and cities of Belgium. General Erich von Manstein, the chief of staff of Army Group A, had similar misgivings and in a series of memos to the OKW between October and December 1939 he recommended a surprise attack through the Ardennes directly into France. The Ardennes was an area of steep river valleys with thick forest and was an unlikely place for a major attack. The OKW dismissed Manstein's plans as fanciful, but on 9 November Hitler arrived at similar conclusions and ordered a rethink of the attack plan to transfer the weight of the attack to the south. His inspiration was apparently due to German intelligence breaking French military traffic and identifying the weakly defended Ardennes sector, but the author Martin Allen makes a more sensational claim. Allen asserts that the Duke of Windsor betrayed Britain and France and provided Hitler with vital intelligence after he toured the defences of the Western Front on 6 October and received a briefing on the Allied defence strategy over dinner with Gamelin. On 9 October the Duke dined with a known double agent, Charles Bedaux, and Dutch intelligence later observed Bedaux entering Hitler's Chancellery on the key date of 9 November. If this account is true, it places a traitor within the British Royal Family and offers a more convincing explanation for the lifelong exile of the Duke of Windsor than the scandal of his abdication and marriage to Wallace Simpson an American divorcee.

The weather achieved what Brauchitsch could not. On 7 November weather reports of heavy rain and low cloud forced Hitler to postpone the attack scheduled for 12 November. On 20 November, Hitler ordered the OKW to implement Operation

Fall Gelb as soon as the weather cleared. To win over the doubters he addressed his senior commanders on 23 November and demanded their faith and loyalty. He emphasised the advantage of fighting a one-front war and declared: 'My decision is unchangeable. I shall attack France and England at the most favourable and quickest moment.'[6] Brauchitsch still had major doubts and immediately after the meeting he tendered his resignation, but Hitler refused to accept it and instructed him to 'obey orders'. Mussolini, in a letter to Hitler, also tried to dissuade him from an attack in the west and urged Hitler to stay true to his anti-Bolshevik roots and attack in the east. Only days before, Hitler had remarked that once the West was defeated, he would turn east 'and show who was the master there'.[7] Mussolini failed to recognise that before he turned east Hitler had to gain security from attack in the west.

The poor weather did not deter Stalin who, following a border dispute with Finland in October and November, ordered an invasion of Finland, without warning, on 30 November. It was the opening of the Winter War that lasted to March 1940.

The war at sea remained the active front line. By the end of December 1939, after four months of warfare, the U-boats had sunk 114 Allied ships. The U-boats and the surface raiders were the greatest threats to Allied shipping, although there were others. On 22 November one of Hitler's much-vaunted 'secret weapons', a magnetic mine, was recovered from the mud of the Thames Estuary near Shoeburyness. Magnetic mines had sunk fifty-nine ships and damaged many more, including the cruiser HMS *Belfast* which was put out of action for three years. The mines were difficult to detect because they lay inert on the seabed until triggered by the magnetic field generated by a passing ship. The captured mine was dismantled and examined, and by March 1940 the countermeasure of 'degaussing' was perfected. An electric current was passed around ship hulls and this successfully neutralised the magnetic field and limited the danger. Many mines were also cleared by wooden minesweepers which towed cables to generate a magnetic field and thus explode the mines safely. Allied merchant ships were also targeted by fast-attack motorboats (E-boats), operating in the approaches to the English Channel and, after the fall of France, from bases in the Channel Islands and along the French coast. A further danger was from German merchant ships armed with concealed guns. One of the most successful merchant raiders was the *Atlantis* which sank twenty two Allied ships before being intercepted and sunk on 22 November 1941 by HMS *Devonshire* in the South Atlantic.

Against this background of rising losses at sea the Royal Navy scored a dramatic success in December 1939 with the interception of the *Admiral Graf Spee* off the River Plate, Uruguay. The *Graf Spee* had sunk nine merchant ships in the South Atlantic since the start of the war and was a key target for the Royal Navy. At dawn on 13 December, the Royal Navy Hunting Group G, HMS *Exeter*, *Ajax* and *Achilles* engaged the *Graf Spee*. The *Graf Spee*, heavily armed with six 11-inch guns and protected by heavy armour, possessed the advantage. By 7.40 a.m. the more lightly armed HMS *Achilles* and *Ajax* were both badly damaged, on fire, and forced to break off the action. However, the *Graf Spee* was sufficiently damaged by the exchange for Captain Langsdorff to enter Montevideo harbour, Uruguay, to seek emergency repairs. It proved to be a gross error because it gave the Royal Navy time to regroup. British propaganda successfully convinced Langsdorff that the more powerful Royal Navy Hunting Group K, including the aircraft carrier *Ark Royal* and the battleship *Renown*, was waiting off the coast for his return to sea. Under the neutrality rules the *Graf Spee* was granted a maximum stay of 72 hours in harbour. On the evening of

17 December, as thousands of spectators watched from the shoreline, the *Graf Spee* turned to sea. But rather than enter into battle with the the superior force believed to be lying in wait, Langsdorff opted to spare the crew and he ordered the *Graf Spee* to be scuttled. On 20 December Langsdorff shot himself in his hotel bedroom wrapped in the German flag. By December 1939, the immediate threat from the Kriegsmarine was largely contained. Britain had lost 422,230 tons of shipping – approximately 2 per cent of the merchant marine – since the start of the war against the loss of 224,372 tons for Germany. However, the German losses represented 5 per cent of her much-smaller merchant marine.

On 10 January, Hitler set 17 January as the date for the attack in the west, but an intelligence blunder rather than the weather further frustrated his plans. On 10 January, the attack plans fell into Allied hands when a Luftwaffe courier, Major Reinberger, was forced to make a crash landing in Belgium. However, the Allies were suspicious of their good fortune and discounted the captured plans as clumsy Nazi disinformation. Hitler cancelled the attack plan and the OKW were forced back to the drawing board. General Schmundt, Hitler's adjutant, advocated Manstein's plan and arranged a meeting between Hitler and Manstein on 17 February. Hitler seized upon Manstein's plans for a major attack through the Ardennes because it matched his own earlier instinct for a surprise attack to the south. By the end of February, the military plan that would give Hitler victory in the west was ready for action, with Manstein's sweep to the Channel appropriately named 'Sickle Cut'.

However, heavy snowfalls across Europe in one of the worst winters on record forced Hitler to postpone the attack to the spring. In his diary, Goebbels recorded temperatures of 20 to 25 below zero in Berlin throughout January, and on 10 February he noted: 'more cold weather and heavy snowfalls'. Two days later he wrote: 'the barbarically cold weather continues'.[8] In Britain, the worst winter since 1895 was recorded. The Thames froze over, as did the sea in harbours along the south coast; deep snowdrifts blocked roads and railways across the country.

In February 1940 President Roosevelt sent a personal envoy, Sumner Welles, to tour Europe to seek a basis for a peace settlement. He returned to the United States on 20 March 1940 without success, primarily because Hitler saw no need to relinquish his gains. Hitler was confident of delivering a knock-out blow to the west in a matter of months. Chamberlain was equally confident of victory because the Allied forces had increased their strength on Germany's border and their defences against air attack.

In a speech to the Conservative Party on 5 April 1940 on the eve of British naval action to secure Norwegian waters, Chamberlain, confident that the 'phoney war' had worked to the Allies' advantage by permitting the build-up of a major Allied army on the German border, proclaimed: 'Hitler has missed the bus.'[9] It was a misjudgement that would return to haunt him because, unknown to Chamberlain, German forces were already at sea and also en route to Norway. The phoney war was about to end with the first German military action in the west from Copenhagen to Narvik.

References

1. Fred Taylor (ed.), *The Goebbels Diaries 1939–41*, Sphere, 1983, p. 24.
2. William L. Shirer, *The Collapse of The Third Republic*, Pan, 1972, p. 606.
3. Montgomery, *The Memoirs of Field Marshal The Viscount Montgomery of Alamein K.G.*, Collins, 1958, p. 58.
4. Martin Gilbert, *Second World War*, Orion, 1989, p. 19.

5. *Manchester Guardian*, 4 September 1939.
6. Alan Bullock, *Hitler: A Study in Tyranny*, Penguin, 1962, p. 569.
7. Martin Gilbert, *Second World War*, Orion, 1989, p. 23.
8. Fred Taylor (ed.), *The Goebbels Diaries 1939–41*, Sphere, 1983, pp. 118–20.
9. A.J.P. Taylor, *English History 1914–45*, Oxford University Press, 1988, p. 470.

8   The Winter War

The Finnish army, well organised, armed and trained for local conditions and tasks, turned out to be highly manoeuvrable, staunch in defence and well disciplined . . . many top commanders were not up to the task. Headquarters had to remove many senior officers and staff chiefs.[1]

The report of Commissar of Defence Voroshilov to the Soviet Central Committee, prior to his sacking by Stalin in March 1940

The Winter War of 1939–40 between Finland and the USSR was a war of David and Goliath. Finland had a population of some 4 million compared to a population of 170 million in the USSR. The Finnish armed forces comprised an army of nine divisions, no tanks, 145 aircraft, two lightly armed patrol ships and five submarines. In comparison, the USSR maintained an army of 180 divisions, 1,500 tanks, 3,000 aircraft, twenty-eight warships and eleven submarines. In addition, a standard Soviet division deployed 18,000 soldiers against 15,000 soldiers in a Finnish division. Such was the scale of the Soviet advantage that Khrushchev, in his memoirs which were published in 1971, recalled the air of confidence in the Kremlin: 'All we had to do was raise our voice a little bit and the Finns would obey. If that didn't work, we could fire one shot and the Finns would put up their hands and surrender.'[2] With this casual assessment of the likely Finnish opposition, the Soviet Union confidently declared war on Finland on 30 November 1939.

The war was not pre-planned but followed the unexpected failure of border negotiations between Finland and the USSR between October and November 1939. It was a war of frustration. Stalin had expected Finland to comply with his demands for adjustments to their joint border. He offered a series of compromises before finally resorting to military force to impose his will. The war was expected to be short and decisive but instead continued to 13 March 1940 and, to Hitler's delight, served to expose the military weakness of the USSR. Stalin's motive was defence coupled with a general desire to restore to the USSR territory lost after the collapse of Tsarist Russia in 1917. This was reflected in the secret protocol of the Nazi–Soviet Pact, agreed between Hitler and Stalin in August 1939. It placed eastern Poland, the Baltic States and Finland into the Soviet 'sphere of influence'. Once Hitler invaded Poland on 1 September 1939, Stalin wasted little time in acting to secure his western borders.

The Red Army invaded eastern Poland on 17 September 1939 and assisted Hitler to defeat Poland. On 10 October 1939 the tiny Baltic states of Latvia, Lithuania and

Estonia yielded to Soviet pressure and accepted Red Army bases on their territory. Stalin firmly mistrusted the anti-communist West. His aim was the creation of a defensive buffer zone against the west, but Finland represented a dangerous gap in the line. Finland had a long 800-mile land border with the USSR that came within twenty miles of Leningrad, the cradle of the Bolshevik Revolution. The city was well within artillery range from Finnish territory and, as Stalin noted, the population of Leningrad numbered 4 million: equivalent to the whole population of Finland. The city could not be moved; consequently Stalin's logic dictated the roll-back of the Finnish border. Similar concerns dictated Soviet demands in the far north, within the Arctic Circle, where the principal Russian naval port of Murmansk was under the shadow of the nearby Finnish port of Petsamo. For Stalin, Finland's territory offered any hostile western power an open door into the USSR, and it was a door that he was determined to close.

On 12 October 1939 the first major talks were held in Moscow. The USSR sought to control the approaches to the Soviet border in the Baltic and Arctic regions by a combination of pushing the Finnish border back and by agreeing long-term leases on strategic Finnish ports and islands. In the Arctic, to protect Murmansk, the Soviet Union proposed to occupy the Finnish port of Petsamo. In the Baltic, the Soviet interest was to gain a long-term lease on the port of Hango which guarded the entrance to the Gulf of Finland and Leningrad beyond. In total, the Soviet Union requested the annexation of approximately 1,066 square miles of Finnish territory and, in exchange, offered Finland 2,134 square miles of Soviet territory. At face value it was an attractive and reasonable offer, but in essence it meant exchanging vital ports for large empty tracts of Soviet marshland and forest adjacent to central Finland. Finland was not short of forests, but its few ports were all vital for trade. The border adjustments would also have made Finland indefensible and vulnerable to a future Soviet occupation. Finland had gained sovereignty from Russia in 1917 and feared a step-by-step re-annexation by her giant neighbour. The president of Finland, Cajander, was prepared to compromise and accept some adjustments to the border, but he refused to contemplate handing over ports to the USSR and was determined to uphold Finnish sovereignty.

A second round of talks was held between 23 and 25 October, but the Finnish refusal to grant the Soviet requests in full enraged the Soviet foreign commissar Vyacheslav Molotov. He denounced Finland's intransigence in a public speech on 31 October 1939. However, during the final round of talks held between 3 and 9 November, Molotov, in an attempt to achieve a settlement, moderated the Soviet demands. Field Marshal Baron Karl Mannerheim, the Finnish commander-in-chief, urged the acceptance of Molotov's terms and warned that Finland would be defeated in any outbreak of war. His advice was rejected because Cajander was convinced that Stalin would not risk war, and on 13 November all negotiations were broken off. Cajander was unaware of the depth of co-operation within the Nazi–Soviet Pact and assumed that Stalin would not commit his forces north while the Germans were on his western border. When Khrushchev predicted a swift Soviet victory Stalin replied: 'Let's get started today.'[3]

The war came swiftly. On 26 November 1939, near Mainila on the southern Finnish–Soviet border, a brief artillery exchange killed some Soviet troops and provided the USSR with an excuse for action. Two days later the Soviet Union revoked the Russo-Finnish Non-Aggression Pact of 1932, and insisted that Finland must immediately dismantle its border fortifications. Without further warning, on 30 November 1939, Soviet forces attacked at sixteen points along the common frontier. The capital Helsinki was heavily bombed in the opening hours of the war in tactics similar to the

Luftwaffe bombing of Warsaw. The scale of the attack was designed to intimidate and to produce an early capitulation, but instead the Finnish people responded with intense anger to the death of so many defenceless civilians and volunteered, in high numbers, to defend their country.

The defence of Finland was placed into the hands of 72-year-old Field Marshal Mannerheim, who had given his name to the 'Mannerheim Line'. This was Finland's Maginot Line. It was not on the scale of the French fortifications, but it nevertheless presented a formidable obstacle to any attacker, with a network of anti-tank ditches, minefields, barbed wire entanglements and reinforced concrete pillboxes. The main section of the Mannerheim Line stretched for 40 miles across the Karelian Isthmus from the natural boundaries of the Gulf of Finland in the west to the shores of Lake Lagoda in the east. It blocked the most direct Soviet pathway into Finland and consequently became the main battleground of the war. The other significant points of Soviet attack were around Suomussalmi in Central Finland and, in the far north, a strike towards the port of Petsamo. The confidence of the USSR in an early victory was highlighted on 2 December when a Finnish communist, Otto Kuusinen, was named as the leader of a new Soviet government for Finland to be based in Terijoki. In consequence, Stalin rebuffed all attempts at mediation by Sweden and the League of Nations.

An estimated fourteen Soviet divisions were deployed on the southern front spanning both sides of Lake Lagoda, four divisions in central Finland and one division in the north. To counter the invasion Finland possessed only nine divisions. The Soviet advantage was three to one, and in the air the USSR enjoyed almost total supremacy with an estimated 1,000 Soviet aircraft against only 145 largely obsolete Finnish aircraft. However, geography and the rapid onset of winter came to Finland's aid and, to the chagrin of the Red Army, skis and Molotov cocktails proved to be decisive weapons in Finnish hands. Finland was largely a land of narrow, twisting mountain roads, steep ravines and thick forest, all covered by a thick blanket of snow and ice. The terrain funnelled the superior Soviet forces along the few major roads into long columns of men, trucks and tanks and left them vulnerable to flank attack. With no room for the tanks or trucks to manoeuvre off-road the advantage lay with the Finns, who were accomplished skiers and familiar with the landscape. They traversed the deep snowfields with ease and attacked from the cover of the thick forest, invisible to the Soviet Air Force. Initial Soviet attempts to operate cross-country were hampered by a shortage of compasses, and many Soviet soldiers found themselves lost and unable to get their bearings in the vast tracts of featureless forest.

As early as 11 December 1939 the Soviet Union experienced its first major defeat when the 163rd Division at Suomussalmi in central Finland was surrounded and defeated. The victory was achieved by the simple tactic of using road blocks of felled trees and landmines to chop the strung-out Soviet column into a series of *mottis* or isolated pockets. Each pocket of Soviet troops was then subjected to sustained hit-and-run attacks from the cover of the thick forest. In the absence of anti-tank weapons the Finns improvised with the ubiquitous empty vodka bottle. Filled with petrol and some tar, the petrol bombs named – Molotov cocktails in a defiant gesture to Soviet Foreign Commissar Molotov – were potent weapons. The blazing sticky tar destroyed the Soviet tanks by dripping through the engine air intake grills. The Soviet soldiers were also ill-equipped for winter temperatures that plummeted to 35 below zero on a daily basis. Confident of a rapid victory, they had gone to war without winter clothing whereas the Finns were clad in fur-lined boots and white camouflage fur-lined parka jackets. The Soviet soldiers spoke of the *Bielaja Smert* or the white death, when the Finns, invisible against the snow, launched surprise attacks and withdrew before the trapped defenders could respond.

The Soviet offensive on the southern front which favoured the preferred Soviet tactic of a frontal assault stalled on the well-prepared defences of the Mannerheim Line. Separate, rigid command structures between the different Soviet forces, and a failure to co-operate and launch co-ordinated attacks, squandered the Soviet advantage in armour, aircraft and artillery. Few of the Soviet commanders had previous experience of war or directing whole divisions because the purge of the Red Army from 1938 to 1939 had removed its experienced core with the execution of 403 out of 706 generals. Consequently the major tactic was the mass infantry charge and the result was very high losses for little gain. The entire Soviet 7th and 8th armies were sacrificed in a reprise of outdated Great War tactics. Only at Petsamo, in the far north, did the Soviet Union achieve an outright victory – but it was a hollow triumph against a tiny force of only 700 Finns.

The Finns were not only victorious in defence, but by mid-December were confident enough to go on the offensive. Stalin's 60th birthday celebrations on 21 December were marred by news of the defeat of a further two Soviet divisions, the 28th and 44th at Suomussalmi. By Christmas Day, the Finns had crossed the border, advanced into the Soviet Union and taken some 36,000 Soviet prisoners. Soviet losses were estimated at 27,000 killed compared to only 900 Finns. Many of the Soviet soldiers froze to death during the long, bitterly cold nights. On all fronts the Soviet Union was placed on the defensive and on 8 January 1940 the jubilant Finns declared a day of national victory and celebration. In reply the Soviet Air Force launched regular air attacks on Helsinki, but the casual brutality of the bombing of civilians stirred greater resistance and earned the Soviet Union further international condemnation.

The response in the west was one of considerable support and sympathy for Finland. Britain and France were keen to lend assistance to the beleaguered Finns but were blocked from giving direct military assistance by the refusal of Norway and Sweden to compromise their neutrality. Both nations were warned by Hitler not to permit the basing of any Allied troops on their territory, although the transit of military supplies and volunteers was tolerated. A flow of arms and aircraft to Finland was maintained by Sweden, Britain and France, but Finland's key shortage was trained soldiers.

In January 1940 the Soviet Union invited the Finns to accept its territorial demands and to end the war, but the Finns – aware of the high Soviet losses, variously estimated at 50,000 to 200,000, and a rising tide of western support – refused to compromise. Finland foolishly believed that the Soviet Union might accept defeat; but the Soviet Union was far from defeated. In a nation of unlimited manpower the Soviet retreat was only the outgoing tide and a Soviet counter-attack of tidal-wave proportions was in preparation. Generals Voroshilov and Meretskov were both sacked and replaced by General Timoshenko, who was given full authority to direct all aspects of the war. On 1 February, Timoshenko unleashed a force of twenty-four infantry divisions, twenty artillery regiments and seven armoured brigades in a co-ordinated attack on the Mannerheim Line. Too late, Britain and France decided on 5 February to send a joint expeditionary force of three divisions to assist Finland. It was a token force to underline solidarity and to encourage the USSR to end the war, but one that also held the attraction of occupying the port of Narvik in Norway and cutting off shipments of Swedish iron ore to Germany.

Finland's time had run out. On 11 February 1940 Soviet forces breached the Mannerheim Line at Summa and by 17 February it was overrun. Marshal Mannerheim ordered a general retreat to a secondary line of defences, but by 4 March the thick ice of the Gulf of Finland was strong enough to bear the weight of tanks and heavy artillery. The Red Army seized the advantage, bypassed the Finnish defences, launched direct attacks on Viipuri and threatened the capital Helsinki.

Defeat was certain and on 7 March the newly appointed Finnish premier Risto Ryti flew to Moscow to negotiate an end to the war. He had little choice but to accept Stalin's terms because by 9 March 1940 an estimated fifty-four Soviet divisions were pouring into Finland against only fifteen scattered Finnish divisions. A peace treaty was signed on 12 March, and a cease-fire was declared at 11 a.m. on 13 March 1940. The Winter War was over and Stalin gained his defensive perimeter – but at a significant cost. Molotov declared that 58,000 Soviet soldiers had been killed, but the actual figure was probably considerably higher. Khrushchev, writing in his memoirs, declared: 'I'd say we lost as many as a million lives.'[4] The Finns lost an estimated 27,000 killed in the fighting, and 470,000 were subsequently uprooted from their homes along the border to create the new Soviet security zones.

The Winter War was ultimately a cul-de-sac in the wider war, but as Khrushchev noted: 'our miserable conduct of the Finnish campaign encouraged Hitler in his plans for the Blitzkrieg, his Operation Barbarossa.'[5] The entire Soviet aim had been to make the Soviet border more secure, but the new forward defences gained from Finland at such high cost were overrun in the first days of Operation Barbarossa in June 1941.

References

1. Dmitri Volkogonov, *Stalin: Triumph and Tragedy*, Weidenfeld and Nicolson, 1991, p. 365.
2. Nikita Khrushchev, *Khrushchev Remembers* (trans. Strobe Talbot), Sphere, 1971, p. 135.
3. Ibid.
4. Ibid.
5. Ibid., p. 139.

Advance

9 Copenhagen to Narvik

> [T]he Germans under the mask of friendship tried to extinguish the nation in one dark
> night, silently, murderously without any declaration of war, without any warning given.[1]
> Carl J Hambro, president of the Norwegian parliament, 1940

At 5.25 p.m. on 16 February 1940 Winston Churchill, as First Lord of the Admiralty, ordered the seizure of the German supply ship *Altmark*. After months of trying to slip back to Germany undetected by the Royal Navy the *Altmark* was finally spotted by an RAF patrol on 14 February emerging from the Arctic Ocean and entering Norwegian territorial waters after a long circuitous voyage from the South Atlantic. The *Altmark* intended to hug the 1,000-mile Norwegian coastline all the way south to the safety of the Baltic and Germany. Norway was a neutral country and under the rules of war all non-combatant ships enjoyed freedom of passage within the *leads*, Norway's territorial waters. On board there were known to be British prisoners of war (POWs), survivors of the attacks on Allied shipping in the South Atlantic by the German pocket battleship *Admiral Graf Spee*. At the insistence of Britain the Norwegian Navy conducted two searches of the *Altmark* but unexpectedly upheld the German claim that the *Altmark* was an innocent merchantman with no POWs on board.

Churchill refused to accept the Norwegian assurance, and his order authorised Captain Philip Vian of HMS *Cossack* to use all necessary force to board the *Altmark* with or without the permission of the Norwegian Navy. The *Altmark* was cornered in the Josenfjord and ran aground while trying to evade capture. During hand-to-hand combat with a boarding party from the *Cossack* four of the German crew were killed and five were injured. Below decks 299 British prisoners of war were discovered locked into storerooms. In breach of neutrality rules, the *Altmark* was also armed with two concealed pom-pom guns and four machine-guns.

The search by the Norwegian Navy had been cursory and reflected a desire to avoid any Allied military action within Norwegian territory that might provoke a German response. Norway feared a German invasion, and their fear was justified.

Four days later on 20 February 1940 Hitler reacted. At 12 noon he appointed General Nikolaus von Falkenhorst commander of Operation Weserburg, the code name for the invasion of Norway. It was not merely an impulse reaction. As early as 10 October 1939, Admiral Raeder, chief of the German naval staff, had discussed with Hitler the strategic importance of Norway. The long coastline with deep fjords was attractive to the Kriegsmarine because it offered the German fleet, and especially U-boats, numerous naval bases from where they could easily slip into the Atlantic to harry Allied shipping. The ports and airfields of southern Norway were also attractive to guard the approaches to the Skagerrak Straits between Denmark and Norway, and the Baltic beyond, and secure Germany's coastline against any Allied attack. A further key interest was to safeguard Germany's supplies of iron ore from the Gallivare ore fields in Sweden. Approximately 11.5 million tons representing 77 per cent of Germany's annual iron ore requirements were imported from Sweden. However, in the winter months when ice closed the Swedish port of Lulea all the ore was shipped from Narvik in northern Norway.

Raeder proposed a German-sponsored coup, and Alfred Rosenberg, Hitler's chief race ideologist, introduced Raeder to Vidkun Quisling. Quisling was the leader of the small Norwegian Fascist party, Nasjonal Samling (National Unity), and he had ambitions to head a Fascist government in Norway. In December 1939 Raeder invited Quisling to Berlin and over the course of three meetings with Hitler requested money and weapons to support a Fascist coup in Norway. Hitler reacted with caution because

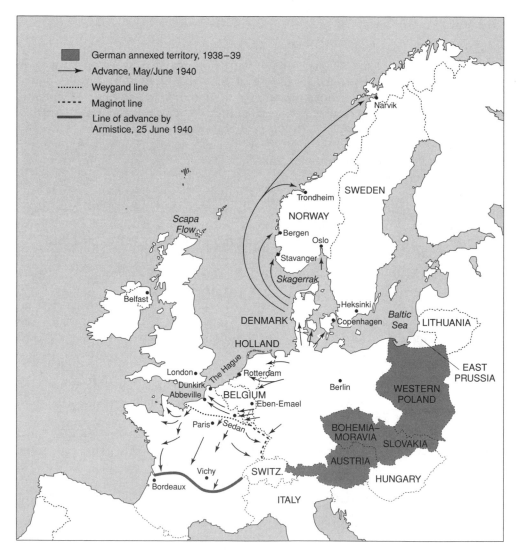

Map 2 The German advance west

uppermost in his mind was the invasion of western Europe planned for January 1940. He had no wish for the distraction of a second front, especially when victory in the west would rob Norway of its strategic significance. Nazi propaganda also promoted the Norwegians as fellow members of the Aryan race, and Hitler expected that following victory in the west a combination of propaganda, backed by economic pressure, would be sufficient to draw Norway into Germany's orbit. However, in January 1940 Hitler agreed to support Quisling following the decision of Britain and France to support Finland in the Winter War. It raised the possibility of the Allies using Norwegian ports and an Allied presence in Norway would threaten Germany's iron ore supplies and, ultimately, control over the Baltic. When poor weather forecasts for January and February 1940 forced the postponement of the attack in the west to the spring, Hitler decided to seize the opportunity to safeguard his northern flank. On 27 January he ordered Field Marshal Wihelm Keitel to prepare feasibility plans for the invasion of Norway. The *Altmark* incident alarmed Hitler and on 1 March 1940 he issued orders for Operation Weserbung (Exercise North) to take precedence over Fall Gelb (Case Yellow), the invasion of the west to stave off any Allied action in Norway

Hitler's instinct was correct. Churchill was an advocate of action in Norway – particularly action to mine the *leads* to deny German shipping safe passage. Churchill first raised the issue in cabinet on 27 November 1939, but the illegality of placing mines in neutral waters caused the cabinet to reject the proposal. The plans were shelved, but in December 1940, when the Allies resolved to assist Finland in the Winter War, Churchill proposed the seizure of Narvik as an Allied base for the onward transport of supplies to Finland. He also, as Hitler had feared, proposed to cut off supplies of iron ore to Germany. Approval was given for a joint expeditionary force of three divisions to land at Narvik (5 February), but disagreements with France over the objectives were not finally resolved until 12 March. By then it was too late. The next day Finland surrendered to the USSR and the imperative for action was removed. The delays and lack of decisive action forced the resignation of the French prime minister, Edouard Daladier, on 20 March. His successor, Paul Reynaud, was keen to take action but found himself in conflict with the commander-in-chief of the French Army, General Maurice Gamelin, who basically advised a 'wait and see' policy. At a meeting of the Allied Supreme War Council in London on 28 March Reynaud ignored Gamelin's advice and endorsed plans for the immediate mining of the *leads*. Plans were also set for Allied landings at Narvik, Stravanger, Bergen and Trondheim to secure the Norwegian coastline for the Allies.

Consequently, by the end of March 1940 both Germany and the Allies were committed to the invasion of Norway, a neutral country in the war. On 2 April Falkenhorst met with Hitler and agreed dawn on 9 April for the implementation of the Weserbung exercise. His invasion plan included the occupation of Denmark as a stepping stone to Norway and the seizure of all major ports from Copenhagen to Narvik. The Allies unwittingly acted in parallel and fixed 5 April for the Allied landings, but after further objections and hesitation from Gamelin the date was rescheduled to 8 April. It was to prove to be a crucial delay because the first forces ashore would hold the advantage.

Churchill, the principal architect of the Allied plan, was fully confident of victory because the Royal Navy significantly outmatched the Kriegsmarine, and he expected minimum opposition. In 1940 the Allies possessed 107 major warships, 135 submarines and seven aircraft carriers, compared to the Kriegmarine's thirteen major warships, twenty-seven submarines and no aircraft carriers. There was even hope in some Allied quarters that the Allied landings might lure the Kriegsmarine out of the security of the Baltic and present the Royal Navy with an opportunity for a victorious naval engagement. As a result, intelligence warnings of German military and naval activity in the Baltic ports did not provoke alarm but rather the opposite.

On 5 April 1940 the Royal Navy's advance force, comprising the battle cruiser *Renown* accompanied by four destroyers, sailed from Scapa Flow to commence mine-laying operations in the Norwegian *leads*. On the same day Prime Minister Chamberlain, sharing Churchill's optimism for a decisive Allied advance, stated in triumphant terms to a meeting of the Conservative Party that 'Hitler has missed the bus.' On the afternoon of 7 April air reconnaissance reported German warships in the Skagerrak. It was the opportunity many in the Admiralty had hoped for and in a flurry of orders all available ships were ordered to sea to intercept and destroy the German fleet. In its eagerness to confront and engage the German fleet the Admiralty shelved the military objectives. Allied troops already embarked and waiting to sail to Norway were hurriedly disembarked as the looming naval engagement was given priority over landings.

In the *leads* off Narvik the first minefields were laid without incident between 4.30 and 5.00 a.m. on 8 April, and at 5.30 a.m. the Norwegian government was informed of the Allied action. Everything was apparently going to plan, but at 9 a.m. the first encounter with the German fleet proved disastrous for the Royal Navy. HMS *Glowworm* had detached herself from the advance task force to search for a man overboard, but unfortunately encountered the German heavy cruiser *Admiral Hipper* escorted by two destroyers en route to Trondheim to land the 138th Regiment. The *Glowworm* radioed her position and engaged the superior force but was outgunned and soon set ablaze by several direct hits. With his ship sinking under him Captain Gerard Roope, under the cover of a smokescreen, rammed the *Hipper* and tore a 40-metre gash in her side. The *Glowworm* sank, leaving only forty survivors, but the *Hipper* was seriously damaged. Roope was posthumously awarded the Victoria Cross for his gallant action in the face of a superior enemy. There was also action in the Skagerrak where a Polish submarine sank the German troopship *Rio de Janeiro*, but despite the evidence from the survivors that they were bound for Bergen the Admiralty and the Norwegian government discounted the possibility of German landings in Norway. The Allies also ignored direct warnings of Hitler's invasion plans from Colonel Oster and Colonel Beck and other dissidents in the German High Command relayed through Dutch intelligence. Within hours Britain and Norway paid a high price for their complacency and Churchill, in his history of the campaign first published in 1948, admitted: 'we have been completely outwitted'.[2]

The Nazi action was both daring and decisive. At 5 a.m. on 9 April three German troopships sailed into Copenhagen harbour while simultaneously the Wehrmacht crossed the Danish border at Flensburg and Trondern. The Luftwaffe hurriedly took possession of the airfields of the strategic Jutland peninsula that projected into the Skagerrak. It was shaped like an arrowhead pointing towards Norway and gave the Luftwaffe an unsinkable aircraft carrier. Tiny Denmark was largely subdued within an hour, and at 6 a.m King Christian X ordered a cease-fire. The commander-in-chief of Danish forces, General Pyor, defied the order and continued to organise resistance, but at 6.45 a.m. he finally obeyed a direct order from the king to cease fire.

At dawn on 9 April five German naval task forces were in position off their target Norwegian ports. The targets from south to north were Oslo, Kristiansand, Bergen, Trondheim and Narvik. Only at Oslo was there significant opposition to the invasion, aided by the geography of the narrow Oslofjord and determined resistance from Norwegian forces. The German naval task force was severely mauled. One German minesweeper was sunk and two destroyers, the light cruiser *Emden* and the pocket battleship *Lutzow* were all badly damaged and forced to withdraw. When the heavy cruiser *Blucher* entered the fjord to bring her big guns to bear she was sunk by torpedoes fired from Fort Oscarsborg. A total of 1,600 were drowned, including most of the senior Nazi and Gestapo officials designated to administer Norway. The landing at Oslo was abandoned, but airborne troops, despite heavy fog, managed to land and seize Fornebu airport. Paratroopers were also used for the first time in the history of warfare and proved their worth by seizing Sola and Stavanger airfields. The Luftwaffe enjoyed complete air supremacy and supported the invasion with an overwhelming force of 290 bombers, forty dive-bombers, 100 fighters and 500 transport aircraft. With the key airfields in German hands a continuous stream of Ju-52 transport aircraft ferried 3,000 airborne troops to subdue and occupy Oslo and a further 2,500 airborne troops to occupy Kristiansand. In the confusion King Haakon and his government escaped a hundred miles north to Hamar and ordered national resistance to the German invasion under the command of General Otto Ruge. By then it was all over. Apart from a few minor upsets the other landings were all highly successful. At Narvik two lightly armed Norwegian coastal defence ships, *Norge* and *Eidsvold*, refused to yield passage to the superior German fleet of ten destroyers but within minutes both were sunk by torpedoes. The destroyers landed a force of 2,000 mountain warfare troops of the 139th Gebirgsjager Regiment under the command of General Eduard Dietl. There was no opposition. The defending forces were led by Colonel Sundlo, a Quisling supporter, and he was easily convinced by Dietl that any resistance would be futile. By the close of 9 April the Germans controlled Norway and Quisling was installed in Oslo as the puppet leader of a new Nazi government.

In the course of a single day the Allies had lost Norway, but Churchill was confident that the German positions were untenable and that counter-attacks would soon force the Germans out. Allied confidence was high because the total number of German troops occupying Norway was estimated to be 10,000, and most were confined to isolated pockets in the vicinity of their invasion ports. General Dietl at Narvik was particularly vulnerable. The mountainous terrain, deep snow and 'guerrilla' actions by the Norwegian Army in blocking roads outlawed the prospect of any reinforcement overland. The Royal Navy controlled the sea and could with ease transport large numbers of troops to land at Narvik and Trondheim and restore northern and central Norway to Norwegian rule.

The counter-attack began immediately and at first there were Allied successes. Captain Warburton-Lee, commanding a flotilla of five Royal Navy destroyers, entered Ofotfjord, Narvik, on the morning of 10 April without waiting to determine the strength of the German opposition. They were outnumbered but managed to sink two German destroyers and six supply ships before being forced to withdraw. On regaining the open sea they encountered and sunk the German supply ship *Ravenfels*, fully laden with supplies and munitions for Dietl's *Gebirgsjäger*. HMS *Hardy* was lost. The bridge suffered a direct hit which killed Warburton-Lee and most of his senior officers, and the ship was subsequently disabled and beached. Warburton-Lee was posthumously awarded the Victoria Cross for his leadership. However, the German ships were trapped in Narvik and on 13 April a force of nine Royal Navy destroyers re-entered Narvik Ofotfjord and sank all eight remaining German destroyers. There was no resistance from the shore and Allied troops landed at Harstad, some sixty miles from Narvik, under the command of Major-General Mackesy and were advised to advance on Narvik without delay. To the south, Allied troops also landed at the small fishing ports of Namos and Andalsnes to support a direct assault on Trondheim by a major naval task force. By 17 April the Germans were faced with superior concentrations of Allied troops and it appeared that the Allies had regained the initiative. Hitler expected the worst and advised his troops to hold on as long as possible; in a brief moment of panic he advised Dietl to seek internment in neutral Sweden.

Hesitation, lack of equipment, and the dominance of the Luftwaffe handed the Germans an unexpected victory. General Mackesy, to the intense irritation of the commander of the Royal Navy forces, Lord Cork, refused to storm Narvik. He firmly believed that the Germans were too well dug in and opted to wait for further troop reinforcements, and in particular the arrival of French trained mountain warfare troops the Chasseur Alpins. As the commander on the spot he could not be overruled, but Churchill angrily contrasted his hesitation with the bravery of the earlier Royal Navy attack on Narvik.

There was also inaction off Trondheim when the chiefs of staff rejected Churchill's plan for a direct naval assault in favour of a pincer attack to be launched from Namos and Andalsnes, to the north and south of Trondheim respectively. The decision ignored the reality of the military situation. Both ports were too tiny to support large-scale landings of munitions and the number of troops and ships attempting to cram into both ports made easy targets for the Luftwaffe. German intelligence had broken Royal Navy signal traffic and was able to provide the Luftwaffe with notice of ship movements. Worse still there were no anti-aircraft guns to fend off the Luftwaffe, which attacked at will. The French supply ship *Ville D'Alger*, loaded with AA guns, transport vehicles and tanks, was unable to dock because she was too big for both Namos and Andalsnes. A second supply ship was sunk by a U-boat. Despite the absence of full equipment or supplies the Allied forces ashore marched on Trondheim, which was 80 miles distant from Namos and 150 miles from Andalsnes, in deep snow and freezing conditions. To support the advance a squadron of antiquated RAF Gloster Gladiator biplanes attempted to use the ice of Lesjeskog lake forty miles from Trondheim as a landing strip, but it was futile. The majority were destroyed in a single Luftwaffe raid, and those that could fly were unable to climb to 20,000 feet and match the operating height of the Luftwaffe. The Allied troops made valiant attempts to reach Trondheim with support from elements of the exhausted Norwegian Army, but to no avail. The advance from Namos was blocked by an unexpected flank attack when the Germans took advantage of their control of the fjords to move troops by boat. The advance from Andalsnes fared little better and stalled at Lillehammer when the Allies came under attack from German forces advancing north from Oslo. The Germans had the advantage of artillery and some tanks and also enjoyed full air cover. The Allies were forced to accept defeat and Namos was evacuated on 28 April and Andalsnes on 1 May.

Hitler was delighted by the victory and, with the Allies reeling in disarray, he met with his senior military commanders on 30 April and ordered the Wehrmacht to be ready to invade western Europe by 5 May. Days earlier, on 24 April, he had replaced Quisling as the leader of Norway's new government with the Nazi Josef Terboren because Quisling's promises of popular support for the Nazis had come to nothing. However, Quisling remained in the government and was restored to the leadership in 1942. He was captured and executed for treason at the end of the war in 1945. Hitler also authorised the formation of a Norwegian SS formation, SS Nord, for those of a suitable bloodstock.

Norway was a triumph for Hitler but a personal disaster for Prime Minister Chamberlain. The Labour opposition demanded a Commons debate on the failures of the Norwegian campaign, and when Chamberlain entered the Chamber on 7 May he was taunted with cries of 'missed the bus'. The House and the nation were exasperated with Chamberlain's complacency and it fell to a personal friend, Leo Amery, to put into words the frustration of the House. Amery addressed Chamberlain with the words of Cromwell to the Long Parliament: 'you have sat too long for any good you have been doing. Depart, I say, and let us have done with you. In the name of God, go!'[3] Churchill was the main architect of the failed campaign and although he accepted full responsibility for any naval failings the House absolved him of any blame. Churchill's political stock was high. He had warned of the dangers of trusting Hitler in 1936 and 1938 and had sought action to secure Norway as early as November 1939. The target was Chamberlain. For three days Chamberlain battled to retain his premiership by drawing the Labour Party into his government, but on 10 May, as the Wehrmacht suddenly swept into Belgium and Holland, the Labour Party refused to accept his leadership. He was reluctantly forced to resign. There were also repercussions in France. Prime Minister Reynaud attacked General Gamelin as 'gutless' and an 'utter failure', and provoked a government crisis by demanding his resignation. Gamelin blamed the failings on the Royal Navy, but he was saved by the opening of the German invasion of the west on 10 May 1940. Reynaud decided not to pursue his dismissal at such a crucial moment for France.

On the same day at 6.00 p.m. Winston Churchill was appointed prime minister during an audience with King George VI at Buckingham Palace. He was sixty-five, and in his later writings he recalled his emotional response: 'I felt as if I was walking with destiny, and that all my past life had been but a preparation for this hour and this trial.'[4] Churchill, despite the urgent need to combat the German advance in western Europe, still hoped to seize Narvik and to salvage some small element of victory from the Norwegian campaign. Major-General Mackesy was replaced by Lieutenant-General Auchinleck, and on 28 May a combined Allied force of 25,000 British, French, Polish and Norwegian troops finally retook Narvik. Dietl had gained some reinforcements from a parachute landing and he also pressed into service the surviving crews of the German destroyers sunk in Narvik harbour as 'naval marines', but he still only commanded approximately 5,000 troops. The Germans were driven back to the Swedish border, but just as they accepted defeat Narvik was unexpectedly regained. On 7 June the Allies destroyed the port installations and withdrew. Following the defeat at Dunkirk, the defence of France and Britain required every division. Churchill had decided to abandon Norway. During the evacuation the Royal Navy suffered one final humiliation. On 8 June in clear skies the Royal Navy aircraft carrier HMS *Glorious* and two destroyers, *Ardent* and *Acasta*, were sunk in a chance encounter with the German battleships *Scharnhorst*, *Gneisenau* and *Admiral Hipper*. There were only forty-three survivors in total and overall 1,515 were drowned. The *Glorious* had failed to place any sentry aircraft aloft and was caught by surprise with its aircraft on deck. Two whole squadrons were also lost at a time when every aircraft was vital to the defence of Britain. The only compensation was that all troopships safely returned to Great Britain, including the *Devonshire* carrying King Haakon and Norway's gold reserves.

On 10 June, Norway formally accepted defeat when General Ruge signed surrender papers, but in a final act of defiance he refused to acknowledge German rule and was subsequently imprisoned in Konigstein Castle for the remainder of the war.

The naval losses were similar in number, but proportionately heavier, for the small Kriegsmarine. The Royal Navy lost one aircraft carrier, one cruiser, seven destroyers and eight submarines, whereas Germany lost three cruisers, ten destroyers and eight submarines. In addition, two German battle cruisers and three cruisers were severely damaged and laid-up in dry dock. The Royal Navy took comfort from the fact that it could more easily absorb and replace the losses and that the rump of the Kriegsmarine was too weak to force a passage for the Wehrmacht across the English Channel. For that, Hitler would have to rely upon the Luftwaffe as the battle for France entered its final stages and he turned his attention towards Britain.

References

1. Winston Churchill, *The Second World War: The Gathering Storm*, Cassell, 1950, p. 485.
2. Ibid., p. 480.
3. Martin Gilbert, *Churchill: A Life*, Heinemann, 1992, p. 638.
4. Winston Churchill, *The Second World War: The Gathering Storm*, Cassell, 1950, p. 532.

10 Blitzkrieg in the west

> Departure with Führer train at 17.00 hours from Finkenkrug. After report that weather situation will be favourable on the 10th the codeword 'Danzig' is given at 21.00.[1]
>
> Entry in the personal diary of General Jodl,
> Wehrmacht chief of operations, 9 May 1940

At 9 p.m. on 9 May 1940, the single codeword 'Danzig' was flashed to the German forces arrayed along the borders of Holland, Belgium, Luxembourg and France. After seven months of delay, primarily a result of the extreme winter weather of 1939–40 and a decision to give priority to the occupation of Norway, Hitler finally authorised the invasion of western Europe for dawn on 10 May. For Hitler it was a strategic war to secure his western frontier following the rejection of his peace overtures by Britain and France. It was not a war he had expected or wanted to fight. To monitor the attack, Hitler travelled west on board his armoured train *Amerika* to a forward military headquarters at Munstereifel, 25 miles south-west of Bonn.

Zero hour for the German forces positioned along the Western Front was 5.30 a.m. on 10 May 1940. This was later than the preferred attack time of 3.00 a.m. but the glider pilots who were to open the offensive by landing on the roof of Fort Eben-Emael on the Belgium frontier needed daylight to ensure a safe landing.

Fort Eben-Emael guarded the approaches to the principal bridges of the Albert Canal and river Maas ('Meuse' in France) on the German–Belgian border near Maastricht. The fort had been built into the side of a hill in the years 1932 to 1935, with a main armament of sixteen 75 mm guns and two 120 mm guns, and was widely regarded as impregnable. The garrison of 1,200 troops, of whom only 750 were present on the morning of the attack (the rest were on leave), was protected against enemy bombardment by deep underground shelters. Eben-Emael was also well-protected against a direct infantry assault by a steep embankment rising sharply from the edge of the broad Albert Canal, anti-tank ditches, four-metre high walls, barbed-wire entanglements and numerous machine-gun emplacements. However, the infantry-minded Belgian High Command had failed to consider air assault and left the roof, which was level with the fields beyond, unprotected.

At approximately 5.25 a.m nine gliders out of eleven successfully landed an elite force of eighty-five *Fallschirm-Pioniere* or combat engineers on the roof of Eben-Emael under the command of Lieutenant Rudolf Witzig. Simultaneously a further thirty gliders landed the main assault force of over four hundred troops under the command of Captain Walter Koch directly alongside the key Veldwezelt and Vroenhoven bridges. Both bridges were seized before the Belgian defenders could respond, but at nearby Kanne a third bridge was successfully blown up before it could be captured. Overhead, wave after wave of Stuka dive-bombers acting as flying artillery kept the defending Belgian 7th Army 'heads down' and prevented any significant counter-attack. Some defensive fire was raised by the garrison of Eben-Emael, but the garrison was quickly cowed by flamethrowers and by explosives dropped down the air vents and the stair-wells. The large garrison was kept bottled up while the *Fallschirm-Pioniere*, operating in small groups, knocked out all the major gun emplacements. They used pre-prepared 'hollow' charges to destroy the heavily armoured gun cupolas and destroyed the two 120 mm guns by the expedient technique of pushing explosives straight down the gun barrels. Such was the speed and success of the attack that for years afterwards it was assumed that the Germans had employed an unknown secret weapon; a fiction that Propaganda Minister Josef Goebbels was happy to encourage. The only secrets were surprise and the perfection of hollow charges: a shaped cavity which directed the force of the explosives downwards in one concentrated jet of energy. The blast punched holes through the reinforced concrete and steel of Eben-Emael and showered those inside with red hot steel fragments. On 11 May the exhausted and battered garrison finally surrendered when German reinforcements succeeded in crossing the Albert Canal and securing the fort perimeter. Only six of the German detachment were killed as against twenty-three Belgian defenders. However, had the 750-strong garrison emerged from the fort they would have undoubtedly overwhelmed the much smaller German forces. Surprise and daring tactics gave the Wehrmacht their first major victory in the west.

The German forces advanced west along a 175-mile front line from Holland to the Ardennes in three major army groups deploying a total of ninety-four divisions. The main strike arm was Army Group A commanded by General von Rundstedt, with a total of forty-five infantry divisions and seven out of Germany's ten armoured divisions. At dawn on 10 May, with Allied attention fixed on the assault at Eben-Emael and the simultaneous German invasion of Holland, this massive concentration of armour slowly threaded its way south through the Ardennes. The Ardennes straddled the borders of Belgium, Luxembourg and France and was unlikely tank country, given a succession of steep river valleys, twisting mountain roads and thick forest. The concentration of armour was the spearhead of the 'Sickle Cut' attack plan first presented to Hitler by General Manstein in February 1940 and thereafter enthusiastically embraced by Hitler as his own. The aim was to catch the Allies off guard by invading France through the lightly defended Ardennes region at Sedan and from there sweeping west towards the English Channel to isolate and cut off the Allied forces in Belgium. It was a high-risk strategy, but it appealed to Hitler because he feared a slow advance through the heavily populated urban areas of Belgium and a repeat of the stalemate of the Great War. As a soldier in the trenches around Ypres from 1914 to 1918, Hitler had bitter memories of the slow degradation of the German Army and nation wrought by a long war of attrition.

Army Group B, under the command of General Fedor von Bock, was composed of twenty-nine divisions, including Germany's three remaining armoured divisions, and was tasked with the invasion of Holland and Belgium. Holland was included in the attack plan primarily to speed the invasion of Belgium by taking advantage of the unfortified border between Holland and Belgium.

Army Group C faced the heavily fortified Maginot Line on the German–French border under the command of General von Leeb. It was the weakest of the three army groups with no armoured divisions, but Leeb was not expected to breach the Maginot Line. His task was to keep the French garrison engaged and to add to the Allied uncertainty about where the main weight of the German attack would fall. In total the assembled German invasion force comprised approximately 2,350,000 troops, 2,700 tanks and a Luftwaffe fleet of 3,200 aircraft.

This was not an overwhelming force. France deployed 2,000,000 troops, Britain 237,000, Belgium 375,000 and Holland 250,000. Nor were the Allies short of armour. Whereas Britain was just on the point of forming its first armoured division, France possessed 3,000 tanks and most of them were better armoured and armed than the German panzers. Half the German tank force was composed of light Mark 1 and Mark 2 panzers. The former were only armed with machine-guns and the latter additionally mounted minor 20 mm guns. In contrast, the majority of the French tanks mounted 37 mm guns and the French B1 tank was armed with a 75 mm gun, making it the most powerful tank in Europe in 1940. In the air the Luftwaffe enjoyed a two-to-one superiority, but both sides were roughly equal in fighter aircraft at around 1,000 each, with the RAF Spitfire outclassing the best Luftwaffe fighter the Me-109. The only key Allied deficiency was the lack of ground attack aircraft – they had nothing comparable to the Stuka dive-bomber. Ultimately it was superior tactics rather than superior strength that defeated the Allied powers – in particular the high speed of the German advance. In the Great War the western front was locked in stalemate with neither side able to gain an advantage, but in May 1940 Blitzkrieg tactics broke the Allied defence in only five days and defeated the whole of western Europe inside only six weeks.

First to fall was Holland. To a neutral state, last involved in war in 1830, the attack was a complete shock. Command and control of Holland meant occupying the major cities of Rotterdam, Amsterdam, Utrecht and the seat of government The Hague. All were located in 'Vesting Holland' or Fortress Holland, so called because they all lay behind an easily defended criss-cross of rivers and canals. Consequently the Dutch military strategy was to fall back from the more exposed border regions and to maximise its firepower along the shorter frontline of Vesting Holland. As in Norway, the German answer was airpower. The primary target was *Den Haag*, with the intention of capturing Queen Wilhelmina and the Dutch government and forcing an immediate surrender. Such was the German confidence that the commander of the 22nd Airborne Division, General Hans Graf von Sponeck, packed a full dress uniform in expectation of an audience with Queen Wilhelmina to receive her formal surrender. It was not to be. Although parachutists successfully seized the main airfields of Ockenburg, Ypenburg and Valkenburg, in striking distance of *Den Haag*, such was the ferocity of Dutch resistance that most of the following Junker (Ju-52) transports carrying reinforcements were shot down or forced to abandon the landings because the runways were blocked by burning wreckage. At Ypenburg alone eleven out of thirteen aircraft in the first wave were shot down. The lightly armed parachutists were soon outnumbered and forced to surrender, and approximately a thousand were shipped to England as POWs. The battle was won, but Holland lost the war at Rotterdam. The 7th Parachute Division, commanded by General Kurt Student, successfully seized Waalhaven airport south of Rotterdam and a series of key bridges across Holland and successfully secured a pathway for the panzers into Vesting Holland. The extent of Nazi planning was demonstrated by the seizure of a key border bridge at Gennap. Here a detachment of German soldiers dressed in the uniforms of Dutch military police escorted some German 'prisoners' onto the bridge and overwhelmed the defenders. In one of the most daring actions a small detachment of 150 airborne troops seized the Willems Bridge in central Rotterdam by landing on the river Maas in twelve ancient Heinkel float planes. They successfully held the bridge with paratroop reinforcements from Waalhaven until the arrival of panzer reinforcements on 12 May.

The extent of the resistance in Holland concerned Hitler because the German forces in Belgium and France were vulnerable to a determined Allied counter-attack. Hitler urged a rapid defeat of Holland to release German forces, especially the panzers, for service in Belgium. Airpower was again the decisive weapon. The Luftwaffe threatened to destroy Rotterdam from the air if the Dutch forces refused to surrender the city and, by implication, all other major Dutch cities. The threat of large-scale civilian deaths worked, but as the surrender terms were still being negotiated the Luftwaffe bombed Rotterdam, destroying over one square mile of the city and killing an estimated 980 people. At the time it was thought to be a deliberate Nazi terror bombing, and panicked reports put the death toll as high as 30,000. However, after the war it emerged that the Wehrmacht commanders on the ground had made frantic efforts to call off the air raid by firing red signal flares into the air and did manage to turn back most of the bombers. It would seem that the large-scale destruction of Rotterdam was not the result of sustained terror bombing but of fierce fires that raged out of control after some of the first bombs unluckily ignited dockside margarine warehouses. However, whether the scale of the destruction was deliberate or not the outcome was the same. Holland had no effective means of defence against the Luftwaffe and to protect civilian lives the Dutch commander-in-chief General Winkelman signed an unconditional surrender at 9.30 a.m. on 15 May. Similar fears later undermined the French will to resist. One prominent German casualty in the fighting was General Kurt Student who was shot in the head, but his life was saved by the skills of a Dutch surgeon. Student had been finalising plans for an airborne assault on Great Britain but he was hospitalised for eight months, and his plans that might have altered the course of the later Battle of Britain were never completed. Queen Wilhelmina avoided capture and hoped to continue resistance from Zeeland but the military situation was hopeless and Zeeland fell on 17 May. Queen Wilhelmina, along with the Dutch Navy and merchant marine, was evacuated to Britain. Blitzkrieg had overwhelmed Holland in only five days, but the Allies comforted themselves with the fact that Holland was beyond their effective military reach. Only a token Allied force, the French 7th Army had crossed the border into Holland to assist the Dutch defence. The surprise for the Allies was not the defeat of Holland but the rapid encirclement and defeat of the Allied forces in Belgium.

At 6.30 a.m. on 10 May, as the German Army began to flood across the Belgian border, King Leopold of Belgium requested Allied military assistance. This was a contingency planned for by the French commander-in-chief of Allied forces, Field Marshal Maurice Gamelin. His strategy was for a forward defence. Rather than sit and wait for the German Army to reach the French border Gamelin planned to join forces with the Belgian Army because their combined strength would match if not outnumber the German invaders. Consequently, within an hour of the German assault on Fort Eben-Emael, Gamelin authorised the immediate implementation of Plan D, the Dyle Plan. As planned, fifty-one Allied divisions, or approximately 800,000 troops, positioned along the Belgian border from the edge of the Maginot Line to the English Channel wheeled north into Belgium to establish a forward defensive line along the river Dyle. Hitler, on hearing of the Allied move, remarked: 'I could have cried with joy. They were walking into a trap.'[2] The most northerly point of the Dyle Line was Antwerp on the coast and from there the line snaked south-east across Belgium along the line of the river Dyle to connect with the river Meuse and the impregnable fortresses of the Maginot Line at Mezieres-Charleville near Sedan. The Dyle Line was to be held by three armies. To the north, from Antwerp to Louvain, the Belgian Army was deployed under the command of General Robert Overstraeten with support from the French 7th Army which had withdrawn from Holland. Next in the centre of the line from Louvain to Wavre was the British Expeditionary Force (BEF) under the command of Lord Gort. Finally, to the south and picking up the natural defensive line of the river Meuse ('Maas' in Belgium and Holland) were the French 1st and 9th armies, commanded by Generals Blanchard and Corap respectively, facing the western edge of the Ardennes. Only a light screening force guarded the Ardennes because the heavily forested terrain was considered to be impenetrable. In theory all three armies were united under one command structure. The designated commander-in-chief of Allied forces was Gamelin. Next in command, as the operational commander of the entire North-eastern Front, was General Alphonse Georges. In practice, however, the Belgians refused to accept direct commands from Gamelin, and Lord Gort similarly preferred all commands to be relayed and confirmed through London. The situation was further complicated by the remoteness of Allied headquarters. Gamelin's headquarters were at Vincennes in the suburbs of Paris; Georges' were at La Ferte-sous-Joarre 35 miles from Paris; and the General Staff headquarters were located at Montry 18 miles from Paris. The French Air Force and the RAF also maintained their own entirely separate command structures and headquarters. Worse still, Gamelin's headquarters had no radio, and Gamelin, a veteran of the Great War, relied upon motorcycle couriers to deliver orders; this meant an average time delay of 48 hours between the transmission and receipt of an order. In contrast, the German supreme military command, the Oberkommando de Wehrmacht (OKW), under Hitler's direction, controlled all military operations and had the advantage of a highly efficient radio network that extended as far as radio communication between individual panzers.

The Allied strategy was to hold the Dyle, and despite the lessons of Poland and Norway they expected trench warfare and a long war of attrition similar to the Great War. But it was the wrong war and the wrong battleground. The real war was Blitzkrieg and the real battleground was the Ardennes. While the Allies focused on events in Holland and on digging-in along the rivers Dyle and Meuse, the armoured spearheads of Army Group A were travelling south through the Ardennes largely undetected and unmolested. A French pilot, on routine patrol, reported the headlights of a nose-to-tail convoy stretching back 100 km from the Ardennes to the Rhine on 9 May, but his report was dismissed as a mistake. No additional air reconnaissance was ordered to check the report, but as a precaution on 10 May four divisions of French cavalry were ordered to scout the Ardennes. They and a force of lightly armed Belgian *Chasseurs Ardennais* (forest riflemen) encountered the advancing panzers but retreated without pausing to block or destroy the numerous river bridges behind them. An immediate Allied counter-attack by artillery or air would have destroyed the closely packed column of German armour, but the main French artillery was still in storage and the Allied air effort was focused on the defence of the Dyle. The Allied command was also highly complacent and firmly believed that the Ardennes was a feint. General d'Astier of the French Army dismissed news of the Ardennes advance as merely an 'energetic thrust'.

Unchecked, the German spearhead of seven panzer divisions deploying approximately 1,800 tanks raced towards the French border and the river Meuse in three separate Korps. First to reach the Meuse near Dinant on 12 May was the little-known General Erwin Rommel in command of the 7 Panzer Division. Twenty-four hours later, and further to the east, Heinz Guderian, the pre-war exponent of tank warfare, emerged from the cover of the Ardennes at Sedan on the banks of the Meuse. Despite Gamelin's entreaty to hold Sedan at all costs the French garrison and the retreating cavalry abandoned Sedan to the Germans and crossed to the safety of the west bank of the Meuse. It was an ominous decision. On 2 September 1870 Prussia had defeated the armies of Napoleon III at Sedan and caused the collapse of the French Second Empire. Now the Third Republic, born from the defeat of the Second Empire in 1875, was also facing its nemesis at Sedan. The 41st Panzer Korps under the command of Reinhardt was the last to reach the Meuse at Montherme on 13 May after a slow passage through the most heavily wooded sector of the Ardennes. The defence of the Third Republic now rested on holding the Meuse, but facing the panzers were the B-class conscript troops of the French 9th Army who were not expected to see action. Most were described by their commanders as 'fat, flabby and over 30', and all had little or no experience of battle let alone the onslaught of Blitzkrieg.

Rommel was Blitzkrieg personified and his unflagging energy marked him out for later promotion. Although the retreating French had blown all the bridges along the Meuse, Rommel's scouts, using motorcyles, discovered an intact stone weir at Houx. Under cover of darkness the German infantry crossed the weir to the far bank. Further upriver at Bouvignes Rommel personally led a flotilla of rubber boats across the Meuse under heavy fire and again achieved a foothold on the far bank. In both cases the French had made the vital mistake of not digging in along the river bank but holding the cliffs above the river. This mistake allowed the German infantry to establish a bridgehead across the river and under cover of darkness to pick their way up the slopes. The German infantry attacked at night at close quarters and the inexperienced French defenders panicked and fled. By 13 May Rommel had established a bridgehead across the Meuse approximately three miles wide and two miles deep, and by the morning of 14 May he pushed his first fifteen panzers across on a rudimentary pontoon bridge. Reinhardt's force at Montherme encountered much fiercer resistance and although he managed to get infantry across the Meuse his panzers remained stranded on the east bank.

At Sedan Guderian's crossing of the Meuse was preceded by five hours of continuous air attacks by Stuka dive-bombers dropping their bombs directly into the French trenches. At one point over a thousand aircraft relentlessly bombed and strafed the French defenders, and Guderian used his 8.8 anti-aircraft (AA) guns to fire directly across the river into the French pillboxes and machine-gun posts. The French 55th and 71st divisions were entirely broken by the attack, and at 4 p.m., as the last bombs fell, Guderian's infantry crossed the Meuse against minimal resistance. By nightfall the first of Guderian's panzers were rafted across the Meuse and established a bridgehead on the Marfee heights to shield the main crossing. Most of the French troops were in a state of nervous collapse and, stunned and dazed by the ferocity of the attack, simply dropped their weapons and fled in an undisciplined retreat. Some mistook their own advancing tanks for panzers and sowed complete disorder in the French ranks. The 55th Division entirely disintegrated and ceased to exist as a fighting unit, with some soldiers fleeing in panic as far as Rheims 60 miles from the front.

The sense of panic rapidly moved up the chain of command. In a hurriedly convened meeting at 3 a.m. on 14 May General Georges burst into tears as he reported the German breakthrough at Sedan. Gamelin immediately ordered reinforcements to close a reported gap of 44 miles in the French line and throughout 14 May the French Air Force and RAF attempted to destroy the German pontoon bridges across the Meuse to stem the panzer advance. No bridges were destroyed and eighty-five RAF and French aircraft were lost to intense German AA fire and Luftwaffe fighter cover. The RAF losses were the highest of the entire war for a single mission, with forty out of the seventy-one bombers shot down. All hope was vested in a counter-attack by the French 1st and 3rd armoured divisions, but their punch was wasted by scattered deployment and a failure to intercept and engage the German armoured columns directly. The French commanders were stuck in a Great War mindset and put their efforts into 'digging-in' to form a defensive front line, but the panzers bypassed the static French positions. With the panzers streaming out from the Ardennes towards the English Channel, Gamelin informed the French minister of defence, Daladier, that there were no reserves to intercept or stop the German advance. Subsequently, a shocked Prime Minister Reynaud telephoned Churchill in London at 7.30 a.m. on 15 May and stated: 'We have been defeated. We have lost the battle.'[3] This was followed at 7.30 p.m. by his urgent SOS: 'The route to Paris is open. Please send all the troops and planes you can.'[4] Only a determined Allied counter-attack could now prevent the fall of France.

References

1. William L. Shirer, *The Rise and Fall of The Third Reich*, Pan, 1960, p. 863.
2. William L. Shirer, *The Collapse of The Third Republic*, Pan, 1972, p. 728.
3. Len Deighton, Blitzkrieg: *From the Rise of Hitler to the Fall of Dunkirk*, Jonathan Cape, 1979, p. 261.
4. William L. Shirer, *The Collapse of The Third Republic*, Pan, 1972, p. 778.

11 Fall of France

Along the roads from the north flowed lamentable convoys of refugees. I noticed among them many soldiers without arms. At this spectacle of a lost people and a military rout and from the reports of the scornful insolence of the Germans I was filled with a terrible fury. It was too awful . . . I would fight on wherever I could as long as necessary until the enemy was defeated and this stain wiped out.[1]

General de Gaulle, commander of the
4th Armoured Division, 16 May 1940

At 5.20 p.m. on the same day as General de Gaulle made his observation Prime Minister Winston Churchill was ushered into the offices of the Quai d'Orsay, the French Foreign Ministry in Paris. He had arrived in response to an urgent summons from the prime minister of France, Paul Reynaud. It was Churchill's sixth day as British prime minister and it was also the sixth day of the German blitzkreig west. Churchill listened in mounting astonishment as the commander-in-chief of Allied forces, Maurice Gamelin, reported the collapse of the French Army at Sedan, the breakthrough of a powerful panzer column driving towards the Channel and the threat of a sudden German dash to Paris. While Gamelin delivered his briefing smoke drifted past the windows as officials in the courtyard below burned government documents in readiness for a rapid evacuation of Paris. Churchill asked Gamelin, 'Ou est la masse de manoeuvre?' (reserve forces) only to receive the one word reply, 'Aucune' (none).[2] In his later history of the war, Churchill admitted that he was 'dumbfounded' by Gamelin's admission – but he also underestimated the scale of the unfolding military catastrophe. The panzer advance was threatening to cut off the bulk of the Allied forces in Belgium. Churchill dismissed the threat and advised the Allied forces in Belgium to stand firm and not to fall back into France. He was confident that the panzers, operating far in advance of the German infantry, would be vulnerable to a French counter-attack once they stopped to replenish their fuel and ammunition supplies. Churchill was guilty of conventional military thinking, but he was not alone. Hitler and his more conservative generals shared Churchill's assessment. By 16 May the panzers had advanced 50 miles towards Cambrai without meeting any significant French opposition, and Hitler was fearful of a successful Allied counter-attack. In a panicked outburst, that would increasingly characterise his later conduct of the war, he ordered the panzers to wait for infantry support. Heinz Guderian, who had masterminded the breakthrough at Sedan, objected to the order because it would offer the Allies valuable time to regroup. Nor did the panzers need to stop for re-supply. Motorised support, including mobile repair workshops, kept pace with the advance and fuel was trucked to each panzer in lightweight refillable cans thereby avoiding dependence on slow fuel bowsers. The ubiquitous petrol cans were later nicknamed jerricans by the Allied troops. After threatening his resignation Guderian received permission from General Kleist to conduct a 'reconnaissance in force'. It was all the permission Guderian needed and on 17 May he ordered the 1st and 2nd Panzer divisions to resume their dash west towards the Channel.

In an attempt to bolster the French defence, Reynaud relieved Gamelin of his command of Allied forces on 17 May. In his place he recalled 73-year-old Maxime Weygand from Syria and appointed 84-year-old Marshal Petain, the staunch defender of Verdun in the Great War, as deputy prime minister.

Over the course of two days (20–21 May) the new commander in chief consulted and assessed the military situation while the panzers advanced. For Weygand, a veteran of the Great War, two days for consultation was insignificant but by 20 May the 2nd Panzer Division had reached the Channel coast at Abbeville and Noyelles having covered 63 miles in a single day. It was an astounding military success. In only eleven days the panzers had advanced 250 miles from the Ardennes to the Channel and cut off the BEF and the French 1st Army in Belgium. It was the fulfilment of Manstein's 'sickle cut' attack plan and a triumph for the theory of blitzkreig.

In northern Belgium the Dyle Line was breached on 17 May, and the Germans entered Antwerp on 18 May. To avoid defeat Lord Gort, in command of the BEF, attempted to direct a breakthrough of the panzer cordon at Arras on 21 May, but the attack failed following confusion over the timing of the attack plan. However, the BEF did inflict a large dent in Rommel's 7th Panzer Division and had the satisfaction of putting to flight the SS Totenkopf (Death's-Head regiment). A relieved Hitler awarded Rommel the Knight's Cross for his prevention of an Allied breakout. Hitler and Keitel both feared a simultaneous north–south Allied counter-attack and a turning point in the war.

This was precisely Weygand's plan and at Ypres in Belgium on 21 May he ordered a co-ordinated north–south Allied attack for 23 May. To support the Weygand's counter-attack Churchill agreed to transfer a further six RAF fighter squadrons to France. The attrition rate was high and RAF Chief Air Marshal Sir Hugh Dowding informed Churchill that he would resign if any further RAF squadrons were transferred to France. One of the most bizarre aspects of the fall of France was the assumption that the French Air Force had been destroyed in the first hours of fighting. After the war it was revealed that approximately two-thirds of the French Air Force sat out the war in the safety of remote civilian and private airfields, forcing Gamelin to admit to an enquiry: 'we have the right to be astonished'.[3] The French aircraft industry was also unaffected by the war and between 10 May and 12 June it delivered a further 1,131 new bombers and fighters to the air force. Few if any entered combat and France actually ended the war with more aircraft than it started with.

The initiative lay with the Germans and on 22 May, after a two-day pause to regroup, the panzers turned north to cut off the flow of Allied supplies from the Channel ports. Boulogne was isolated on 22 May and Calais on 23 May, and by nightfall the panzers were on the river Aa within striking distance of Dunkirk. Churchill ordered the British forces in Calais to fight to the last to delay the German assault on Dunkirk. For those troops there was to be no evacuation. Churchill later saluted their bravery with the words: 'the bit of grit that saved us'.[4] From the north the German 18th Army broke the Belgian line at Courtrai and forced Lord Gort to take a momentous decision. Short of ammunition, and certain of defeat if he attempted to fulfil the Weygand plan, he ordered a retreat to the coast and the port of Dunkirk on 25 May. It was a controversial decision that caused much bitterness within the French command because it exposed the French 1st Army around Lille to encirclement and resulted in formal protests to Churchill by Weygand and French premier Reynaud. However, compared to the size of the French Army the BEF was a tiny force and the success or otherwise of Weygand's offensive was always bound to depend upon French forces. Weygand claimed an advance of 25 miles, but there was no evidence of a sustained offensive and the French Army put its efforts into digging-in along a new defensive line. The subsequent 'Weygand' Line stretched for 400 miles along the rivers Somme and Aisne to link with the Maginot Line and was France's last line of defence.

The stationary French army assisted the Germans because it permitted the Wehrmacht to turn north and concentrate all its forces upon the defeat of the Allied forces marooned in Belgium. The BEF was fighting a desperate battle for survival trapped in a pocket approximately 25 kilometres wide by 12 kilometres deep, with their backs to Dunkirk. They were assisted by the bravery of the French 1st Army, trapped in a pocket around Lille, who despite overwhelming odds refused to surrender. The Belgium Army shielded Dunkirk to the north, but it was steadily losing ground to the superior German forces. On 24 May the German Panzer divisions were poised for a full-scale attack to destroy the Allied pockets when Hitler made his first major military mistake of the war. He issued an irrevocable 'Führer Order' which ordered the panzers to hold their positions. Hitler's decision has been subject to intense speculation as to his motives, including the possibility that he wanted to smooth the path for a peace settlement with Great Britain. This theory was given currency by a discussion between Hitler and Rundstedt on 24 May when Hitler praised the British empire and in essence declared Britain to rule the world and Germany the Continent. However, there were also compelling military reasons for the decision. The Flanders terrain, as Hitler well remembered from his service in the Great War, was marshy and criss-crossed by canals, and General Runstedt also advised Hitler to reserve the panzers for the greater battle to come against the bulk of the French Army to the south. In addition, in what was perhaps the clinching argument, Göring insisted that the Luftwaffe could bomb the BEF and French into submission. The possibility of the escape of the BEF by sea was apparently not considered, but as early as 19 May Churchill had ordered Vice-Admiral Bertram Ramsay to prepare plans for an evacuation.

The trigger for the evacuation was the decision of King Leopold of Belgium to surrender. He informed Churchill and Reynaud of his decision on the afternoon of 26 May, and at 7 p.m. Churchill ordered the evacuation of the BEF, codenamed Operation Dynamo, to commence.

Operation Dynamo stirred fresh controversy with France because the French Navy and Army were not forewarned of the escape plan, and there were bitter accusations that Britain was abandoning France. There was also considerable political controversy in Belgium when King Leopold defied the wishes of his prime minister and government and refused to join the government in London to lead continued Belgian resistance. After some negotiations, deliberately prolonged to grant the Allies as much time as possible, the Belgium Army declared a cease-fire at 4 a.m. on 28 May. After the war, King Leopold was accused of betraying his country and was forced into exile in Switzerland.

The 'miracle of Dunkirk' commenced at 9 p.m. on 26 May when the first ship, *Mona's Isle*, sailed from Dover and returned the next day with 1,420 troops crammed onto her decks. The evacuation ended at 2.30 p.m. on 4 June, and between the two dates a total of 338,226 British troops and 123,095 French troops were safely conveyed to Britain. It was a remarkable achievement against an original target of only 45,000. The troops waded chest deep into the sea and under constant strafing from the Luftwaffe they scrambled on board small ships and were transferred to larger ships anchored off the coast. Thousands of ordinary civilian 'weekend' sailors volunteered to assist the Royal Navy as the nation answered a call to save the BEF, and thousands more staffed railway platforms to feed the exhausted troops as they were moved inland from Dover. At first the evacuation gave preference to the BEF, but after furious French protests Churchill personally intervened and directed the Royal Navy to evacuate both French and British troops equally, 'arm in arm'. As Dunkirk finally fell on 4 June 1940 approximately 30,000 French troops were left on the beaches, and during a lunch with the US ambassador on 4 June, Petain angrily accused Britain of intending to fight 'until the last available drop of French blood'.[5] It was the beginning of a dangerous rift in Anglo-French relations.

Dunkirk raised a cheer in Britain, but Churchill was quick to dampen any talk of a victory with the words, 'we must be careful not to assign to this deliverance the attributes of a victory. Wars are not won by evacuations.'[6] The victory belonged to Germany. A delighted Hitler ordered church bells across Germany to toll for three days in celebration of a victory he claimed as the 'greatest battle in world history'.[7] However, for many in Britain the 'Dunkirk spirit' was a victory, and at a time when the nation was at its lowest ebb it significantly boosted national morale. Britain also regained its most experienced officers and soldiers to carry forward the war.

On 5 June, a day after the fall of Dunkirk, Hitler ordered the commencement of Operation Red, the final battle for France. The German Army was reorganised into five Corps deploying a total of 104 divisions to assault at best sixty French divisions dug-in along the 'Weygand' line. Britain was able to contribute two divisions – the 1st Armoured Division and the 51st Division – and planned to land a further two divisions. The Polish government in exile also planned to field two divisions. The German strategy was threefold: first, to secure the Brittany coastline to isolate France; second, to bypass Paris and occupy central France; finally, to sweep behind the Maginot Line to the Swiss border and trap the 400,000 strong garrison in their underground bunkers. Weygand tried to learn from earlier mistakes and deployed the French forces in a 'hedgehog' pattern of heavily fortified positions, but he had no defence against the panzers. The first major German breakthrough was achieved on 7 June when Rommel, in command of the 7th Panzer Division, once again distinguished himself in battle and broke the French line between Abbeville and Amiens. He occupied Rouen on 8 June and trapped the British 51st Division and the French 9th Corps, accepting the surrender of 45,000 Allied troops, including twelve generals.

With the German Army only 50 miles from Paris the French government held its last Cabinet meeting in Paris on 9 June. Weygand advised surrender. It was not the resolve Reynaud expected from his new commander-in-chief and it presaged a political as well as a military collapse of France. Weygand was supported by Petain, whereas Reynaud was supported by General Charles de Gaulle who had been appointed under-minister of national defence on 5 June. Both Reynaud and de Gaulle favoured a stubborn slow retreat and once France was lost to rally French forces and the powerful French Navy to carry forward the war from exile in French North Africa.

The debate was suspended when the French government hurriedly relocated to Tours on 10 June. Here they received news of a further damaging blow: Italy, under Mussolini's leadership, had declared war on France. President Roosevelt summed-up Allied outrage with the words, 'the hand that held the dagger has stuck it into the back of his neighbour'.[8] In September 1939 Mussolini had failed to join Hitler in war, but now with France virtually defeated he feared missing out on the spoils of war. A total of thirty-two divisions of the Italian Army were pitted against only six French divisions guarding the Alpine border. The Italian attack petered-out after an advance of only 2 kilometres, with 5,000 losses to only eight French troops. In contrast to the Italian debacle the Wehrmacht ranged across France virtually unchallenged. To avoid destruction by the Luftwaffe, Paris was declared an open city on 11 June. It was surrender in all but name and across France most people were resigned to defeat. In some towns and villages local people protested and prevented the retreating French Army from blowing bridges and railway lines. Churchill arrived at Tours on 11 June and returned for a second meeting on 13 June to urge Reynaud to stand firm, but the government was in political crisis. Reynaud was under sustained pressure from Weygand to seek an armistice, the latter advising that the war was lost; he was supported by Admiral Darlan who commanded the French Navy. The next day, 14 June, as the government relocated to the greater safety of Bordeaux, the first German soldiers of the 18th Army entered Paris without a shot being fired, and within hours they were relaxed and swarming over the major tourist spots. Swastika flags were raised on the Eiffel Tower and the Arc d'Triumph, and with the capital bowed in defeat the French government finally collapsed over the weekend of 15–16 June. Reynaud was mentally exhausted. He had hoped that a telegram to President Roosevelt, sent with Churchill's strong encouragement, would produce US support, but on the evening of 15 June Roosevelt ruled out any possibility of intervention. The US army had saved France from defeat in March 1918 in the Great War, but the US public were firmly set against any repeat. On 16 June Churchill sought assurances on the position of the French Navy and in a last-minute attempt to bolster French resolve he offered France, on de Gaulle's initiative, political union with joint citizenship and a united British and French government to continue the war. Reynaud eagerly grasped the proposal, but at a cabinet meeting called at 5 p.m. the proposal was received in stony silence and one minister offered the opinion that uniting with Britain would be as useful as uniting with a cadaver. The remark illuminated the depth of French defeatism. Most assumed that Britain would be defeated within weeks and that without US military intervention the only realistic policy was to negotiate with Hitler and aim to preserve as much French independence as possible within the new German continent. At 10 p.m. a broken Reynaud submitted the resignation of his government to President Lebrun, and at 11 p.m. Lebrun invited Marshal Petain, the deputy prime minister, to form a new government. Petain appointed Weygand as his minister of defence and accepted his recommendation for an immediate armistice.

Negotiations were opened via the German embassy in Madrid, and Petain addressed the French people by radio to urge non-resistance and acceptance of defeat. In London, on 18 June, de Gaulle gave a defiant reply and implored the French people not to give up but to support the newly formed 'Free French' forces under his command in London. By default, Petain and his government were rejected as collaborators and Charles de Gaulle, a virtually unknown 49-year-old brigadier-general in the French Army, assumed the mantle of leader in exile. In return, Weygand ordered a military tribunal to try de Gaulle *in absentia* for desertion and decreed at first a prison sentence and later a death sentence. All along the French Atlantic coast British troops flooded into the ports and most were evacuated to the safety of England in a mini Dunkirk. A total of 163,225 troops were safely returned, including some French soldiers who answered de Gaulle's appeal. In the midst of this dispiriting defeat an estimated 5,000 soldiers were drowned on 17 June when HMS *Lancastria* was sunk off St Nazaire following four direct hits from Stuka dive-bombers. It was Britain's highest maritime death-toll of the war, but on Churchill's direct orders it was not reported on order to avoid damaging the already low morale in Britain.

At 3.15 p.m. on 21 June Hitler stepped out of his Mercedes at Rethondes in the Forest of Compiègne on the French–German border. He paused to read the inscription on the stone monument that marked the location as the place of Germany's defeat and surrender in November 1918. Around him the world's press watched as he crossed the forest clearing and entered an old railway dining car to receive the French surrender. It was perhaps the moment Hitler relished most in the entire war. The dining car was the same carriage used by the French High Command in 1918 to receive Germany's surrender. On Hitler's orders it had been removed from a museum and restored to its original position. After the armistice was signed it was transported in triumph to a museum in Berlin; it was destroyed in a later air raid. Hitler only stayed long enough to hear General Keitel read aloud a denunciation of the French victory in 1918 before leaving. The surrender terms were generous and designed to encourage a swift settlement because Hitler wanted to avoid a dispute that might build support for de Gaulle in London or provoke a continuation of the war from North Africa. Consequently, to Mussolini's intense irritation, Hitler made no claims on the French empire territory in North Africa or the French Navy and offered Petain two-fifths of France as a continuation of a French sovereign state. Hitler's only major condition was the occupation of the French coastline and border areas to secure Germany's new frontiers. The moderate settlement was also an unspoken encouragement to Britain to end the war because it held out the promise of a similar deal in return for peace and an acceptance of the 'new order' in Europe. A different British prime minister might have negotiated a peace settlement. At the height of the Dunkirk evacuation on 28 May ex-Prime Minister Chamberlain supported the views of Foreign Secretary Halifax to open peace talks with Hitler. However, Churchill emphatically ruled out any consideration of surrender and rallied his cabinet with the words: 'if this long island story of ours is to end at last, let it end only when each one of us lies choking in his own blood upon the ground'.[9] The majority of the cabinet overwhelmingly supported Churchill. To reinforce the decision, Churchill issued a statement to the whole government and Civil Service urging all to offer Hitler nothing but defiance. Consequently, when Hitler offered Britain a formal peace settlement on 19 July his proposal fell on stony ground.

Petain questioned some of the armistice details, but faced with an ultimatum he authorised acceptance and at 6.50 p.m. on 22 June 1940 France formally surrendered. The next day Hitler enjoyed an early morning tour of Paris, and like any tourist he had his picture taken against a backdrop of the Eiffel Tower.

With France defeated Churchill feared the transfer of the French fleet to Germany and in the absence of firm guarantees from Petain he refused, on 24 June, to recognise the new 'Vichy' government. Churchill condemned Petain for collaboration with the Nazis, but French public opinion rallied to him and it was de Gaulle, with his message of continued resistance, who was isolated and ignored. Petain privately expressed the opinion that within three weeks 'England's neck will be wrung like a chicken's.'[10]

Churchill's attitude hardened. On 1 July Admiral Sir James Somerville, in command of Royal Navy Force H at Gibraltar, was ordered to confront the French Navy and secure its transfer to British ports, a transfer to the remote French West Indies, or its destruction. Most of the French fleet was at anchor in the French Algerian port of Mers el-Kebir near Oran. After some hours of negotiation no agreement was reached with Admiral Gensoul, and the French fleet was deemed hostile. At 6 p.m. the Royal Navy opened fire and sunk the *Bretagne* and disabled the *Dunkerque* and *Provence*. However, most of the French fleet escaped to Toulon.

The fall of France was confirmed on 11 July when Petain formally dissolved the French Third Republic and declared himself head of state of the new Etat Français, or French State, with its capital in the spa town of Vichy. Petain later refused a request from Hitler for French forces to join the war against Britain, but he did offer Hitler 200 pilots to assist the Luftwaffe during the Battle of Britain and implemented Hitler's racial war in France by removing citizenship from all French Jews. Later French officials and police collaborated with the round-up and transport of French Jews to their deaths in Auschwitz. Petain offered France a 'new order' with the Fascist values of 'work, family and country'. The France of liberty, equality and fraternity had fallen.

References

1. William L. Shirer, *The Collapse of The Third Republic*, Pan, 1972, p. 790.
2. Ibid., p. 784.
3. Ibid., p. 704.

4. Winston Churchill, *The Second World War: The Gathering Storm*, Cassell, 1950, p. 650.
5. William L. Shirer, *The Collapse of The Third Republic*, Pan, 1972, p. 865.
6. Martin Gilbert, *Churchill: A Life*, Heinemann, 1992, p. 655.
7. A.J. Barber, *Dunkirk: The Great Escape*, Dent and Sons, 1977, p. 209.
8. Martin Gilbert, *Second World War*, Orion, 1989, p. 90.
9. Martin Gilbert, *Churchill: A Life*, Heinemann, 1992, p. 651.
10. William L. Shirer, *The Collapse of The Third Republic*, Pan, 1972, p. 938.

12 Battle of Britain

We shall defend our island whatever the cost may be. We shall fight on the beaches, We shall fight on the landing grounds, in the fields, in the streets and in the hills. We shall never surrender . . .[1]

> Extract from Churchill's address to the
> House of Commons, 4 June 1940

Churchill made his defiant call to arms as the last Allied troops were evacuated from the beaches of Dunkirk. It was an emotive rallying cry to the British nation at a time of defeat and a clear message not only to Hitler but also to those in Britain who were sympathetic to Nazism and open to suggestions of a negotiated peace settlement. Ten days earlier on 23 May 1940 Sir Oswald Mosley, the leader of the British Union of Fascists, had been arrested and was later interned along with 1,678 other suspected Nazi sympathisers. Most belonged to the pro-Nazi 'Anglo-German Fellowship' and 'Link' organisations which had thirty-five active branches across Great Britain with an estimated 4,300 members. They enjoyed influence far beyond their numbers. The most prominent members were the 11th Duke of Bedford, the 2nd Duke of Westminster, and sixteen other peers of the realm. Other significant members were the governor of the Bank of England, Frank Tiarks; the chairman of ICI, Lord McGowan; the chairman of Morris Motors, Lord Nuffield; the chief political adviser to the Foreign Office, William Strang; and the MP for Peebles, Captain Ramsay. However, the figurehead for all British Nazi sympathisers was the Duke of Windsor, formerly King Edward VIII, who had abdicated in 1936 in order to marry the American divorcee Wallace Simpson. In June 1940 the Duke, temporarily resident in Lisbon, was approached by Nazi emissaries with the offer of a return to the throne of the United Kingdom under future Nazi rule. The Duke refused to conspire against his brother King George V but, on 4 July, Churchill appointed him as the governor of the remote Bahamas Islands. It was in effect a banishment and one that the Royal family resolutely maintained after the war.

Churchill tried to encourage US intervention in the war on 18 June by asserting that Hitler's threat was world-wide with the words: 'if we fail then the whole world, including the United States . . . will sink into the abyss of new dark age'.[2] However, he was aware of the strength of isolationist opinion in the United States and fully prepared for Britain to stand alone. He ended his speech with the emotive appeal to arms: 'if the British Empire and its Commonwealth last for a thousand years, men will still say, this was their finest hour'.[3]

The battle for Britain was not what Hitler had expected or envisaged. If anything, he had envisaged future partnership with Great Britain and for the whole of western Europe to unite under the Fascist flag for a anti-communist war against the USSR. Consequently, no advance plans for an invasion of Great Britain existed. On 2 July 1940 Hitler ordered the Wehrmacht to prepare preliminary plans for invasion, but he remained hopeful that the threat of invasion alone would push Britain into capitulation.

The preliminary invasion plan was submitted to Hitler on 12 July by General Jodl. He proposed an initial landing by thirteen divisions, supported by airborne troops, along the south coast from Lyme Bay to Ramsgate. Once the ports were secure Jodl expected to land a further twenty-eight divisions, including armoured divisions, to drive inland. Hitler demanded swift action and on 16 July he issued military directive No. 16, code-named '*Seelöwe*' or 'Sea-lion', with a target of mid-August for the invasion of Great Britain. During victory celebrations in Berlin on 19 July Hitler offered Great Britain a final opportunity for peace and indicated his reluctance to invade with the words: 'a great empire will be destroyed – an empire which it was never my intention to destroy or even harm'.[4] The Luftwaffe also dropped 'peace' leaflets over Great Britain entitled 'A last appeal to Reason' which urged the British people to accept a peace settlement. Hitler celebrated the triumph of German military forces in western Europe by promoting twelve generals to the rank of Field Marshal and by elevating Göring to the unique rank of reichsmarschall. It was honour Göring relished and he personally designed a new sky-blue uniform for the occasion.

The detailed military planning for Operation Sea-lion was conducted at a series of military conferences in late July, but the discussions produced a series of angry disagreements between Generals Jodl and Keitel and Admiral Raeder and the Kriegsmarine. The Norwegian campaign had severely depleted the Kriegsmarine and Raeder only had four cruisers and eight destroyers at his command to escort the proposed invasion fleet of 1,500 barges and 180 transport ships across the English Channel. It was a woefully weak force. The forward defensive screen of the Royal Navy alone comprised thirty-six destroyers, and the main home battle fleet was anchored in the safety of Scapa Flow and poised to intercept any German naval activity. Consequently Raeder would only commit the Kriegsmarine to the defence of a single landing point around Dover and to initially transport 150,000 troops rather than the 250,000 proposed by Jodl. The only point of unity between the Wehrmacht and the Kriegsmarine was deep pessimism for the success of the operation. Not for the first time in history, the English Channel was proving to be Britain's best defence.

The answer appeared to be air power, because during the Norwegian campaign the Luftwaffe had demonstrated its ability to drive off the Royal Navy. There were hopeful signs. From mid-June onwards the Luftwaffe had begun to probe RAF defences and to bomb targets in Great Britain, and on 10 July the Luftwaffe opened the *Kanalkampf*, or Channel Battle, with sustained air attacks against British shipping and the Channel ports. Dover was nicknamed 'hellfire corner', given the frequency of the air raids. Göring was delighted by the results because the Luftwaffe sank some 30,000 tons of British shipping and forced the withdrawal of the Royal Navy's capital ships from south coast ports to the safety of the more remote Scapa Flow naval base in Scotland. The attacks cost the Luftwaffe 180 aircraft to seventy RAF losses, but Göring believed that the larger Luftwaffe could sustain the losses and win. His confidence appeared to be well placed because at the end of July 1940 the RAF only had 591 fighters compared to 1,100 Luftwaffe fighters. In addition the Luftwaffe possessed a bomber force of 1,400 light and medium bombers and 400 dive-bombers, whereas at best RAF Bomber Command deployed 275 bombers. Göring was confident that the Luftwaffe could rapidly knock out all RAF airfields and destroy RAF aircraft on the runways and in their hangars, as had been the case in Poland, Holland and France.

On 1 August Hitler accepted the misgivings of the Wehrmacht and Kriegsmarine. He resolved not to commit his prized panzers to vulnerable sea transports until he was assured of their safe arrival. Consequently, he amended the target date for invasion to mid-September subject to the Luftwaffe gaining command of the skies to protect the invasion fleet. It was a demanding target and Admiral Raeder advised a postponement to spring 1941 unaware that Hitler had issued orders for the Wehrmacht to be ready to invade the USSR by May 1941. The *Aufbau-Ost*, or 'build-up east', had commenced in August 1940 and caused considerable consternation within the ranks of the OKW at the thought of fighting a two-front war. However, Hitler's increasing belief that he was a military genius made him deaf to all entreaties.

After some delays due to poor weather Hitler's Directive No. 17 finally fixed 13 August for *Adlertag*, or Eagle Day, and the commencement of the Battle of Britain. In Britain the battle was dated from 10 July, the start of the *Kanalkampf*, but for Hitler and Göring *Adlertag* marked the start of the strategic air war. Göring expected to destroy the RAF fighter command inside four days, but *Adlertag* was not the success he had hoped for. Low cloud forced the cancellation of most of the morning sorties, and although 1,485 sorties were flown against airfields along the south coast the damage was minimal. Only two airfields, Eastchurch and Detling, were hit and temporarily put out of action. The weather worsened on 14 August and reduced the attacks to little more than a third of *Adlertag*, but on 15 August the Luftwaffe delivered approximately 2,000 sorties, the largest air raid of the entire war. Driffield, Lympne, Martlesham and West Malling airbases were heavily bombed, as was the Shorts aircraft factory at Rochester, but otherwise the damage was insignificant. The Luftwaffe lost seventy-five aircraft and the RAF lost thirty-four and largely forced the bombers off target. However, air raids on 16 August resulted in substantial damage to the RAF airbases at West Malling, Tangmere and Brize Norton. On the same day in the skies above Gosport airbase Flight-Lieutenant James Nicholson won the only Victoria Cross of the Battle of Britain when despite a fire in his cockpit and suffering severe burns he refused to bail out until he had successfully pursued and shot down an Me 109 fighter. The Luftwaffe paused to regroup its aircraft on 17 August and the next day it returned to the attack and caused some of the heaviest damage of the air war with substantial raids on Biggin Hill and Kenley airbases.

Göring had promised to destroy the RAF in four days but by 18 August after four days of air attacks the Luftwaffe had lost 236 aircraft to ninety-five for the RAF. During an urgent reassessment of tactics on 18 August Göring personally rebuked his pilots, but when he asked them what they needed to win air ace Adolf Galland gave the uncomfortable reply: 'give me a squadron of Spitfires'.[5] In contrast Churchill was delighted by the performance of the RAF, and in commending their bravery in the House of Commons on 20 August he memorably stated: 'Never in the field of human conflict was so much owed by so many to so few.'[6]

Galland's comment to Göring highlighted that for the first time in the war the Luftwaffe had met not just an equal air force but in many respects a superior one. At the opening of the Battle of Britain the RAF had thirty-two squadrons of Hawker Hurricanes and nineteen squadrons of Vickers Supermarine Spitfires. Although the Spitfire became the symbol of the Battle of Britain it was the Hurricane that was the mainstay of the air war, with two Hurricanes for every Spitfire in the air. Both were powered by Rolls-Royce Merlin engines, but the Spitfire was the faster aircraft with a top speed of 360 m.p.h. The Messerschmitt 109 was the Luftwaffe's main fighter and although it outclassed the Spitfires and Hurricanes in both speed and armament it could not match the tighter turning circles of the British fighters. In dog-fights this proved its undoing. The Me-109 was also hampered by the distance to target and only had sufficient fuel to spend twenty minutes over southern England. Consequently the British fighters largely held the advantage and completely outmatched the slow Ju-87 Stuka dive-bombers and the two-man Messerschmitt 110 fighter that was designed to fly alongside and protect the bombers. So many Stukas were being shot down that the RAF pilots nicknamed them 'flying coffins', and as early as 18 August they were withdrawn from the battle to preserve them for the invasion. The Me-110 also proved to be so vulnerable to attack that the Me-109 had to abandon its role as an advance guard and stay close to the bomber formations to protect not only the bombers but also their Me-110 fighter escorts. The above factors allowed the RAF to maintain an overall two to one kill ratio during the air war. Nor was the RAF short of aircraft. The main Shorts and Vickers aircraft factories maintained high production levels, and whereas German intelligence estimated the production rate at 180 new fighters per month the RAF was actually receiving 460 fighters per month. The key RAF weakness was the lack of experienced pilots, a situation not helped by a strict social class divide. Before the war most pilots were selected from elite university backgrounds, but in 1936 with the threat of war the selection process was relaxed and many pilots from ordinary backgrounds were enlisted. They were not welcomed by the serving RAF officers and were denied officer status and restricted to the rank of sergeant-pilot. Their subservient positions were underscored by separate messes, and worse, many officers refused to accept orders or directions from sergeant-pilots despite in many cases their having greater flying and combat experience. However, one member of the volunteer reserve, Johnnie Johnson, managed to breach the class barrier. After being initially rejected by the RAF he became Britain's greatest fighter ace of the war with the confirmation of thirty-eight 'kills', and after the war he rose to the rank of air vice-marshal.

At the height of the battle, training for new RAF pilots was cut from four weeks to two weeks and many entered combat without any prior target shooting practice. To ease the shortfall pilots were recruited from other Allied countries. In total, thirteen other nationalities joined the RAF during the Battle of Britain, including some American volunteers. The biggest non-British contingent was 147 Polish pilots. However, the total number of foreign pilots only accounted for 10 per cent of all RAF pilots. With their minimal training and flight experience all the pilots exhibited considerable bravery against the experienced and battle-hardened Luftwaffe pilots.

The RAF's most significant advantage in the battle was the ability to detect and plot the height and direction of attacking Luftwaffe aircraft by radio direction finding (RDF) technology. RDF technology was first perfected in Britain by Robert Watson-Watt of the National Physical Laboratory in 1935, and by 1940 Great Britain had a chain of twenty-two long-distance RDF stations, codenamed 'Chain Home'. They wrapped around the British coast from Sumburgh in the Shetlands to Strumble Head in Pembrokeshire. In addition, thirty 'Chain Low ' stations detected low-flying intruders, and 30,000 volunteers joined the Observer Corps and staffed 1,000 observation stations to report the number, direction and estimated height of enemy aircraft. In ideal conditions the RDF detection range was 120–150 miles, but in operational practice it tended to be 60–80 miles. However, this was more than sufficient to grant the RAF thirty minutes' warning time of approaching 'bandit' aircraft. The early warning permitted the RAF pilots to be in position, fully fuelled and armed above the flight line of the approaching Luftwaffe aircraft and, whenever possible, in sufficient concentration to outnumber the attacking force. The Luftwaffe failed to recognise the importance of RDF technology and although RDF stations were bombed no sustained attempt was made to 'blind' the RAF. The US military did recognise the importance of the new technology and as part of a deal struck by Churchill on 16 August 1940 Britain traded RDF technology, along with 99-year leases on British naval bases in the Caribbean, in return for fifty US destroyers to protect Atlantic convoys. The US military gave RDF technology its more familiar acronym of RADAR, or *RA*dio, *De*tection *A*nd *R*anging.

The Luftwaffe absorbed the lessons of the first phase of the battle and reassessed its tactics during a period of poor flying weather from 19–23 August. The new tactics were immediately apparent when the Luftwaffe attacked and heavily damaged Manston, Hornchurch and North Weald RAF fighter stations on 24 August. The Luftwaffe lured the RAF into the air with a first strike and timed a second wave of bombers to arrive just as the RAF were landing to refuel and rearm. In addition the Luftwaffe also launched many feint attacks to trigger RAF 'scrambles' in order to keep the RAF uncertain about when and where a real attack would be pressed home and, ultimately, to exhaust the RAF crews. To reduce its losses the Luftwaffe also increased the ratio of fighters to bombers.

Although this meant fewer bombers the larger fighter screen meant that most of the bombers successfully reached and hit their targets. The main target was the RAF's fighter stations, and many were put out of action as the daily toll of bomb damage to runways and support facilities outstripped the capacity of the ground crews for repair and renewal. The new Luftwaffe tactics stretched the RAF to breaking point and on 31 August the RAF endured its worst single day of the air war when thirty-nine aircraft were shot down and fourteen pilots killed. The RAF could not sustain such high daily losses of men and machines and in early September, with the pilots at the point of total exhaustion, the outlook was bleak. The Luftwaffe was winning the air war by sheer weight of numbers and Göring's willingness to trade high losses for victory. Hitler congratulated Göring, and with the RAF apparently beaten he authorised a major change of tactics to force Britain to surrender.

On 7 September 1940 the full weight of the Luftwaffe air assault was switched to London. Göring was convinced that a major attack on London would force the RAF to commit all its reserves and present the Luftwaffe with a final opportunity to clear the skies. By demonstrating that the RAF could not defend London, Göring also hoped to destroy civilian morale and place public pressure on the government to surrender. The switch in tactics was also an emotional reaction to the bombing of Berlin by the RAF on 25 August, following an accidental bombing of London by the Luftwaffe on 24 August. The bombing of Berlin was a deep embarrassment to Göring and on 4 September, speaking in the Sportpalast, an enraged Hitler threatened: 'We'll wipe out their cities.'[7] From 4–6 September the Luftwaffe launched minor raids to test air defences, and on 7 September the first major Luftwaffe attack on London sparked invasion fears. Since 1 September the number of invasion barges in the Channel ports had tripled in number and the sudden heavy bombing of London was regarded as the prelude to the invasion with its aim being the disruption of government and the sowing of terror among the civilian population. The RAF was caught by surprise with its fighters north of London ready to repel further attacks on its airfields. Faced with little opposition, the Luftwaffe bombers set the docks and housing districts around the East End of London ablaze, killing approximately 430 civilians and injuring 1,600. At 8.07 p.m. on 7 September the British chiefs of staff, with the expectation of a dawn invasion, flashed the single code word, 'Cromwell' to all army and Home Guard forces. The Home Guard was a force of approximately 1.5 million civilian volunteers (originally raised in May 1940 as local defence volunteers), and all were pledged to defend their home areas. The direction to the British public in the event of invasion was to stay at home because during the blitzkrieg in Holland and Belgium fleeing masses of civilians had blocked the roads and hindered the movement of military reinforcements. The Home Guard was hopelessly under-equipped. The best-equipped units deployed in coastal areas possessed only one rifle per three volunteers, and many volunteers were armed with nothing more than hastily fashioned steel pikes. Defeat at Dunkirk had stripped the British Army of most of its weapons, and there was little likelihood of defeating the Germans if they gained a foothold in Great Britain. However, Churchill was adamant that Britons would fight to the last and in a speech given in July he stated: 'There will be no placid lying down of the people in submission . . . as we have seen, alas in other countries. We shall defend every village, every town and every city . . . we would rather see London laid in ruin and ashes than it should be tamely and abjectly enslaved.'[8] It was a commitment to total war and a commitment readily accepted by the British people.

No invasion came on 8 September because Hitler was waiting for the Luftwaffe to eliminate the RAF. However, Hitler had unwittingly assisted the recovery of the RAF. The Luftwaffe focus on London granted the RAF time to repair its runways and aircraft and to train and roster new pilots. Consequently, as the Luftwaffe continued to bomb London on 8, 9 and 11 September, the RAF regrouped. The ordinary people of London and Liverpool were placed in the front line and although there was public anger at the lack of sufficient public air-raid shelters morale remained high, this being epitomised by the comment 'we can take it' from one Londoner when Churchill visited an air-raid shelter in East London. Londoners introduced their own solution to the shortage of air-raid shelters. They bought platform tickets for the Underground and in defiance of the authorities stayed the night on the platforms. The Underground soon played host to approximately 177,000 Londoners every night, but surprisingly only 40 per cent of Londoners sought shelter and most took their chances in their own beds. King George VI and Queen Elizabeth also toured the East End, and to recognise that civilians were in the front line the king instituted the 'George Medal' on 23 September for acts of civilian bravery. The continued high levels of RAF resistance caused Hitler to postpone his invasion order to 17 September, and with this in mind Göring planned a major Luftwaffe attack for 15 September to break the RAF. To the shock of the Luftwaffe the decisive strike turned into a rout when they were intercepted by wave after wave of attacking Spitfires and Hurricanes. Many bombers were forced off target and the Luftwaffe lost sixty aircraft to twenty-six RAF.

On 17 September Hitler accepted defeat and postponed the invasion until 'further notice'. Göring retained his optimism that the Luftwaffe would yet succeed, but on 12 October, with winter weather making the English Channel impassable to barges, Hitler cancelled Operation Sea-lion. It was Hitler's first defeat, but one that he dismissed as unimportant because he regarded Great Britain as isolated and militarily insignificant.

The battle was won by Britain but the air war continued. The Luftwaffe changed tactics to night-time raids to operate under the cover of darkness, and from October 1940 to May 1941 Great Britain endured the Blitz. Most major cities were heavily bombed. On the night of 14 November central Coventry was destroyed, with over 500 killed, and on 29 December a firestorm ignited by over 22,000 incendiary bombs destroyed most of the City of London. In Hull only 6,000 homes out of 93,000 escaped bomb damage because the docks attracted regular Luftwaffe raids. The misery of the Blitz only ended in May 1941 when in preparation for the invasion of the USSR most of the Luftwaffe was transferred to the Eastern Front. In total approximately 40,000 civilians lost their lives, with just over half of the deaths in London.

Over the course of the battle the RAF lost 915 aircraft and 515 pilots in total, ninety-seven being non-British nationals. The Luftwaffe lost 1,733 aircraft and 1,644 pilots and aircrew. With the danger passed, Air Marshal of Fighter Command Sir Hugh Dowding was unceremoniously retired from active command on 25 November by a curt letter of dismissal. Whereas his tactics had produced victory, his blunt, no-nonsense manner and lack of deference even to Churchill had made him unpopular.

Apart from the Channel Islands, Britain was not invaded or occupied, and the survival of Britain against all the odds forced Hitler to divert considerable military resources to build and maintain coastal defences from Holland to the Spanish border.

References

1. Winston Churchill, *Great War Speeches*, Corgi, 1957, p. 28.
2. Ibid., p. 41.
3. Ibid.
4. Alan Bullock, *Hitler: A Study in Tyranny*, Penguin, 1962, p. 592.
5. Roger Manvell and Heinrich Fraenkel, *Göring*, Mentor Books, 1968, p. 181.
6. Winston Churchill, *Great War Speeches*, Corgi, 1957, p. 67.
7. Ian Kershaw, *Hitler 1936–45: Nemesis*, Penguin, 2000, p. 309.
8. Winston Churchill, *Great War Speeches*, Corgi, 1957, p. 55.

13 Italy on the march

Führer, we are on the march. This morning a victorious Italian army has crossed the Greek border.'[1]
                    Mussolini's greeting to Hitler upon his
                    arrival in Florence, 28 October 1940

As Hitler stepped down from his armoured train *Amerika* onto the platform of Florence railway station on 28 October 1940, Mussolini's greeting confirmed what he already knew. At dawn that morning Italy had commenced the invasion of Greece. It was unwelcome news, but during their talks in the medieval Pitti Palace Hitler suppressed his anger and offered Mussolini his full support.

The invasion of Greece broke an understanding arrived at between Mussolini and Hitler in July, and reconfirmed in September 1940, to focus all efforts on the defeat of Great Britain. Hitler expected to lead and Mussolini to follow, but Mussolini was determined to match Hitler's military successes in western Europe and to fulfil his own territorial ambitions with a parallel war of expansion in the Mediterranean.

Mussolini first outlined his strategy to the Italian High Command in February 1939 and confirmed his aims in a memo to King Victor Emmanuel III on 31 March 1940. He planned a return to the glory days of ancient Rome with the renewal of a Mediterranean empire that encompassed North Africa and the Balkans and redefined the Mediterranean as *mare nostrum* ('our sea'). In particular he wanted to end Britain's role as gatekeeper of the Mediterranean through its control of Gibraltar and the Suez Canal.

Following the success of the German blitzkrieg west in April and June Mussolini declared war on Britain and France on 10 June. It was an opportunist act designed to win a place at the victors' conference table and to stake a claim to North Africa and the Balkans. However, to his disappointment Hitler's peace settlement with France was benevolent rather than punitive and all Italy gained was an adjustment of Alpine borders, the province of Nice and a slice of Savoy.

Mussolini resolved to assert Italy's military independence by invading Greece and extending Italian leadership over the Balkan region. Whereas Hitler had no objections to Mussolini's plans his priority was the defeat of Great Britain, followed by the conquest of the Soviet Union to fulfil his primary goal of *Lebensraum*. He expected the subsequent rise of the Nazi new order in Europe to isolate the Balkan States and leave them with no alternative but to align themselves with the policies and interests of the Axis powers. It was a matter of patience and timing. Consequently Hitler planned to woo the smaller states of Eastern Europe and the Balkans to support a Fascist, anti-communist Europe and to gain their passive if not active collusion in the invasion of the Soviet Union. In this context, Greece was a potential ally rather than an enemy: in 1936 Greece had fallen under the right-wing military dictatorship of General Ioannis Metaxas. He was sympathetic to Hitler and modelled his secret police, the Asfalia, on the Gestapo and aped Nazi youth movements with a Greek version, the Ethniki Neolea. Therefore Hitler played down Mussolini's frequent complaints that Greece was providing covert support to Britain and betraying the positions of Italian ships and submarines to the Royal Navy. Hitler urged Mussolini to invade British Egypt rather than Greece. Hitler's interest was the closure of the Suez Canal to threaten the survival of the British Indian and Far Eastern empires. Faced with a choice between the continuation of empire or a peace treaty Hitler expected Churchill to capitulate. An invasion of England was Hitler's last resort, given the high risks for the Wehrmacht in forcing a passage across the English Channel.

Mussolini was responsive because Egypt and the adjacent British colonies of Somaliland, Kenya and Sudan in East Africa were attractive prizes. Beyond was the even greater prize of the British Middle East and oil. Consequently, Mussolini embraced Hitler's strategy and on 28 June he ordered the commander-in-chief of Italian forces in Libya, Marshall Italo Balbo, to invade Egypt. His order was never implemented because, on the same day, Balbo was killed when his reconnaissance flight over Tobruk was abruptly terminated by Italian anti-aircraft fire. It was an inauspicious start. Mussolini rescheduled the invasion for 15 July, but the new commander-in-chief of the Italian Army, Marshal Rodolfo Graziani, was reluctant to comply and complained that there were insufficient trucks and supplies to support the invasion. There was some truth in this because Mussolini, with an eye still focused on Greece, had husbanded military resources in Albania. To spearhead the invasion Hitler offered Mussolini a panzer division, but this was more than Mussolini's sense of national pride could bear and he declined the offer. He was determined to conquer Egypt unaided and at first there were some military successes. On 5 August Italian troops crossed the border from Abyssinia into British Somaliland on the Horn of Africa and captured the capital, Berbera, on 19 August 1940. It was a minor victory. The Somaliland defence force was outnumbered five to one, but it contributed to Hitler's strategy by posing a threat to the British empire in Africa and forcing Britain to divert troops and supplies. However, the Italian Army showed little interest in advancing further and, apart from a few border incursions into Kenya and Sudan, the Italian armies in Abyssinia and Libya remained dormant.

The lack of any major advance frustrated Mussolini and he threatened to dismiss Graziani if the Italian Army had not invaded Egypt by 15 September. A reluctant Graziani complied and on 13 September five divisions of the Italian Army advanced into Egypt in temperatures of up to 50°C. Mussolini had timed his invasion to coincide with the expected invasion of Great Britain by the Wehrmacht on 15 September, unaware that Hitler had cancelled Operation Sea-lion.

To increase the pressure on Britain to capitulate Hitler also courted the support of Vichy France, Spain and Japan. Hitler was encouraged when forces loyal to Vichy France repulsed an attempted landing by Free French forces under the command of General de Gaulle between 23 and 26 September in the French colony of Dakar in West Africa. The landings were supported by the Royal Navy, and in reprisal the French Air Force bombed Gibraltar and raised the prospect of war between Vichy France and Great Britain. Hitler's courtship of Japan brought immediate success and on 27 September Japan signed the Tripartite Pact with Germany and Italy and joined the Axis alliance. Hitler subsequently fanned Japanese expansionist plans in the Pacific to threaten Britain's Far East empire and as a useful foil to the USA.

On 4 October 1940 Hitler met Mussolini at the Brenner Pass in the Alps for a brief meeting to discuss and confirm their joint strategy. No formal minutes were kept, but it would appear that Mussolini renewed his case for an invasion of Greece by emphasising that the occupation of Greece would contribute to the defeat of Britain in Egypt by allowing naval and airbases to be established on the island of Crete. Hitler was apparently unmoved and reiterated his support for an invasion of Greece, but only after the defeat of Britain in Egypt.

Three days after their meeting at the Brenner Pass German troops entered Romania in fulfilment of a secret defence pact struck between Hitler and the anti-communist leader of Romania, General Ion Antonescu. Hitler's interest was oil and the protection of the strategic Ploesti oilfields in Romania. In June 1940 the Soviet Union had annexed the Romanian province of Bessarabia and Hitler feared further Soviet encroachment that might threaten Germany's oil supplies. It was a further unilateral act by Hitler and breached his own declared strategy of avoiding military action in the Balkans.

Mussolini felt humiliated by Hitler's lack of consultation and the disagreement introduced the first significant discord into the Axis relationship. Hitler realised his error and attempted to appease Mussolini by hurriedly arranging for a contingent of Italian troops to enter Burcharest alongside the Wehrmacht, but Mussolini was stung into action. He remarked to Ciano: 'Hitler always faces me with a fait accompli. This time I am going to pay him back in his own coin. He will find out from the newspapers that I have occupied Greece.'[2] The immediate invasion of Greece was attractive to Mussolini, not just as riposte to Hitler but also to distract attention away from the slow, hesitant progress of the Italian Army in Egypt. The invasion was rapidly becoming an embarrassment for Mussolini and Italian arms. After an unchallenged advance of only 60 miles along the Egyptian coast to the town of Sidi Barrini, Graziani had chosen to dig in. Graziani had an army of 215,000 against a British army in Egypt of only 30,000, but he refused to advance further until he received more trucks – especially water tankers – to support the advance. His strategy was threefold: first, to fortify Sidi Barrini as a forward supply base; second, to advance a further 75 miles to the oasis of Mersa Matruh; third, to advance the final 170 miles from Mersa Matruh to Alexandria and Suez. Mussolini urged Graziani forward but his ponderous staged advance was far removed from the display of Fascist, fighting spirit that Mussolini expected, and a pale shadow of Germany's blitzkrieg in Europe. Consequently, the promise of a swift, decisive victory over Greece was all the more attractive to Mussolini as a demonstration of the prowess of the Italian armed forces and to remind Hitler that he was an independent military leader. To guarantee a glorious Italian victory Mussolini took the advance precaution of distributing millions of lire in bribes to Greek generals and officials. His military commander in Albania, General Prasca, expected minimal Greek opposition and promised Mussolini not a war but a 'colpo di mano in grande'[3] – a triumphant military parade. Without consulting his High Command Mussolini issued orders on 15 October for the invasion of Greece to take place on 26 October. The order was later amended by Marshal Badoglio to 28 October, the eighteenth anniversary of Mussolini's seizure of power in the 'March on Rome' in 1922. It was to be his last independent military action, but the first of many military humiliations.

Oblivious to Mussolini's resolve Hitler embarked on a 4,000-mile round trip in his armoured train *Amerika* on 20 October to persuade Vichy France and Spain to join the Axis alliance and to enter the war against Great Britain. However, the most he was able to gain from talks with Vichy Foreign Minister Pierre Laval and Prime Minister Marshal Petain was a statement of joint interests and increased collaboration. He expected a more positive response from General Franco because German forces had assisted his seizure of power during the Spanish Civil War of 1936–39. Hitler met Franco in the Spanish border town of Hendaye on 23 October and offered the services of German airborne troops to seize Gibraltar, but the talks stalled when Franco demanded the restoration of a Spanish empire in North Africa and extensive economic and military aid. After a full day of inconclusive negotiations Hitler later confided to Mussolini in Florence: 'rather than go through that again I'd prefer to have three or four teeth taken out'.[4] It was a very rare event, but Hitler had met his match in negotiations. The failure to gain Spain as an ally was a significant strategic setback for Hitler. The seizure of Gibraltar, codenamed 'Operation Felix' had been pencilled in for 10 January 1941 and, if successful, it would have closed the Mediterranean to British shipping. In addition, the construction of U-boat bases in the Canary Islands and the Azores would have dramatically extended Germany's reach in the Atlantic war.

The refusal of Vichy France and Spain to enter into a firm military alliance largely ended Hitler's consideration of a plan favoured by General Jodl, Admiral Raeder, Foreign Minister Ribbentrop and Reichsmarschall Göring for an advance south into the Mediterranean region. Jodl promoted the benefits of an 'extension of the war to the periphery'[5] as a means of draining Britain's resources in defence of her empire in a battleground chosen by Germany. Göring enthusiastically embraced the proposal and directed detailed military planning for a three-pronged invasion of the Mediterranean region to trigger the collapse of the British empire in the Middle East and India and to force Britain to come to terms. Hitler refused to be drawn. In a rare argument with Göring he reiterated that his unwavering goal was for *Lebensraum* to the east, and whereas he was keen to promote and aid a Fascist alliance of Italy, France and Spain to eject Britain from the Mediterranean, he regarded the Mediterranean as lying within the Italian sphere of interest and of marginal interest to Germany. Göring pressed his argument by reminding Hitler of his promise to the Wehrmacht not to repeat the kaiser's mistake in the Great War of fighting a war on two fronts, but Hitler countered by dismissing Britain as a spent military force. He argued that the key to Britain's surrender lay not in the Mediterranean but in the defeat of the Soviet Union as, in his opinion, 'Churchill was hanging on and waiting for Stalin to come into the war.'[6] Consequently, Hitler regarded the early conquest of the Soviet Union as pivotal to final victory. Not only would it end British hopes of Soviet support but the occupation of the Soviet Union would feed German industry with an inexhaustible supply of raw materials and secure the new German continent against any future threat from the USA.

As Hitler travelled back to Germany on 25 October he received a letter from Mussolini that confirmed earlier reports from German military intelligence of Mussolini's decision to invade Greece. The letter, dated 19 October, was deliberately not despatched by Mussolini until 22 October to reduce Hitler's time for reaction. Mussolini defended his decision by asserting: 'Greece is to the Mediterranean what Norway was to the North Sea.'[7] Although Hitler had ample opportunity to telephone or telegraph Mussolini to forestall the invasion he resigned himself to the news.

At 3 a.m. on 28 October 1940 General Metaxas was awakened by the arrival of the Italian minister in Athens who presented him with an ultimatum to surrender his country by 6 a.m. Metaxas remarked that it was insufficient time to consider selling his home let alone his country, and ordered full national resistance. At 5.30 a.m., in advance of the deadline, an Italian army of approximately 125,000 began to cross the Albanian border into Greece. Churchill immediately offered Greece full support and ordered British forces in the Mediterranean and Egypt to lend all possible assistance. Churchill gave the defeat of the Italian forces in Greece priority over Egypt. A day after the invasion the first British troops landed on Crete to establish forward military bases, and the RAF bombed Naples on 31 October.

The strategy pursued by General Visconti Prasca was to overwhelm Greece by a simultaneous advance by three Italian armies to seize the north, centre and south of the country. At first there was little resistance because the Greek Army was caught unprepared with only four of its sixteen divisions mobilised. However, the Italians had not learnt the lessons of the Winter War a year earlier and repeated the mistakes of the Red Army in Finland. As they penetrated the valleys the Greek Army took to the mountains and launched flank attacks against the vulnerable Italian supply convoys. The Italians were forced to pursue the Greeks into the mountains but they lacked maps and winter clothing, and once above the snowline they made slow, hesitant progress. The bare hillsides also provided little cover and as they advanced uphill they made easy targets for the Greek defenders. The superior Italian Air Force might have made a difference, but Mussolini had made the mistake of ordering the invasion during the rainy season. Low cloud cover regularly shrouded the mountains and kept the Italian Air Force grounded for most of the war.

Prasca committed most of his troops to the mountainous central sector of Greece in an advance towards Koritas and Metsovon. By sheer weight of numbers Koritas was captured, but the Italian armies to the north and south made little progress: after five days of fighting the Italians had, at best, advanced 25 miles into Greece. Without waiting for full mobilisation the commander-in-chief of the Greek Army, General Alexander Papagos, launched a counter-attack on 2 November. He surprised the Italians by marching four divisions across the border into Albania into the Italian rear and captured the Pissoderi mountain commanding the road to Koritas. The unexpected move cut off supplies and reinforcements to the crack Julia Division of the Italian Alpine forces in Koritas. In his diary entry for 2 November, Goebbels recorded Hitler's disapproval of the Italian invasion, and noted: 'It has been badly conceived and does not present an elevating spectacle, at least at present.'[8]

The implied expression of hope by Goebbels for an improvement in the Italian military position was dashed by the failure of Italian counter-attacks from 6–10 November and the collapse of Italian resistance with 5,000 prisoners and 25,000 casualties. Mussolini blamed Prasca for the failure and replaced him as commander-in-chief by General Ubaldo Soddu. However, this defeat was followed by an equally humiliating defeat at sea when in a single stroke the Royal Navy ended Italian naval superiority in the Mediterranean. On 11 November, twenty-one Swordfish torpedo bombers, launched from the aircraft carrier HMS *Illustrious*, surprised the Italian Navy at anchor in Taranto harbour in southern Italy. The battleships *Littorio, Caio Duile* and *Conte di Cavour*, and four other ships, all sustained heavy damage for the loss of only two Swordfish. This successful use of air-launched torpedoes was closely studied by Admiral Isoroku Yamamoto in Japan and by the US Secretary of State for the Navy Frank Knox, who suggested the installation of anti-torpedo nets at Pearl Harbor. His suggestion was never acted upon.

On 12 November Hitler issued War Directive No. 18 which renewed his pursuit of anti-British alliances with Spain and Vichy France. However, both countries politely refused his overtures and later, on 10 December, Franco firmly ruled out any co-operation with Hitler's plan to seize Gibraltar. To guard against the increased Allied military activity in the Mediterranean Hitler signed War Directive No. 19 on 10 December and set contingency plans for the occupation of Vichy France. Ever the opportunist, he also attempted to enlist Soviet support against Great Britain. During talks with Soviet Foreign Minister Molotov in Berlin on 12 and 13 November Hitler encouraged Molotov to consider an advance south to the Indian Ocean at the expense of the British empire in Asia. The talks floundered when Molotov not only showed no interest in the proposal but reaffirmed Soviet strategic interests in the Baltic and the Balkans. Any further Soviet encroachment into Europe was anathema to Hitler and it strengthened his resolve to invade the USSR. Ribbentrop gamely attempted to persuade Molotov to reconsider, but he only confirmed his reputation for inept diplomacy when he suggested to Molotov, during an RAF bombing raid, that Britain was finished, prompting Molotov to remark: 'and whose are these bombs which fall?'[9]

After three weeks of intense fighting in Greece at altitudes as high as 5,000 feet the Italian focus was the relief of Koritas, but on 22 November the besieged Italian 9th Army was forced to surrender. The next day the last Italian soldiers withdrew from

Greece and, aided by newly formed Albanian League, the Greek Army went on the offensive. The intention was to drive the Italians out of Albania, but as they moved out of the mountains the Italian superiority in aircraft, artillery and tanks forced the Greeks to a standstill. The RAF established airbases in Greece and provided air support, but a stalemate ensued across a ragged front line from Progradec in the north-east of Albania to Himare on the south-west coast. Mussolini found himself in a war he could not win and he had no alternative but to seek military assistance from Hitler. It was not a prospect he relished, and the Italian ambassador to Germany noted: 'I found the Duce plunged into the depths of depression. I have never before seen him looking so dispirited.'[10] Ciano met Hitler at Salzberg on 18 November and endured Hitler's verbal criticism, and on 20 November Mussolini received a letter of rebuke from Hitler causing him to remark: 'he has really smacked my fingers'.[11]

Mussolini's humiliation was not over. In the western desert the British 'desert rats' of the Western Desert Force under the command of Major General Richard O'Connor launched an attack against the stationary Italian Army at Sidi Barrani on 9 December and delivered a crushing defeat. The Italian Army broke and fell into a general retreat, and O'Connor's army of 30,000 soldiers accepted the surrender of some 38,000 Italians, including four generals. Hitler had little choice but to intervene and support Italy in Greece and North Africa. He could not permit his only ally in the Mediterranean to be defeated, and he could not tolerate RAF bases in Greece within striking distance of the Romanian oilfields. Consequently, it was the failure of the Italian Army rather than the arguments of Göring and the Nazi hierarchy that finally persuaded Hitler to turn his attention south.

On 13 December Hitler issued War Directive No. 20 and ordered the Wehrmacht to mass twenty-four divisions in Romania ready for a spring invasion of Greece, code-named 'Operation Maritsa'. His intention was to secure his southern flank before the invasion of the Soviet Union.

On 6 December General Jodl presented Hitler with the first draft plan for the invasion of the Soviet Union, codenamed 'Operation Fritz'. Hitler approved the plan but renamed it 'Operation Barbarossa' after Emperor Frederick Barbarossa who had expanded the Holy Roman Empire eastwards in 1190. On 18 December Hitler signed War Directive No. 21, which ordered the Wehrmacht to be prepared to 'crush Soviet Russia in a quick campaign before the end of the war against England'.[12] The target date for action was 15 May 1941.

By the close of 1940 Mussolini's grandiose ambition for Italian greatness was at an end. His parallel war in the Mediterranean was subsumed as Hitler's peripheral war and, for the rest of the war he meekly accepted Hitler's direction and ultimately presided over the German annexation of his country.

References

1. Martin van Creveld, *Hitler's Strategy 1940–41: The Balkan Clue*, Cambridge University Press, 1973, p. 49.
2. Alan Bullock, *Hitler: A Study in Tyranny*, Penguin, 1962, p. 614.
3. Martin van Creveld, *Hitler's Strategy 1940–41: The Balkan Clue*, Cambridge University Press, 1973, p. 26.
4. Alan Bullock, *Hitler: A Study in Tyranny*, Penguin, 1962, p. 605.
5. Martin van Creveld, *Hitler's Strategy 1940–41: The Balkan Clue*, Cambridge University Press, 1973, p. 28.

6. L. Mosley, *The Reich Marshal*, London, 1974, p. 270.
7. Martin van Creveld, *Hitler's Strategy 1940–41: The Balkan Clue*, Cambridge University Press, 1973, p. 45.
8. Fred Taylor (ed.), *The Goebbels Diaries 1939–41*, Sphere, 1983, p. 161.
9. Michael Bloch, *Ribbentrop*, Bantam, 1992, p. 315.
10. Christopher Hibbert, *Benito Mussolini: The Rise and Fall of Il Duce*, Penguin, 1986, p. 160.
11. Alan Bullock, *Hitler: A Study in Tyranny*, Penguin, 1962, p. 623.
12. Ibid., p. 625.

Expansion

14 North Africa and the Balkans

> The Italians have brought the entire military reputation of the Axis crashing down in ruins. That is why the Balkan states are being so obstinate . . . Now we shall have to attack. Not to help them but to chase out the English.[1]
>
> Extract from Goebbels' diary, 22 December 1940

Goebbels' diary entry encapsulated the new strategic direction forced upon Hitler in December 1940 by the failure of the Italian armed forces in Greece and North Africa. The Balkans and North Africa held no attraction for Hitler but he could not permit Britain to defeat Italy and establish a front on Germany's southern border. Consequently, his aim was not to furnish Italy with an empire but rather to secure the borders of the new German Europe. Hitler shared his strategic thinking with his military commanders at the Berghof, his Alpine retreat, on 8 and 9 January and confirmed his orders for a Mediterranean offensive in War Directive No. 22 issued on 11 January 1941. On 19 January it was Mussolini's turn. Hitler greeted Mussolini on the platform of Pusch railway station in Austria and escorted him up the steep, winding road to the Berghof. It was a meeting Mussolini had tried to avoid, such was his deep embarrassment at the rout of the Italian forces in Greece and North Africa. By January 1941 Italy's forces were retreating on all fronts. In Albania the Italian Army was being driven back towards Valona and, in an attempt to arrest the Greek advance, Mussolini had sacked General Soddu on 13 January and replaced him with General Ugo Cavellore. In East Africa the British had entered Abyssinia and on 15 January restored Emperor Haile Selassie to the throne to lead opposition to Italian colonial rule. Of greater concern was defeat in North Africa, where British forces had not only repelled the Italian invasion of Egypt but pursued the Italians across the border into the Libyan province of Cyrenaica and seized Bardia on 3 January, taking 30,000 Italians prisoner. Hitler made no reference to any of these Italian defeats. His mood was upbeat and he dazzled Mussolini's entourage with his command of military strategy and confidence in an overall Axis victory. As always, he was less than candid with his Axis ally and Mussolini returned to Italy unaware of the plans for Operation Barbarossa. To Mussolini's relief, he was back in Italy and not in Hitler's company when news was received of the fall of Tobruk on 22 January as the victorious British pushed deeper into Cyrenaica. The victory was largely won by Australian forces and in the absence of a Union Jack the triumphant Australians hoisted a 'Digger's hat' up the main flagpole. Throughout January 1941 the British advance continued unchecked and General Richard O'Connor's desert rats fanned out across Cyrenaica and seized the port of Benghazi on 7 February. The Italians fell into a general retreat and in an audacious pincer movement the Italian Army was intercepted south of Benghazi at Beda Fomm. Here, a brigade of only twenty-nine British tanks engaged an Italian armoured column, destroying sixty Italian tanks and forcing the abandonment of a further forty. The British lost only three tanks, and the tiny force of 3,000 troops took 20,000 Italian prisoners. In only eight weeks O'Connor's desert rats had liberated the whole of Cyrenaica and had advanced some 400 miles to the edge of the western province of Libya, Tripolitania, within striking range of the capital of Italian Libya, Tripoli.

This was Britain's first major offensive of the war and was a considerable boost to British morale at a time when Britain was enduring the Luftwaffe blitz and heavy losses in the battle for the Atlantic. Hope for future victory was also raised by the growing anti-Axis stance of US President Roosevelt. Whereas public opinion in the US remained sternly in favour of neutrality, Roosevelt's speeches and actions increasingly steered the US towards intervention. On 6 January Roosevelt addressed the American nation and characterised the war as a war between dictatorship and liberty, and he placed the USA foursquare behind liberty by declaring the US to be 'the arsenal of democracy'. The practical expression of this commitment was Roosevelt's personal support for 'Lend-Lease' legislation to allow Britain unlimited access to the resources of the US economy. On 10 January Roosevelt took a more significant step for the future when he linked US foreign policy to the pursuit of the four fundamental human freedoms of speech, religion, and from want and fear. It was an ideological commitment that would ultimately end the US foreign policy of isolationism and pitch the US not only against the Axis powers but, after 1945, against Soviet totalitarianism.

The British military successes and the evidence of Roosevelt's hostility stirred Hitler's anger. In a speech marking the eighth anniversary of his accession to power on 30 January 1941 at the Sportpalast in Berlin, he condemned Britain for holding back the advancement of Germany in Europe and the world. In evidence he cited Britain's

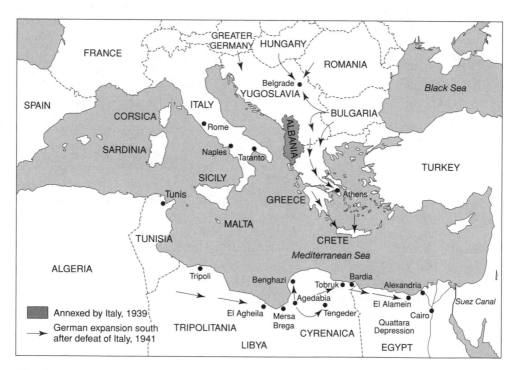

Map 3 German expansion south, 1941

hostility to the kaiser Wilhelm II's policy of *Weltpolitik* (world policy), Britain's declaration of war in 1914, Britain's imposition of the Treaty of Versailles in 1919 and Britain's declaration of war in 1939. In a bitter outburst he attested that he had only ever sought peace with Britain: 'I have offered Britain my hand again and again. It was the very essence of my programme to come to an understanding . . . we have been drawn into war against our will.'[2] Hitler ended his speech with a firm prediction for a conclusive German victory in 1941: 'The year 1941 will be, I am convinced, the historical year of a great European new order.'[3] Unknown to his audience, Hitler was already relishing the prospect of the defeat of the Soviet Union and the exploitation of economic resources that would make Germany wholly independent and impervious to attack even from the USA. Such was his ebullient mood that he renewed his prewar prophecy that the war would result in the destruction of the Jewish race.

Hitler's confidence appeared to be well-placed. On 1 January the X Fliegerkorps (Air Corps), composed of 150 fighters and bombers, was deployed to Sicily and scored an early success. On 10 January the aircraft carrier HMS *Illustrious* was attacked and crippled by thirty Stuka dive-bombers. In opposition the RAF based on the nearby island of Malta could only muster a single squadron of fifteen Hurricanes.

The job of the X Fliegerkorps was to secure the sea lanes to Tripoli because on 6 February Hitler ordered the transport of the 5th Light Division and the 15th Panzer Division to North Africa to form the Deutsches Afrika Korps under the command of General Erwin Rommel. Rommel had become a public figure in Germany after his flamboyant command of the 7th Panzer 'ghost' Division in the battle for France, and he was one of Hitler's favourite generals. His orders were to assist the Italian Army in the defence of Tripolitania under the overall command of Italian General Italo Garibaldi, and at best was expected to recapture Benghazi. Rommel arrived in Tripoli on 12 February and true to his reputation he decided within a matter of hours 'to depart from instructions . . . and to take command at the front into my own hands as soon as possible'.[4] On 14 February the first of Rommel's advance forces arrived and moved directly to the front line on reconnaissance missions. To fool British intelligence, while he impatiently waited for his Panzers to arrive, Rommel deployed dummy tanks made out of wood and canvas and mounted on the chassis of Volkswagen cars. The 5th Panzer Division, with 120 tanks, reached Tripoli on 11 March and were unloaded in the course of a single night under Rommel's restless direction. Rommel pushed his panzers into immediate action and on 24 March they retook the minor fort and airstrip at El Agheila against minimal British opposition. Only a light screen of British troops remained from the victorious desert rats because in response to Churchill's orders General Wavell had withdrawn most of his experienced desert command for service in Greece. The victorious 7th Armoured Division and 6th Australian Division had been replaced by the inexperienced 2nd Armoured Divison and 9th Australian Division. General Richard O'Connor, the architect of British victory in Cyrenaica, had also been withdrawn and his command of the Western Desert group had passed to the inexperienced Lieutenant-General Philip Neame. On 31 March Rommel probed east along the coast road and regained Mersa Brega and, by 2 April, Agedabia. This success placed Rommel and his panzers at a strategic gateway into British-occupied Cyrenaica with a choice of three major routes forward. As Rommel pondered his next move there was astonishment in Berlin, Rome and London as Rommel's reconnaissance mission turned into a major advance.

Hitler's attention was fixed on Greece rather than on Africa because Rommel was not expected to take any action until after the arrival of the 15th Panzer Division in

May. With the invasion of Greece set for 6 April Hitler's priority was in gaining the co-operation of the Balkan nations surrounding Greece to permit the transit of German troops. Romania and Hungary had both joined the Axis alliance in November 1940, but the keys to the rapid invasion of Greece were Bulgaria and Yugoslavia because both shared a border with Greece. Bulgaria was the first to yield to Hitler after months of economic and military pressure and joined the Axis alliance on 1 March 1941. Yugoslavia was more resistant to Hitler's demands, but on 4 March, after enduring several hours of persistent badgering and invasion threats from Hitler at the Berghof, the regent of Yugoslavia, Prince Paul, agreed to join the Axis alliance. However, within days the decision plunged the government of Yugoslavia into political crisis. On 21 March four cabinet ministers resigned rather than co-operate with Hitler, and when Prime Minister Dragisa Cvetkovich insisted on signing the Axis alliance on 25 March in a formal ceremony in Vienna his actions triggered a coup.

The next day ordinary Serbs took to the streets of the capital Belgrade in protest. Cvetkovich was forced out of office and a new government of national resistance under the leadership of chief of staff of the air force, General Dusan Simovic, was formed on 27 March. The decision precipitated the internal collapse of Yugoslavia because the Croat minority were largely pro-Axis. Hitler was enraged by this sudden reversal and in War Directive No. 25, signed on 27 March, he ordered the invasion of Yugoslavia as well as Greece on 6 April. His anger was reflected in his order for an *ohne Gnade*, or a merciless campaign, to punish the people of Yugoslavia for their defiance. His determination to enforce his will was underlined by his decision to postpone Operation Barbarossa for four weeks to grant the Wehrmacht and Luftwaffe sufficient time to crush Yugoslavia. Thus it was the unexpected invasion of Yugoslavia rather than Greece that was to delay Barbarossa.

At 5.20 a.m. on 6 April, German forces began the simultaneous invasion of Yugoslavia and Greece. To monitor the progress of the attack Hitler travelled to the southern Austrian border near Monchkirchen in his train *Amerika*. The first air raids overwhelmed the Yugoslavian Air Force of 450 largely obsolete aircraft, and the majority were destroyed on the ground. In fulfilment of Hitler's command for *ohne Gnade* the Luftwaffe repeatedly bombed Belgrade and killed an estimated 17,000 civilians. On the ground four panzer columns brushed past the weak border defences and penetrated deep into the interior. Their advance was virtually unimpeded because the Yugoslavian Army had made the mistake of deploying along the length of the 1,000-mile border, with no strong central reserves to counter the inevitable German breakthroughs. A German victory was assured when the Fascist-orientated Croat-Ustahi movement sided with Hitler on 10 April and declared an independent pro-Axis Croatia. Yugoslavia imploded into civil war and after only ten days of fighting Yugoslavia surrendered on 17 April.

The brutal treatment meted out to Yugoslavian civilians contrasted with the strict military etiquette observed in Greece. Athens was not bombed and the Greeks were shown respect for their stubborn and brave defence of their country. Little was contributed to the defence of Greece by the hastily formed British Expeditionary Force of approximately 60,000 British troops under the command of General Sir Henry Maitland. With only a hundred light tanks at their disposal and minimal RAF cover the British forces were dwarfed by the substantial military resources of the Wehrmacht and Luftwaffe. Churchill's decision to aid Greece made more political than military sense. He wanted to demonstrate that Britain would stand by any country that opposed the Axis powers, but in stripping North Africa of experienced troops he merely aided

Rommel's advance and lost all the gains made in Cyrenaica, exposing the British Army and Royal Navy to needless losses during the evacuation of Greece.

The Greek Army expected the main weight of the German attack to fall on the border with Bulgaria but with the collapse of Yugoslavia the Wehrmacht poured across the lightly defended Yugoslavian border in strength. The Greek Army, in the front line against Italy in Albania, was trapped and cut off from supplies or reinforcement and the Wehrmacht drove a deep wedge into the heart of Greece. The Greek and British armies had no forces capable of stopping the advancing panzers or the relentless Luftwaffe attacks. Within days Maitland's forces were reduced to a fighting retreat and gradually fell back to Kalamata on the southern tip of the Peloponnese. The prime minister of Greece, Alexander Koryzis, committed suicide on 18 April, and on 23 April his replacement, Emmanouil Tsouderos, and King George evacuated the Greek government to Crete. It signalled the collapse of resistance, and on 27 April the panzers reached Athens and the victorious Wehrmacht draped a swastika over the Acropolis. The only option left was evacuation and in the face of sustained Luftwaffe attacks the Royal Navy implemented a mini Dunkirk and evacuated over 50,000 troops to Crete and Egypt minus all their heavy weapons and trucks. Inside only three weeks, Hitler had achieved his aim of securing southern Europe and, to his delight, with minimal losses. Only 151 German troops were killed in Yugoslavia and 1,518 in Greece.

The British remained in control of the island of Crete and from here the RAF could target the strategic Polesti oilfields in Romania and the whole of southern Italy. It was an uncomfortable prospect, but with the Royal Navy dominant Hitler had no plans for the invasion of Crete. Kurt Student, the commander of Germany's airborne forces, offered Hitler a solution and proposed a major parachute drop to seize Crete. Student was keen to prove that his elite shock troops could do more than simply seize bridges, which had been their major operational role in Norway and Holland. Hitler was sceptical, but he authorised the plan with the codename 'Operation Merkur' (Mercury) on 25 April. It was to prove to be one of the most audacious attacks of the war.

In parallel to the military successes in the Balkans, Rommel added to the invincible reputation of the Wehrmacht, and to his own reputation as a military strategist, by retaking Cyrenaica. His frequent comment to his commanders that he liked to sniff the air before a battle like a fox quickly earned him the nickname of 'the Desert Fox'. Faced with a choice of three routes into British-held Cyrenica, Rommel advanced along all three. On 4 April he retook Benghazi and, as the British Army retreated along the semi-circular coast road, he punched a corridor east across the open desert and cut off the retreat at Coefia and further east at Derne. The swift action trapped many British troops, among them General Richard O'Connor, the mastermind of the earlier British victory, and the commander of the British forces Lieutenant-General Neame. They were captured when their car ran into a German roadblock on the coast road north of Derne. By 11 April Rommel had cleared the whole of Cyrenica apart from the port of Tobruk, and after the failure of attacks on 10–11 and 14 April he paused to regroup. Britain was at bay and by the end of April 1941 Germany was the master in both Europe and North Africa.

Hitler returned to Berlin on 28 April as the victorious warlord and, with his southern flank firmly secured, he set dawn on 22 June for the commencement of Operation Barbarossa, the invasion of the Soviet Union. His judgement and strategy appeared to be flawless and as a result he refused to be moved by renewed concerns about the dangers of fighting a two-front war against Britain and the Soviet Union. He dismissed the Red Army as a demoralised force and predicted a rapid victory that would permit the panzers to roll south from Soviet Caucasus into the oilfields of the Middle East and from there to link up with the Afrika Korps and force Britain to surrender. However, the continued defiance of Britain was clearly an irritant and it appears to have prompted Hitler's deputy Rudolf Hess to undertake a daring but half-baked personal mission to negotiate a peace settlement with Great Britain. On 10 May he piloted a Messerschmitt 110 to Scotland and parachuted out with the intention of making contact with the Duke of Hamilton, a suspected Nazi sympathiser, and inviting him to act as an intermediary with Churchill. Churchill refused to meet Hess, who was bundled into captivity and remained in captivity for the rest of his life. Hitler declared him insane, but Hess had gambled everything on a major political coup that would end the war with Britain and restore his faded fortunes within the Nazi hierarchy. Like many of Hitler's dinner guests Hess had regularly absorbed Hitler's wish for an alliance with Britain, and as late as August 1941 Hitler was still regaling his dinner guests with talk of a future partnership with England: 'One day we will see England and Germany marching together against America.'[5]

The final act in securing southern Europe commenced at 8 a.m. on 20 May when approximately 280 bombers, 200 fighters and 150 Stuka dive-bombers of the Luftwaffe 4th Air Fleet bombed and strafed Allied positions on Crete. There was little Allied response because the last six RAF fighters on Crete had been withdrawn the day before for their own preservation, and there were few anti-aircraft guns. As the attack faded the sky filled with parachutes as a fleet of approximately 500 Junkers 52 transports disgorged over 6,000 paratroopers. Their targets were the three major airfields along the northern coast of Crete at Maleme, Retimo and Heraklion, with the aim of securing the airfields to establish an airbridge for transports to land reinforcements and heavy weapons. Further reinforcements were expected to arrive by sea, with a planned landing of 7,000 troops of the 100th Mountain Rifle Regiment from a flotilla of Greek caiques and barges. The attack was not a surprise. The codebreakers at Bletchley Park had broken the Luftwaffe codes and followed every detail of the build-up to the invasion. The only surprise was the eventual German victory. The paratroopers suffered high casualties and at first the British press claimed a British victory. The paratroopers were dropped directly over defended positions and made easy targets during their 30-second descent. Many more were injured by landing awkwardly on the rough terrain or were entangled in the dense olive groves, and at least 300 drifted out into the sea where they drowned under the weight of their heavy equipment. Little mercy was shown to the injured and many were killed at close quarters. Some German units like the 1st Assault Company were almost entirely wiped out with 112 out of 126 troops killed. The initial Allied success on land was followed by success at sea with the interception and sinking of the major part of the German and Italian naval flotilla by the Royal Navy. On the second day of the battle the Germans were surrounded in isolated pockets and appeared to be on the point of defeat, but the high morale and determination of the elite German parachutists turned the tide of the battle. The fulcrum was Maleme airfield and the command of the neighbouring high ground, Hill 107. Student, who was directing the invasion from a hotel in Athens, ordered further parachute drops over Maleme and forty Junkers 52 transports crash-landed, under heavy fire, onto the airstrip and delivered further reinforcements. The additional troops were sufficient to secure Hill 107 and the airfield, and over the next three days the Luftwaffe flew in further reinforcements. The German breakout commenced on 24 May, and without heavy weapons or air cover the Allies were forced into a steady retreat. Fierce fighting erupted around Kastelli, Galatas and Suda Bay, but by 28 May the Germans were victorious across the north of the island. The British retreated to the tiny port of Sphakia on the south coast and under heavy Luftwaffe attack the Royal Navy staged an evacuation. Approximately 18,000 British troops were rescued before the Germans established control over the entire island on 31 May, taking 12,000 prisoners. Crete had fallen and the losses on both sides were heavy. Approximately 2,000 Allied troops were killed. The Royal Navy also lost 2,000 men and, in a testimony to air power, three cruisers and six destroyers were sunk by the Luftwaffe. The Germans lost approximately 7,000 troops – more than in the entire battle for Yugoslavia and Greece combined – and this alone convinced Hitler that lightly armed parachutists were too vulnerable for a main battlefield role. Publicly the seizure of Crete was hailed as a tremendous victory, but in private Hitler remarked: 'Crete has become the graveyard of the German paratrooper.'[6] He refused to authorise any further mass parachute attacks, but in Britain Churchill reached the opposite conclusion and ordered the creation of Britain's first parachute regiment from among the ranks of the British commando forces. Most of Student's paratroopers were later attached to the infantry and saw service on the Eastern Front and, in a bizarre twist, assisted in the defeat of the Allied parachute drop at Arnhem in 1944.

Against the tide of German advances the only Allied successes were the defeat of Italian forces in East Africa and the defeat of the pro-Axis leadership of Rashid Ali in Iraq which had threatened Allied control over the Middle Eastern oilfields. An attempt to regain the initiative in North Africa with the launch of Operation Battleaxe on 17 June was also a dismal failure. General Wavell had hoped to break Rommel's line and relieve the besieged port of Tobruk, but the attack collapsed under the weight of a firm counter-attack which allowed the Germans to breach the border of British Egypt. Churchill reacted by replacing General Wavell with General Claude Auchinlech, or 'Auk' to the troops, as commander-in-chief Middle East with orders not only to hold Egypt but to drive Rommel back.

With Britain under siege and Operation Barbarossa imminent, Hitler was fully confident of winning the war by Christmas 1941. While waiting for victory Hitler filled his days studying plans for the redesign of Berlin to transform it into Europe's leading city and poring over plans for the Germanisation of western Russia with projected German settlements stretching to the shores of the Black Sea. The soldiers of the demobilised Wehrmacht were to be offered farms and lordship over the Russian population, and Hitler planned to transport the surplus Russian population east of the Ural mountains to survive as best they could in the permafrost of Siberia. Hitler envisaged the Urals as a natural Hadrian's Wall to keep the barbarians out of the new German Europe.

References

1. Fred Taylor (ed.), *The Goebbels Diaries 1939–41*, Sphere, 1983, p. 214.
2. Alan Bullock, *Hitler: A Study in Tyranny*, Penguin, 1962, p. 633.
3. Ibid.
4. *Purnell's History of the Second World War, Volume One*, Purnell, p. 438.
5. Hugh Trevor-Roper, *Hitler's Table Talk 1941–1944*, Phoenix Press, 2000, p. 26.
6. BBC Two, *Timewatch*, 16 February 2001.

15 Battle of the Atlantic

Distressing! It is terrifying. If it goes on it will be the end of us . . .
This mortal danger to our life-line gnawed my bowels.'[1]
        Churchill's comment on shipping losses, 26 February 1941

On 23 January 1941 the German battlecruisers *Gneisenau* and *Scharnhorst,* under the direct command of Vice-Admiral Lujens, slipped out into the Atlantic Ocean undetected by the Royal Navy. Their aim was to hit and run. The German surface fleet was too weak to confront the Royal Navy directly. Consequently, the few capital ships of the Kriegsmarine relied upon their speed and surprise to attack Allied merchant ships and to retreat to port before the more powerful Royal Navy could close and engage. After June 1940 their task was made easier with the acquisition of naval bases in conquered Norway and France. Both coastlines offered the Kriegsmarine raiders a choice of bolt-holes and ended the disadvantage of trying to slip in and out of the narrow Baltic Sea. The *Gneisenau* and *Scharnhorst* successfully eluded the Royal Navy and after twenty days at sea they took refuge in Brest in France, having sunk twenty-two unescorted Allied merchant ships.

The raid highlighted the vulnerability of Allied shipping and offered Hitler a new strategic direction to defeat Great Britain. Hitler had expected the high death toll inflicted by the Luftwaffe blitz of 1940–41, coupled with the threat of invasion in spring 1941, to force Great Britain to capitulate. But in a review of tactics on 6 February 1941 Hitler concluded that the blitz had failed. The deliberate 'terror bombing' of Britain's major cities had not produced the expected collapse in civilian morale and public support for Churchill, but the opposite. Hitler had hoped that public distress would manifest itself in the rise of a peace party around Lord Halifax or David Lloyd-George and push Churchill out of power. However, after five months of intensive bombing there were no stirrings of public protest against Churchill or the war. Consequently, Hitler decided to intensify the U-boat campaign against Allied shipping in the Atlantic to disrupt Britain's war production and to starve Britain into submission. Directive 23, 'Directions for Operations against the English War Economy', identified control of the Atlantic shipping lanes as a major strategic goal.

It was a significant threat. As an island nation Britain was dependent upon regular imports. Moreover, in wartime half of Britain's food, all oil and a constant flow of munitions all crossed the Atlantic, mainly from the USA. The focus of Hitler's Directive was to cut this 'Atlantic life-line' by expanding the *Unterseebootflotte* (U-boat Fleet) and by ordering the Luftwaffe to target Britain's major ports. Churchill publicly acknowledged the new danger in a radio broadcast on 9 February 1941 when he stated: 'Herr Hitler will do his utmost to prey upon our shipping and to reduce the volume of American supplies reaching these islands.' He conceded the advantage to Germany of naval bases in France and Norway with the words: 'his clutching fingers reach out on both sides of us into the ocean'.[2]

The renewed focus on the defeat of Great Britain also assisted Hitler to beguile Stalin. Hitler encouraged Stalin's assumptions that the new Atlantic campaign was part of his preparations for the invasion of Great Britain in the spring of 1941. The Kriegsmarine found it impossible to fulfil Hitler's new directive immediately because whereas it had gained many new naval bases it only commanded a minor surface and U-boat fleet. War had not been expected until 1943 at the earliest, and the Kriegsmarine had been thrust into the war with only fifty-six U-boats and a surface fleet pegged at 35 per cent of the tonnage of the Royal Navy by the pre-war agreement of 1935. Although both sides possessed equal numbers of submarines, only twenty-six of Germany's U-boats were Type IX, these having an operational range of 12,000 miles and thereby capable of operating in the Atlantic. Despite these limitations, the first major successes in the naval war of 1939–40 were scored by the Kriegsmarine (see Chapter 7).

The Luftwaffe also contributed to the battle of the Atlantic but its threat was largely confined to coastal waters. The Kriegsmarine had no aircraft carriers to support air strikes out into the Atlantic, but after 1940 the four-engined Focke-Wulf Kondor (FW-200) based in Merignac in Bordeaux and Stravanger in Norway gave the Luftwaffe a long-range bomber capable of Atlantic operations.

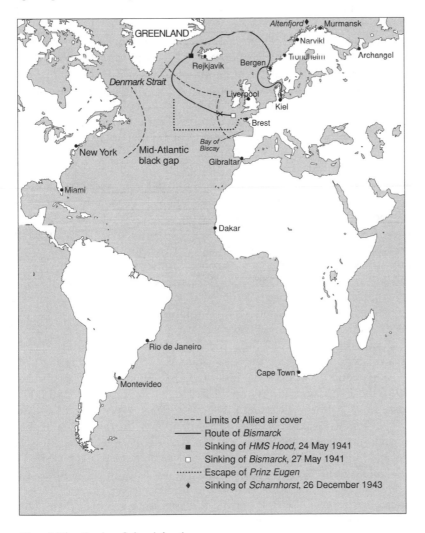

Map 4 The Battle of the Atlantic

The greatest threat to Allied shipping was, by far, the U-boat. By the end of 1940, 1,059 Allied ships had been sunk and 60 per cent of these were accounted for by U-boats. At the outbreak of war, Britain had possessed the largest merchant fleet in the world with 3,000 ships, and in July 1940 this had increased by 34 per cent following the transfer to Great Britain of merchant fleets from defeated Norway, Holland and Belgium. Churchill was nevertheless concerned that a major increase in U-boat activity would outpace the replacement capacity of the shipyards. His fears were confirmed on 24 February 1941 when, in a speech to Nazi Party stalwarts in Munich, Hitler boasted of his plans for a massive expansion of the U-boat fleet to knock Britain out of the war. Two days later Goebbels recorded in his diary: 'Our U-Boats have sunk 250,000 tons. First results of the intensified campaign . . . The U-Boat campaign is being taken very seriously in London. People are very anxious after the Fuhrer's speech. And rightly so.'[3] The commander-in-chief of the U-boat fleet, Karl Donitz, requested a fleet of at least 600 U-boats in order to maintain 300 U-boats at sea at any one time. He established his headquarters at Kernevel, near Lorient, and to protect his U-boats he built U-boat 'pens' at Lorient, Brest and Bordeaux with roofs of reinforced concrete, twelve-feet thick, impervious to air attack. The RAF missed an opportunity to destroy the pens during the construction phase. They chose to focus their efforts on bombing the main U-boat construction yards at Wilhelmshaven and Kiel, but with minimal results.

To counter the U-boat threat, Churchill formed the Atlantic Committee which met daily from March 1941, and he appointed Admiral Sir Percy Noble, commander-in-chief of Western Approaches, to direct Britain's battle of the Atlantic. Noble established his headquarters in Liverpool from where he maintained direct control over all convoy and escort movements. A large map of the Atlantic Ocean dominated one wall of his operations room, showing the 'trade plot' of the merchant ships at sea and the positions of the twenty-five escort groups under his command. The map also plotted the last reported positions of any U-boats and any movement from port by surface raiders revealed by Enigma intercepts and air reconnaissance. The Royal Naval Intelligence unit based in Hut 8 of Bletchley Park had broken the Kriegsmarine Enigma naval code and were able to read U-boat radio traffic and plot their positions. Armed with this vital intelligence, the Royal Navy regularly re-routed convoys out of harm's way. The Royal Navy possessed nothing as sophisticated as the German Enigma machine to encode its radio traffic but nevertheless believed that German naval intelligence had not broken its radio traffic. It was a mistaken assumption. The Kriegsmarine B-Dienst (observer service) routinely read Royal Navy signals, but its intelligence activity was rudimentary and largely consisted of sifting the data for convoy departure dates and destinations. Had they looked deeper the correlation between Enigma traffic and the movements of Allied convoys would have indicated that Enigma had been broken.

In March 1941 the U-boats sank forty-one Allied ships amounting to 243,000 tons – but at the cost of five U-boats, including three of the *Unterseebootflotte*'s most decorated captains. The first to be lost was Gunther Prien on 7 March, when U-47 was depth-charged and sunk by HMS *Wolverine*. He was responsible for sinking HMS *Royal Oak* in Scapa Flow in the early months of the war. On 16 March, HMS *Vanoc* rammed U-100 and crushed Captain Joachim Schephe to death in the conning tower. The next day, HMS *Vanoc* was again in action and forced the surrender of U-99 after she was depth-charged to the surface by HMS *Walker*. Among the survivors plucked from the sea was Captain Otto Kretschmer who held the record for sinking the highest tonnage of Allied shipping and had the status of Germany's leading U-boat ace. His new status as a POW was a welcome gift for Allied propaganda and his tonnage record remained unbroken for the remainder of the war.

Britain also received welcome news from the United States. On 8 March the US Congress passed Lend-Lease Act by 60 votes to 31 which significantly eased Britain's ability to pay for munitions and foodstuffs. However, Churchill privately commented: 'we are not only to be skinned but flayed to the bone'.[4] His comment indicated the scale of Britain's mounting debt to the USA which had resulted in the earlier forced sale of Britain's assets in the USA and the release of naval bases to the US Navy (USN) in Bermuda. On 15 March President Roosevelt publicly declared the US to be anti-Nazi, and he committed the US to grant all possible aid to Britain short of war. In secret, on 27 March, the US and British military staffs concluded Defence Plan 1. It gave priority to the war against Nazi Germany, over the Pacific, in any future joint military action. On 10 April the first US naval action against the Kriegsmarine occurred when the USN destroyer *Niblack* sighted and engaged a U-boat. The action was to enforce the declaration of a 200-mile security zone for Allied ships by the USN, off the US east coast, following earlier U-boat attacks on US merchant ships.

The greater involvement of the US and Canadian navies in the protection of Allied convoys off the US and Canadian seaboards allowed the Royal Navy to concentrate its efforts in the Western Approaches. This left the mid-Atlantic, known as the 'black gap', as the key danger zone for Allied shipping because it was beyond the operating range of the three navies and Allied aircraft. In consequence the U-boats focused their attacks in the mid-Atlantic and, as Donitz deployed more U-boats, the Allied losses mushroomed. During the single month of April 1941 the Allies lost 488,124 tons of merchant ships to U-boat attacks – a 50 per cent increase on the March total. Goebbels noted in his diary on 11 May: 'A big British propaganda effort. She is now forced to admit to 500,000 tons of shipping lost in April. The highest monthly total so far.'[5]

The U-boat successes reflected the perfection of wolf-pack tactics. Donitz used intelligence gleaned from Royal Navy radio traffic and from agents operating in the major US ports to direct a 'wolf pack', or flotilla of U-boats, to intercept the Allied convoys in mid Atlantic. This tactic overwhelmed the Royal Navy escorts and permitted the U-boats to scatter the convoys and to subsequently pick out and sink the most valuable targets, particularly oil tankers. The U-boats also attacked on the surface and at night. This not only increased their speed but avoided detection by ASDIC. The Royal Navy used ASDIC detection equipment (known as SONAR in the USN) to track submerged U-boats, but the system was blind to U-boats on the surface. Attacking on the surface also neutralised the primary anti-U-boat weapon of depth charges, and at night the U-boats were all but invisible to lookouts.

The Royal Navy was the superior navy, but it was fully stretched by the scale of the challenge in the Atlantic and by the need to maintain a fleet in the Mediterranean and a Home Fleet to guard against invasion. The key shortage was escort destroyers. Consequently, most convoys sailed with insufficient escorts, and sometimes no escorts, to counter the wolf-pack attacks. The civilian merchant seamen were on the front line of the Atlantic war. Only troop convoys received a major and continuous escort to and from port. The survivors of torpedoed ships had minimal chance of rescue because the ships in a convoy were under standing orders not to stop to pick up survivors, both to avoid collisions and to avoid offering any circling U-boats stationary targets. Life expectancy in the freezing waters of the North Atlantic, and for those on the later Arctic convoy routes, was at best measured in hours. Air reconnaissance was a vital weapon in the Atlantic war, but owing to inter-force rivalry the RAF insisted upon full operational control of all aircraft and pointedly refused to co-ordinate its operations with convoy movements. Churchill resolved the situation in April 1941 by placing RAF Coastal Command under the direct command of the Admiralty.

The Luftwaffe contributed to Hitler's Atlantic strategy by targeting Britain's major ports to sink ships in the harbours and to destroy the port facilities. In April and May 1941, large tracts of London, Belfast, Hull and Liverpool were entirely destroyed. The Luftwaffe also heavily bombed Coventry and Birmingham. A new two-ton bomb, dropped by parachute, was capable of destroying whole streets at a time, and during the first two weeks of May the centre of Liverpool and the East End of London around the docks were all but destroyed. Liverpool docks were bombed for seven consecutive nights 1–7 May, killing 1,450 people. An ammunition ship, the *Malkand*, was set on fire and exploded with such force that six other ships were sunk at their moorings and the entire Huskisson dock was destroyed. Within a week, the raids had destroyed sixty-nine out of 144 moorings and most of Liverpool was reduced to rubble. London continued to be the major target of the bombers and on the single night of 11 May 1,440 Londoners were killed and much of central London was made impassable with over 2,000 fires raging beyond fire brigade control. The House of Commons received a direct hit forcing parliament to convene in the assembly rooms of Church House.

By May 1941 the twin assault of the bomber and the U-boat was steadily sapping the ability of Great Britain to survive and against a background of defeat in Greece, Crete and North Africa the outlook was grim. Consequently, there was a major sense of relief in Britain when in late May and early June the Luftwaffe raids suddenly diminished and all but stopped. From Engima intercepts Churchill knew the reason why. Hitler had transferred the Luftwaffe to the Eastern Front to prepare for the invasion of the Soviet Union. Churchill passed warnings to Stalin, but Stalin refused to heed them because he was suspicious that Churchill was trying to draw the Soviet Union into war to relieve the pressure on Great Britain.

Public morale in Britain was also raised in late May by the defeat of a bold bid by Admiral Raeder to use his surface fleet, in conjunction with the U-boats, to sever the Atlantic lifeline. Raeder wanted to force Britain's surrender, or at the very least to severely curtail Britain's war effort in advance of the invasion of the Soviet Union. He intended to direct all four of Germany's most powerful battleships, *Bismarck*, *Prinz Eugen*, *Scharnhorst* and *Gneisenau* as a hunting group to attack and scatter Allied convoys in the mid-Atlantic and thereby provide the U-boats with defenceless targets. The plan went wrong from the outset when *Gneisenau* was damaged at anchor in Brest by RAF bomb attacks. Raeder, however, refused to abandon the operation and decided to press ahead with the *Bismarck* and *Prinz Eugen* under the direct command of Admiral Lujens. He expected a repeat of Lujens' earlier Atlantic raid in command of the *Scharnhorst* and *Gneisenau*, but everything depended upon the element of surprise.

At dawn on 20 May 1941 surprise was denied. A patrol aircraft from the Swedish cruiser *Gotland* spotted both battleships in the Kattegat Straits leaving the Baltic, and within hours the Admiralty were informed via the British naval attaché in Stockholm. After a brief stop in Bergen, Norway, on 21 May to take on fuel, both battleships steamed for the Atlantic, taking the northern route around Iceland. They narrowly escaped an RAF bomb attack on Bergen by the margin of a few hours. The Home Fleet at Scapa Flow under Commander-in-chief Admiral Jack Tovey immediately put to sea and, unaware of the *Bismarck*'s direction, established patrol lines to the west and east of Iceland. For added protection Royal Navy Force H, based in Gibraltar under the command of Admiral Somerville, was ordered to steam for the mid-Atlantic to be in position should the *Bismarck* and *Prinz Eugen* attempt to run the cordon. Lujens was aware from the intense increase in Royal Navy radio traffic that he had been spotted but, rather than return to port or hide in the Arctic Ocean, he decided to press ahead into the Atlantic. HMS *Hood* and HMS *Prince of Wales* intercepted the *Bismarck* and *Prinz Eugen* at 5.30 a.m. on 24 May and opened fire at 5.53 a.m. In their haste to engage the *Bismarck* both Royal Navy ships closed at a poor angle of attack and failed to bring all their guns to bear. It was a fatal error. Highly accurate fire from the *Bismarck* scored three direct hits on the *Hood* and set the stern alight. The damage was minor, but a fourth shell penetrated the lightly armoured decks of the *Hood* and hurled red-hot metal splinters into the main aft magazine, which exploded with catastrophic results. The *Hood* sank inside three minutes and only three of the 1,400 crew survived by being blown overboard. An investigation of the wreck of the *Hood* lying on the seabed by the deep-sea explorer David Mearns in 2001 has revealed that the ship was torn asunder, with the bow lying a mile and a half away from the main hull. The spread of the debris field indicates that the *Hood* was destroyed by not one but by two massive explosions occurring only seconds apart. It would appear that a jet of flame from the aft explosion flashed the length of the ship and ignited the cordite store for the forward turret. The force of twin explosions aft and forward would explain why the *Hood* sank so rapidly without time to abandon ship.

The *Prince of Wales* broke off the engagement at 6.13 a.m. after further accurate fire from the *Bismarck* had inflicted heavy damage. The *Bismarck* was victorious, but at a price. During the exchange a shell had ripped a hole in her bow and not only flooded the forward compartments with 1,000 tons of sea water but also cut off fuel oil from the forward oil bunkers. The damaged *Bismarck* was forced to reduce speed to conserve fuel and to head for the safety of Brest or St Nazaire in France for repairs. The *Bismarck* was no longer the hunter but the quarry as the most powerful battleships of the Royal Navy converged on her position. Lujens turned briefly towards his pursuers and used the confusion of a renewed engagement to cover a dash into the Atlantic by the *Prinz Eugen* with orders to seek out and engage Allied convoys. The Royal Navy maintained contact with the *Bismarck,* the greater of the two prizes, but during the early hours of 25 May all contact was lost in thick rain mist as the lead cruisers conducted zigzag manoeuvres to guard against possible U-boat attack. In a twist of fate that proved fatal for the *Bismarck*, General Hans Jeschonnek, chief of staff of the Luftwaffe in Athens, radioed Berlin for the latest information on the *Bismarck* on behalf of one of his staff whose son was serving on board as a midshipman. The Luftwaffe 'Red Key' was broken by the signals staff at Bletchley Park in January 1940 and after May 1940 they routinely listened in to all Luftwaffe radio traffic. Jeschonnek was reassured that the *Bismarck* was safe and en route to Brest, but the signal betrayed *Bismarck*'s position and within an hour the Royal Navy was on an intercept course.

At 10.36 a.m. on 26 May a long-range Catalina flying boat out of Lough Erne, Northern Ireland, spotted the *Bismarck* and all available ships, including Swordfish torpedo planes from *Ark Royal*, were ordered to attack. A series of continuous attacks on 26 May exhausted the crew of the *Bismarck* and left them in little doubt about the final outcome. Vice-Admiral Lujens sent a last defiant radio message to Berlin: 'Ship unmanageable. We shall fight to the last shell. Long live the Fuhrer.'[6] It was his fifty-second birthday.

At 8.47 a.m. on 27 May the battleships HMS *King George V* and HMS *Rodney* closed on the *Bismarck* and opened fire. The *Rodney* carried nine 16-inch guns and its fourth salvo destroyed the *Bismarck*'s forward A-turret. Thereafter the *Bismarck* was raked by continuous direct hits which smashed the superstructure and set the ship alight from bow to stern. By 9.30 a.m. the *Bismarck* was crippled and unable to return answering fire, and was finally sunk at 10.36 a.m. by torpedoes launched from the cruiser HMS *Dorsetshire*. Only 110 of the 2,000 crew survived. Churchill received the news as he sat down in the House of Commons having delivered a sombre report on the loss of HMS *Hood*. He immediately returned to his feet and flatly added: 'I might venture with great respect to intervene for one moment. I have just received the news that *Bismarck* is sunk.'[7] The reaction in Berlin was more emotional. Goebbels recorded in his diary: 'A black day . . . a fearful blow which will be felt by the entire nation.'[8] Hitler received the news with disbelief and criticised Raeder for exposing the *Bismarck* to attack from the entire Royal Navy Home Fleet. The only good news for Germany was the safe arrival of *Prinz Eugen* in Brest on 1 June where she joined the cruisers *Scharnhorst* and *Gneisenau*. But six of the supply ships attached to the raid were also tracked by Enigma intercepts and sunk.

The *Bismarck* raid was the last major action of the Kriegsmarine surface fleet, but the battle of the Atlantic remained in the balance. The U-boat threat was increasing rather than diminishing as Donitz's expanded fleet took to the Atlantic. In May 1941 the U-boats sank fifty-eight Allied ships, taking the total tonnage lost in the period April–May 1941 to 1.1 million tons. Hitler was aware that Allied losses on this scale were unsustainable and with his *Panzerarmees* poised to invade the Soviet Union he expected to achieve overall victory in the summer of 1941.

References

1. Martin Gilbert, *Churchill: A Life*, Heinemann, 1992, p. 691.
2. Winston Churchill, *Great War Speeches*, Corgi, 1957, p. 116.
3. Fred Taylor (ed.), *The Goebbels Diaries 1939–41*, Sphere, 1983, p. 247.
4. Martin Gilbert, *Churchill: A Life*, Heinemann, 1992, p. 692.
5. Fred Taylor (ed.), *The Goebbels Diaries 1939–41*, Sphere, 1983, p. 358.
6. Michael Smith, *Station X: The Codebreakers of Bletchley Park*, Channel 4 Books, 2000, p. 58.
7. Winston Churchill, *Great War Speeches*, Corgi, 1957, p. 134.
8. Fred Taylor (ed.), *The Goebbels Diaries 1939–41*, Sphere, 1983, p. 384.

16 Barbarossa

What India was for England, the territories of Russia will be for us. If only I could make the German people understand what this space means for our future. We must no longer allow Germans to emigrate to America. On the contrary we must attract the Norwegians, the Swedes, the Danes and the Dutch into our Eastern territories. They'll become members of the German Reich. Our duty is methodically to pursue a racial policy . . . one day we will see England and Germany marching together against America.[1]

Hitler, in discussion with his dinner guests, 8 August 1941

During the early evening of Saturday, 21 June 1941 Sergeant-Major Alfred Lishof of the German 74th Infantry Division deserted his post, slipped across the Soviet border and entered the Ukrainian border town of Vladimir-Volynsk. He warned the local Soviet commander, General Purkayev, that the Wehrmacht was poised to invade the Soviet Union at 4 a.m. Purkayev took the warning seriously and at 9 p.m. he telephoned the chief of staff of the Soviet Army, Marshal Zhukov, in Moscow, and recommended an immediate military alert. Lishof's warning confirmed many earlier warnings of invasion received by the Soviet High Command. The first warning had been received by the Soviet Embassy in Berlin on Christmas Day 1940, only a week after Hitler had first approved plans for Operation Barbarossa. The Soviet Embassy received a further, more potent warning on 15 February when copy of a new Wehrmacht German–Russian phrase book was anonymously handed in. Among the many non-tourist phrases was the telling direction, 'Hands up or I shoot.' The warnings of invasion were given credence by a steady build-up of three major Wehrmacht army groups along the Soviet border. The chief of Soviet military intelligence, General Golikov, monitored the German build-up and reported to Stalin, in March 1941, that 180 Wehrmacht divisions were stationed along the border. Stalin also received warnings that Hitler was planning to invade the Soviet Union from Churchill, US intelligence, the Lucy spy ring in Sweden, and from the Soviet Union's most prolific and reliable spy, Richard Sorge, in Tokyo. Sorge not only provided details of the German invasion plans from contacts in the German embassy in Tokyo but in an intelligence report sent to Moscow on 15 May he accurately predicted the date of attack as 22 June.

Stalin dismissed all the warnings as Allied misinformation and, in particular, as a clumsy attempt by Churchill to embroil the USSR in a war with Nazi Germany. He accepted the explanation from Hitler that the Wehrmacht was regrouping to the east out of range of RAF bomb raids and was preparing for the invasion of England. Consequently he ignored all evidence to the contrary, including a sharp increase in Luftwaffe surveillance flights across the Soviet border throughout May and June. Stalin was convinced that the Nazi–Soviet Pact of August 1939, and the occupation of Poland, had satisfied Hitler's appetite and removed the threat of invasion. Consequently, at 00.30 hours on 22 June, he rejected a joint appeal from Marshal Zhukov and Marshal Timoshenko to heed Lishof's warning and to place Soviet forces on full battle alert. His only concession to caution was to raise the alert status of the border units to Combat Alert Two, but he forbade Soviet forces to open fire on any German incursions without his direct authorisation. Confident that there would be no attack Stalin had left the Kremlin for his dacha at Kuntsevo on the outskirts of Moscow in the early hours of 22 June. Others were unable to relax. In his memoirs, the first secretary of the Ukraine, Nikita Khrushchev, noted: 'Instead of returning home that night, I waited till three o'clock to see what would happen.'[2]

At 3.15 a.m. on Sunday, 22 June, German artillery along the 1,800-mile Axis border with the Soviet Union from the Baltic to the Carpathian mountains opened fire. At 3.40 a.m. the Luftwaffe began to bomb and strafe all forward Soviet airfields. The majority of the Soviet planes were neatly lined-up and made easy targets for the highly experienced Luftwaffe pilots. Most were destroyed before their pilots were awake and air supremacy was achieved within a matter of hours. At 4.15 a.m. the first advance panzer units of the Army Group Centre crossed the river Bug and entered the Soviet Union. The Germans achieved almost total surprise. Sundays were a traditional family

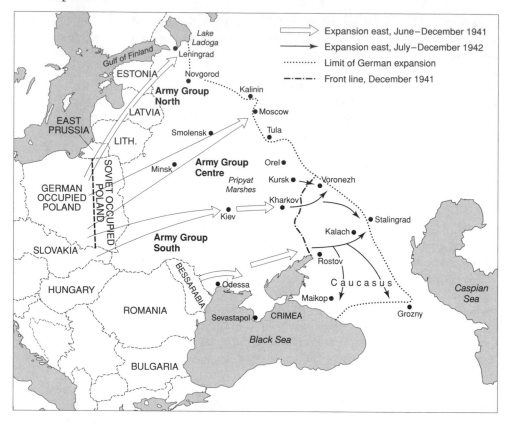

Map 5 German expansion east, 1941–42

day in the Soviet Army and time for the troops to sober up after the night before. There was some sporadic resistance, but most Soviet commanders refused to return fire without direct orders from Moscow.

All awaited Stalin's command. At 4.30 a.m. he arrived in the Kremlin, but his first orders were for diplomatic rather than military action. Despite the evidence of invasion he clung to the hope that the border incursions were the acts of a few renegade Nazi officers rather than a planned invasion sanctioned by Hitler. The German Ambassador, Schulenberg, was summoned to the Kremlin but confirmed to Foreign Minister Molotov that there was no mistake. Hitler had declared war. Earlier, at 3 a.m. in Berlin, a clearly drunk Foreign Minister Ribbentrop had informed Soviet ambassador Dekanozov of the German declaration of war. Simultaneously in Rome, Mussolini was awoken to receive news of the invasion in a personal letter from Hitler. He complained to Foreign Minister Ciano: 'I do not disturb even my servants at night but the Germans make me jump out of bed at any hour without any consideration.'[3] However, he offered Hitler Italy's full support, including an Italian expeditionary force to join the invasion. In Berlin Hitler had gone to bed and left Propaganda Minister Goebbels to announce the news to the world on the radio at 5.30 a.m. To Stalin's evident shock there were no German demands and no request for negotiations. He froze in silent panic as he digested the enormity of his personal miscalculation. Only a week before he had permitted the Soviet press to publish a lengthy government statement rebutting the rumours of a possible German invasion and restating the benefits of the Nazi–Soviet Pact. It was not until 7.15 a.m. that Stalin was finally persuaded to issue his first military command. He ordered Soviet forces to engage and destroy all invading forces, but not to cross the border because he expected a limited military engagement.

Stalin was used to being obeyed, but his order was detached from reality and demonstrated his ignorance, rather than command, of the military situation. The Soviet Army was reeling backwards as the largest military force ever assembled in world history, totalling 3,360,000 soldiers, 3,600 tanks, 7,200 guns and 2,500 fighters and bombers punched through the unprepared Soviet border units and into the Soviet interior. Stalin seemed unable to comprehend events and it was Foreign Commissar Molotov rather than Stalin who addressed the Soviet nation with news of the German invasion. By the end of the first day the Wehrmacht had overcome or bypassed all Soviet border defences and penetrated up to 50 miles into the Soviet Union against minimal resistance. The Luftwaffe had attacked sixty-six airfields and destroyed 1,489 Soviet planes for the cost of only thirty-five Luftwaffe fighters. The air commander of the Baltic district, Lieutenant-General Rychagov, was summoned to Moscow and shot, as was the commander of the western district military forces General Dmitri. The commander of the western air district, Lieutenant-General Kopet, didn't wait for a summons and shot himself.

During the evening of 23 June Hitler travelled to his eastern military headquarters, codenamed *Wolfsschanze*, or 'Wolf's Lair' deep in a forest 5 miles east of Rastenburg in East Prussia to monitor the invasion. *Wolfsschanze* was no more than ten reinforced concrete bunkers with minimal concessions to comfort and plagued by swarms of midges. However, Hitler only expected to spend a few weeks there before returning in triumph to Berlin. The few weeks became 3.5 years and ended Hitler's lazy days at the Berghof in the company of his mistress Eva Braun. Although he routinely made affectionate telephone calls to her every evening at 10 p.m. they rarely met again before Eva elected to join him in the Berlin bunker during February to April 1945.

In June 1941 victory seemed assured when the Wehrmacht, operating in three major army groups, swept across western Russia. Army Group North, composed of twenty-six divisions under the command of Field Marshal von Leeb, drove through the Baltic States towards Leningrad. Army Group Centre, with fifty-one divisions under the command of Field Marshal von Bock, advanced directly east towards Moscow. Army Group South, deploying forty divisions under the command of Field Marshal von Runstedt, invaded the Ukraine and targeted the regional capital Kiev. In addition, fourteen Romanian divisions and two Hungarian divisions joined the invasion and marched on the Crimea. On 26 June Finland also declared war on the Soviet Union to restore her independence from Soviet rule, followed by tiny Albania on 28 June.

All seemed to be lost. Stalin lapsed into open despair and apparently suffered a nervous breakdown. On 27 June, after receiving details of the scale of the German advance, he snapped at those around him: 'Lenin left us a great inheritance and we his heirs have fucked it all up.'[4] He retreated to his dacha and reportedly drank himself into a stupor. On 30 June, after three days without contact, representatives of the Politburo paid him an unexpected visit. He was evidently startled by their arrival, and enquired: 'Why have you come?'[5] Stalin apparently feared that he was about to be arrested and charged with negligence, but there were no plans for a coup. The delegation was submissive and invited Stalin to chair a newly formed State Committee for Defence (Stavka Glavnogo

Komandovaniia) or Stavka. Stalin's leadership was secure. His regular purges of the ruling Politburo, and his major purge of the army during 1937 and 1938, had removed anyone capable of raising a challenge to his leadership and on 1 July he returned to the Kremlin and resumed command. Whereas he normally delegated responsibility he appointed himself supreme commander of the armed forces on 10 July, and on 19 July he personally replaced Marshal Timoshenko as commissar for defence and adopted the title *Generalissimo*. To combat the three-pronged German advance Stalin reorganised the Soviet forces into three matching commands: North-western, Western and South-western under Marshals Voroshilov, Timoshenko and Budenny respectively. The orders in each case were absolute; hold the line and no retreat.

On 3 July 1941 Stalin gave his first radio broadcast to the Russian people. He appealed to their patriotism and love of country, though revealingly not to their loyalty to communism, and ordered a 'scorched earth' policy. As the Germans advanced, he ordered the land to be stripped of all shelter, livestock and food. All factories were ordered to be dismantled and transported east. Some 50,000 factories were eventually moved east beyond the war zone. Anything that could not be moved out of the path of the German advance was to be destroyed. The aim was to present the Germans with a wasteland and to deny the Wehrmacht the ability to live off the land. It meant that for every mile of their advance the Wehrmacht had a mile further to haul the essentials of petrol, food, ammunition and spare parts for their trucks and panzers. With Moscow 800 miles distant it was a potent weapon, but it was a long-term weapon and the Wehrmacht was initially unconcerned because they expected to win the war within weeks. On the same day as Stalin's speech General Halder stated: 'it is thus probably no overstatement to say that the Russian campaign has been won in the space of two weeks'.[6]

The Wehrmacht had made startling progress. Against the advice of his own military staff Stalin had insisted upon the forward deployment of the Red Army, allowing the Wehrmacht to repeat the blitzkreig tactics that so successfully overwhelmed Poland. Fast moving panzer spearheads punched holes in the front and chopped the Red Army into a series of isolated pockets and left them to be engaged by the slower-moving Wehrmacht infantry. Each pocket was relentlessly bombed by the Luftwaffe and bombarded by artillery, and once food and ammunition were exhausted the encircled Soviet forces had little choice but to surrender. On 29 June the first major encirclement of the war, by Army Group Centre, netted 400,000 Soviet prisoners around Minsk. This was followed by the capture of a further 300,000 prisoners at Smolensk on 16 July, opening the road to Moscow. In the north Latvia and Lithuania had fallen and the panzers were on the river Luga only 60 miles from Leningrad. In the south, although the progress was slower, Soviet forces were being steadily pushed back.

It all confirmed Hitler's prediction of a rapid victory within six to eight weeks, despite the fact that the Soviet Army in the west possessed as many troops and nearly three times as many tanks as the Wehrmacht. Hitler's confidence was so high that he made no provision for winter equipment or clothing. He expected the war to be over by September and he silenced all military doubts among his generals by declaring: 'we only have to kick in the door and the whole rotten structure will come crashing down'.[7] The British and US intelligence services shared Hitler's assessment of a rapid German victory. Hitler's table talk to his dinner guests throughout July and August 1941 was dominated by his future plans for the colonisation of the Soviet Union. On 27 July he expressed his admiration for the British empire and stated: 'let's learn from the English, who, with two hundred and fifty thousand men in all, including fifty thousand soldiers govern four hundred million Indians'.[8] On the eve of the invasion of the Soviet Union Goebbels had noted in his diary: 'The Fuhrer has high hopes of the peace party in England.'[9] Hitler hoped that Churchill, who was a long-standing opponent of communism, might welcome and support the invasion of the Soviet Union, but Churchill moved swiftly to end any such speculation. On the first day of the Nazi invasion Churchill declared on radio: 'Hitler is a monster of wickedness', and although he openly acknowledged his opposition to communism he stated that 'any man or state who fights on against Nazism will have our aid'.[10] Churchill immediately offered the Soviet Union a military alliance and this was accepted by Stalin on 27 June and signed on 12 July. On 15 July Churchill emphasised that the alliance was against the common enemy: 'we are not fighting the battle of communism'.[11] This answered the disquiet in many quarters concerning the Soviet Union's aggressive record in invading western Poland in September 1939, invading Finland in November 1939, occupying the Baltic States in 1940 and annexing Bessarabia in 1940. In secret, Churchill insisted that Stalin treat the Poles as allies and release approximately 1.7 million Poles who had been herded into cattle trucks and deported to Soviet slave labour camps in Siberia and Kazakhstan by the Soviet secret police, the NKVD. Over a million had perished, but the survivors were marched south and formed a Polish army in Persia and fought on the Allied side for the rest of the war. The intervention came too late for the 15,000 Polish army officers and 7,000 Polish intellectuals who were also deported from Poland and held in prison camps near Katyn in western Russia. They were all executed by the NKVD, each with a single bullet in the back of the head, in April 1940.

All across western Russia as the Germans advanced the NKVD either evacuated their prisoners or more often than not executed them. Consequently, during the first weeks of the war the Nazis were greeted with warmth and enthusiasm as liberators from Soviet rule. Activists from the Organisation of Ukrainian Nationalists (OUN) joined the German invasion and urged the local population to rise up against Soviet rule. General Guderian recalled: 'women came out from their villages onto the very battlefield bringing wooden platters of bread and butter and eggs'.[12] This reservoir of anti-communism support was squandered by Hitler who dismissed the entire population as sub-human and fit only to serve as slave labourers for future German colonists.

Stalin ordered all Soviet troops to fight to the last or to face execution. NKVD units were deployed to shoot any Soviet soldiers falling back from the front line. All were condemned as traitors and the punishment was death. Any commander who ordered a retreat was also charged with treason and executed. Stalin also regarded prisoners with deep suspicion and in an order signed on 16 August he ordered the families of all Soviet POWs to be deprived of state benefits and the wives and families of captured officers to be imprisoned. Stalin extended this harsh ruling to his own son Yakov Djugashvili who was captured at Smolensk on 16 July 1941. He refused to consider a German offer of a prisoner exchange for his son and ordered the arrest of his daughter-in-law, who was imprisoned in a labour camp. Yakov was later shot dead in 1943 by a German guard as he attempted to reach the wire of the POW camp.

By August 1941 the harsh discipline imposed by Stalin and the NKVD succeeded in producing fierce resistance to the German invasion. The Soviet soldiers, often drunk on the free daily supply of vodka, displayed reckless bravery and charged the German lines with or without weapons. German casualties began to rise sharply, and not only on the front line. Soviet soldiers trapped behind the lines formed partisan units and emerged from the cover of thick forests to attack supply lines and depots.

On 30 March 1941 Hitler had instructed his senior commanders preparing for the invasion to be ruthless and to fight 'a war of extermination'.[13] Hitler firmly believed that the large Slav population of the Soviet Union were *Untermenschen*, or sub-humans; a barbarian horde that threatened western Europe and western civilization. He declared his war to be a preventative war; a crusade to attack and destroy the Bolshevik danger to Europe. Consequently, from the outset Operation Barbarossa was no ordinary war. It was a war of survival – against Aryan *Untermenschen*. To win the racial war Hitler planned to execute the entire communist leadership, including all communist commissars, and to reduce the Slav population of western Russia by 30 million through deliberate starvation. Hitler directly instructed his commanders to suspend the normal rules of war and to punish all resistance with summary justice and reprisal executions. He also made no provision for prisoners of war (POWs). The fate of Soviet prisoners was to be herded behind barbed wire in the open and to be starved into weakness. No treatment was provided for injured prisoners and approximately 3.5 million Soviet POWS out of 5 million died in German captivity. The end of the war brought further tragedy when Stalin condemned the survivors as collaborators who should have fought to the death. Most were sentenced to hard labour in Siberia and few survived.

Hitler had offered the Wehrmacht a licence to murder and it was a licence accepted by most senior army commanders. Field marshals Keitel, Reichenau, Hoth and Manstein, in particular, exhorted the troops in their command to show no mercy. A printed order found on a dead German lieutenant read: 'Free yourself from your feelings of compassion and sympathy – kill every Russian, every Soviet person. Don't stop whether you have an old man, a woman, a girl or a boy before you – kill!'[14] To remove the burden of the thousands of executions from the Wehrmacht Himmler directed four *SS* Einsatzgruppen, or action squads, to follow behind the Wehrmacht. Einsatzgruppe A was attached to Army Group North, Einsatzgruppe B was attached to Army Group Centre and Einsatzgruppen C and D were attached to Army Group South. The killings started within days with the murder of 2,000 Jews on 27 June at Bialystok. It was the precursor of the Final Solution. Those who objected to the racial war were few and mute. Most of the Wehrmacht, to a greater or lesser degree, endorsed Hitler's vision of a German empire stretching to the shores of the Black Sea and welcomed the promise of free land to farm once the war was won.

Hitler's dream of an early victory began to go sour in late July. In the south the Wehrmacht advance faltered as Army Group South encountered fierce resistance from fifty-six Soviet divisions equipped with 5,580 tanks, including 1,000 KV and T-34 tanks, both superior to the panzer. The terrain also hampered the German advance, as the natural barriers of the Pripyat Marshes to the north and the Carpathian Mountains to the south denied the preferred tactic of encirclement. Consequently, Army Group South was forced to engage the Soviet forces blocking its path directly; the result was a high attrition rate in men and panzers that the Wehrmacht could ill afford. In the north the battle for Leningrad had also stalled. The ordinary citizens of Leningrad – men, women and children – volunteered to fight the Germans and fought and died in their thousands in the front-line trenches along the line of the river Luga approximately 60 miles west of the city. Their immense courage successfully stemmed the German advance for a month and ultimately saved the city by granting sufficient time to improve the defences. Hitler opposed any further advance on Moscow by Army Group Centre until his northern and southern flanks were secure. He feared that an advance towards Moscow on a narrow front would leave Army Group Centre vulnerable to a Soviet encirclement. Hitler insisted upon a broad front advance and ordered the OKW to redeploy the panzers of Army Group Centre to assist with the capture of Leningrad in the north and Kiev in the south. The OKW fiercely resisted Hitler's plan. With Moscow only 200 miles distant and the Soviet front in disarray the OKW favoured a dash to Moscow to decapitate the leadership and force surrender. It produced the first of many bitter divisions between Hitler and his generals. In his diary General Halder recorded his anger at having to listen to Hitler's lengthy diatribes on military tactics: 'hours of gibberish and the outcome is there is only one man who understands how to wage war'.[15] General Guderian, in command of Army Group Centre's panzer spearhead, also strongly opposed Hitler's decision and travelled to *Wolfsschanze* on 23 August to try and persuade Hitler to change his mind. Hitler listened to Guderian but he remained unmoved. Hitler criticised Guderian and the OKW for failing to appreciate the importance of resources – especially oil – to the war effort. He upheld his primary goal as the seizure of the oil, coal and grain of the Ukraine and he dismissed the occupation of the capital Moscow as a symbolic gesture of little importance. Two weeks were lost in prevarication before Guderian finally turned his panzers south-west towards Kiev. On 19 September Hitler's decision appeared to be vindicated when the capital of the Ukraine, Kiev, was captured, along with 600,000 Soviet troops in the largest single encirclement of the war. The scale of the defeat was largely due to Stalin who had ordered the Soviet forces to stand fast against the advice of Marshal Budenny who favoured a strategic withdrawal. He was sacked and replaced by Marshal Timoshenko and when Chief of the General Staff Marshal Zhukov also pressed the case for retreat he too was relieved of his command.

Army Group North was also successful and overran the Luga line. On 1 September they captured Mga on the outskirts of Leningrad and cut off the last road and rail link to the city. It was the start of a 900-day siege that would reduce the population of Leningrad by half and cause suffering on a scale barely appreciated in the West. The death toll in this single Soviet city, at approximately 1.7 million, was three times greater than Britain's entire wartime losses. Hitler ordered Leningrad to be wiped off the face of the earth and for the ground it stood on to be ploughed over. Leningrad was the city where Lenin had declared the communist revolution in 1917 and it was a chapter of history that Hitler was determined to erase physically. In a rare redemption Stalin restored Zhukov to active command on 13 September and ordered him to take all and any measures to save the city.

The Soviet Union was at bay and a euphoric Hitler declared victory. In ten weeks of fighting Germany had taken 3.5 million prisoners, destroyed 18,000 tanks, 22,000 guns and 14,000 aircraft. With the north and south secure Hitler assembled all available forces for a final drive to Moscow, codenamed 'Operation Typhoon', to win the war before the onset of winter. Hitler believed that overall victory was only weeks away, and on 4 October he made a rare return to Berlin. In front of an ecstatic crowd in the Sportpalast Hitler announced: 'I can say today that this enemy is already broken and will not rise up again.'[16]

At first Hitler's confidence seemed well placed. Operation Typhoon commenced on 2 October and the first target, the city of Orel, fell on 3 October. In Moscow, panic gripped the population and government. Looting was widespread and people flooded the roads and railways trying to escape east. On 15 October plans were finalised to evacuate the government to Kuibyshev 500 miles to the east. An early evacuee was Lenin. His mummified body was unceremoniously removed from its Red Square mausoleum and transported east to Tyumen in a purpose-built refrigerated train carriage. As the Germans closed on Moscow and reached Kalinin only 100 miles from the city there is some evidence that Stalin contemplated surrender. However, on 17 October he unexpectedly cancelled the government evacuation of Moscow and on 19 October proclaimed: 'Moscow will be defended to the last.'[17] Stalin appeared to have been buoyed up by Zhukov's successful defence of Leningrad. On 10 October he recalled Zhukov from Leningrad and gave him full command and authority over the Moscow front. To restore order the NKVD began to execute looters and anyone considered defeatist. Non-essential workers were driven out of the city to the front line. With the Germans only 65 miles away, approximately 500,000 men, women and children were ordered to labour night and day to dig 5,000 miles of trenches and anti-tank ditches to defend the city.

Zhukov gained a valuable ally in the weather when early snow showers in the first fortnight of October dropped up to 10 inches of snow across the battlefield. Heavy rain followed on 18 October as the Russian rainy season closed in – the *rasputiza*, literally 'the time of mud'. Men and machines ground to a halt as the dirt roads dissolved into thick, glutinous mud and ended all prospects of a rapid north–south encirclement of Moscow. The lack of modern roads did as much as the Russian winter to stem the German advance. Stalin also gained a valuable intelligence report from the spy Richard Sorge in Tokyo just prior to his disclosure and arrest on 18 October. Sorge was able to confirm that Japan had no plans to invade Siberia. Stalin immediately ordered the transfer of eight divisions of the Siberian Army, complete with 1,000 tanks and 800 aircraft, to the Moscow front to form the spearhead of a new reserve army.

Hitler retained his confidence and ordered the Wehrmacht to wait for the ground to harden with the first frost of winter before launching the final push for Moscow. His order exposed his gamble. The Wehrmacht was about to enter a Russian winter in summer uniforms and with no shelter or anti-freeze for their panzers, trucks or aircraft. In Berlin, Goebbels organised collections of fur coats and warm clothing for the troops in the east. It was the first public indication that Hitler's announcement of victory was premature. Heavy snow fell on 25 October and within days the entire landscape was cloaked in a metre of snow as the temperature dropped below freezing. On 6 November, on the eve of the 24th anniversary of the communist revolution, Stalin gave a speech calling for total war. He remarked: 'If they want a war of extermination they shall have it . . . death to the German invaders.'[18] The next day the troops taking part in the traditional Moscow military review marched straight to the front line.

Operation Typhoon recommenced on 15 November and the Wehrmacht closed to within 20 miles of Moscow. On 4 December a forward reconnaissance patrol led by Walter Schaefer-Kehnert entered the suburbs of Moscow, only 12 miles from the Kremlin. They were beaten back. It was the high water mark of the Wehrmacht advance as men and machines succumbed to temperatures as low as minus 40°C. Without anti-freeze the panzers could only be started by lighting fires under their engines, guns misfired, and with no shelter more troops began to be lost to frostbite than to enemy bullets. The last working panzer, nicknamed 'Anthony the last' by the troops, broke down on 4 December. The Luftwaffe was also grounded as planes exposed to the elements on open airstrips iced over, whereas Soviet planes were maintained in heated hangars.

On 5 December the Wehrmacht received a major shock when the reserve army husbanded by Stalin launched an unexpected counter-attack spearheaded by Siberian troops. They were fully equipped for winter warfare in white camouflage uniforms, fur-lined mitts, snow goggles, skis and felt boots and were accustomed to temperatures in Siberia that plummeted as low as minus 60°C. The Wehrmacht advance was over. Hitler's immediate concern was to avoid panic and a full-scale rout: the fate of Napoleon in 1812. He ordered 'not a single backward step', and for the Wehrmacht to stand and die where they stood. When General Guderian returned to the *Wolfsschanze* on 20 December to protest and to request permission to retreat to a prepared defensive line, Hitler berated him for defeatism. On 26 December Guderian was sacked, closely followed by six other senior commanders whom Hitler blamed for the defeat. Field Marshal von Brauchitsch, who had held the position of commander-in-chief of the Wehrmacht from 1938, offered his resignation, which Hitler accepted. Operation Barbarossa had cost the Wehrmacht 164,000 casualties, as opposed to 70,751 casualties for the conquest of the whole of western Europe, but without victory. In comparison, the human wave attacks made by the Soviet Army and the widespread murder of civilians by the Wehrmacht and by the NKVD to enforce Soviet rule had cost approximately 2,663,000 Soviet lives. The final tally was to climb to over 20 million.

As Hitler enforced total obedience to his stand-fast order the Japanese unexpectedly attacked the US Pacific Fleet at Pearl Harbor on 7 December 1941. Hitler was delighted. He believed that the Pacific war would fully stretch and occupy the USA and end the threat of their intervention in the war in Europe. He also believed that Britain would be unable to sustain the war in Europe while fighting the Japanese in the Pacific and would accept a peace settlement. Consequently, on 14 January 1942 Hitler permitted the Wehrmacht to withdraw approximately 20 miles to a more secure defensive line – the Koenigsberg Line, or K-Line – and planned for victory in the spring with the deployment of a new panzer army. To demonstrate solidarity with his Axis ally, Hitler declared war on the USA on 11 December fully aware that Germany possessed no means to attack the USA. The decision reflected Hitler's confidence that the defeat and exploitation of the resources of the Soviet Union would make Germany a match for the USA, and he believed that the US army would not risk crossing the Atlantic Ocean, given the U-boat threat. His impulsive declaration of war on the USA joined the European and Pacific wars and created a truly global world war.

References

1. Hugh Trevor-Roper, *Hitler's Table Talk 1941–44*, Phoenix, 2000, p. 24.
2. Nikita Khrushchev, *Khrushchev Remembers* (trans. Strobe Talbot), Sphere, 1971, p. 149.
3. Alan Bullock, *Hitler: A Study in Tyranny*, Penguin, 1962, p. 649.
4. Dmitri Volkogonov, *Stalin: Triumph and Tragedy*, Weidenfeld and Nicolson, 1991, p. 410.
5. Richard Overy, *Russia's War*, Penguin, 1998, p. 79.
6. Ian Kershaw, *Hitler 1936–45: Nemesis*, Penguin, 2000, p. 399.
7. Martin Gilbert, *Second World War*, Phoenix, 1989, p. 199.
8. Hugh Trevor-Roper, *Hitler's Table Talk 1941–44*, Phoenix, 2000, p. 15.
9. Fred Taylor (ed.), *The Goebbels Diaries 1939–41*, Sphere, 1983, p. 424.
10. Winston Churchill, *Great War Speeches*, Corgi, 1957, p. 138.
11. Ibid., p. 139.
12. Heinz Guderian, *Panzer Leader*, Penguin, 1996, p. 193.

13. Peter Padfield, *Himmler: Reichsfuhrer SS*, Papermac, 1991, p. 333.
14. Edwin P. Hoyt, *199 Days: The Battle for Stalingrad*, Robson Books, 1993, p. 49.
15. John Keegan, *The Second World War*, Hutchinson, 1989, p. 193.
16. Ian Kershaw, *Hitler 1936–45: Nemesis*, Penguin, 2000, p. 432.
17. Martin Gilbert, *Second World War*, Orion, 1989, p. 246.
18. Richard Overy, *Russia's War*, Penguin, 1998, p. 114.

17 Final Solution

The Jews are the sworn enemies of the German people and must be eradicated. Every Jew that we can lay our hands on is to be destroyed now during the war, without exception. If we cannot now obliterate the biological basis of Jewry, the Jews will one day destroy the German people.[1]

> Reichsfeuhrer SS Henrich Himmler, speaking to Rudolf Hoess, commandant of Auschwitz, at an unspecified date, summer 1941

Precisely when the Final Solution order to murder all European Jewry was taken remains unknown due to the absence of a written record. It would appear that all orders relating to the Final Solution were deliberately communicated verbally to dissociate Hitler and the Nazi state from the formal decision to enact genocide. As Himmler stated to the SS executioners gathered in Posen on 4 October 1943: 'we will never speak of it publicly . . . the extermination of the Jewish race . . . this is a page of glory in our history which has never been written and is never to be written'.[2] Consequently, deliberate Nazi obfuscation concerning the meaning of the term 'Final Solution' and who gave the orders and when, has been a licence for confusion and Holocaust deniers ever since 1945. However, the events cannot be denied and the events leave the indelible signature of the lifelong obsessive desire of Adolf Hitler to erase Jewry.

In 1919 when Hitler was aged 30 and a political education officer in the army in Munich he blamed the Jews for the intervention of the USA in the Great War and for Germany's defeat. He advised his army superiors of the need to act against the Jews and stated: 'the final objective must be the complete removal of the Jews'.[3] In 1922, as the leader of the infant Nazi Party, he remarked to the journalist Josef Hell:

> Once I really am in power, my first and foremost task will be the annihilation of the Jews . . . I will have gallows built in rows . . . the Jews will be hanged indiscriminately and they will remain hanging until they stink . . . as soon as they have been untied the next batch will be strung up . . . until all of Germany has been completely cleansed of Jews.[4]

In his autobiography *Mein Kampf* (My Struggle), published in 1924, he advocated the mass murder of Jews, and in a prophetic statement he foreshadowed the use of poison gas: 'at the beginning of the war or even during the war if twelve or fifteen thousand of these Jews had been forced to submit to poison gas . . . then the millions of sacrifices at the front would not have been in vain'.[5] Hitler ended his political career and life at the age of 56 with a final burst of anti-Semitic venom. In his 'Last Will and Testament', dictated 24 hours before his suicide in April 1945, he issued a final injunction to his successors: 'Above all I charge the leaders of the nation and those under them to the scrupulous observance of the laws of race and to merciless opposition to the universal poisoner of all peoples, international Jewry.'[6]

The evidence indicates that Hitler's entire political life from beginning to end was governed by an unswerving desire to destroy Jewry and, given the resources involved, it is not tenable that the Final Solution was enacted without his knowledge or approval. The Final Solution was a conscious declaration of total war on the Jewish people by Hitler, born of his absolute conviction that the Jews were behind the Bolshevik revolution of 1917 and were inciting communist revolutions across Europe to further a goal of Jewish world domination. This was the theme of his infamous threat of the annihilation of the Jews when he addressed the Reichstag on 30 January 1939:

> if international finance Jewry inside and outside Europe should succeed in plunging nations once more into a world war the result will be not the bolshevization of the earth and thereby victory of Jewry, but the annihilation of the Jewish race in Europe.[7]

There are no innocent definitions of the word 'annihilation' and it is striking that Hitler repeated the same word in a speech of January 1942 at a time when the Final Solution was firmly underway. It is highly unlikely that Hitler possessed a step-by-step plan to execute the entire Jewish population of Europe – rather it probably emerged as a choice during the dislocation of war. The choice was offered to Hitler by a steady escalation of anti-Semitic actions from 1933–40 that left Jews largely dispossessed, displaced and devoid of any champions to protest their fate.

Following the rise to power of Hitler in 1933 most German Jews who could afford to emigrate did so, and on 24 January 1939 emigration was confirmed as the official Nazi policy towards the Jews. Göring directed Reinhard Heydrich to establish a central office for Jewish emigration and to force the Jews out of Germany 'by all possible means'.[8] SS Sturmbannführer (Major) Adolf Eichmann, a self-proclaimed expert on Judaism, was installed in plush new offices at 116 Kurfurstenstrasse, Berlin to direct Jewish emigration; but he found few countries willing to accept large numbers of Jewish immigrants. The preferred Jewish destination was Palestine, but strong opposition from the local Arab population resulted in Britain refusing settlement rights. The German Foreign Office proposed confinement on the island of Madagascar in the revival of a plan first proposed by French anti-Semites in 1885.

The German invasion of Poland in September 1939 closed European borders to any further Jewish emigration and placed a further 3 million Jews into German hands. To co-ordinate security across the expanding Reich Himmler established the Reichssicherheitshauptamt (RSHA), or Reich Security Main Office, on 27 September 1939. The RSHA, under the leadership of his deputy Reinhard Heydrich, treated all Jews as enemies of the state and was eventually responsible for the implementation of the Final Solution. In every town and village across Poland the Jews were singled out for brutal torture and forced to perform heavy labour and physical exercise while being whipped, clubbed or stabbed with bayonets. By October this onslaught had resulted in the public murder of approximately 5,000 Jews, often with the active participation of the local Polish community who frequently drove their Jewish neighbours out of their homes and declared streets and villages to be Jew free.

With the outlet of emigration closed Eichmann proposed the resettlement of all Jews into controlled reservations in the Nisko region south-west of Lublin in central Poland. Heydrich was enthusiastic and announced the new policy of 'resettlement' on 21 September 1939. Between October and December 1939 approximately 93,000 Jews were forcibly driven from their homes in Czechoslovakia and Austria and transported in sealed railway carriages to Nisko. The first transports of Jews were greeted by Eichmann and directed across the river San with orders to build a settlement if they wanted to survive the winter. Within the major cities the Jews were progressively confined to ghettos to await resettlement. The first was established in Piotrkow in October 1939, but it was short-lived and it was not until 1940 that the ghetto policy was firmly enacted. The resettlement plan was ended in March 1940 when the governor-general of the general government region of Poland, Hans Frank, protested to Göring and Hitler that no more Jews could be adequately policed or controlled in the Nisko region. It is noteworthy that earlier in December 1939 Hans Frank had complained: 'we cannot shoot 2,500,000 Jews . . . neither can we poison them'.[9] Clearly murder on this scale was not yet contemplated, and the Nazi policy being pursued in Nisko was resettlement and hard labour. This is given credence by a memo from Himmler to Hitler, dated 25 May 1940, which reopened the Madagascar option. Following victory in the west Himmler suggested the creation of a Jew-free Europe via 'large-scale emigration of all Jews to Africa or some other colony'.[10] Confirmation that this was a serious intention was later provided by the deportation of 9,000 Jews from Alsace and Lorraine to a concentration camp at Gurs in the French Pyrenees, apparently in readiness for onward transportation to Madagascar. However, the failure to arrive at a peace settlement with Great Britain ended any prospects of overseas deportations.

The winter of 1940/41 was dominated by the round-up and concentration of Poland's Jewish population in the major ghettos in the cities. The largest ghettos were Lodz, with 163,000 inhabitants, and Warsaw, with 500,000 inhabitants, established in May and October 1940 respectively. Within the ghettos approximately 2,000 died each month from starvation and disease from the unsanitary conditions. In contrast to the horrors in Poland the Jewish population to the west was largely unmolested. Anti-Semitism was not as pronounced or as popular in the west due to the widespread integration of the Jewish population. The sub-human stereotypes of Nazi propaganda were at odds with the highly literate and cultured Jewish population of western Europe, and even in Fascist Italy and Spain there was no enthusiasm for anti-Semitic laws. The exception was the French Vichy regime which voluntarily enacted Nazi anti-Semitic laws in October 1940.

The first evidence of an ominous new policy that would threaten all Jews in Europe emerged on 20 May 1941 when the Central Office of Emigration in Berlin issued a Europe-wide directive ending any further Jewish emigration, pending the 'imminent final solution'.[11] The timing is significant. The Wehrmacht was poised to invade the Soviet Union and Göring, in his role as head of the Wirtschaftsstab Ost (Economic Staff for the East), was ordered by Hitler to submit plans to strip the Soviet Union of all economic and food resources to make Germany and the Wehrmacht fully self-sufficient and capable of sustaining a long war. Göring's collective orders for the East, known as the Green File, were published on 23 May and he predicted the mass starvation of 'many tens of millions of people'[12] following the diversion of all food supplies to the Reich. The future of the remaining Slav population and Jews was to be slave labourers.

Hitler also ordered Himmler to support the invasion by deploying Einsatzgruppen (execution squads) to round up and execute all communist commissars or anyone who might organise resistance to the German invasion. To fulfil Hitler's orders Himmler formed four Einsatzgruppen, totalling some 3,000 men largely made up of volunteers from the Gestapo, SD, Waffen SS and transfers from police forces in Germany, to form police battalions for special duty in the east. Heydrich addressed the 120 commanders of the Einsatzgruppen at Pretsch near Wittengburg in late May and ordered them to execute without mercy communist commissars, gypsies, saboteurs and any civilians, especially Jews, for any actual or suspected acts of defiance. It was a tactic that had been employed during the invasion of Poland as a pacification measure rather than the commencement of the Final Solution.

On 23 June, twenty-four hours after the invasion of the Soviet Union had commenced, the Einsatzgruppen entered the Soviet Union. The largest was Einsatzgruppe A with 990 men attached to Army Group North and the smallest was Einsatzgruppe D with only 500 men attached to Army Group South. In their path were approximately 5 million Jews scattered across the western Soviet Union. The size of the Einsatzgruppen in relation to the size of the Jewish population indicates that their task was confined to pacification because they did not possess the capacity to round up and execute the entire Jewish population. Across the Soviet Union the Einsatzgruppen combed towns and villages for commissars and government officials and routinely selected Jews for execution, often at the urgings of the local population.

On 16 July 1941 Hitler held a conference at the *Wolfsschanze* attended by the key policy-makers for the east – namely, Göring, Rosenberg, Bormann, Field Marshal Keitel and Hans Lammers (head of the Reich Chancellery). Himmler was also a guest at the *Wolfsschanze* from 15–20 July. No minutes or documents survive beyond a confirmation that the major topic of discussion was the exploitation of the east. Given the subsequent events it would appear that during this meeting Hitler issued a verbal order for the commencement of the Final Solution. All Jews in Europe were to be transported east to work as slave labourers and all incapable of work, including women and children, were to be executed. Ultimately all would disappear, and famine, war, disease and popular pogroms would eventually explain and disguise their deaths.

The Final Solution order was formally issued on 31 July 1941 in Göring's name and addressed to Reinhard Heydrich who was directly responsible for Jewish policy as head of the RSHA. The order had been drafted by Heydrich's own RSHA office but signed by Göring in his role as head of the economic staff for the east and as Hitler's intermediary. The fact that Hitler's signature does not appear on the order has fostered some speculation that Hitler was ignorant of events, but the order was taken with the knowledge and active involvement of the entire Nazi hierarchy – indeed, only a Führer directive could bind all to the policy. The key words of the Final Solution order were as follows:

> Complementing the task that was assigned to you on 24th January, 1939 . . . I hereby charge you with making all necessary preparations in regard to organisational and financial matters for bringing about a complete solution of the Jewish question in the German sphere in Europe . . . Wherever other government agencies are involved these are to co-operate with you . . . I charge you furthermore to send me before long an overall plan.[13]

The subsequent events indicate a two-stage plan of action. First, an immediate authorisation for the Einsatzgruppen to execute all Jews in the Soviet Union incapable of work, rather than just those suspected of being commissars or partisans. Second, following the defeat of the Soviet Union the transport of all Jews in the 'German sphere in Europe' to the Soviet Gulag, with slave labour for the able bodied and execution for all others. The precedent existed. Stalin had sentenced an estimated 28 million 'enemies of the people' to hard labour in the Gulag from 1934–41. Half of this number had died from beatings, starvation, random executions and exhaustion in Stalin's concealed 'holocaust'.

The actual meaning of the words 'Final Solution' has permitted claims of ignorance of the events that followed. At his trial in Nuremberg in 1946 Göring stated under cross-examination that neither he nor Hitler had any knowledge of the mass execution of Jews. He dismissed the 'Final Solution' order as 'a policy for emigration not liquidation of the Jews'.[14] However, it is not credible that Himmler and Heydrich misunderstood the order and transmuted emigration into mass execution. Corroboration that an execution order had been issued was supplied by Rudolf Hoess, the commandant of Auschwitz, who recorded in his memoirs being summoned to Berlin for a meeting with Himmler during the summer of 1941. He was uncertain of the exact date of the meeting but his record of Himmler's words, as quoted at the start of this chapter, are a stark commitment to mass murder. Within weeks of this discussion Eichmann visited Hoess at Auschwitz and identified a newly constructed secondary camp at the nearby village of Birkenau for the location of gas chambers capable of gassing 800 at a time. He also pinpointed adjacent meadows as suitable for burial plots since there were as yet no plans for crematoria. It would appear that Auschwitz-Birkenau was to be designated as a transit camp to the east for the able bodied and a killing centre for those incapable of work – mainly the women and children. Hoess was not given a target date for the receipt of the first transports because the decision to commence deportations was still awaited. That decision could only come from Hitler and indicates caution on his part and the need to wait for the defeat of the Soviet Union. Hitler was not immune to challenge. In April 1941, following rising protests from the Vatican and the general public against the compulsory euthanasia of Germany's mentally and physically handicapped, Hitler felt obliged to disown the programme and it was ended in August 1941. By this stage approximately 70,000 had been gassed within Germany's hospitals under the direction of Dr Karl Brandt and Christian Wirth who had perfected a system of disguising gas chambers as showers. Consequently, Hitler was probably waiting to monitor reactions to the implementation of the Final Solution in the Soviet Union. Many ordinary soldiers and officers in the Wehrmacht were openly disgusted by the actions of the Einsatzgruppen – especially by the execution of women, children and babies. Gauleiter Wilhelm Kube of the occupied territory of White Ruthenia bitterly opposed the execution of the Jews and directly sabotaged round-ups in his district by warning the Jews that they were going to be executed. He was not alone, but to Himmler's and Hitler's undoubted relief such men were in the minority and the majority of the Wehrmacht and Nazi leadership co-operated with the Einsatzgruppen in the Soviet Union. Hitler undoubtedly distanced himself from the Final Solution order so that in the event of widespread protests from the Wehrmacht or the western world he could be seen to intervene to stop the executions. Unfortunately for the Jews of Europe most people within Germany and occupied Europe, together with the Vatican and the Allies, largely ignored their fate. From Hitler's point of view, silence was assent.

The compelling evidence that the Final Solution order was an order for murder and not resettlement was provided by the quantum leap in executions from August 1941 onwards. Across the Soviet Union the random executions were superseded by the systematic round up and execution of the Jewish population. The numbers being executed rose from hundreds to thousands, and by September to tens of thousand. As the killings expanded so did the numbers serving in the Einsatzgruppen. In early August the original Einsatzgruppen force of 3,000 was considerably expanded by the attachment of 11,000 troops from two SS brigades and thereafter expansion to a total force of 60,000. This was more than sufficient manpower to implement the Final Solution. Most were ordinary family men who got drunk to cope with their daily task of murdering men, women and children in cold blood. Many experienced nervous breakdowns and were excused execution duty. Perversely, this psychological burden on his men was Himmler's chief concern. To express his concern and to offer support Himmler travelled to watch an execution at Minsk at an undetermined date in late July or early August 1941. He watched as a hundred Jews were shot and pushed into a pit and, as his liaison officer General Karl Wolff recalled, 'he got a splash of brains on his coat and I think it also splashed into his face and he went very green and pale'.[15] Once he had recovered his composure Himmler gathered the executioners together and thanked them for their work and urged them to 'be hard and stand firm . . . in the interests of the Reich'.[16] The most notorious massacre conducted by the Einsatzgruppen occurred at Babi Yar, a ravine on the outskirts of Kiev. Here, over three days from 29 September 1941, a total of 33,771 Jews were whipped and beaten in a continuous procession to the edge of the 25-metre deep Yar by Ukrainian policemen and shot a hundred at a time by machine-gun. An eyewitness to the massacre noted that the policemen 'took the children by the legs and threw them alive down into the Yar'.[17] The steep slopes of the Yar were subsequently dynamited and collapsed down on top of the living and the dead.

By September 1941 Himmler was actively seeking for a method of mass execution that removed the psychological stress on the SS and was less public. At first the answer appeared to be supplied by the 'experts' from the disbanded Department T4 euthanasia programme. They had found re-employment in the concentration camps implementing the *Sonderbehandlung*, or special treatment programme, by which SS doctors selected those unfit for work and handed them over to Department T4 for gassing. To speed the process small gas chambers utilising carbon monoxide gas from truck engines were added to many concentration camps, and gas trucks, invented by SS Dr Karl Becker, were also deployed and offered to the Einsatzgruppen. They were subsequently used on the Eastern Front and in Serbia. At Auschwitz-Birkenau on 3 September an estimated 600 Soviet POWs and 250 Jews were crammed into the cellars of Block 11 for an experiment in mass murder. They were gassed with Zyklon B, a hydrocyanic acid gas (HCN) manufactured in crystal form by Tesch/Stabenow and Degesch and originally supplied to the camp as rat poison. Once exposed to the air the crystals vaporised and the observers noted that death was virtually instantaneous.

In September 1941 Hitler apparently advanced his plans for the first transports of western Jews to the east following a brutal round-up and deportation to Siberia of approximately 600,000 ethnic Germans by Stalin from the Volga region. Stalin suspected their loyalty and few were to survive. On 18 September, following a meeting between Himmler and Hitler two days earlier at the *Wolfsschanze*, the first western Jews were beaten and driven into cattle trucks and transported from Vienna and Prague to the Lodz ghetto in Poland. It was the start of regular transports of Jews from Germany, Austria and Czechoslovakia to the ghettos, and their arrival exacerbated the severe overcrowding and shortages of food. Within the ghettos thousands were suffering and dying from typhus, dysentery, tuberculosis and heart disease, and most were incapable of work. The unsanitary conditions also provoked fears of cholera epidemics and placed Himmler under increasing pressure for a solution. As late as October 1941 the action favoured by Himmler and Hitler still appeared to be the transport of all Jews to their deaths in the wastelands of the Soviet Gulag. On 25 October, over dinner with Himmler and Heydrich at *Wolfschannze*, Hitler remarked:

> I prophesied to Jewry that, in the event of wars proving inevitable, the Jew would disappear from Europe . . . Let nobody tell me that all the same we can't park them in the marshy parts of Russia . . . It's not a bad idea, by the way, that public rumour attributes to us a plan to exterminate the Jews. Terror is a salutary thing.[18]

The subsequent defeat of the Wehrmacht from November to December 1941 closed the option of the Soviet Gulag and with the conditions in the ghettos of Poland at crisis point Himmler turned to the experts of the *Sonderbehandlung* for a solution. Herbert Lange was ordered to assemble an execution team to clear all Jews in the Lodz ghetto and the surrounding Wartheland region. In early November 1941 Lange identified an old mansion surrounded by forest at Chelmno as a suitable site for the gassing and burial of all Jews in the region. Under pressure from Odilo Globocnik, the chief of police in Lublin, Himmler extended the gassing order to all Jews in the General Government region of Poland. This decision to commence the 'local' murder of all Jews in Poland was the catalyst for the Holocaust of 1942–44. There is no written record, but at some point in November – or at the latest in early December 1941 – Hitler, Himmler and Heydrich took the major decision to build *vernich-tungslager* (extermination) camps in Poland with a capacity to gas the Jewish population of Europe. Felix Kersten, Himmler's personal masseur, recorded in his diary on 11 November 1941 that Himmler, on his return from a meeting in Hitler's Chancellery, told him that the 'destruction' of the Jews was being planned. Ultimately Poland rather than the Soviet Gulag was confirmed as the killing ground for the systematic murder of Europe's Jews.

References

1. Ronnie S. Landau, *Studying the Holocaust: Issues, Readings and Documents*, Routledge, 1998, p. 80.
2. Henry A. Zeiger (ed.), *The Case Against Adolf Eichmann*, Signet, 1960, p. 82.
3. Ronnie S. Landau, *Studying the Holocaust: Issues, Readings and Documents*, Routledge, 1998, p. 56.
4. Gerald Fleming, *Hitler and the Final Solution*, Hamish Hamilton, 1985, p. 17.
5. Martin Gilbert, *The Holocaust: The Jewish Tragedy*, Fontana, 1986, p. 28.
6. Alan Bullock, *Hitler and Stalin: Parallel Lives*, HarperCollins, 1991, p. 982.
7. Ian Kershaw, *Hitler 1936–45: Nemesis*, Penguin, 2000, p. 153.
8. Yehuda Bauer, *Jews For Sale: Nazi-Jewish Negotiations 1939–45*, Yale University Press, 1994, p. 38.
9. Martin Gilbert, *The Holocaust: The Jewish Tragedy*, Fontana, 1986, p. 106.
10. Ibid., p. 119.

11. Ibid., p. 152.
12. Roger Manvell and Heinrich Fraenkel, *Göring*, Mentor, 1968, p. 186.
13. Henry A. Zeiger (ed.), *The Case Against Adolf Eichmann*, Signet, 1960, p. 100.
14. Roger Manvell and Heinrich Fraenkel, *Göring*, Mentor, 1968, p. 269.
15. Martin Gilbert, *The Holocaust: The Jewish Tragedy*, Fontana, 1986, p. 191.
16. Ibid.
17. Ibid., p. 203.
18. Hugh Trevor-Roper, *Hitler's Table Talk 1941–44*, Phoenix, 2000, p. 87.

18 Pearl Harbor

[E]nemy carriers, naval escorts and transports will begin to come under air attack at a distance of approximately 750 miles. This attack will increase in intensity until within 200 miles of the objective the enemy forces will be subject to attack by all types of bombardment closely supported by our most modern pursuit . . . with this force available a major attack against Oahu is considered impracticable.[1]

Defence review of Pearl Harbor sent to President Roosevelt by
General George Marshall, chief of staff US forces, May 1941

At 6.45 a.m on Sunday 7 December, after a two-hour search, the USN destroyer *Ward* located and sank a midget submarine spotted in the approaches to Pearl Harbor, off the Hawaiian island of Oahu. No general alert was sounded. At 7.02 a.m. two army radar operators, Privates Joseph Lockard and George Elliot, manning a mobile radar station on the high ground of Kahuku Point, reported a formation of aircraft at a distance of 132 miles approaching Oahu from the north-west. The duty officer in command of the communications centre, Kermit Tyler, assured them that the planes were an expected flight of USAF B-17 Flying Fortresses bound for Hickam Field airbase. The communications centre had no designated air corridors to monitor inbound air traffic and no pre-set call signs to identify friend or foe. No general alert was sounded, but even if an alarm had been raised no fighter aircraft were on standby to intercept hostile radar contacts. Both incidents highlighted the extraordinary level of complacency in the defence of Pearl Harbor and both serve to undermine the popular belief in the existence of a high-ranking American conspiracy to invite a Japanese attack in order to bounce a reluctant Congress into the war. No conspiracy could script such complacency at all levels of command from ordinary service personnel in Oahu to Washington. The possibility of an attack on Pearl Harbor was discussed in Washington as early as 24 January 1941 when the Secretary for the Navy Frank Knox warned that if war did break out with Japan 'hostilities would be initiated by a surprise attack upon the Fleet or the naval base at Pearl Harbor'.[2] His warning was discounted as improbable. Japan was 3,400 miles distant. For the military professionals it was unthinkable that a hostile fleet could travel that distance undetected. The chief of staff, General George Catlett Marshall, assured President Roosevelt (as quoted at the start of this chapter) that any enemy fleet foolish enough to try and attack Pearl Harbor would be intercepted and engaged 750 miles out to sea and destroyed no closer to Oahu than 200 miles. Marshall's confidence rested on the powerful USN Pacific Fleet, which included three aircraft carriers (the *Saratoga* was being refitted in the US at the time of the attack), eight battleships and thirty-eight other warships. Pearl Harbor was also protected by a significant force of over 350 fighter aircraft based at five airfields. However, both advantages were nullified by the poor military judgement of the commander-in-chief of the Pacific Fleet, Admiral Husband E. Kimmel, and the commander of the army, General Walter C. Short.

A fleet at sea is powerful but a fleet at anchor is vulnerable. Japanese intelligence monitored the regular habit of the Pacific Fleet to return to port at the weekend and to moor in a straight line, two by two, in Battleship Row lying parallel to Ford Island in the centre of Pearl Harbor. No fleet rotation was enacted to keep half the fleet at sea at any one time. No anti-torpedo nets were used to protect the ships in port because the harbour waters were deemed to be too shallow for air-dropped torpedoes. The fighter aircraft were not dispersed around the airfields but drawn-up in rows, wing tip to wing tip, to make it easier for sentries to patrol and guard against intruders. It reflected that the greatest security fear in Pearl Harbor was not air attack but sabotage from enemy agents operating within the indigenous Japanese population. While the fleet was in harbour no reconnaissance aircraft were placed aloft and no picket ships were placed far out to sea. Oahu was blind, even though in the weeks before the attack the exact location of Japan's aircraft carriers was unknown. While discussing the possible whereabouts of the Japanese carriers with his intelligence officer, Kimmel joked: 'do you mean to say that they could be rounding Diamond Head and you wouldn't know it?'[3] On 26 November the Secretary of State for War Henry L. Stimson in Washington issued a general war alert to all US commands in the Pacific following intelligence intercepts that Japan was preparing to break off all negotiations. Washington was able to read all Japanese diplomatic traffic, codenamed 'purple', routinely. In comparison there was only a partial ability to read Japanese military traffic coded JN25 and its upgrade JN25b. This was the official position, but those wedded to conspiracy theories believe that the USA and British governments concealed their ability to read Japanese military traffic and deliberately withheld vital intelligence of the planned attack on Pearl Harbor from their own forces. The military alert received by Kimmel opened with the words: 'This dispatch is to be considered a war warning.'[4] The separate military alert received by General Short contained the warning: 'Japanese future action unpredictable but hostile action possible at any moment.'[5] After the war Kimmel, in his defence, stated that he did not associate this general warning with a direct threat to Pearl Harbor because all intelligence assessments indicated that the Philippines and Thailand were the likely Japanese targets. Whereas the warning was non-specific, it was a war warning and it was issued to all Pacific commands. This falls short of a conspiracy of silence. General Short did act in response to the war warning but only to review and further tighten the defence of the airfields against possible saboteurs. He reported his anti-sabotage measures to Washington but no one questioned his very limited response to a war alert. No fighter aircraft or anti-aircraft batteries were placed on alert. Both commanders firmly believed that Japan did not possess the capability to launch an air attack on Pearl Harbor despite their marked superiority in aircraft carriers. The only threats they regarded as credible and did respectively guard against were submarine attacks and sabotage. The breakdown in diplomatic relations between the USA and Japan was public knowledge and made headline news across the US. Only days before the attack on Pearl Harbor the *Honolulu Times* printed the headline: 'Japanese may strike over the weekend.'[6] On the morning of Sunday, 7 December 1941 Admiral Kimmel and General Short were due to meet for a round of golf before lunch. Complacency at all levels, not conspiracy, was the Japanese ally.

At 7.49 a.m. the first Japanese attack wave of forty-three fighters, fifty-one dive-bombers, seventy torpedo planes and fifty high-level bombers, led by Commander Mitsuo Fuchida, swept across the northern coast of Oahu. There was total surprise. The immediate target was the airfields to counter any US air opposition. The tightly parked aircraft on the Army Air Corps airfields at Wheeler, Bellows and Hickam were largely destroyed by cannon fire from the Mitsubishi A6M2 Zero-sen, or Zero fighters, within the opening minutes of the attack. The Marine Corps airbase at Ewa and the naval air units at Ford Island and Kaneohe Bay were similarly strafed and bombed. At 7.53 a.m., as the first torpedo planes dived to attack Battleship Row, Fuchida sent the short message *Tora, Tora Tora* (Tiger) to inform Vice-Admiral Chuichi Nagumo on board the flagship *Akagi* and Admiral Yamamoto in Japan that total surprise had been achieved. Most American sailors stared skyward in disbelief and the only opposition raised was some minor machine-gun fire as the Aichi Type 99 dive-bombers ('Vals' to the Americans) and Nakajima B5N2 torpedo planes ('Kates' to the Americans) commenced their attack runs. The battleships *Arizona, West Virginia, Nevada, Oklahoma* and the *California* all took torpedo hits within the first 12 minutes of the attack. It had taken Japanese naval technicians many months of trials to perfect a torpedo capable of operating in the shallow waters of Pearl Harbor. Their answer was the attachment of wooden fins to prevent the torpedoes from sinking too deep when they first entered the water. The startled crews of the stationary battleships were helpless and could only watch as the torpedoes streaked towards them. The *Tennessee, Arizona, Maryland* and *California* were also targeted by high-level bombers and all were struck by armour-piercing bombs designed to penetrate the decks of the heavily armoured battleships. The only American success was the detection and sinking of a second midget submarine within the harbour (to add to the catalogue of defence woes the anti-submarine nets across the harbour mouth had been left open) by the destroyer *Monaghan*, while a third ran aground trying to outrun the destroyer *Helm*. Its pilot, Ensign Kazua Sakamaki, was captured and became the first Japanese prisoner of war of the Pacific War. Five midget submarines took part in the attack on Pearl Harbor; the remaining two were reported missing and presumed sunk. A scene of utter devastation confronted Admiral Kimmel when he reached his harbour-side headquarters. As he watched the attack a 50-calibre bullet casing stuck his chest and he remarked: 'I wish it had killed me.'[7] The *Arizona* exploded after an armour-piercing bomb ignited its forward magazine stores. It sank within minutes with the loss of 1,177 crew and to this day remains where it rested as a permanent war grave. The *Tennessee* was set ablaze. The *California* was crippled and sinking. The *Oklahoma* capsized, trapping many of her crew below decks. The *Utah* was sunk, and the light cruiser *Raleigh* was half-submerged and only kept afloat by its mooring lines. As the first wave attack subsided at 8.25 a.m. Kimmel entered his private office and demoted himself. To the dismay of his staff he removed his four-star shoulder boards of a full (acting) admiral and replaced them with his permanent rank of a two-star rear-admiral.

At 8.55 a.m. a second Japanese attack wave of eighty dive-bombers, thirty-six fighters and fifty-four high-level bombers, commanded by Lieutenant-Commander Shimazaki, renewed the attack. In the interim some American fighters had made it into the air and, against considerable odds, succeeded in shooting down some of the Japanese aircraft. During the lull the badly damaged *Nevada* succeeded in making steam and attempted to escape to sea, but under further attack and fear of imminent sinking the captain beached the ship on Hospital Point to ensure that it did not block the main shipping channel. The *Pennsylvania*, under repair in the dry dock, was badly damaged, along with two destroyers, and as the second wave faded a total of twenty-one ships, including all eight battleships, were either sunk or badly damaged. The air force was effectively wiped out as a fighting force with 188 aircraft destroyed and 159 damaged. The American death toll was 2,403 and 1,178 injured.

By 10.00. a.m. it was over. The victorious Japanese pilots expected to be re-fuelled and rearmed and to return to destroy the harbour facilities and fuel dumps, but Vice-Admiral Nagumo opted for caution. He was concerned by the absence of the two most important targets for attack – the USN aircraft carriers *Lexington* and *Enterprise*. He feared an American carrier strike while his planes were at their most vulnerable being refuelled. His fears were justified because aircraft from the *Enterprise* were actively searching for the Japanese Fleet. The *Enterprise* was en route to Pearl Harbor following a delivery of aircraft to Wake and Midway islands. However, in a final defence failure for the USN, poor intelligence resulted in the *Enterprise* conducting a search to the south of Oahu while the Japanese Fleet was positioned 200 miles to the north. It escaped into the central Pacific as it had arrived, unseen and largely unscathed. The Japanese losses were twenty-nine aircraft, one submarine and all five midget submarines.

Washington was alerted to the attack at 7.58 a.m. (1.50 p.m. Washington time) with the direct uncoded message: 'Air raid on Pearl Harbor this is not a drill.'[8] At 2.05 p.m. Secretary of State Cordell Hull received the Japanese ambassador, Admiral Nomura, and emissary, Saburo Kurusu, for a meeting at their request. They had spent a feverish 24 hours destroying all confidential documents in their embassy and patiently waiting for the full transmission of a lengthy fourteen-part message from Tokyo which contained a declaration of war in the last paragraph. Tokyo intended the message to be handed over by the two diplomats approximately twenty minutes in advance of the attack. The differential time zones between Washington, Hawaii, Tokyo and London added a further layer of complexity to the timings. The two diplomats were unaware that they were too late, or in fact that the US intelligence 'purple' intercepts were so efficient that Hull and Roosevelt had already read the transcript of the message they were about to deliver. Hull bitterly admonished both men and the Japanese government for its treachery and set the tone for President Roosevelt's speech to Congress at 12.30 p.m. on 8 December. Roosevelt declared:

> Yesterday, December 7 1941 – a date which will live in infamy – the United States of America was suddenly and deliberately attacked by naval and air forces of the Empire of Japan . . . no matter how long it may take us . . . the American people in their righteous might will win through to absolute victory.[9]

Congress approved the declaration of war by 388 votes to one. The single dissenter was the pacifist Jeannette Rankin, who had also voted against war with Germany in 1917.

Churchill was dining at his official country house, Chequers, with the American ambassador Gilbert Winant and American envoy Averell Harriman at 9 p.m. (11 a.m. in Pearl Harbor) when he was alerted to the attack by a BBC radio broadcast. There is some evidence to suggest that Churchill was not surprised by the news. Central to this is the speculation that he had received intelligence of a Japanese coded war alert to all its embassies, known as the 'winds' message. The 'winds' alert was first intercepted on 19 November 1941 when Tokyo warned all its diplomats to listen out for a future war alert to be disguised as a weather report. Reference to 'easterly wind rain' would indicate war with the United States, 'northerly wind cloudy', war with the Soviet Union, and 'Westerly wind fine', war with Great Britain. There is some speculation that Churchill had been informed as early as 4 December of the transmission of a 'winds' message which indicated war with both the United States and Great Britain, but chose not to reveal it because he wanted a Japanese attack to force the United States into the war. Churchill was known to be keen to involve the United States in the war, but the 'winds' message would have added little to what was already known on both sides of the Atlantic. War was expected in the first week in December and a war alert was in force.

Churchill conferred with Roosevelt by telephone and offered to wait for a US declaration of war before issuing a separate British declaration of war. However, the next day, 8 December 1941, British Malaya was invaded by Japanese troops and thrust Britain directly into war with Japan. Churchill reported the invasion to the House of Commons and, given the time difference, he declared war on Japan some six hours in advance of the USA. The Netherland forces in the Dutch East Indies also declared war, and common cause was made with the leader of Nationalist China, Jiang Jieshi, at war with the Japanese since July 1937.

At the *Wolfsschanze* Hitler responded with delight to the news and declared to those around him: 'we can't lose the war'.[10] He declared war on the USA on 11 December and thereby linked the European and Pacific wars into a global world war. Without his action it was possible that the American public would have continued to veto US involvement in the war in Europe in preference for *their* war

The Japanese attack on Pearl Harbor and the simultaneous advance into the South Pacific was a calculated declaration of war on the ABD powers – the Americans, British and Dutch. It was a high-risk strategy that most Japanese diplomats and many military staff had opposed, including Admiral Yamamoto, but by December 1941 Japan's options had narrowed to a choice of bowing to ABD pressure to withdraw from China, or war. For the Japanese military there was only ever one choice.

The spark for war was the announcement by President Roosevelt on 1 August of a total ban on all oil exports to Japan as part of an overall trade embargo. It fulfilled his preferred strategy of placing Japan into 'quarantine' to force a less aggressive stance in the Pacific. The Japanese military regarded the ban on oil as an unspoken declaration of war. Japan only produced 2.3 million barrels of oil out of an annual consumption of 35.8 million barrels. The USA was Japan's major supplier, delivering 27.2 million barrels; the Dutch East Indies supplied 4.8 million barrels; and 1.5 million barrels were imported from the world spot market. Japan held reserves of oil sufficient for three years of peacetime use and eighteen months of warfare. Consequently, time was against the Japanese military, and the prospect of a future inability to sustain military action produced a clamour for immediate war. Covetous eyes lit on the Dutch East Indian islands of Sumatra, Borneo and Java in the South Pacific. Their combined annual oil production was 65 million barrels: more than enough to make Japan self-sufficient. But the US Pacific Fleet at Pearl Harbor exercised a latent veto over any Japanese expansion into the South Pacific, and most naval commanders regarded it as an immovable check. The commander of the combined fleet, Admiral Yamamoto, was more sanguine. As early as April 1941 he had directed Rear-Admiral Takijiro Onishi to undertake a feasibility study for a surprise attack on Pearl Harbor. He was largely prompted by the success of the British torpedo attack on the Italian Fleet in Taranto harbour on 11 November 1940 which sank three of Italy's most powerful warships. The tactic of a surprise attack was a celebrated feature of Japanese naval strategy. Yamamoto was a veteran of Japan's crushing defeat of the Russian Navy by Admiral Togo at the battle of Tsushima Straits in 1905, a war which Japan had opened in 1904 with a surprise attack on the Russian Fleet in Port Arthur. At the time Japan was a British ally and the British government, and the press congratulated the Japanese for an 'act of daring'.[11] It is also notable that the Royal Navy had used the tactic of a surprise attack in April 1801 when Admiral Nelson destroyed the Danish Navy in Copenhagen harbour prior to a declaration of war. Hitler had also employed surprise attacks against Poland, Norway, western Europe and the Soviet Union from 1939–41. It is generally incumbent upon any military commander, especially in a warlike atmosphere, to maintain a high state of readiness.

The attack plan against Pearl Harbor was drafted by Admiral Onishi in May 1941 with assistance from Commander Minoru Genda, a leading exponent of naval aviation. At first it was not well received because few believed that a surprise attack was possible. The prime minister of Japan, Prince Fumimaro Koyone, opposed the plan and recommended a settlement with China and the normalisation of relations with the western powers. He signalled his desire for a rapprochement in July by manoeuvring Foreign Minister Matsuoka Yosuke, the author of Japan's entry into the Axis alliance, out of office and requesting a summit meeting with Roosevelt. His olive branch was firmly opposed by Churchill, who warned against any form of appeasement for fear of another Munich. The British, Chinese and Dutch (BCD) preconditions for the commencement of any talks was a commitment from Japan to withdraw from China, but this was not in Koyone's gift. The army represented in Koyone's new cabinet by Minister of War General Hideki Tojo refused to bow to ABCD (addition of American) pressure and undermined Koyone's initiative. The choice between diplomacy or war was debated by the Japanese government on 6 September in the presence of the emperor. Emperor Hirohito refused to reject the option of war and Koyone was given to 15 October to arrive at a diplomatic breakthrough that would lift the oil embargo.

On 16 October, with no significant shift in US policy to report, Koyone was forced to resign and Tojo was appointed as Japan's new prime minister with a mandate from the emperor to reach a settlement with the USA or to take Japan into war. Tojo convened a conference from 1–2 November to re-examine Japan's options. The conference ruled out an immediate declaration of war or an acceptance of ABCD demands, and settled on a twin-track approach. New negotiations for peace were authorised, with a deadline of 30 November for a diplomatic settlement, while the navy and army prepared to implement war. Few expected a settlement and the twin track was in effect a tramline to war. The Japanese ambassador in Washington, Admiral Nomura, was joined by the experienced diplomat Kurusu Saburo to conduct the negotiations while the navy prepared for war. The negotiations in Washington ended with an ABCD demand for withdrawal from China, and on 29 November the emperor sought the advice of the eight *jushin* or senior statesmen, all of whom had previously held office as prime minister. The clear majority counselled against war, as did the emperor's brother Prince Takamatsu. However, on 1 December the emperor formally received his entire government and endorsed the view of the president of the privy council,

Hara: 'the existence of our empire is threatened . . . there is nothing else we can do'.[12] Hirohito was not a remote bystander ignorant of events but was actively involved in the decision for war and the subsequent direction of the war.

The attack order – *niitaka yama nobore* (climb Mount Niitaka) – was transmitted to the First Air Fleet under the command of Vice-Admiral Nagumo on 1 December as it hove to 1,000 nautical miles north of Oahu. The six carriers, *Akagi, Hiryu, Kaga, Shokaku, Soryu* and *Zuikaku*, in full black-out conditions and shrouded by heavy rain, moved to their launch position 200 miles north of Oahu undetected. At 9 p.m. on the eve of the attack Admiral Nagumo, to the cheers of the assembled crew and airmen, hoisted the battle flag flown by Admiral Togo at the historic victory of Tsushima in 1905 to the masthead of the flagship carrier *Akagi*. The next morning at 6.15 a.m. the first wave of strike aircraft lifted off.

Despite the image of US defeat conveyed by the pictures of the burning and broken US Pacific Fleet the Japanese victory was relatively minor. The US Fleet lay in only 40 feet of water and within six months all but three battleships were salvaged. Pearl Harbor was not invaded or disabled and the aircraft carriers were untouched. Admiral Yamamoto remarked: 'I fear we have only awakened a sleeping giant and his reaction will be terrible.'[13]

References

1. John Toland, *Infamy: Pearl Harbor and Its Aftermath*, Methuen, 1982, p. 254.
2. Martin Gilbert, *Second World War*, Phoenix, 1989, p. 154.
3. John Toland, *Infamy: Pearl Harbor and Its Aftermath*, Methuen, 1982, p. 283.
4. Ibid., p. 7.
5. Ibid., p. 6.
6. Gordon W. Prange, *At Dawn We Slept: The Untold Story of Pearl Harbor*, 1982, Penguin, p. 447.
7. John Toland, *Infamy: Pearl Harbor and Its Aftermath*, Methuen, 1982, p. 11.
8. Ibid., p. 12.
9. Henry Steele Commanger, *Documents of American History, Volume 2: Since 1898* (9th edn), Prentice-Hall, 1973, p. 451.
10. Ian Kershaw, *Hitler 1936–45: Nemesis*, Penguin, 2000, p. 442.
11. B.H. Liddell-Hart, *History of the Second World War*, Cassell, 1971, p. 218.
12. Herbert P. Bix, *Hirohito and the Making of Modern Japan*, Duckworth Press, 2000, p. 433.
13. A.J.P. Taylor, *The Warlords*, Hamish Hamilton, 1978, p. 180.

19 Pacific hegemony

There must at this stage be no thought of saving the troops or sparing the population . . . Commanders and senior officers should die with their troops. The honour of the British Empire and the British army is at stake.[1]

Churchill's order concerning the battle for Singapore, 20 January 1941

At 00.25 a.m. on 8 December 1941 the first wave of Japanese troops of the 56th Infantry Regiment under the command of Colonel Nasu landed on the beaches of Kota Bharu in British Malaya. There was no surprise. For over a week British intelligence and RAF surveillance flights had been monitoring the movement south into the Gulf of Siam of a large Japanese naval fleet, including twenty-two troop transports. Its destination was unknown, but Malaya was an obvious target and the British forces were alert and dug-in. The exception was Singapore at the tip of the Malay Peninsula where to their surprise the first Japanese bombers found a brightly lit city and harbour. Like their counterparts in Pearl Harbor few British officers believed that the Japanese had the ability or capability to launch an attack on 'fortress' Singapore. The governor of Singapore, Sir Shelton Thomas, on being informed of the invasion by General Percival, remarked: 'I trust you'll chase the little men off.'[2] Casual anti-Japanese racism was endemic in the British Far East, and it was widely repeated that a single British soldier was worth ten Japanese.

On the beaches of Kota Bharu the Japanese troops were swept with machine-gun fire as they struggled to disembark from their landing craft under a monsoon downpour and against heavy six-foot surf. Many were drowned under the weight of their equipment and those who reached the beaches were pinned down by highly accurate fire from the 8th Indian Infantry Brigade under the command of Brigadier Key. Two miles out to sea the troop transports and their naval escorts were bombed by Hudson bombers of the Royal Air Force (RAF). The command ship *Awajisan Maru* received a direct hit and was abandoned. Some consideration was given to abandoning the landings, but Major-General Takumi, the force commander, personally led reinforce-

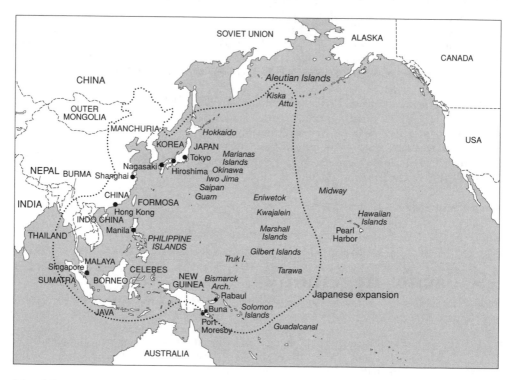

Map 6 Japanese expansion in the Pacific

ments ashore and rallied his officers and men to charge inland. Key's troops were thinly stretched over 25 miles of shoreline, and, with no reserves to call upon, he ordered a retreat. The Japanese breakthrough caused widespread panic and at Kota Bharu airfield, the principal Japanese target, the troops mutinied and commandeered trucks to flee. The Japanese occupied the airfield virtually unopposed and found the runways and even the petrol stores intact. Low morale to the point of actual desertion of the Allied forces (British, Australian, Indian and Malayan troops) became the hallmark of the Malayan campaign. Defeatism was rife – among the Australian troops in particular – and lay behind Churchill's rare exhortation (as quoted at the start of this chapter) for the Allied forces to stand and die. The Japanese landings at Kota Bharu on the east coast were largely diversionary in nature. Malaya forms the broad end of a long spoon-shaped peninsula with the island and major naval base of Singapore at its tip. To the immediate north of Malaya was Siam (Thailand), positioned across the narrow Kra isthmus (or handle of the spoon), and further north the major landmass of Siam and neighbouring British Burma. Siam was attractive to the Japanese Army as a gateway into Malaya and Burma because the borders were largely undefended. The Japanese 15th Army, under the command of General Yamshita, landed at the Siam ports of Singpora and Patani and quickly overwhelmed the minor Thai forces. They crossed Thailand to the west coast of the isthmus, while British attention was fixed on Kota Bharu on the east coast, and advanced down the two major west coast highways that ran in parallel from the Siam border to Singapore 250 miles to the south. Singapore was home to the British Far East Command under Commander-in-chief Air Marshal Sir Robert Brooke-Popham and widely regarded as impregnable. Powerful 15-inch shore batteries pointed seaward to protect the harbour, but there were only minor defences against a landward attack. Landward defences were considered to be unnecessary because it was widely assumed that any enemy invasion force would be engaged and defeated at sea by the Royal Navy and RAF, and that few if any enemy troops would ever make it ashore. Britain was primarily a naval power and Singapore was above all a naval base, but the harbour was empty following the withdrawal of the Far East Fleet. On 2 December, on Churchill's direct orders, HMS *Repulse* and HMS *Prince of Wales* arrived at Singapore as a deterrent against any Japanese aggression. Fighter cover was meant to be supplied by the aircraft carrier HMS *Indomitable*, but the *Indomitable* was under repair in the US after running aground and Churchill overrode the concerns of the Admiralty in the belief that shore-based aircraft could provide the necessary air cover.

The scale of Japan's imperial ambition was grossly underestimated in both London and Washington. Japan intended to seize all European possessions in the Pacific and to hold sway over the entire Pacific region stretching north–south from the Kurile Islands to Australia and east–west from Hawaii in the mid-Pacific to India. Consequently Japan's principal military targets were the British Far East Command in Singapore, the US Pacific Command in the Philippines and the powerful USN Pacific Fleet based at Pearl Harbor. All three were attacked within hours of each other, but appear a day apart (7–8 December) due to the division of the International Date Line.

The US forces on the Philippines under the command of General Douglas MacArthur came under Japanese air attack only five and a half hours after the Pearl Harbor attack. Implausibly the Japanese achieved surprise and found the majority of the US aircraft neatly lined-up along the airfield aprons. The majority of US planes were destroyed on the ground for the loss of only seven Japanese planes. It was the first in a succession of clumsy defence failures by MacArthur. The US islands of Guam, Wake and Midway were also attacked on 8 December, and in China the Japanese Army crossed the border into British Hong Kong and seized the US garrisons in Shanghai and Tientsin. The only distinguished Allied military action in the first days of the Pacific War was on the island of Wake, where a tiny force of 524 US marines and 1,216 civilian workers fiercely resisted Japanese air attacks and on 11 December forced the withdrawal of a Japanese invasion force after sinking two Japanese destroyers with the loss of 5,350 Japanese servicemen. Wake eventually succumbed to vastly superior Japanese forces on 23 December.

With the Japanese forces firmly ashore in Malaya and Siam, Brooke-Popham ordered the 11th Indian Division to form a defensive line across the west coast highways at Jitra in northern Malaya and to hold the main Japanese advance. The result was one of the worst disasters in British military history. The defensive line was thinly spread and little attempt was made to make the roads impassable with mines, roadblocks or blown bridges. The British line was penetrated by a minor column of Japanese tanks supported by only 581 infantry, and, in scenes of complete disorder, the vastly superior Allied troops abandoned their weapons and retreated. In doing so they were exposed to Japanese machine-gun and shell-fire and suffered thousands of casualties, compared to only fifty Japanese. In their haste to retreat, large stockpiles of ammunition, food, trucks and petrol were left behind for the Japanese. It was the commencement of the worst rout in British military history in which a Japanese army of some 35,000 troops defeated a British-led Allied army of 76,300 troops. When support and administrative staff are included the total forces were 75,000 and 140,000 respectively. At Alor Star airfield, 15 miles south of Jitra, the Japanese breakthrough caused a repeat of the chaotic scenes experienced at Kota Bharu. The ground troops fled and the airfield was abandoned with further stores of food, ammunition and petrol left intact. It was all to the delight of the Japanese who were existing on basic ration packs. Brooke-Popham later formally rebuked his RAF commanders with the words: 'aerodromes appear to have been abandoned in a state approaching panic . . . stores that will assist the enemy have been left behind . . . this is utterly opposed to all the tradition of the airforce'.[3] When all surviving RAF planes in northern Malaya were ordered to regroup further south at Butterworth airfield only ten out of 110 planes reported.

Within 48 hours of landing in Malaya, the Japanese had broken the British Army and the RAF, but there was hope that the Royal Navy battleships *Repulse* and *Prince of Wales* would destroy the Japanese invasion fleet. The battleships designated Force Z, commanded by Admiral Philips, sailed north from Singapore to intercept the Japanese fleet. At 11.07 a.m. on 10 December action stations were sounded when a wave of Japanese bombers appeared on the horizon. Both battleships were subjected to a relentless onslaught of bombing and torpedo attacks from three separate waves of Japanese fighters and torpedo bombers, and in little over two hours both were fatally damaged. Admiral Philips and Captain Leach both refused to leave the bridge and went down with the *Prince of Wales,* the newest and most powerful battleship in the Royal Navy and the proud platform for Churchill's Atlantic meeting with Roosevelt in August 1941. Escorting destroyers plucked most of the crews from the water, but 513 of the *Repulse* crew of 1,309 were lost and 327 out of the *Prince of Wales* crew of 1,612. It was a grievous loss to the Royal Navy and to a nation that prided itself as being invincible at sea. Churchill remarked: 'In all the war I never received a more direct shock.'[4]

News of the defeat swept Malaya and crushed British morale, and at no point did Britain recover the initiative. The British Army was forced into a continuous retreat punctuated by half-hearted attempts to form defensive lines along the major rivers. The Japanese responded by outflanking the British positions by pushing through the jungle and by commandeering small boats left undamaged in the harbours to leapfrog down the coast. The Allied troops had all been directed to regard the jungle as impenetrable and consequently defensive lines were not extended into the jungle. The Japanese, in an inspired tactic, also made the best use of the smooth tarmac roads by supplying their troops with bicycles. Most soon lost their tyres and the clatter of the wheel rims on the roads was often mistaken by the Allied troops for approaching tanks and caused many to flee in panic. Although the Allied troops had no tanks or heavy guns to confront the few Japanese tanks that did exist it is notable that only twenty-four anti-tank mines out of a stock of 1,400 were laid. Only a handful of the 250 bridges down the west coast highway were blown, and the few that were destroyed were rapidly repaired by Japanese engineer battalions attached to the spearhead units. By Christmas 1941 the Japanese had occupied the entire northern half of Malaya against minimal resistance. On 27 December Brooke-Popham was relieved of command and replaced by Lieutenant-General Sir Henry Pownall. On the first day of war Brooke Popham's official war com munique had stated: 'we are ready. We have had plenty of warning and our preparations are made and tested.'[5] Churchill considered abandoning Singapore, but the symbolism attached to Singapore as the seat of British power in the Far East, and entreaties from Prime Minister Curtin of Australia who regarded Singapore as Australia's front line, caused him to commit Britain to defend it to the last.

On Christmas Day the 12,000 strong British garrison of Hong Kong, under siege since 10 December, surrendered. The victorious Japanese troops went on a murderous rampage and bayoneted hundreds of prisoners, including the wounded and, most notoriously, many patients lying in bed in St Stephen's Hospital. The Japanese military code was punitive and encouraged victorious soldiers to regard a conquered people as the spoils of war to be murdered, raped, tortured or worked to death. All were deemed worthless and devoid of any rights by virtue of conquest. The Japanese massacre of defenceless prisoners and civilians was first noted as early as 1894 when the Japanese sacked Port Arthur in Manchuria. A New York newspaper, *The World*, reported: 'at least two thousand helpless people butchered by Japanese soldiers . . . streets cloaked with mutilated bodies of men, women and children while the soldiers laughed'.[6]

On 22 December 43,000 Japanese troops landed, largely unopposed, on the main island of the Philippines, Luzon, 120 miles from the capital Manila. A further 7,000 landed on the east coast. MacArthur had deployed 110,000 Filipino troops around the coast as a tripwire and concentrated the US troops and crack Filipino scouts to defend Manila, but once the Japanese landing zones were apparent he failed to take the war to the enemy as originally intended and adopted an entirely defensive posture. Despite possessing a larger army he inexplicably decided that he could not defend Manila and declared it an open city on 26 December, retreating into the inhospitable mosquito-ridden mountainous Bataan peninsula. The peninsula was 25 miles long and 20 miles wide and at its tip, in Manila Bay, was the heavily garrisoned island of Corregidor that dominated the sea approach to Manila. MacArthur regarded the peninsula as a good defensive position to concentrate his forces, but all he achieved was to hand the Philippines to the Japanese and imprison his men. The warehouses of the city of Manila were left fully stocked with all manner of food and military stores, including 3 million gallons of petrol, 500,000 artillery rounds, five months' supply of rice for the entire garrison, and even a large stockpile of the vital anti-malaria drug quinine. The Japanese contented themselves with guarding the perimeter of the peninsula and shelling the US positions. Despite outnumbering the Japanese, MacArthur never took the offensive and as the weeks passed his troops grew steadily weaker from food shortages and outbreaks of malaria. The Japanese were also stricken by malaria, with 10,000 incapacitated; their numbers fell to only 3,000 when the 48th Division was transferred to the Dutch East Indies. The US garrison of the island of Corregidor alone was 15,000, but at no stage did MacArthur attempt to probe the Japanese strength or to lift the siege. The ordinary American soldiers fought with considerable courage in a desperate siege that was to last for six months and openly criticised their commander-in-chief for his poor tactics and lack of leadership.

The Japanese offensive in Malaya continued unabated as a hastily prepared defensive line at Slim river collapsed on 7 January and opened the road into the southernmost province of Johore. Panic gripped the capital Kuala Lumpur and a stream of European refugees flooded south to Singapore to try and secure passage on any ships to India or Australia. Non-Europeans were forbidden to travel or to take up evacuation places. It was an unsavoury decision that assisted Japanese propaganda that the 'Whites' were exploiters who cared nothing for Asians. In response, many Indian troops flocked to join the Indian National Army, led by Major Mohan Singh, to fight alongside the Japanese to liberate Malaya, Burma and India from British rule. The city was occupied on 11 January and although petrol dumps were fired the troops charged with destroying all military equipment and military stores failed to do so and joined the undisciplined retreat south.

Reinforcements were rushed to Singapore to fulfil Churchill's pledge to hold the island while a last defensive line was prepared in Johore province. Fifty-one Hurricanes arrived in crates on 13 January and the 18th British Division landed on 20 January, followed on 22 January by the 44th Indian Infantry Brigade and a further 1,900 Australian troops. All were unprepared for the chaotic scenes that greeted them, and rather than finding themselves reinforcing a coherent plan for a counter-attack in Johore province they stood around on the shores of Singapore island to await the Japanese attack. The island was sealed on 31 January by blowing the causeway to the mainland, and General Percival deployed 70,000 Allied troops and 15,000 administrative staff to defend the island. The Japanese Army across the narrow Johore Straits was at best 30,000 strong and, unknown to the British, very low on ammunition. Their major advantage was almost total air supremacy, and approximately 2,000 were killed per day in Singapore from bombing raids. The newly arrived Hurricane fighters firmly engaged the Japanese and twenty-six were shot down, but on the ground there was no fighting spirit. Beaches were not mined or blocked with barbed wire and few trenches or gun emplacements were built to provide a prepared defensive line. During the night of 8 February after a fifteen-hour artillery bombardment the Japanese landed on the western shores of Singapore island. The sector was guarded by Australian troops, but most deserted their posts and refused orders to stand firm. By dawn on the 9th the Japanese had established a strong beachhead and fanned out across the island. There was a complete breakdown of military discipline, with wild scenes of drunken Allied troops refusing orders, looting shops and bars, stealing boats and fighting their way onto any ship leaving Singapore harbour. Nor was it just the ordinary troops. Major-General Gordon Bennett handed his command of the 8th Australian Division to a junior officer and fled Singapore on one of the last civilian ships. The end was certain. At 6.10 p.m. on 15 February after a short meeting with General Yamashita, General Percival surrendered Singapore. It was one of the lowest points of British military history. The Japanese were contemptuous of their captives and, as in Hong Kong, they murdered civilians and prisoners alike. Approximately 5,000 Chinese citizens of Singapore were beheaded, hundreds of prisoners were bayoneted and the patients of Alexandra Hospital were murdered in their beds, including a patient on an operating table along with the surgeons and nurses. Those who survived faced an ordeal of regular beatings and a battle for survival against hunger and disease in prisoner of war camps. The most notorious was Changi where 50,000 prisoners were crammed into four barracks of an old army camp.

As Singapore fell, the Japanese Navy was massing in the Java Sea to secure the oil-rich islands of the Dutch East Indies. To ward off any intervention from the Allied forces in Australia, Darwin was heavily bombed on 20 February. All seventeen ships in the harbour including the USN destroyer *Peary*, were sunk and the surrounding harbour installations and airfields were destroyed for the cost of five Japanese aircraft. On 25 February, the Allied Command under General Wavell was evacuated to Australia from Java as a Japanese invasion fleet entered the Java Sea. It was intercepted by an Allied naval task force comprising two Dutch cruisers, two British destroyers, a USN cruiser and an Australian cruiser under the command of Dutch admiral Karel Doorman. One Japanese troopship was sunk, but within 24 hours the entire Allied naval force was destroyed. The Japanese controlled the sea and air, and the 100,000 Dutch, British and American defenders of Java surrendered on 7 March. Many thousands were to perish in Japanese captivity as the Japanese troops executed prisoners and civilians at random all over the Dutch East Indies.

In Burma the capital Rangoon was evacuated by British and Indian troops under the command of General Slim on 7 March, and so began a long fighting retreat northwards through the dense jungle of the Burmese interior towards the Indian border. The last significant outpost of allied resistance in the Pacific was provided by the beleaguered US troops trapped in the Bataan peninsula, Luzon. Emperor Hirohito overrode his military commanders, who were content to shell the Americans into submission, and ordered an offensive to hasten their defeat. In an admission of defeat President Roosevelt ordered General MacArthur to sneak out of the Philippines, and on 11 March he escaped by motor boat to Mindanao and from there by plane to the safety of Australia. The massive defeat across the Pacific had damaged national morale and Roosevelt wished to deny the Japanese the propaganda triumph of the capture of the US commander-in-chief Pacific. Whereas Admiral Kimmel was cashiered for the loss of the US Pacific Fleet at Pearl Harbor, MacArthur escaped any censure for his appalling lapses of defence in the Philippines. The US and Filipino troops valiantly fought on for six weeks but surrendered on 9 April broken by hunger and disease and constant artillery bombardment. Some escaped to Corrigedor, but 15,000 US and 60,000 Filipino troops were captured. Their suffering was not at an end as their Japanese captors insisted that they march 65 miles to a railhead at San Fernando to be transported to the POW camp, Camp O'Donnell in Tarlac province. The Bataan 'Death March' was the epitome of cruelty. All were denied food, water and shelter from the tropical sun, and those who paused or could not march further were savagely beaten, bayoneted or beheaded at the side of the road. At least 6,000 died on the road, and a further 26,000 shortly after arrival in Camp O'Donnell from the dehydration and injuries endured on the march.

In Burma, the Japanese achieved their strategic goal of cutting the Burma Road when they occupied Lashio on 29 April. The longest fighting retreat in British military history of approximately a thousand miles ended on 20 May when the Allied survivors crossed the Indian border into Assam racked by malaria and dysentery.

The last Allied foothold in the South Pacific, the island of Corregidor in Manila Bay, fell on 6 May after an unrelenting 27-day artillery barrage and consigned a further 12,000 US troops into Japanese captivity.

Inside six months the Japanese had achieved a string of stupendous military victories on a par with Hitler's invasion of western Europe and vanquished the ABD powers in the Pacific. To secure the boundaries of their new empire a carrier group had penetrated deep into the Indian Ocean from 6–9 April where it had bombed Ceylon and forced the withdrawal of the Royal Navy Eastern Fleet to the safety of Kenya. The only other possible threat was from the USN aircraft carriers. On 4 May, in the battle of the Coral Sea, the *Yorktown* and *Lexington* intercepted and prevented Japanese landings in New Guinea. The *Lexington* was lost in the engagement and the *Yorktown* was badly damaged, but the Japanese also lost an aircraft carrier, the *Shoku*. It was the first Japanese reversal in the Pacific and, like the earlier Doolittle raid on Tokyo on 16 April, a warning that US military forces in the Pacific had been rolled back rather than decisively defeated. The air raid led by General James Doolittle was a daring strike by sixteen B-25 bombers from the deck of the carrier *Hornet*. After successfully bombing Tokyo they flew on to China hoping to land in territory controlled by the Chinese nationalist forces. Most, including Doolittle, fell into friendly hands but eight were captured by the Japanese Army in China and transported to Tokyo. Here Emperor Hirohito refused to treat them as POWs and signed death warrants for five of the pilots as a deterrent to American fliers.

To protect Japan, and to provide time to build the defences of their newly won empire, the Japanese Navy needed to destroy the US naval presence in the Pacific totally. The answer was to lure the US Navy into defending Midway Island and to correct the mistake of Pearl Harbor by destroying the USN aircraft carriers.

References

1. Gilbert Mant, *The Singapore Surrender: The Greatest Disaster in British Military History*, Kangaroo Press, 1992, p. 12.
2. Jonathan Lewis and Ben Steele, *Hell in the Pacific: From Pearl Harbor to Hiroshima and Beyond*, Channel 4 Books, 2001, p. 25.
3. Sir Andrew Gilchrist, *Malaya 1941: The Fall of a Fighting Empire*, Robert Hale, 1992, p. 151.
4. Martin Gilbert, *Churchill: A Life*, Heinemann, 1992, p. 712.
5. Jonathan Lewis and Ben Steele, *Hell in the Pacific: From Pearl Harbor to Hiroshima and Beyond*, Channel 4 Books, 2001, p. 19.
6. Ibid., p. 64.

Containment

30 Midway

> The parachute opened with a bang and I hurtled to sea. When I looked around, I saw three pillars of fire, Akagi Kaga and Soryu, had been destroyed . . . we had no carriers to counter attack. There was nothing we could do.[1]
>
> The recollection of Pilot Iyozo Fujita after he was forced to bale-out from his stricken Zero

After the failure to provide a warning of the Japanese attack on Pearl Harbor on 7 December 1941, US naval intelligence placed every effort into breaking the Japanese naval code referred to as JN-25b. The structure and coding methodology of JN-25b was understood, but prior to Pearl Harbor there was insufficient manpower to study the 500–1,000 messages being intercepted each day and to identify and break the 50,000 different code groups that were randomly selected by the Japanese Navy to encode their naval traffic. In Washington the headquarters of naval intelligence, designated OP-20-G, employed thirty-six code-breakers, but only a few of those worked full-time on JN-25b. The office of naval intelligence in Pearl Harbor, designated Station Hypo, was similarly handicapped with a staff of only twenty-three to cover all naval intelligence activity. IBM punch card readers were installed to help with the work, but they proved too efficient and generated 3 million punch cards a month, outpacing the ability of the staff to read and digest the intelligence output. After Pearl Harbor the number of staff devoted to breaking JN-25b was sharply increased in both OP-20-G and Station Hypo, and by March 1942 JN-25b was successfully broken. It was read with few breaks for the rest of the war. The Midway intercepts were the first and most dramatic evidence of this intelligence breakthrough. On 14 May 1942 the commander of naval intelligence at Pearl Harbor, Commander Joseph J. Rochefort, reported Japanese naval traffic relating to preparations for a *Koryaku butai* (invasion force) to occupy 'AF'. Rochefort was fairly certain that AF was an indicator for Midway Island, but his hunch was not good enough for Commander of the Pacific Fleet Admiral Chester Nimitz. On 19 May Rochefort directed Midway to report in an open signal to Pearl Harbor that its desalination plant had broken down and there was a shortage of fresh water. Two days later a JN-25b decrypt revealed that the desalination plant on AF was broken. The confirmation resulted in feverish activity in Station Hypo and OP-20-G in Washington to decode any previous or incoming signal relating to AF, and piece by piece they successfully collated the full Japanese plan of attack. On 27 May Rochefort briefed Nimitz and his senior commanders on the Japanese plan of attack. Rarely in any war has any commander enjoyed advance intelligence of his enemy's battle plan, but Rochefort was able to detail dates, times, positions and enemy strength.

The Japanese plan of attack was a highly ambitious plan drawn up by the admiral of the combined fleet and author of the Pearl Harbor attack, Isoroku Yamamoto. His aim was to correct the mistake of Pearl Harbor and destroy the US carrier force in the Pacific with a single knock-out blow. With the US Navy defeated, Yamamoto intended to occupy the Aleutian, Midway and Hawaiian islands to deny the US any naval or airbases within range of the new Japanese empire. He estimated that it would take the US a year to eighteen months to recover from this blow and to build a new Pacific fleet, but with no forward bases it would have to cross 3,000 miles of empty ocean just to reach the outer fringes of the Japanese empire. Coupled with the expected defeat of Britain and the USSR by Germany, Yamamoto was confident that the USA would have little choice but to accept the new Axis world order and sign a peace treaty. Yamamoto's strategy was initially rejected by the Army High Command because their immediate priority was to consolidate the gains won in the South Pacific and to subdue China before opening a new front. However, the military landscape altered dramatically in April 1942 when the Doolittle raid by sixteen B-17 bombers from the USN *Yorktown* successfully bombed Tokyo, to the considerable embarrassment of the Army High Command. There was an assumption that the planes had flown from Midway because it was deemed impossible for a B-17 to take off from a short carrier runway. Roosevelt teased the Japanese by stating that the planes had appeared from Shangri-la. The Japanese military accorded the highest priority to the defence of the homeland and consequently Yamamoto's plan to push the USN out of the Pacific was adopted. The Doolittle raid had been mounted to boost American morale and had caused little damage, but it sparked a chain of events that ended with the destruction of Japanese naval power in the Pacific.

To fulfil his plan, Yamamoto assembled five separate battle groups deploying eleven battleships, eight carriers, twenty-three cruisers, sixty-five destroyers, twenty submarines and 350 aircraft. In a series of interlocking steps, Yamamoto planned to lure the US carriers out of Pearl Harbor and to destroy the entire US fleet in one surprise blow. The first step, scheduled for 3 June, was for the Northern Force, comprising the small carriers *Ryujo* and *Junyo*, together with two cruisers and three destroyers, to attack Dutch Harbor in the Aleutian Islands and to occupy the tiny Aleutian islands of Kiska and Attu. This was primarily a diversionary raid to draw off some of the US fleet. The second step was for the Striking Force, comprising the four major aircraft carriers *Akagi*, *Kaga*, *Hiryu* and *Soryu* and two battleships, to destroy the air and sea defences of Midway Island. All four carriers were part of the strike force that had launched the surprise attack on Pearl Harbor and were again operating under the overall command of Vice-Admiral Nagumo. The third step was for the troopships of the Occupation Force, escorted by four cruisers and one carrier, to land 5,000 troops on Midway and to prepare the airstrip as a base for the attack on Hawaii. The fourth step was for a screen of twenty submarines to form a picket line from Midway to Hawaii and to warn of the approach and direction of the US carriers and fleet as they steamed to counter-attack the Japanese forces at Midway and the Aleutians. Yamamoto had reserved the fifth and final step for himself. He commanded the Main Body, comprising seven battleships and a carrier, and he planned to stand off and wait for the US carriers to commit themselves before closing and using the powerful guns of the battleships to sink the entire US fleet. Yamamoto's flagship was the *Yamato*, the most powerful battleship in the world with eight 18-inch guns, capable of firing a shell 25 miles.

Nimitz's counter was simple but bold. He intended to move first and to place the much-weaker US fleet inside the Japanese operation zone in order to spring his own surprise attack. His problem was scraping together a fleet capable of challenging the Japanese, following the losses and damage sustained by the USN during the battle of the Coral Sea on 4 May. The carrier *Lexington* had been sunk and the *Yorktown* had suffered severe bomb and fire damage. The Japanese were convinced that they had also sunk the *Yorktown,* but she had limped into Pearl Harbor on 27 May, blackened and with her flight deck twisted and inoperable, for an estimated three months of repair work. Nimitz gave the yard-workers three days to make *Yorktown* battle-worthy and after 48 hours of non-stop work by 1,500 workers working in relays, the *Yorktown* left Pearl Harbor on 30 May with workers still on board. This gave Nimitiz two task forces. TF16 was the more powerful, composed of the carriers *Hornet* and *Enterprise*, with six cruisers and nine destroyers under the command of Rear-Admiral Raymond Spruance. TF17 comprised the single carrier *Yorktown*, under the command of Vice-Admiral Fletcher, with two cruisers and five destroyers. Nimitz also ordered immediate improvements to the anti-aircraft defences of Midway and deployed additional fighters and B-17 bombers to help defend the island. The US carriers took up station 200 miles north of Midway and waited for the Japanese fleet.

At 3 a.m. on 3 June the Japanese Northern Force bombed Dutch Harbor and later successfully landed troops on the barren rocky islands of Kiska and Attu. At dawn the following day the Striking Force of four carriers launched the first wave of Japanese fighters and bombers to attack Midway as a preliminary to invasion. The flight of thirty-six torpedo bombers, thirty-six dive-bombers and thirty-six Zero fighters, commanded by Lieutenant Joichi Tomonaga, arrived over Midway at 6.15 a.m. but flew into a heavy barrage of anti-aircraft fire and discovered that all the US planes were airborne and waiting. Twenty-six US fighters engaged the Japanese, but most of the planes were obsolete F2A-3 Buffaloes which were unable to keep pace with the Zeros. All but two were destroyed. However, the furious anti-aircraft fire downed sixty-seven Japanese planes, prompting Tomonaga to radio Vice-Admiral Nagumo on board the flagship *Akagi* to request an immediate second strike. This was unexpected, but minutes later the carriers were attacked by six Gruman Avenger and four Marauder torpedo-bombers from Midway. All were easily beaten-off by the Zero defence screen and seven of the US planes were shot down without scoring a single hit. Nagumo accepted that a second strike was essential to destroy Midway's air power and with no reports from the submarine picket line of the approach of US carriers Nagumo ordered his remaining aircraft to be armed for a further ground attack. After six months of continual victories the Japanese carriers were in the grip of 'victory fever' and there was a prevailing attitude of an unstoppable force. Nagumo made the fatal error of not staggering the air attacks from his four carriers to ensure that at any one time two of his carriers could provide full air cover during the vulnerable time of take-offs and landings.

At 7.28 a.m. a Japanese surveillance flight spotted TF16, but at first reported only the presence of battleships and destroyers. Nagumo's relief was short lived because at 8.20 the surveillance plane belatedly reported a US carrier. Tension and confusion mounted as Nagumo realised the enormity of his mistake. He immediately abandoned the preparations for a further attack on Midway and ordered the planes to be rearmed with torpedoes and armour-piercing bombs to attack the US carrier; but first he had to recover Tomonaga's returning flight. The recovery and rearming would take at least one hour.

The unexpected appearance of the Japanese spotter plane also caused consternation on the *Enterprise* and *Hornet*. Spruance was still assembling his air strike but, concerned that he was about to lose the element of surprise, he ordered the Dauntless dive-bombers and Devastator torpedo bombers, already airborne and flying a holding pattern, into the attack. The result was high losses because the bombers and their fighter escorts never managed to link up and launch a single co-ordinated attack as originally planned. Worst of all, the planes were operating at the extreme range of their fuel supplies and the best hope for the pilots after the attack was to reach Midway or to ditch. At 9.30 a.m. the US torpedo bombers spotted the carriers *Akagi*, *Kaga* and *Soryu* and, despite the absence of fighter cover, the forty-one slow Devastators commenced their torpedo runs. All were knocked out of the sky by the fast-moving Zeros without scoring a single torpedo hit. Only one of the pilots, George Gray, survived the attack. However, their sacrifice was not in vain because the Zeros failed to notice the arrival high overhead of the US Dauntless dive-bombers. The four carriers were at their most vulnerable, with their decks crowded with fully fuelled and armed aircraft ready for take-off. Led by Lieutenant-Commander McClusky, the dive-bombers, operating at a height of 19,000 feet, dropped into near vertical dives and aimed their 1,000 pound bombs at the broad carrier flight decks. *Akagi* was struck by two bombs. The first plunged straight through the flight deck midships and exploded in the torpedo stores setting off a devastating series of explosions that ripped out the core of the ship. The second hit the rear of the flight deck and exploded among the tightly packed aircraft setting off multiple explosions and fierce fires. Nagumo was forced to abandon ship. The *Kaga* was similarly disabled. The first bomb hit a petrol tanker below the bridge and engulfed the bridge in a firestorm killing everyone on it including the captain. Three further bombs exploded on the flight deck and within minutes the entire ship was a mass of flames from bow to stern. The *Soryu* was equally devastated after three bombs struck the flight deck and set off a chain reaction of fierce fires and explosions among the heavily laden aircraft on the flight deck. Within 20 minutes the crew had also abandoned ship. The entire attack had only taken five minutes and left the three carriers still afloat, but on fire and crippled. In the haze and confusion of battle the *Hiryu* escaped attack and managed to clear her flight deck to launch eighteen dive-bombers and ten torpedo bombers. The dive-bombers found the *Yorktown* at 11.58 a.m. Ten were shot down by Wildcat fighters and two were shot down by anti-aircraft fire in a furious air battle, but the remaining six scored direct bomb hits. One bomb immobilised the *Yorktown* by smashing through the funnel and exploding in the middle of the ship's boilers and furnaces, and two other bomb hits started serious fires. Despite the heavy damage, the ship was saved by damage control parties and was again making steam and underway when the ten torpedo-bombers from the *Hiryu* renewed the attack. Two torpedoes struck the portside and tore gaping holes in the ship. A heavy list raised the fear of a capsize and in consequence the order to abandon ship was sounded at 3 p.m. It proved premature.

The *Hiryu* was hunted down by aircraft from the *Enterprise* and *Hornet* and attacked just after she had recovered the few surviving aircraft from the *Yorktown* attack. Dauntless dive-bombers repeated their earlier deadly performance and left the *Hiryu* afloat but with fires raging out of control. None of the Japanese carriers survived. The first to sink was the *Soryu*. Rent by multiple explosions, the *Soryu* slipped beneath the waves at 7.13 p.m. with her captain on the bridge. The *Kaga* followed at 7.25 p.m., after two large explosions tore the ship asunder. The *Hiryu*, beyond any hope of recovery, was scuttled at 2.30 a.m. on 5 June by torpedoes fired from a Japanese destroyer. The *Akagi* lasted to dawn, but at 5 a.m. with all hope of salvage exhausted she too was despatched by torpedoes from a Japanese destroyer.

Before the last carrier had sunk, a shaken Yamamoto abandoned the landings on Midway and the attack by the Main Force. The US fleet had withdrawn under the umbrella of air support offered by Midway and their own air cover, and whereas his battleships and cruisers could significantly outgun the US fleet they could not survive a mass aerial attack. It was a decision that, coupled with the earlier sinking of HMS *Repulse* and HMS *Prince of Wales* by Japanese dive-bombers off Malaya, indicated that the age of the heavyweight battleship was over. Air power was king.

The final act occurred on 7 June when the *Yorktown*'s nine lives finally ran out. She had been successfully salvaged on 6 June, but while she was under tow back to Pearl Harbor the Japanese submarine I-168 slipped through the destroyer screen and fatally holed the *Yorktown* with two torpedoes at 6 a.m. on 7 June. Some hours later *Yorktown* sank after a final desperate bid to save her.

In the course of a single day Japan's offensive in the Pacific was curtailed. Before the attack on Pearl Harbor Yamamoto had remarked: 'I can run wild for the first six months but after that . . . the enemy will not necessarily adhere to the classic idea of a battleship to battleship showdown.'[2] His prediction was more accurate than he dared to admit. The scale of the defeat was hidden from the nation and was not even revealed to the Army High Command lest it cause a defeatist mood. Japan had lost four of the six carriers that had launched the attack on Pearl Harbor, a cruiser, 332 aircraft and 3,500 men, among them her most experienced and skilled navy aviators. In contrast the USN lost one aircraft carrier, one destroyer, 150 aircraft and 307 men. Midway was an overwhelming US victory and the burgeoning economic and military power of the USA indicated only one possible outcome. In January 1942 Roosevelt had announced that by the year end US industry would produce 45,000 aircraft, 45,000 tanks and 8 million tons of shipping. It was a colossal industrial capacity that neither Japan nor her Axis allies could hope to match. To highlight the point, in September 1942 a 'Liberty' ship, *Robert E. Peary*, was built from prefabricated steel panels and launched inside four days. The US triumph was also a significant victory for the intelligence services. Commander Rochefort, who alerted the US fleet to the Japanese plan, was nominated for a Distinguished Service Medal, but petty professional jealously and rivalry from the OP-20-G in Washington muddied the water as to who was responsible for the vital intelligence breakthrough. Rochefort lost the political battle with Washington and in October 1942 he was sidelined into managing a dry dock in San Francisco. His key role in the defeat of Japanese naval power was not officially recognised until 1985, nine years after his death, when he was posthumously awarded the DSM.

Midway ended Japan's tide of conquest, but the battle to liberate the territory seized by Japan and held by troops who preferred death to surrender was to take a further gruelling three years.

References

1. Jonathan Lewis and Ben Steele, *Hell in the Pacific: From Pearl Harbor to Hiroshima and Beyond*, Channel 4 Books, 2001, p. 111.
2. Edwin P. Hoyt, *Hirohito: The Emperor and the Man*, Praeger Press, 1992, p. 121.

21 El Alamein

> This is not the end. It is not even the beginning of the end. But it is, perhaps, the end of the beginning.[1]
>
> Churchill speaking at the Lord Mayor of London's luncheon,
> Mansion House, London, 10 November 1942

Churchill arrived in Cairo on 1 August 1942 in a depressurised Liberator bomber, which meant that he had to wear an oxygen mask for the duration of the ten-hour flight. However, as a concession to personal comfort his mask had been specially adapted to permit him to smoke his trademark cigars. Churchill's visit marked his deep concern about the scale of the German victories in North Africa and the imminent danger of defeat in Egypt. A German victory in Egypt would close the Suez Canal to Allied shipping and threaten Allied oil supplies from the Middle East.

To Churchill's immense frustration, it was the second time that Rommel's Afrika Korps had menaced Egypt. Over a year earlier in June 1941 Churchill had responded to a similar danger to Egypt by replacing the commander-in-chief Middle East, General Wavell, with General Claude Auchinleck following the failure of Wavell's 'Battleaxe' offensive from 15–19 June 1941. Auchinleck had fulfilled Churchill's expectations by delivering a notable victory when Operation Crusader, launched in November 1941, liberated the whole of the Libyan province of Cyrenaica. In the process the key Mediterranean port of Tobruk, under siege since April 1941 and tenaciously defended by its largely Australian garrison, had been relieved on 10 December. However, Auchinleck's advance had ended at El Agheila in January 1942 when he paused to regroup following the transfer of his most experienced divisions to the more critical defence of Burma and Singapore. The replacements Auchinleck received were untried and untrained, but although he was not expected to advance further, he was expected to hold his gains. As the British position weakened, Rommel was gaining in strength: the Afrika Korps took delivery of two convoys of replacement panzers and was redesignated the Panzerarmee Afrika on 21 January 1942. Probing attacks from Rommel revealed the British weaknesses, and on 21 January he launched a determined attack at El Agheila and forced the British 1st Armoured Division into retreat. Against all expectations Rommel maintained his offensive and by June 1942 he had successfully rolled back all the hard-won British gains in a repeat of his 1941 advances. Tobruk was recaptured on 21 June and a jubilant Hitler promoted Rommel to the rank of field marshal. Tobruk gave the German–Italian forces a much-needed forward port to ease their supply problems. The Panzerarmee Afrika was at the end of a very long supply chain and all military supplies, especially petrol for the panzers, were in short supply. The greatest problem was the regular sinking of supply convoys by the RAF and Royal Navy forces operating out of Malta. The island sat astride the main shipping routes from Italy to the key Axis ports of Tripoli and Benghazi in Libya and could also easily intercept shipping to Tobruk. Despite intensive bombing by the Luftwaffe based in Sicily, the island of Malta acted as an unsinkable Allied aircraft carrier. The tenacity of the entire population in refusing to surrender was recognised in April 1942 with the award of the George Cross. The problem was so great that Hitler had refused permission for any troop transports to cross the Mediterranean to reinforce Rommel's steadily shrinking army. Consequently, Mussolini and Hitler had agreed that once Tobruk had fallen Operation Hercules would be mounted to invade Malta to end the shipping losses and to ensure that the Panzerarmee Afrika was fully resupplied before advancing into Egypt to drive the Allies out of Africa. On the day Tobruk fell, Field Marshal Kesselring visited Rommel to confirm the standstill by the Panzerarmee Afrika and the arrangements for Operation Hercules. Rommel made a fateful decision. Buoyed-up by continual retreat of the Allied forces and the capture of extensive supply dumps in Tobruk, including 2,000 vehicles, 5,000 tons of food and 2,000 tons of petrol, Rommel argued for a hot pursuit into Egypt to deny the Allies time to regroup. Kesselring was unconvinced, but Rommel appealed over his head to Hitler and Mussolini and requested permission for a final push to Cairo with the promise of overall victory within three weeks. It was a dazzling prospect, and Rommel cleverly played upon Mussolini's vanity by offering him a victory parade through Cairo. Hitler was also receptive as he was harbouring doubts about the ability of the Italians to land troops on Malta, and it fitted in with his overall strategy for the German advance in the Caucasus to eventual link-up via Persia (Iran) with the Panzerarmee in the Middle East. Approval was granted and Rommel was promised the immediate shipment of 5,000 tons of petrol – his minimum estimate of the fuel required to take his panzers to Cairo. It was a significant gamble, but Rommel was convinced that the Allies were a spent force.

On the evening of 23 June the Panzerarmee Afrika crossed the border into Egypt. It was undefended, and within two days the Axis forces reached Mersa Matruh, over 100 miles deep inside Egypt. Auchinleck sacked the commander of the 8th Army, Lieutenant-General Neil Ritchie, and placed himself in direct command. A hastily constructed defensive line at Mersa Matruh was attacked on 26 June. Despite some initial reverses, Rommel was victorious and forced the 8th Army to fall back towards El Alamein on 28 June. Here a new Allied defensive line was established only 60 miles from the major port of Alexandria and 200 miles from Cairo. The swift advance confirmed Rommel's judgement that the 8th Army was prostrate, and an ebullient Mussolini arrived in North Africa complete with a white charger to lead the victory parade in Cairo.

Churchill was determined to hold the line, and on 4 August, three days after his arrival in Egypt, he sacked General Auchinleck and replaced him with General Sir Harold Rupert Alexander as commander-in-chief Middle East. He also elevated Lieutenant-General William Gott from commander 13th Corps to commander of the 8th Army. Gott's appointment was regarded as questionable following his decision to order a retreat at Mersa Matruh, but on 7 August, only 24 hours into his new command, Gott was killed when his transport plane was shot down by the Luftwaffe. Only the day before Churchill had flown the same route. His place was taken by the largely unknown Lieutenant-General Bernard Law Montgomery, but this was also not a popular appointment because Montgomery was widely regarded to be too abrasive and too difficult to work with. Churchill's response was: 'if he is disagreeable to those about him, he is also disagreeable to the enemy'.[2]

Churchill's order to his new commander-in-chief before he flew onward to Moscow on 11 August to confer with Stalin was brief and direct: 'your prime and main duty will be to take or destroy at the earliest opportunity the German–Italian army commanded by Field Marshal Rommel together with all its supplies and establishments in Egypt and Libya'.[3] In Moscow, Churchill received a hostile reception from Stalin when he explained that the US and British forces were not in a position to open an immediate second front in Europe. Stalin was anxious for a second front to relieve the intense German pressure on Stalingrad. However, Churchill did appease Stalin with news that a joint US–British landing, Operation Torch, was planned for the coast of Morocco in November 1942, and, coupled with an advance from Egypt by Montgomery, he promised to drive the Germans from North Africa. They parted on amicable terms and on 17 August Churchill retraced his route to Cairo and visited Montgomery at his headquarters at Burg el-Arab on the Egyptian coast. Churchill spoke to Montgomery at length and visited the front line to speak to the troops about the importance of the coming offensive. He also took a rare opportunity to swim in the Mediterranean, from a caravan Montgomery had placed on shore, before returning to London on 24 August. At the age of 74 he had flown 10,000 miles and crossed some of the most active fronts in the war, but he was not free from criticism. Prior to his journey, Churchill had been forced to defend his record in the House of Commons on 1 July and to answer a vote of no confidence. It reflected a thirst for victory in Britain after three years of defeat, and especially the reversals in the Far East and the fall of Tobruk. Churchill won the vote by 475 votes to 25, but the dissenters were increasing in number. In January 1942, following the loss of Malaya, Churchill had defeated a vote of no confidence by 464 votes to one. El Alamein was to provide his critics with a decisive answer.

Montgomery disagreed with Churchill's direction for action at the earliest opportunity. Churchill wanted a September offensive but Montgomery argued for more time to restore the morale of the battered 8th Army and to allow for in-depth training and the resupply of his forces. After some discussion with General Alexander the date for the Allied offensive was pushed back to 23 October when the new full moon would aid the sappers and the advance teams.

Rommel launched his final push for Cairo on 31 August against the El Alamein line in a three-pronged attack. He directed his main thrust south, intending to skirt the high ground of Alam Halfa (Hill 132 to the Germans) and to sweep behind the Allied positions, while largely diversionary attacks were made to the north and centre of the Allied lines. Unfortunately for Rommel, this was a weak point Montgomery had identified on his initial survey of the battlefield and the area had been reinforced only days before. Rommel's forces also hit extensive minefields and after losing the cover of a fierce dust storm his panzers came under heavy attack from the RAF. Rommel could not sustain a lengthy engagement because his panzers were critically short of petrol. He had counted upon a surgical strike rather than a prolonged battle. Out of the immediate 5,000 tons of petrol promised by Mussolini and Field-Marshal Kesselring to support his drive to Cairo, 2,600 tons had been lost at sea to Allied action and 1,400 tons were still in Italian ports awaiting shipment. Little made it to the front where it was needed because it had to be trucked 370 miles from Tobruk or 660 miles from Benghazi. Rommel was a victim of his own success because the further he advanced the longer his supply line became. The long supply lines attracted the attention of British special forces raised to harry the German and Italian supply columns and to attack supply dumps and airfields. The Long Range Desert Group (LRDG) was formed in 1940, with the more celebrated Special Air Service (SAS) being formed in 1941 to specialise in hit and run raids. It all combined to starve the Panzerarmee Afrika of resources, of which petrol was the most critical. To conserve his meagre supplies Rommel pulled back to the safety of his defensive positions and, instead of his promised drive to Cairo, his attack petered out after only six days. The Axis forces had no choice but to dig in and put their energy into building a defensive line and await the inevitable British attack. Mussolini, who had waited for three weeks in Libya to lead the victory parade, returned to Rome and took to his bed complaining of amoebic dysentery. One of his less than loyal ministers remarked: 'It is a less common-place disease. It's called humiliation.'[4] Rommel was more seriously ill with a flare-up of intestinal and circulation complaints and returned to Germany to convalesce on 23 September, leaving the Panzerarmee Afrika in the hands of General Georg Stumme. While in Berlin he was received by Hitler and presented with his field marshal's baton on 1 October.

Montgomery made meeting the officers and men of the 8th Army his first priority. Most were delighted to hear his plans at first hand, and he quickly gained respect for a general who lived at the front in a caravan and regularly visited their front-line positions; many, though, were dismissive of his school-boyish enthusiasm for the war with exhortations like 'hit the enemy for six out of Africa'. For the men facing death on a daily basis the war was far from a game of cricket. However, confidence and morale was raised by the inflow of new tanks, aircraft and guns to support the planned offensive. The US dividend appeared in the form of 300 Sherman tanks and 100 howitzers, and contributed to the development of an overwhelmingly superior force. Montgomery enjoyed a two to one superiority in men, tanks and artillery, and 530 RAF planes compared to 350 Axis planes. His supply line from the main port of Alexandria was also only 55 miles long and untroubled by any Axis commando activity in the rear. However, the impact of Allied commando raids was minor. On the night of 13–14 September three major raids by the LRDG and SAS against Benghazi, Barce and Tobruk were dismal failures. The Axis forces were alerted to the sabotage attacks by Axis agents who picked up full details of the planned operations from over-confident talk in Cairo's bars and clubs. The re-equipment and reinforcement of the 8th Army placed Montgomery in a commanding position and anything less than total victory would have been questionable. However, Montgomery faced tactical difficulties that had the potential to deny victory. The front line at El Alamein was only 37 miles long and bounded on the north by the sea and on the south by the impassable sinking sands of the Quattara Depression. This precluded any outflanking manoeuvres by Montgomery's armour and restricted the advance to a Great War-style frontal assault against prepared defensive positions. Rommel's highly experienced troops were well dug-in and had used their time to lay 445,000 mines in minefields up to 5 miles deep (nicknamed 'Devil's Gardens') to break up and channel the 8th Army into narrow corridors leading to concentrations of German armour and anti-tank guns located in concealed positions. It was a tactic that made the best use of Rommel's weaker force; he hoped to make the attack so costly for the 8th Army that Montgomery would break off the attack and give the Panzerarmee time to re-equip, and in particular to restore its supply of petrol.

Montgomery was aware of the risks and, although he could not surprise Rommel with an outflanking manoeuvre, he went to considerable lengths to conceal the disposition of the 8th Army and to keep Rommel uncertain as to the positions and likely directions of his main strike arm. This was achieved by moving only at night and by maintaining a balance across the front of tanks, trucks, guns and men to deny German reconnaissance any pointer to the coming offensive. The balance was an illusion because Montgomery created hundreds of dummy tanks, guns, ammunition dumps, fuel dumps and empty tents to disguise the true concentrations of his men and armour. Montgomery's plan was for the main weight of the attack to fall on the northern sector of the front in a two-stage attack. First, the 30th Corps was charged with clearing two major pathways through the minefields and, in Montgomery's terminology, to 'crumble' the German defenders by using their superior numbers of men to rotate and rest the Allied troops regularly and thereby maintain the momentum of the attack. Once the pathways across the minefields were secured, the 10th Armoured Corps was directed to pour through into the German rear and to engage and destroy the enemy armour. To reinforce German uncertainty for as long as possible Montgomery also planned for an attack in the southern sector by the 13th Corps. To maintain the illusion of a major force in the south dummy fuel pipes travelled across the desert to empty fuel tanks and, in the days preceding the attack, fake radio traffic was generated across the southern sector. A professional magician advised on how best to fool German reconnaissance. Montgomery warned his commanders to expect a twelve-day slogging match and to be prepared to take heavy initial losses.

At 9.40 p.m. on 23 October the appropriately named Operation Lightfoot to clear the minefields commenced. A line of 1,000 guns (only 908 were operational) opened fire along the front in a continuous deafening roar and rained shells down on the enemy positions while 30th Corps in the north and 13th Corps in the south advanced. A feint landing on the coast behind the Axis lines was also simultaneously launched to sow further confusion about the direction of the main Allied thrust. Some of the first Allied casualties were self-inflicted when some shells fell short and exploded among the advancing troops of 13th Corps in the south. The sappers of 30th Corps were aided by tanks fitted with rotating flails, known as 'Scorpions', to beat the ground to safely explode the mines, but most broke down when thick clouds of dust and sand enveloped their engine air intakes. It reduced the advance to a literal crawl as the sappers moved cautiously forward probing the ground with bayonets and marking a safe passage with white tape. Behind was a frustrated queue of tanks and trucks under fire, and although the first tanks cleared the minefields by 2 a.m. the majority remained marooned and unable to manoeuvre in the minefields. It had the potential for disaster, and at a hastily called conference of senior officers at 3.30 a.m. on 24 October there was some dissension and a request for a change of tactics from Major-General Gatehouse, the commander of the 10th Armoured Division. Montgomery refused to alter his plan and insisted that his tank commanders accept the losses. Later that same morning General Stumme, commanding the Panzerarmee in Rommel's absence, died from a heart attack when his car was caught up in an artillery barrage on the edge of the front line. Rommel returned to command on 25 October. He found a battle of attrition in progress and after a full week of close-quarter fighting it was becoming obvious that whereas the 8th Army could absorb the losses Rommel, with his slender resources, could not. His Achilles' heel was petrol. On 27 November a long-awaited convoy carrying petrol was sunk at the entrance to Tobruk harbour. Montgomery opted for a final knock-out blow against the steadily weakening Axis forces, codenamed Operation Supercharge, at the mid-point of the line at Tel el-Aqqaquir. At 1.05 a.m. on 2 November a barrage of shells from 800 guns punched a hole through the weakened Axis front line and tanks and infantry poured through the breach. There was fierce resistance that at one point threatened to arrest the advance. However, Montgomery informed the commander of the 9 Armoured Brigade, Brigadier John Currie, that he was prepared, if necessary, 'to accept 100% losses in his formation in order to achieve success'.[5] In the subsequent action Currie lost seventy-five out of his ninety-four tanks, but a full breakthrough was achieved and the 51st Highland Division and the 4th Indian Infantry Division poured into the Axis rear.

The end was sudden and complete. On 2 November Rommel was informed that his Panzer divisions had been reduced to thirty-five operational tanks out of a starting force of 489. In comparison, the Allies had started the battle with 1,029 tanks. Further resistance was impossible, and Rommel admitted defeat and ordered a full retreat back 60 miles to Fuka. The code-breakers at Bletchley Park intercepted his report to Hitler in Berlin and Churchill knew it was over before the troops on the ground. Hitler replied with a standfast 'victory or death' order, but it was pointless and after an appeal to Kesselring by Rommel the order was rescinded. During the night of 3–4 November the Axis troops abandoned hundreds of vehicles and many undamaged tanks for want of petrol and streamed back across the desert. Only twelve tanks and 4,000 troops made it back to Fuka. The Panzerarmee Afrika was not just defeated but vanquished. Any hope of future resurgence was ruled-out by the news on 8 November of Operation Torch and the commencement of US and British landings on the coast of Morocco. The liberation of North Africa was only a matter of time. El Alamein was the first major British and Allied victory of the war, and on 15 November 1942 the church bells rang out across Great Britain in celebration. (Churchill had delayed the celebration until he was certain that Operation Torch had been successful.) Churchill commented: 'before Alamein we never had a victory, while after Alamein we never had a defeat'.[6] The tide of war had turned.

References

1. Martin Gilbert, *Churchill: A Life*, Heinemann, 1992, p. 734.
2. Ibid., p. 726.
3. Ibid.
4. Christopher Hibbert, *Benito Mussolini: The Rise and Fall of Il Duce*, Penguin, 1986, p. 168.
5. Stephen Badsey (ed.), *World War Two Battle Plans*, Hutchinson, 2000, p. 109.
6. Ibid., p. 110.

22 Stalingrad

Not one more step backwards! . . . Panic mongers and cowards must be destroyed on the spot . . . three to five well armed detachments should be formed and placed directly behind unreliable divisions and they must be made to shoot the panic mongers and cowards on the spot . . .[1]

Military Order 227, issued by Stalin on 28 July 1942

On 16 July 1942 a fleet of sixteen Luftwaffe Ju-25 transport planes transported Hitler and his headquarters staff from the *Wolfsschanze* in East Prussia to a new forward military headquarters at Vinnista in the Ukraine, codenamed *Werwolf*. More comfortable log cabins replaced the austere concrete bunkers of *Wolfsschanze*, but Hitler was soon to complain that swarms of mosquitoes and the stifling summer heat made Vinnista unbearable. The relocation was to shorten the lines of communication between Hitler and his senior commanders as the Wehrmacht swept south-east towards Stalingrad and the oilfields of the Caucasus.

Hitler intended to direct personally every step of the new Wehrmacht summer offensive (codenamed Operation Blau or Blue), following the failure of Operation Barbarossa. To Hitler's undiluted rage, the Red Army had beaten the Wehrmacht to a standstill in December 1941 only 20 miles from Moscow and forced the Wehrmacht to bunker-down along a front line that stretched for 1,230 miles from Leningrad in the north to Rostov in the south. Throughout the long winter months of January–April 1942 the Wehrmacht had repelled regular Soviet attacks but otherwise remained stationary waiting not just for the spring thaw but for the summer when the steppes would be firm enough to renew the blitzkrieg east. The Wehrmacht that emerged from the trenches in spring 1942 was not the same confident army of 1941. By 1 March 1942 the Eastern Front had claimed some 1 million Germans. An estimated 202,257 soldiers had been killed, 225,642 wounded, 400,000 taken prisoner and 112,617 had been disabled by severe frostbite. The brutal nature of the fighting on the Eastern Front had filtered back to Germany in letters and photographs home and in the eyes and horrified reports of soldiers on leave. Photographs of the execution of Jews and ordinary Russians had been banned in August 1941, but many were still taken. By 1942 the Eastern Front was a byword for savagery, and later in the war, as the defeats mounted and the Red Army neared Germany, it was the fear of Soviet retribution that kept ordinary Germans fighting to the bitter end.

Hitler presented the details of Operation Blau to his senior commanders on 5 April in Directive 41. He no longer consulted, but issued orders that he expected to be obeyed. Operation Blau directed the full weight of the Wehrmacht south into the Caucasus, with a secondary advance in the far north, codenamed Operation Nordlicht (Northern Lights), to seize Leningrad. To fulfil the plan Army Group South was divided into two operational army groups, A and B, under the respective commands of Field Marshal Wilhelm List and Field Marshal von Bock. However, both were designed to act in concert as hammer and anvil. The first target was Voronezh on the river Don, to be followed by a sweep south to secure Rostov and forward into the Caucasus to seize the key strategic objective of the oilfields of Maikop and Grozny. To safeguard the flank of the southward advance, the Wehrmacht was directed to secure the steppe east to Stalingrad and the river Volga.

To the disappointment of the High Command or OKW (Oberkommando der Wehrmacht), Directive 41 was a return to Hitler's strategy of August 1941 rather than the OKW preference for an all-out drive to Moscow to destroy the command and control of Soviet forces. Hitler's target was the oilfields of the Caucasus, both to fuel Germany and to halt the Soviet Union. He therefore permitted no dialogue within the OKW and insisted upon blind faith in his military judgement. Operation Blau was entirely Hitler's conception and ultimately exploded the myth of his military genius.

In April, as Hitler was finalising his plans for Operation Blau, Stalin attempted to wrest the initiative away from the Wehrmacht by going on the offensive. The Red Army advanced along the Kerch peninsula in the Crimea, at Kharkov in central Russia, and in the far north along the Volkhov river to try to raise the siege of Leningrad. All three advances were spectacular failures. The clumsy Soviet tactics of mass frontal attacks and the scale of the Red Army defeats raised Hitler's optimism for a rapid overall victory. He delayed the start of Operation Blau to 28 June to give time to mop up the last Soviet resistance and to complete a series of anti-partisan sweeps to secure the Wehrmacht supply lines and rear.

The scale of the Wehrmacht advance caught Stalin off guard. He had ignored evidence of a build-up of German troops to the south and believed that Hitler was planning to renew his advance on Moscow. He therefore refused to release troops from the central front to reinforce the south. It took the fall of Voronezh on 12 July and the rapid disintegration of the Soviet front line to convince him to act. He corrected his mistake by forming the Stalingrad Front under the command of Marshal Timoshenko and Political Commissar Nikita Khrushchev, and ordered the 62nd and 64th armies under the command of General Vasily Chulkov to hold the German advance towards Stalingrad west of the Don. As the Red Army raced to intercept the German advance Hitler was becoming dangerously overconfident. He remarked to Chief of Staff Halder: 'The Russian is finished.'[2] He decided to speed the advance by setting Army Group A and Army Group B independent targets. Army Group A was ordered to advance south to seize Rostov, the gateway to the Caucasus, while Army Group B, composed of the 6th Army, 2nd Romanian Army, 8th Italian Army and the 3rd Romanian Army, was ordered to clear the steppe up to the river Don. When Field Marshal Bock recommended caution Hitler admonished him for having failed to close the encirclement of Voronezh. Bock was abruptly sacked and replaced by Colonel-General Freiherr Maximilian von Weichs.

The subsequent fall of Rostov on 23 July appeared to vindicate Hitler's judgement and led him to commit his greatest strategic blunder of the war. Hitler was convinced that army groups A and B were powerful enough to operate as independent forces and, impatient for victory, he ordered Army Group A south into the Caucasus and Army Group B east across the river Don to the river Volga and Stalingrad. It was a fateful decision. Army Group B lost the powerful armoured punch of the 1st and 4th Panzer armies that may have made the difference at Stalingrad. The formal division of Army Group South was confirmed by Hitler on 23 July as Directive 45, codenamed Braunschweig, and was irrevocable. Halder confided in his diary: 'This chronic tendency to underrate enemy capabilities is gradually assuming grotesque proportions and develops into a positive danger.'[3] Hitler's decision sharply reduced the striking power of both army groups and meant that neither possessed the reserves or the firepower to overcome any unexpected resistance.

At first the Wehrmacht made startling progress and there was chaos on the Soviet front line with officers and men openly abandoning their posts. To prevent a rout Stalin issued the draconian Order 227 (as quoted at the start of this chapter) which commanded *ne shagu Nazad* (not a step backwards), and authorised the summary execution of any retreating soldier or officer. Army Group B, under the overall command of General Weichs, cut through the scattered and disorganised ranks of the Soviet 62nd and 64th armies with ease and reached Kalach on the river Don, only 40 miles from Stalingrad, on 7 August. Army Group A was equally successful in advancing south into the Caucasus and reached the oilfields of Maikop on 9 August. The Red Army fell back to the city of Stalingrad in disarray leaving many thousands encircled and trapped against the river Don. General von Paulus, the commander of the 6th Army, the fighting core of Army Group B, predicted victory within weeks. At *Werwolf* on 9 August Hitler addressed his dinner guests in triumphant mood and revelled at the prospect of Soviet resources enriching Germany: 'Timber we shall have in abundance, iron in limitless quantity, the greatest manganese ore mines in the world, oil – we shall swim in it! . . . in a hundred years' time there will be millions of German peasants living here.'[4] At Stalingrad the entire population was mobilised, as they had been in Leningrad and Moscow, to dig anti-tank ditches and trenches. Trainloads of reinforcements poured in with orders to defend the city to the last. To ensure full resistance, and to fulfil Order 227, detachments of NKVD (Narodny Komissariat Vnutrennykh Del) – internal security troops – guarded the east bank of the Volga and executed anyone who attempted to cross the river and leave the city.

On 21 August the Wehrmacht panzer spearheads poured across the Don on pontoon bridges. It had taken two weeks to destroy the Soviet forces trapped in the Don Pocket, but now the panzers raced the short distance towards Stalingrad virtually unopposed. They approached the city in pincer formation with the 6th Army under the command of General von Paulus attacking from the north and the 4th Panzer Army under the command of General Hoth from the south. The flanks of the long extended advance were largely lined and guarded by Romanian, Hungarian and Italian troops. Both panzer columns encountered only minor resistance, and at 11.30 p.m. on 22 August the 79th Panzer Grenadiers reached the Volga at Spartanovka on the northern outskirts of Stalingrad. The city sprawled along the river for some 20 miles and enjoyed a reputation as a garden city with parkland and terraces sweeping down to the broad Volga, full of trees, fruit orchards, grape vines, tomatoes and melon fields. At dawn on 23 August the panzer crews breakfasted as the Luftwaffe 4th Air Fleet with 1,200 aircraft at its disposal and almost total air superiority reduced the city to a wasteland of mud and rubble. On 24 August the panzers probed the outer defences of the city with an expectation that the defenders would abandon the burning city and flee across the Volga – but they encountered fierce resistance. Hoth halted the advance and closed his panzers and artillery into a hedgehog defensive formation until the slower moving infantry had caught up. Overhead the Luftwaffe relentlessly bombed the city and by the end of the first week an estimated 40,000 people had been killed: the same number who died in the entire ten months of the British Blitz of 1940–41. The nature of the battle ahead was underlined by the Regional Communist Party Committee on 25 August with the direction to the population: 'Let us defend every street; transform every district, every block, every house into an impregnable fortress.'[5] It was a battle that favoured the stubborn defender and was contrary to the Wehrmacht blitzkrieg strategy that directed that all enemy cities and strongpoints should be bypassed in favour of wide territorial sweeps to occupy and hold the land. Hitler had endorsed this strategy in relation to the advances on Leningrad and Moscow but, to the dismay of the Wehrmacht, he now insisted that Stalingrad was to be taken. Hitler mistakenly elevated the capture of this single city into a strategic goal. It was a gross mistake against an enemy that thought nothing of forcing thousands of convicts in penal companies to protect tanks by walking in advance across minefields. The Red Army's greatest resource was its unlimited manpower, and Stalin was prepared to trade hundreds of thousands of lives for victory. The Wehrmacht, with its slender manpower and material resources, could ill afford to enter into a battle of attrition.

On 13 September the 6th Army stormed the city in a co-ordinated north–south attack. They expected to crush the defenders within days, but they discovered that the major ruins had taken on the role of fortresses. Each one was fiercely defended and the Wehrmacht was forced into hand-to-hand combat. The 'fortress' ruins from north to south were the Dzerzhinsky tractor factory (converted to produce T-34 tanks), the Barrikady armaments factory, the Red October steel plant, the hilltop park and cemetery of Mamayev which dominated the Volga, the main railway station, the Univermag department store, the main Volga landing stage and the massive reinforced concrete grain elevator. Of these the key strategic targets for the Wehrmacht were the Mamayev Hill and the landing stage to cut off all supplies and reinforcements from the east bank of the Volga. General Chuikov organised his troops into 'storm groups' of 10–12 men and directed them to fight and hold every building in the Germans' path. The Wehrmacht measured progress room by room, building by building and street by street because the Soviet soldiers, fearful of execution by the NKVD if they retreated, fought to the last. The 6th Army referred to it as *Rattenkreig* (rat war) as the storm groups used the sewers to outflank the Wehrmacht and to reoccupy buildings previously cleared. The main railway station changed hands fifteen times over three days before it was secured by the Germans with the aid of a concentrated Stuka attack. The close-quarter fighting caused very high casualty rates on both sides. To hold the line, Chuikov committed the 10,000-strong Soviet 13th Guards Rifle Division to the battle on 14 September. Over 1,000 men were lost crossing the Volga alone, and by 19 September the division was reduced to only 2,500 men. Only 320 were to survive the battle. The heavy concentration of troops made an ideal hunting ground for snipers, and the Red Army deployed a clutch of extraordinary snipers to target German officers to disrupt command and control. The most famous sniper was Vasily Ivanovich Zaitsev, a shepherd from the Urals, who perfected the art of lying motionless for hours until a German officer wandered into his gun-sights. Zaitsev was credited with 149 kills and was selected by Red Army propagandists to be feted as a hero in a 'Stakhanovite' morale-raising campaign. However, eight other highly skilled Soviet snipers were equally active in the Stalingrad ruins and among them one identified only as Zikan claimed 224 kills. Gradually the superior firepower of the Wehrmacht pushed the defenders out of the city centre and left the Red Army holding only the northern industrial zone around the tractor factory and the Barrikady armaments factory. On 25 September, in an attempt to raise morale, Paulus declared victory and ordered the swastika to be flown above the Univermag department store in the city centre.

At *Werwolf* there was no celebration. Hitler's earlier confidence in an overall victory had all but evaporated as a second Russian winter approached with none of his targets for the Eastern Front realised. In the north Operation Nordlicht to seize Leningrad had been repulsed by a Soviet counter-offensive, and at Sukhinichi an advance by Army Group Centre to threaten Moscow had equally failed with heavy losses. The key strategic goal of securing the oil of the Caucasus had also failed. Although Maikop had fallen the oil wells had been expertly destroyed by Soviet engineers, and the entire advance by Army Group A had stalled when the panzers lost their manoeuvrability and speed in the high mountains of the central Caucasus. The first sign of Hitler's brooding anxiety burst into the open on 21 August when news reached him of the 'success' of German mountain troops planting a swastika on the summit of Mount Elbrus, the highest peak in the Caucasus mountains. Hitler exploded into an uncontrolled rage and essentially condemned the action as a frivolous distraction and a theatrical success at a time when Army Group A had yet to achieve its military goals. Days later, on 24 August, his anger erupted more forcibly when Halder suggested a minor withdrawal to consolidate the front line. In front of junior officers Hitler admonished Halder for defeatism. On 7 September Hitler's fury was renewed and unbounded when General Jodl returned from a mission to the Caucasus to investigate the stalled advance and defended List and his command of Army Group A. When Hitler pointed out the lack of success, Jodl angrily remonstrated that List was merely obeying Hitler's direct orders. Hitler broke off the argument and withdrew to his room where he ate alone for several days and refused to speak to anyone. He suspended his daily military conferences until stenographers arrived from Berlin to record his every word. The row was the final break between Hitler and the OKW. Hitler's spell was broken and within the senior ranks of the Wehrmacht the mounting disillusionment with Hitler's leadership resulted in two assassination attempts in March 1943.

Hitler ignored Jodl's report and sacked List on 8 September, taking over personal command of Army Group A. After casting around for a suitable replacement for Halder he finally settled on the virtually unknown Major-General Kurt Zeitzler and promptly sacked Halder on 24 September.

A victory was urgently needed as nightly RAF bomb attacks, defeat in North Africa and setbacks on the Eastern Front combined to shake German confidence. Hitler settled on Stalingrad and at the Sportpalast in Berlin on 30 September he publicly promised the German people victory, stating: 'you can be sure that nobody will get us away from this place again'.[6] His public commitment locked the Wehrmacht into delivering nothing less than victory at Stalingrad at a time when the OKW was tentatively recommending a strategic withdrawal. Paulus had lost 10 per cent of the 250,000 strong 6th Army with no hope of replacements, whereas Chuikov, despite losses of 80,000 men in September, had gained full replacements. On 3 October Paulus advanced on the industrial district of Stalingrad to fulfil Hitler's victory pledge. He encountered fierce resistance but forced the Red Army back into a narrow strip against the Volga, in places only 1,000 yards deep. The final push for victory focused on the Red October and Barrikady works on 14 October. The *Rattenkreig* was remorselessly renewed in the endless dark corridors, machine halls and workshops of the large factory complex and resulted in heavy casualties on both sides. The Soviet defenders lost 13,000 dead in three days of intense close-quarter fighting. The Germans controlled nine-tenths of the city, and at best the Red Army held a one-mile stretch of the Volga river bank. However, every night a succession of tiny boats transferred fresh troops and supplies across the Volga to maintain the Russian presence in Stalingrad. Nothing could dislodge them. As the battle ground on into November Hitler rejected a suggestion from Ribbentrop to seek peace talks with Stalin, and in a defiant speech to the annual party rally in Munich on 7 November he stated that whereas the kaiser in the Great War had capitulated at a quarter to twelve, his resolve was 'always at five past twelve'.[7] Hitler reassured himself and the OKW that although the 6th Army was enduring high losses the determination of Stalin to hold Stalingrad meant that the whole Red Army was slowly being delivered into the gunsights of the Wehrmacht to be steadily annihilated. He therefore ignored reports of the movement of Red Army troops along the flanks of the Wehrmacht supply corridor to Stalingrad. He refused to believe that the Red Army could sustain such heavy losses in Stalingrad and retain sufficient troops to threaten the Wehrmacht rear. Yet this was precisely the Soviet plan.

As early as 12 September Marshal Zhukov and General Aleksandr Vasilevsky had suggested to Stalin an imaginative plan for a pincer attack to cut off and encircle the 6th Army at Stalingrad. The next night Stalin approved a broad outline plan, code-named Operation Uranus. In conditions of top secrecy a force of over a million men, 13,541 guns, 894 tanks and 1,115 aircraft were readied for a simultaneous counter-offensive against the Axis northern and southern flanks.

At 7.20 a.m. on 19 November the Red Army broke the Romanian line at Kletskaya and Bolshoy 100 miles to the north of Stalingrad, using the German blitzkreig tactic of mass tank spearheads. The next morning, the second arm of the Soviet offensive smashed through the Romanian line south of Stalingrad. Within only three days the two Soviet armoured columns joined up at Kalach on the river Don where in August the Wehrmacht had enjoyed a crushing victory over the Red Army. The 6th Army was trapped and encircled in a pocket measuring approximately 20 miles by 35 miles, but in response to Paulus's immediate request to break out from Stalingrad Hitler issued a *Führerbefehl*, an irrevocable decree that ordered them to stand firm and await relief. He gratefully accepted Göring's assurance that the Luftwaffe could keep the 6th Army supplied by air because it avoided any admittance of defeat. It was an entirely unrealistic proposition. The estimated daily needs of the 6th Army were 700 tons of food, fuel and ammunition, but Göring cut this to 500 tons and, given the harsh winter weather and Soviet successes in shooting down the slow Ju-52 transports, the daily average dropped to 97 tons. The result was a progressive reduction in rations and the onset of starvation in the *der Kessel*, or cauldron, as Stalingrad was known to the beleaguered 6th Army. Hitler preferred the term *Festung Stalingrad*, or fortress Stalingrad, and formed all available reserves into Army Group Don under the command of Field Marshal Manstein with orders to break the Soviet encirclement. Manstein prepared a counter-attack, codenamed Winter Storm, but he only commanded fifty panzers and the transfer of the 6th Panzer Army from France added only a further 160 tanks. In contrast Zhukov had over 800 tanks at his disposal and had flung a formidable ring of 1,000 anti-tank guns around Stalingrad. Winter Storm commenced on 12 December and advanced 50 miles in eight days, but ground to a halt on 21 December 30 miles from Stalingrad. Manstein had urged Paulus to break out, but Paulus had few illusions. He was aware that most of his men were too weak from hunger to leave their dugouts and trenches and embark upon a fighting retreat of over 30 miles in deep snow and in temperatures that fell 20°C below zero in the daytime and often double that at night. He believed that the best prospect of survival for the 6th Army was to hold their ground and await relief. Many German soldiers, unable to face the cold and hunger any longer, stood on the parapets to receive a bullet. The dead were stacked up in long piles like logs of wood because the ground was too frozen to dig graves, and the living were plagued by ravenous armies of lice, rats and mice. The starving soldiers cracked open the skulls of long-dead horses to extract brain tissue and sucked marrow from their thigh bones in desperate attempts to sustain life. On Christmas Day the men of the 6th Army clustered around makeshift Christmas trees and drank a small measure of reserved rum. Those who had access to a radio were surprised to hear the broadcast of a Christmas message to the people of Germany from the soldiers of Stalingrad. It was a propaganda broadcast orchestrated by Goebbels in an attempt to preserve an air of normality, because the German people were kept ignorant of the desperate plight of the 6th Army. It was not until 16 January that Hitler permitted Goebbels to prepare the German people for the defeat by announcing news of the encirclement.

Paulus rejected a formal invitation to surrender from the Red Army on 9 January and the next day Zhukov launched Operation Koltso (ring) to crush the 6th Army, commencing with an opening bombardment from 7,000 guns. Paulus, aware that defeat was inevitable, despatched Captain Winrich Behr as a personal emissary to Hitler on 12 January to request permission to surrender. Behr gave Hitler the unvarnished truth, to the point that Field Marshall Keitel tried to silence him, but Hitler was unmoved. His campaign map showed a greater danger. The 6th Army was blocking the Red Army from sweeping south to cut-off Army Group A in the Caucasus and every day the 6th Army survived bought more time to withdraw Army Group A to a more defensible front line. Behr was spiritually broken by the encounter as his commander-in-chief airily dismissed the hardship and sacrifice of the 6th Army and spoke of the formation of a new panzer army to relieve Stalingrad. It was the first of many phantom armies that Hitler would conjure up in the months and years ahead. By 14 January the 6th Army had lost control of its main supply airfield at Pitomnik. Here there were pitiful scenes as the wounded, lying in tents and out in the open without hope of treatment, clung to the wings and wheels of the last departing planes and fell to their deaths. Similar scenes were repeated on 22 January when the tiny headquarters airstrip at Gumrak was also overrun. Paulus relocated his headquarters to the basement of the ruined Univermag department store in the centre of Stalingrad.

At Leningrad the Wehrmacht suffered a further reversal when on 13 January 1943 the Red Army launched Operation Iskra (Spark) and, after five days of fighting, largely against the volunteer Spanish Blue Division, broke the siege of Leningrad south of Lake Lagoda. Only a narrow 10-mile corridor was secured, but it was sufficient to end the 900-day siege. A minimum of 632,253 people, and perhaps as many as 1.1 million, had died during the siege from the daily shelling, starvation and hypothermia during the long winter months. There had been no distinction between civilians and soldiers. All were on the front line and their courage was one of the greatest feats of endurance of the entire war.

On 30 January 1943 Hitler issued a brief but defiant statement to mark his tenth anniversary in power, but across Germany most knew that the days of endless advances were over. The next day he confirmed the promotion of Paulus to the rank of field marshal – an unmistakable signal that he was expected to die a glorious death at the head of his troops. However, at 7.35 a.m. on 31 January 1943, with all German resistance broken, Lieutenant Fyodor Ilchenko cautiously descended into the Univermag basement and accepted the surrender of the 6th Army from a prematurely aged and stooped Field Marshal Paulus. As German radio alerted the public to the defeat by playing Siegfried's Funeral March from Wagner's *Götterdämmerung*, Hitler was openly outraged by Paulus's rejection of a Wagnerian last stand. He condemned Paulus for failure and stated: 'the heroism of so many soldiers is nullified by one single characterless weakling'.[8] In the northern half of the city the 11th Army Corps under the command of General Strecker continued to fight on within the bowels of the tractor plant, but at 4 a.m. on 2 February he too disappointed Hitler and chose to surrender rather than fight to the last round. The Red Army took 91,000 German prisoners, including twenty-two generals and Paulus – the first ever German field marshal to be captured in battle. The entire 6th Army had been destroyed and Operation Blau had cost some 500,000 men for no gain.

Goebbels announced three days of national mourning. At Stalingrad the ordeal was not over because the Red Army, with no facilities to treat so many German wounded, simply shot them where they lay and forced the able bodied to march 20–30 miles to hastily constructed POW camps. Thousands died en route from hunger, exertion and exposure from sleeping out in the open during the harsh winter nights. Once at the camps over 50,000 of the survivors died within three months from hard labour and the lack of any nourishing food. In his memoirs Khrushchev recalled that the ground was too frozen to bury the German dead: 'we gathered thousands of corpses and stacked them in layers alternating with layers of railway ties. Then we set these huge piles on fire.'[9] Ten years after the end of the war, in 1955, the Soviet Union released the last survivors of Stalingrad from captivity. Out of an original 6th Army of approximately 250,000 men only 2,000 ever made it back to Germany. Paulus, who had been treated well in Moscow from 1943–45 and after the war in East Germany, died in Dresden in 1957.

The surviving population of Stalingrad reclaimed the city, but out of a pre-war population of 500,000 only 1,500 were left. Their heroism, and the heroism of the Red Army, was proclaimed by King George VI who commissioned the Sword of Stalingrad to be forged and presented to Stalin by Churchill at Tehran in November 1943. The defeat marked the ascendancy of the Red Army and the end of German optimism for final victory.

References

1. Dmitri Volkogonov, *Stalin: Triumph and Tragedy*, Weidenfeld and Nicolson, 1991, p. 460.
2. Edwin P. Hoyt, *199 Days: The Battle for Stalingrad*, Robson Books, 1993, p. 98.
3. Ian Kershaw, *Hitler 1936–45: Nemesis*, Penguin, 2000, p. 529.
4. Hugh Trevor-Roper, *Hitler's Table Talk 1941–44*, Phoenix, 2000, p. 624.
5. Edwin P. Hoyt, *199 Days: The Battle for Stalingrad*, Robson Books, 1993, p. 134.
6. Ian Kershaw, *Hitler 1936–45: Nemesis*, Penguin, 2000, p. 536.
7. Ibid., p. 540.
8. Antony Beevor, *Stalingrad*, Penguin, 1998, p. 392.
9. Nikita Khrushchev, *Khrushchev Remembers* (trans. Strobe Talbot), Sphere, 1971, p. 176.

Contraction

23 Clearance of North Africa

> All enemy resistance has ceased: we are masters of the North African shores.[1]
> Signal to Churchill from General Alexander,
> 13 May 1943

At dawn on 8 November 1942, only four days after the British victory at El Alamein in Egypt, the first US army to enter combat in the western theatre landed on the shores of Morocco in an operation codenamed Torch. The combined invasion force of approximately 107,000 US and British troops was designated the Allied 1st Army and was placed under the overall command of US Lieutenant-General Dwight D. Eisenhower. The landings had been conceived prior to the British victory at El Alamein, when victory in North Africa was in the balance and Churchill feared the German seizure of Cairo and Suez. The strategy was for an east–west pincer attack from Morocco and Egypt, respectively, to drive the Axis forces out of North Africa. President Roosevelt supported the landings against the advice of his chief of staff General George Catlett Marshall. Marshall's preference was for a focus on the war against Japan, and he also questioned the strategy of landing in Africa. He feared becoming bogged down in a protracted fight against the dragon's tail in the Mediterranean as opposed to chopping off the dragon's head by a direct line of attack across the Channel into Germany and Berlin. Marshall proposed Operation Sledgehammer: a plan to open a second front in Europe in two stages. First, landings in France at the Pas de Calais in September 1942, or along the Contentin Peninsula, followed by a full-scale invasion and drive to Berlin named Operation Round-up. Churchill's strategic priority at the time was to safeguard Suez to protect oil supplies and links with the Far East; consequently, he was never more than lukewarm towards Sledgehammer and Round-up. The planning for Torch was protracted because the Allied staff disagreed on every aspect of the plan from the date of the invasion to the number and location of the landing sites. The Americans had at first opposed any landings inside the Mediterranean in favour of the Atlantic coast of Morocco for fear of sustaining heavy losses from attacks by Axis U-boats and air power operating out of Sicily. The extent of the US caution dismayed the British staff because the Atlantic coast was a thousand miles away from the major military objective of occupying Tunisia and bringing the Allies into striking range of Libya and the main Axis supply port of Tripoli. It was not until 5 September that both military staffs finally reached agreement on three major landing sites: Casablanca and Oran in Morocco and Algiers in Algeria. Roosevelt cabled Churchill with relief at the news of the agreed campaign strategy with the single word, 'Hurrah'. However, the compromise agreement still excluded landings in Tunisia because it was beyond the effective range of Allied air cover. It proved to be a costly omission because it gave the Germans time to convert Tunisia into a fortress, and instead of the expected swift entry into Libya the Allies were forced into an unexpected and protracted battle for Tunisia.

On 4 November, to Churchill's relief, the British 8th Army routed Rommel's forces at El Alamein and forced Rommel into a continuous retreat along the Libyan coast. His only strategy was to maintain a fighting retreat back to Tripoli with hope of eventual resupply and to avoid encirclement by the superior 8th Army. The Torch landings in Morocco and Algeria four days later compounded Rommel's defeat by forcing the Germans to contain this new front in the battle for North Africa. The Allied invasion fleet had crossed the Atlantic without loss, despite Hitler's frequent boast that his U-boat fleet would deny the US army passage across the Atlantic.

Total surprise was achieved, but when the landing craft approached the shores of Morocco and Algeria all three landings were fired upon by the French Army and Navy. It was a battle Roosevelt and Churchill had hoped to avoid, but after the fall of France in June 1940 the commander-in-chief of all French forces in North Africa, Admiral Darlan, had declared his loyalty to the pro-Nazi regime of Marshal Petain and Vichy France against the entreaties of General de Gaulle and Churchill to join the Allies. However, with the tide of war moving sharply against the Axis powers most of the French general staff in North Africa were prepared to switch sides. To encourage their co-operation the British involvement in Torch was downplayed: de Gaulle was given no role in the operation and Churchill even offered to dress the British troops involved in the landings in US uniforms.

In Morocco, General Bethouart declared for the Allies but the French commander-in-chief of Morocco, General Nogues, believed that the Allies were only launching a commando raid, and he ordered the arrest of Bethouart and ordered French forces in Morocco to open fire. The confusion of orders permitted most of the US troops to land safely but thereafter they were pinned down on the beaches by highly effective French fire. General Patton established his reputation as a decisive military leader when he strode along the beach, with pearl-handled revolvers on his hips, and ordered his inexperienced troops to storm the French positions. The greatest threat to the invasion fleet was posed by a squadron of one French cruiser and seven destroyers, but in a series of exchanges four of the French ships were sunk and the four others were severely damaged by superior US naval firepower. At Oran, in Algeria, the French repulsed an attempt by 400 US troops to land directly in the harbour from HMS *Walney* and *Hartland* and killed or captured the entire force, disabling both ships. However, major landings to the east and west of Oran achieved surprise and by 9 a.m. armoured columns were moving inland to surround the port from well-established beachheads.

At Algiers, General Mast declared for the Allies and was promptly arrested. Admiral Darlan, supported by Marshal Petain in France, insisted upon full resistance to the Allied invasion. What followed was a French farce as Darlan and Petain maintained the haughty manners of a French power that no longer existed, and for days debated their terms for French co-operation while on the ground French and Allied soldiers died fighting each other in a pointless conflict. The debate was ended by Hitler who authorised the invasion of Vichy France on 11 November to secure the southern coast of France against any Allied landings. Petain was outraged by his ally's action and the loss of French sovereignty, and promptly agreed to support the Allies. In North Africa, confusion reigned supreme as Darlan and his general staff jockeyed for position and advantage in the changing political landscape, while de Gaulle in London insisted that all should accept his leadership. On 13 November, after two days of cease-fire orders issued and rescinded, an exasperated US general, Clark, threatened to arrest and lock-up the entire French leadership in North Africa unless they gave a clear commitment to the Allied cause. The threat worked. Darlan declared for the Allies and was permitted to remain in command of French forces to ensure their co-operation. However, he was unable to persuade Admiral de Laboude, in command of the powerful French Mediterranean fleet based in Toulon, to sail for Oran and join the Allies. Laboude was equally determined not to allow his ships to fall into the hands of the Germans and when the SS stormed the harbour on 27 November he ordered the entire fleet to be scuttled at anchor. His action fulfilled a pledge given to Churchill in 1940 that the French fleet would never be used against the Royal Navy, but his actions also denied the fleet to the Allies and hindered rather than assisted the Allied cause. News of Darlan's continuation in command provoked strong public protests in Great Britain and the United States because he was widely vilified in the press as a Nazi collaborator, with direct responsibility for the deaths of hundreds of Allied troops. The uneasy relationship ended on Christmas Eve 1942 when a French student opposed to Vichy France shot Darlan dead on the steps of his headquarters.

With the transfer of the French Army in North Africa to the Allied side Churchill and Roosevelt expected victory by Christmas. Instead the battle for North Africa dragged on for six months to May 1943, because the delays imposed by the French forces had given the highly experienced Wehrmacht time to establish strong defensive positions in the mountainous terrain of Tunisia. Hitler insisted that Tunisia be held to buy time to defeat the Red Army on the Eastern Front before turning west to confront the Allied challenge. Field Marshal Kesselring had correctly anticipated Hitler's strategy and built up a reserve of troops and military stores in southern Italy ready to counter any Allied action in the Mediterranean. Within hours of the Allied landings in North Africa Kesselring had ordered an airlift and the shipment of 18,000 German troops, 159 panzers and 127 guns to Tunisia. Kesselring appointed Major-General Nehring to command Axis forces in Tunisia with orders to prepare an impregnable defensive line, while Rommel and the remnants of the Panzerarmee Afrika were ordered to delay the westward advance of Montgomery and the British 8th Army as long as possible. However, after their decisive defeat at El Alamein on 4 November, Rommel and the Panzerarmee Afrika were a broken force. In his regular letters home Rommel despaired of a German victory and believed that the war was lost. With only 36 panzers, and limited fuel and ammunition, Rommel had lost his capacity for offensive action. His strategy amounted to avoiding encirclement and to fighting an ordered retreat back along the Libyan coast to link up with the new Axis army forming in Tunisia.

The Allies closed on Tunisia from Algiers under the overall command of Lieutenant-General Sir Kenneth Anderson. The immediate problem was the existence of only two roads and one railroad track to support an advance of approximately 550 miles across Algeria to the Tunisian border. To speed the advance, the Royal Navy successfully lifted the 36th Brigade 120 miles along the coast to Bougie on 11 November. The next day a parachute drop by the British 1st Parachute Brigade permitted a further hop to Bone on the border with Tunisia to secure the airfield, while a commando force secured the harbour. The major opposition was delivered by Luftwaffe air strikes, but the Allies successfully advanced from Bone along the coast road and, on 16 November, crossed the border into Tunisia and captured the tiny port of Tabarka.

Inland, the 11th Infantry Brigade and the armoured Blade Force moved in parallel to the coastal advance and also crossed the Tunisian border on 16 November at Souk el-Arba. The key objective of the port of Tunis was only 80 miles distant and, unknown to the Allies, only a minor force of 3,000 German troops barred their path. Anderson chose to pause to allow time for his scattered forces to regroup and to build his supply dumps, but by the time he resumed his advance on 25 November the German strength had trebled following the arrival in the line of Kesselring's reinforcements from Italy. An opportunity for an early victory was unwittingly missed.

On the same day, Rommel and the Panzerarmee Afrika prepared to make a stand against Montgomery's pursuing 8th Army at Mersa Brega and nearby El Agheila, the gateway to Tripolitania. His tiny force was dwarfed by the 8th Army, but both Mussolini and Hitler expected him to hold the line to protect the capital of Italian Libya, Tripoli. Rommel requested an additional fifty panzers and reacted with fury when Kesselring refused and directed all reinforcements to Tunisia. On 28 November Rommel flew to the *Wolfsschanze* to appeal directly to Hitler, but his star had fallen. Rommel made the mistake of advising Hitler to abandon North Africa and was treated to a diatribe on the importance of holding the Allied advance. Far from regaining some command authority, Rommel was ordered to act in accordance with orders from Kesselring and Mussolini. The trusted relationship was broken and left Rommel disenchanted with Hitler's leadership. On his return via Rome, Rommel obtained a more flexible response from Mussolini and gained permission to resume his retreat if his position became untenable. On 13 December Rommel activated this escape clause when his forward defence line at Mersa Brega was broken by a heavy British artillery bombardment, and on 14 December he also abandoned El Agheila when an armoured column threatened to outflank his position. Rommel fell back to Buerat and the final approaches to Tripoli.

In Tunisia, Anderson's offensive was slow and cautious and bold German counter-attacks, coupled with concentrated Stuka strikes, reduced the advance to a crawl. Kesselring, in a personal visit to the battlefield on 1 December, ordered a successful block to the Allied advance by the first battlefield deployment of the heavily armoured 56-ton Tiger tank armed with an 88 mm gun. The Tiger could stand out of range of Allied tank fire and destroy Allied tanks with impunity with armour-piercing rounds. A further counter-attack on 10 December pushed the Allies into a disorganised, confused retreat. Eisenhower, who was visiting the front line at the same time, privately despaired of the poor military judgement and clumsy tactics of his inexperienced American commanders.

The success encouraged Hitler to believe that he could reverse his fortunes. A victory in North Africa was attractive as a distraction for the German people from the disastrous encirclement of the 6th Army at Stalingrad and to buy time for a counter-offensive on the Eastern Front. The Axis command structure for Africa was reviewed at the *Wolfsschanze* between 18 and 22 December by Hitler and Kesselring, with Italian representation. The Italian High Command under Mussolini, the *Comando Supremo*, was in theory given leadership over all campaign decisions in North Africa in recognition that it was primarily an area of Italian interest. However, the real authority was vested in Colonel-General Jurgen von Arnim who replaced Nehring as the commander of all Axis forces in Tunisia. Thousands more German troops were poured into Tunisia to reinforce the line. Mussolini offered little practical leadership because he was frequently ill and confined to bed for days at a time. The diagnosis of severe duodenal ulcers reduced his diet to rice and milk, but unconfirmed rumours circulated that he was suffering from the ravages of syphilis following an uninhibited youth. When Mussolini did appear in public or before the *Comando Supremo* it was to recite vague, rambling exhortations for victory and, in his darker moments, to berate the Italian people for being insufficiently warlike and unworthy of his leadership.

Anderson regrouped his forces for a second offensive, to commence on Christmas Eve 1942, but it was postponed because heavy rain resulted in thick clawing mud and prevented movement. However, an Allied victory was never in doubt, given the overwhelming superiority of the Allied forces and the slow but certain closure of the Axis sea and air supply corridor from Sicily.

At Casablanca between 14 and 23 January 1943, Roosevelt and Churchill met with their senior military commanders to end the strategic disagreements that preceded Torch and to agree a future military strategy. Stalin was invited but did not attend, given the demands of the battle for Stalingrad. De Gaulle did attend but studiously ignored his political and military rival General Giraud who was in command of French forces in North Africa. Roosevelt privately denounced de Gaulle as insufferably arrogant and much preferred to deal with Giraud, but Churchill advised Allied support for de Gaulle as the man most likely to carry the widest French support. After days of discussions, Churchill's preferred military strategy was adopted: first, the defeat of Italy; second, Nazi Germany; third, Japan – and in all three cases there was to be no negotiations but a demand for unconditional surrender. This unity of purpose and strategy was never attained by the Axis powers and was a key factor behind their eventual defeat.

The first clear sign of the impending Axis defeat was the fall of Tripoli on 23 January 1943 to the 8th Army. Tripoli had been the administrative centre of the Italian North African empire from 1912 and its loss signalled the end of Italian imperial power and placed Mussolini's leadership under an uncomfortable spotlight. Mussolini railed against Rommel for abandoning the city without a fight, but Rommel saw little point in fighting a battle he could not win and expected his Panzerarmee to be re-equipped in Tunisia. His hope for a major command role in Tunisia was ended on 26 January 1943 when he received an order from Hitler to resume his sick leave (Rommel had returned to Egypt from sick leave in October 1942 to deal with the crisis at El Alamein), and for his Panzerarmee to absorbed into the 1st Italian Army commanded by General Giovanni Messe. It was a bitter blow for the general most associated with Axis victory in North Africa, but he had made the mistake of alienating Kesselring by regularly questioning his orders and strategy.

The battle for Tunisia resumed in earnest in early February 1943, when the port of Tripoli was successfully repaired and cleared of mines. The first Allied convoy docked on 9 February and permitted the full resupply of the 8th Army as it closed on the border of Tunisia and prepared to assault the Axis defensive line at Mareth. In the north-west the Allies pushed the Axis forces back towards the Tunisian coast and the major ports of Birzerta and Tunis, while the Royal Navy patrolled the coast to ensure there was no escape by sea. The terrain of northern Tunisia favoured the Axis defenders and delayed their defeat, because high mountains punctuated by narrow passes channelled the Allied forces into long columns and forced a pitched battle for every defile. The inexperienced US troops regularly broke under attack and could not match the accuracy under fire of the battle-hardened German tank and anti-tank gunners. It was an ideal situation for an experienced commander like Rommel. He directed an unexpected and powerful blow against the Allied forces at the Kassarine

Pass between 20 and 25 February. The US 1st Armoured Division was smashed, with the loss of 183 tanks, and the American troops fled in panic and abandoned hundreds of guns, jeeps and trucks. However, Rommel had insufficient panzers to sustain his planned advance on the main Allied supply dump at Tebessa and from there to drive to the coast at Bone encircling the Allied forces in Tunisia. A confusion of orders and strategies between the *Comando Supremo*, von Arnim, Messe and Kesselring contributed to the failure to reinforce and exploit his initial success. However, the victory did restore his battered reputation and Mussolini offered Rommel full command of Army Group Africa in place of von Arnim. It was an offer he declined. Rommel knew that, whereas he could delay an Allied victory in Tunisia, he could not prevent it because of the shortages of fuel, ammunition and food. On 1 March Rommel had submitted a report to Kesselring and Mussolini requesting either further reinforcement or an Axis withdrawal from Africa, but both options were denied. Heavily disillusioned, he submitted his sick leave order and left North Africa for the last time on 9 March. He reported to Hitler at *Werwolf* in Vinnista and again failed to persuade him to abandon Tunisia, but this time he received a warmer reception and his Iron Cross with oak leaves cluster was embellished with diamonds, Germany's highest military decoration.

On 28 March, the Mareth Line holding back the 8th Army in the south-east was overrun in a major offensive on the scale of El Alamein. By the end of April the Axis forces were pressed against the Tunisian coast defending a pocket which extended in an arc for 100 miles from Enfidaville in the east to Bizerta in the west. The Axis forces were outnumbered and out-gunned by an Allied army of 300,000 deploying 1,200 tanks against only 130 Axis tanks and with full command of the air. However, despite the inevitability of defeat the Germans and the Italians forced the Allies to fight for every metre. On 10 April Hitler held a crisis meeting with Mussolini at Klessheim Castle near Salzburg and was so alarmed by Mussolini's physical decline that he offered the services of German specialists. Mussolini failed to fulfil a promise to his High Command to confront Hitler with demands to open negotiations with the Allies, but Hitler was sufficiently alarmed by his physical weakness to commence planning for the German occupation of Italy.

At approximately 3.45 p.m. on 7 May the 11th Hussars and the 6th Armoured Division entered the centre of Tunis; 30 minutes later Bizerta also fell. The battle for Tunisia and North Africa was effectively over, although it took to 13 May to defeat the last pockets of Axis resistance. General Alexander telegraphed Churchill (as quoted at the start of this chapter) with the declaration that the Allies were masters of the North African shore. Hitler and Mussolini had suffered a major defeat and their decision to heavily reinforce Tunisia had significantly increased the number of those trapped and captured. The Allies claimed 240,000 prisoners whereas the Germans quoted 180,000 captured, including Generals von Arnim and Messe. The higher Allied total was similar to the number encircled and defeated by the Red Army at Stalingrad in February 1943, and may have been a useful answer to Stalin's frequent complaint of Allied inactivity in the west. At both Stalingrad and Tunisia Hitler had ignored the advice of his military commanders to withdraw and thereby preserve his armies for future combat. His shortsighted policy of 'no retreat' undoubtedly assisted the Allies and began to stir and promote considerations of assassination plots within the senior echelons of the Wehrmacht. The disillusioned Rommel was an early convert. Mussolini's position was in greater doubt and, as the Allies prepared to invade Sicily, many Italians openly called for a coup and for the Axis alliance with Germany to be severed. The

Italian ambition for expansion and empire, headily expressed during the 1930s when Italy declared the Mediterranean *mare nostrum,* was over. The cartoonist David Low, in a cartoon published in the *London Evening Standard* on 27 July 1943, underlined the death of Italian ambition with the drawing of the hand of a drowning man in an otherwise empty sea. The only ambition left to the Italian people was to avoid the destruction of their homes and country as the Allies prepared to invade.

Reference

1. Martin Gilbert, *Second World War*, Phoenix, 1989, p. 427.

24 Defeat on the Eastern Front

I want to say goodbye to you . . . I really mean goodbye and forever. We attacked not long ago. If only you knew how disgusting and horrible it was. Our soldiers went forward bravely but the Russian devils wouldn't go back for anything and every metre cost us the lives of our comrades . . . I know they'll kill me, goodbye, but I don't care, what's the point of living if the war's lost and the future black.[1]

Letter written by Otto Richter, a German soldier,
to his brother shortly before his death during the
German defeat at Kursk, August 1943

The German defeat at Stalingrad in February 1943 was a heavy psychological blow to the Wehrmacht and to a German people accustomed to victory, and raised the first widespread doubts about Hitler's leadership and the ability of Germany to win the war. After Stalingrad, Hitler, who had once bewitched the German people with his visionary oratory, remained conspicuously silent and was rarely glimpsed in public. The celebration of his accession to power on 30 January was muted, and in the whole of 1943 he gave only two public speeches and those were the obligatory occasions of Heroes' Day on 21 March and the twentieth anniversary of the abortive Nazi *putsch* on 8 November. On 18 February 1943 at the Sportpalast, Goebbels attempted to fill the silence with a rousing call to total war, but beyond the hall, which had been filled with hand-picked Nazi supporters, there was little enthusiasm. Earlier the same day a small group of anti-Nazi students at Munich University, the 'White Rose' Society, had distributed a leaflet which condemned Hitler and urged a rising against the Nazi regime. It was the first overt public demonstration against the Nazi regime and was triggered by the prospect of defeat and personal knowledge of the atrocities being committed on the Eastern Front. Two of the students, brother and sister Hans and Sophie Scholl, were named and reported to the Gestapo by a university porter, and both were quickly arrested and tortured to reveal the names of the other 'White Rose' members. In all six students, including Hans and Sophie Scholl and a university lecturer,

Professor of Philosophy Kurt Huber who was responsible for writing the leaflet, were found guilty of treason and beheaded by guillotine. It was a salutary warning to all dissidents not to attempt public protests, but anti-Nazi leaflets and graffiti made regular appearances in most major cities, and in private many questioned Hitler's leadership. Even the most loyal member of Hitler's hierarchy Josef Goebbels confided in his diary and to Albert Speer that Germany did not have a leadership crisis but a 'leader' crisis.

Hitler's public remoteness reflected his own doubts and he spent his time largely brooding in silence and eating alone at the *Wolfsschanze* or Berchtesgaden. He rarely visited Berlin and made no attempt to raise national morale by visiting workers in the factories, soldiers at the front line, civilians in the bomb-damaged cities or the doctors and nurses tending the wounded in the hospitals. He was incapable of offering comfort or dealing with defeat, and his words to his inner circle revolved around the weakness of his allies and the need for greater effort and sacrifice from the German people. He was openly shaken by Field Marshal Paulus's decision to surrender to the Red Army at Stalingrad on 31 January 1943 rather than to die at the head of his troops, and cited it as evidence of a lack of will for victory within the Wehrmacht. In a private address on 7 February to the gauleiters who formed the backbone of the Nazi movement, Hitler absolved himself of any responsibility for defeat and placed the responsibility squarely on the shoulders of the German people with the words: 'If the German people fails then it does not deserve that we fight for its future.'[2]

The only success plucked from the military disaster at Stalingrad was the withdrawal intact of Army Group A from the Causcasus. The Caucasus formed a deep cul-de-sac bounded on the west by the Black Sea and on the east by the Caspian Sea, and at its base by the Iranian border. Army Group A had penetrated deep into the Caucasus to seize the oilfields at Maikop and Grozny, but as the Red Army advanced beyond Stalingrad they threatened to close off the mouth of the cul-de-sac and inflict an even greater defeat on the Wehrmacht. Hitler's first instinct had been to order Army Group A to stand fast, but with no reserves to counter the Red Army advance he relented and between 15 January and 1 February Army Group A conducted an ordered retreat of over 400 miles. The Red Army tried to close the escape route, but heavy snow and a shortage of supplies slowed their advance and Army Group A escaped. However, the field belonged to the Red Army and on 14 February they entered Rostov at the western edge of the Caucasus and recovered the entire territory occupied at such high cost by the Wehrmacht during the summer and winter of 1942. Nor was the Soviet success confined to the southern front. The German central front from Orel to Kharkov was threatened with collapse as the Red Army pushed west from Voronezh. Kursk fell on 8 February, followed the next day by Bielgorod, and on 16 February Kharkov, the fourth largest city in the Soviet Union, was retaken. Hitler had ordered the SS divisions, Leibstandarte, Totenkopf and Das Reich, under the command of General Hausser, to fight to the death to defend Kharkov but, faced with impossible odds, Hausser ignored the order and implemented a strategic withdrawal to preserve his panzers and troops.

In mid-February the Red Army offensive faltered as supplies of food, fuel and ammunition struggled to keep pace with the rapid advance which had covered some 450 miles in only ten weeks. The advance had largely been sustained by supplies transported in convoys of American Studebaker heavy trucks and by the expansion of new railway networks and rolling stock delivered to the Soviet Union under Lend-Lease arrangements.

Lend-Lease also introduced Soviet soldiers to the delights of highly portable American canned food, particularly Spam. Although Stalin frequently complained about the inadequacy of US Lend-Lease supplies, the supplies received did bridge a significant production gap from 1941 to 1943 as Soviet industry struggled to re-establish itself after the loss of major industrial areas of the western Soviet Union.

Manstein, sensing that the Red Army had overstretched itself, seized the opportunity to launch a counter-attack against the exposed Red Army salients at Paulograd and Krasnoarmeisk on 21 February. His counter-attack not only stopped the Red Army advance but retook Kharkov on 15 March and Bielgorod on 19 March and pushed the Russians back to the river Donets. A more substantial victory was denied when he was forced to abandon plans to cross the Donets and encircle the Red Army due to a lack of panzers to spearhead the attack. It was a missed opportunity to roll back the entire Soviet front line and to turn the tide of battle in the German favour.

Any further military action on the Eastern Front was ended when an early thaw of the heavy cover of snow and ice at the beginning of March transformed the hard steppe into a quagmire of thick clawing mud that dragged men, trucks, horses, tanks and even aircraft to a standstill. The Luftwaffe operated from grass strips across the front, but the thick mud made it impossible to taxi or take off. The stalemate imposed by the *rasputiza* (time of mud) gave both sides time to regroup and to consider their options.

Within the Wehrmacht and the Nazi hierarchy there was rising support for negotiations and a compromise solution. Ribbentrop suggested peace talks with Stalin, Goebbels proposed a focus on anti-communism in order to win the active support of the civilian population and Rosenberg recommended an offer of future independence to the different national groups in return for their support. Hitler rejected any compromises in the east and to the dismay of his inner circle he insisted upon total victory or national annihilation. Hitler's stark choice prompted the first major assassination plot from within the ranks of the Wehrmacht. On 13 March disaffected officers of Army Group Centre planted a bomb on his plane when he visited their headquarters at Smolensk. The bomb failed to explode in the air as intended, due to a faulty detonator, and was retrieved and disarmed by a fellow conspirator when the plane landed at Rastenburg. The plot was never uncovered, but the fact that it was attempted highlighted the depth of despair among the officers and men on the Eastern Front.

It was against this background of political and military disquiet that Hitler contemplated his next military moves. The Wehrmacht favoured a standstill in the east to release forces to counter the imminent Allied second front in the west, but Hitler was wedded to the notion of a knock-out blow in the east. Hitler, haunted by the downfall of the kaiser and the defeat of Germany in the Great War due to the demands of fighting a war on two fronts, was obsessed with the need for a decisive victory in the east before turning west. The stubborn German defence of Tunisia raised Hitler's spirits and offered a window of opportunity. He hoped to hold Tunisia to at least the autumn of 1943, thereby delaying any Allied invasion of Italy or occupied France to spring 1944 at the earliest. By then Hitler expected to have achieved victory in the east and for a stream of new weapons to guarantee victory in the west. Foremost among them was the new heavily armoured Tiger tank, equipped with an 88 mm gun, and a new medium-weight Panther tank, armed with a 75 mm gun. The first prototypes rolled off the production lines in spring 1943 and with the deployment of a new battlefield fire support aircraft, the Henschel 129, it was hoped that the Wehrmacht would regain its blitzkreig superiority. Experiments were also well advanced into rocket technology with the aim of developing self-propelled bombs to bombard London and to destroy any invasion forces on the beaches. Equally, there was an expectation of jet aircraft to counter the RAF bomber offensive and the launch of a fleet of new, faster U-boats. The one weapon that might have made the difference, the atomic bomb, was scarcely considered by Hitler because the research in Germany was still in its early stages and many years away from a breakthrough. There is also some speculation that the head of Hitler's bomb programme, the German physicist Werner Heisenberg, implemented a deliberate go-slow to deny Hitler the bomb.

Hitler's optimism translated into action when he studied the map of the Eastern Front. The final dispositions of the front line had left the Red Army in possession of a major salient around Kursk. The salient was a lop-sided box approximately 100 miles deep from the north and projecting 100 miles along its northern edge compared to 50 miles along its southern edge. It offered an opportunity for a pincer attack to encircle and destroy a major concentration of the Red Army and to collapse the whole Soviet front line. It was also a major opportunity to restore the morale of the German people and to stiffen the resolve of the Hungarian and Romanian governments who were openly wavering in their commitment to the war. Hitler was also anxious to bolster the position of Mussolini and to combat the growing assumption in Italy that the Axis powers were destined to lose the war, an assumption strengthened by the decision of the Vichy French forces in North Africa to join the Allies.

On 15 April Hitler issued the order for Operation Zitadelle (Citadel), the encirclement of Kursk, with the words: 'Every commander, every private soldier, must be indoctrinated with awareness of the decisive importance of this offensive. Victory at Kursk will be a beacon for the whole world.'[3] The OKW recommended an immediate attack as soon as the ground had hardened in May, but Hitler delayed while he monitored the situation in the Mediterranean. Army Group Africa was defeated on 13 May and Hitler had no wish to commit major forces at Kursk when he might need hurriedly to transfer reinforcements to buttress the Western Front. He also wanted to wait for the production of the new Tiger and Panther tanks in sufficient numbers to contribute to the battle and to turn the tables on the formidable Soviet T-34 main battle tank.

The delay perhaps cost the Hitler the battle, as Marshal Zhukov not only predicted the German target but had his prediction confirmed by the steady build-up of Wehrmacht forces around the Kursk salient and a flow of reliable intelligence. Churchill was able to inform Stalin on 30 April of the German battle plan, and the codename Zitadelle, from Ultra intelligence intercepts. The Lucy spy ring was able to provide even greater detail of Hitler's plans for Zitadelle from a group of anti-Nazi officers within the senior ranks of the Wehrmacht. They had been active since the start of the war and regularly provided a co-conspirator, Rudolf Rossler, who lived in Switzerland, with details of all major operations; he in turn passed the information to Swiss intelligence and to the Allies.

Zhukov was placed in charge of the defence of Kursk and, with his experience of the successful defence of Moscow and Leningrad, he directed the construction of eight concentric defensive belts around the city. Each belt was heavily fortified with gun emplacements and deep minefields, and in total Zhukov deployed 1.3 million troops, 20,000 guns, 3,600 tanks and 2,400 aircraft. The plan was to allow the Germans to exhaust and deplete their forces by trying to force a pathway through the defences and once they were fully engaged to launch a counter-attack from the north towards Orel to attack the German rear. Partisan forces were also briefed to act in concert and to blow German railway lines to deny the movement of reinforcements. The complexity of the plan demonstrated that the Red Army was not only improving its strategies beyond the traditional but costly frontal assault, but was adopting the successful Wehrmacht tactic of blitzkreig with the mass deployment of tanks. The strategy was the product of a new generation of battle-hardened Soviet commanders who had absorbed the lessons of defeat in 1941; Stalin had learned to trust their judgement and more often than not endorsed rather than altered their attack plans. This trust was signalled by his removal of the need for all military orders to be countersigned by the political officer attached to each division. He also restored full military ranks, complete with new uniforms resplendent with gold braid and shoulder boards. The Red Army had also enjoyed a rapid expansion in manpower and equipment. The Soviet Union was reaping the benefits of its relocation of industry to Siberia and a reliable flow of Lend-Lease supplies via the ports of Murmansk, Vladivostok and overland from the Persian Gulf. The number of troops on the front line tripled between 1941 and 1943. However, because of the high losses the expansion was only secured by major movement of women into the factories to release men for the battlefield. In contrast, the Wehrmacht, even with the replacement of men by women in the factories and the use of 6 million slave labourers, was unable to replace its losses and contracted in size. Hitler concealed the reduction in army manpower by maintaining the same number of divisions, but at significantly less than their paper strength. Himmler expressed his deep anxiety about the number of men dying on the Eastern Front, and especially the racial elite of the SS. He therefore ordered all SS troops to visit SS-controlled brothels to impregnate selected Aryan women before departing for the front line.

The Wehrmacht committed all available forces to Operation Zitadelle 900,000 troops, 10,000 guns, 2,700 panzers and 2,000 aircraft – but it was still significantly outnumbered and out-gunned. At 5.30 a.m. on 5 July the Wehrmacht launched Zitadelle with a pincer attack directed against the north and south of the Kursk salient. The 9th Army under the command of Colonel-General Walther Model formed the core of the northern arm, and the 4th Panzer Army and three SS Panzergrenadier divisions under the command of Colonel-General Hermann Hoth comprised the southern arm. A pre-emptive artillery attack by the Red Army at 2.30 a.m. narrowly failed to catch the German troops at their assembly points as expected. A deserter had mistakenly specified the attack time as 3.30 a.m. when it was scheduled for 5.30 a.m., but it confirmed that the Wehrmacht lacked the element of surprise. Marshal Manstein and Heinz Guderian, the inspector-general of armoured forces, had both recommended to Hitler the cancellation of Zitadelle when it became apparent that the Red Army was moving major reinforcements into the area, but Hitler felt compelled to go ahead to regain the initiative on the Eastern Front.

On the first day Model advanced a maximum of 6 miles along a 25-mile front at a cost of 25,000 killed or wounded and the loss of 200 panzers. He managed to penetrate the first defensive belt but was pushed back by furious Soviet counter-attacks. In the south Hoth enjoyed greater success, but only due to a heavier concentration of panzers – including the new Tiger and Panther tanks – and with close air support from the new Henschel 129. His strategy of deploying his panzers in a tightly packed armoured wedge or *Panzerkeil* successfully breached the first Soviet defence belt by the end of the morning, but a rush of Soviet reinforcements to the second defence belt prevented any wider breakthrough. The new Panther tanks were also prone to breakdown, and the new Tiger tanks were not equipped with machine-guns, which left them vulnerable to infantry attack in the close-quarter battles. By 10 July Hoth had penetrated to the third defensive belt in the direction of the town of Prokhoravka, but in the north Model, after five days of intense battle, was still assaulting the second defensive belt. In all he had only advanced 8 miles. All hope of a German victory focused on the southern front at Prokhoravka when Hoth's panzers broke through the third Soviet defence belt. Zhukov committed one of his major reserve forces, the 5th Guard Tank Army, to stem the German advance. They covered 230 miles in two days from the rear to be in position, and on 12 July the biggest tank battle in history commenced when 800 Soviet tanks engaged approximately 450 panzers. Both sides raced into the attack and ended-up firing at each other at point-blank range as the two formations commixed. Overhead an intense air battle also raged as both sides attempted to sway the course of the battle by deploying 'tank buster' aircraft. Hoth successfully entered Prokhorovka, but it was only a temporary hold; by nightfall he was forced to retreat with the loss of 110 panzers to 450 Soviet tanks. The Red Army could sustain its losses but the Wehrmacht could not, and the next morning Hitler accepted defeat and abandoned Zitadelle.

A greater catastrophe for the Wehrmacht was narrowly avoided when the Red Army launched its own offensive north of Kursk towards Orel on 12 July in an attempt to encircle the 9th Army and the 2nd Panzer Army. With no reserves to hold the line, the Wehrmacht was forced to retreat and Orel fell to the Red Army on 5 August. Soviet partisan activity was also highly effective in aiding the Soviet victory, with over a thousand bomb attacks on railway lines and trains moving German supplies and reinforcements up to the front in July and August. The Soviet offensive pushed the Wehrmacht back for approximately 95 miles to the Hagen Line. On the southern front a further Soviet counter-attack commenced on 3 August, and after three weeks of intense fighting Kharkov was taken on 28 August. It marked the end of a summer of triumph for Soviet arms and the decisive defeat of the Wehrmacht in the east. Hitler had blamed the previous Soviet victories before Moscow and Stalingrad on the severity of the Russian winter and the unreliability of his Romanian and Italian allies. However, at Prokhorovka he was forced to digest that the Wehrmacht's elite SS divisions, equipped with the latest Tiger tanks, had been defeated in high summer by Soviet troops he routinely dismissed as *Untermenschen* or sub-human. Zitadelle was the last German offensive in the east, and in the west, as the Allies invaded Sicily, the Wehrmacht found itself stretched to breaking point.

References

1. *Purnell's History of the Second World War, Volume Four*, Purnell, p. 1474.
2. Alan Bullock, *Hitler and Stalin: Parallel Lives*, HarperCollins, 1991, p. 877.
3. *Purnell's History of the Second World War, Volume Four*, Purnell, p. 1465.

25 Bomber offensive

Are we beasts? Are we taking this too far?[1]
Churchill's remark to the Australian representative in the
war cabinet, Richard Casey, after viewing a film of the
destruction of the Ruhr by the RAF, June 1943

On 8 October 1914 Churchill, as First Lord of the Admiralty, had directed four aeroplanes of the Royal Navy Air Service (RNAS) to bomb Cologne in the first British bomb attack of the Great War. Minor damage was caused to a railway station. Twenty-eight years later on 30 May 1942 Churchill, as prime minister, authorised the first 1,000-bomber air raid of the Second World War. The target was again Cologne, but on this occasion the entire city was laid waste. The significant growth in air power between the two air raids reflected the development of a strategic air force in Britain and faith in a bomber offensive as a means to win the war by air power alone. The potential of bombers to attack the enemy beyond the conventional front line was first raised in October 1916 by General Bares of the French Air Service. A year later the idea of a strategic bomber fleet was taken up and formally presented to the British war cabinet by General Jan Christian Smuts. The outcome, on 1 April 1918, was the formation of the Royal Air Force (RAF) as a wholly independent branch of the British armed forces. The war ended on 11 November 1918 before the RAF could put the theory of strategic bombing to the test, but in 1922 the RAF successfully bombed and defeated Kurdish independence forces in Iraq and promoted the concept of bombers as an all-powerful and unstoppable force. The Italian military theorist General Giulio Douhet, in his treatise *Il Dominio dell 'Aria* (The Command of the Air) published in 1921, articulated the potential of a bomber offensive to win wars independently. Douhet predicted that future wars would be won by fleets of battle planes that could reach over the heads of a defending army or navy to destroy the heartland of the enemy and thereby force surrender. No country was expected to be able to sustain the deaths of hundreds of thousands of people from bomb attacks directed against vulnerable city populations, or the wholesale destruction of industry. The first chief of staff of the RAF, Hugh Trenchard (1919–29), arrived at similar conclusions and lobbied for the development of a fleet of heavy bombers to become Britain's first line of defence. He regarded bombers as a future deterrent force and sought to usurp the traditional role of the battleships of the Royal Navy as the principal guardians of the British Isles. Beyond Britain, only the United States, under the enthusiastic influence of Brigadier-General William (Billy) Mitchell, considered the doctrine of a strategic bomber force. His ideas were initially rejected but later took root around the concept of precision bombing and the development of the Boeing B-17 Flying Fortress heavy bomber in 1937. The more common military strategy was for aircraft to act in direct support of army and navy operations. This strategy was honed in Nazi Germany into the offensive strategy of blitzkreig whereby the Luftwaffe attacked in unison with ground forces to subdue and overwhelm the enemy. Hence the Luftwaffe never invested in heavy bombers but instead developed ground-attack aircraft and medium and light bombers to dominate the battlefield. With the outbreak of war in September 1939, the Luftwaffe successfully demonstrated its strategy with a major contribution to the conquest of Poland in 1939 and western Europe in 1940.

Five days after he took power as prime minister of Great Britain on 15 May 1940 Churchill authorised the first major RAF bomb attack of the war with a strike against German industry in the Ruhr valley. The attack by ninety-nine bombers was conducted at night to foil anti-aircraft (AA) guns and Luftwaffe fighters after the RAF bombers had endured heavy losses in daytime raids. The raid was judged to be a significant success because only one Wellington bomber was shot down, and most aircrews reported direct hits on the designated targets of key industrial plants, railroad junctions and German troop concentrations. The commander-in-chief of Bomber Command, Sir Charles Portal, recommended to Churchill the creation of a heavy bomber fleet to reduce German industry to rubble. However, it was fighter production rather than bombers that were given priority in the summer of 1940 during the Battle of Britain. The failure of the Luftwaffe to bomb Britain into submission during the Blitz (1940–41) did not shake the faith of the RAF Bomber Command in strategic bombing because the RAF concluded that the Luftwaffe, rather than the strategy, had failed. RAF Bomber Command highlighted the Luftwaffe's lack of heavy bombers and its delivery of minor bomb loads that in essence disrupted rather than destroyed industrial production and civilian life.

RAF Bomber Command stepped up its bomber offensive in 1941 and conducted regular bomb attacks against oil, railroad, naval and major industrial centres in Germany. The attacks were all conducted at night to reduce losses and despite the absence of electronic navigational aids, and bombing from a high altitude over a blacked-out landscape, few questioned the accuracy of the bomb runs. However, the gradual accumulation of reconnaissance photographs undermined the accuracy claims of the RAF aircrews. On Christmas Eve, 1940, reconnaissance photographs taken of attacks on two oil plants at Gelsenkirchen in the Ruhr by 296 bombers revealed that most bombs had missed by an 'immeasurable distance'.[2] In April 1941 David Butt, a member of the war cabinet secretariat, was directed to investigate the effectiveness of the RAF air raids. Butt studied 650 'before and after' reconnaissance photographs of RAF raids and in August 1941 concluded that only 25 per cent of the bomber force actually found the designated target and only 10 per cent of bombs dropped fell within 5 miles of the target. The problem was primarily one of navigation because the pilots and navigators, often flying in cloud and total darkness, were reduced to navigation by 'dead reckoning', essentially a calculation of speed and distance, to estimate when they were over the target. The air raids with the greatest accuracy were those conducted against naval targets because the bombers followed the coastline to find the designated harbours and dockyards, but even here precision eluded the bombers. Out of 1,100 sorties against the German battleships *Scharnhorst* and *Gneisenau*, in drydock in Brest harbour in July 1941, only four bombs scored hits. The evidence called into question the wisdom of pouring further resources into a bomber fleet at a time when the Royal Navy and the British Army were pressing for re-equipment. Churchill was swayed by the fact that the bomber offensive was Britain's only offensive capability at a time of widespread defeat, but he was sceptical of the claims made on behalf of air power, following the stoicism of the British public under the Blitz and the emergence of a strong German counter-offensive. By mid-1941 the RAF aircrew were confronted by a formidable array of German defences against air attack. The Luftwaffe had invested in a chain of ground radar stations, the Kammbuher Line, in an arc across Holland, Belgium and northern France, to track the RAF bomber streams. The bomber aircrews were forced to fly a gauntlet of night-fighters on both legs of the flight and once over the target they endured heavy fire from the concentrations of *Flugabwehr-Kanone* (flak), or anti-aircraft guns, surrounding the major industrial centres. By the end of 1941 the Luftwaffe night-fighters were winning the air war because the nightly losses were outstripping the ability of Bomber Command to replace the aircraft and, more importantly, the experienced aircrews. This grim reality was underlined on 8 November 1941 when thirty-seven bombers, or 9.25 per cent of the force, were shot down or failed to return from air raids across Germany. The losses were unacceptably high for a single night and on 13 November the RAF suspended operations pending a review of tactics. The Air Staff answered their critics by formulating a new strategy designed to win the war by targeting and destroying Germany's major cities. The strategy was promoted by the development, in 1941, of Gee radio location equipment and the new Lancaster bomber. In combination these gave Bomber Command a reliable means of navigation and a dependable heavy bomber. The first prototype of the Avro Lancaster successfully completed a short test flight from Ringway Airport, Manchester, on 9 January 1941 and was the successor to the lacklustre Manchester bomber. The Lancaster was the most powerful bomber in the world, with a range of 1,600 miles and a design bomb load of 14,000 pounds. Later design modifications increased the range and permitted the Lancaster to deliver the war's biggest conventional bomb, the 10-ton Grand Slam. In comparison the Luftwaffe possessed no heavy bombers and its most powerful medium bomber, the Heinkel He111, had a limited range of 600 miles and could only deliver a maximum bomb load of 4,000 pounds.

The new bombing directive issued to Bomber Command by the Air Staff on 14 February 1942 ordered a focus on 'the morale of the enemy civil population and in particular, of industrial workers'.[3] Stripped of judicious language it authorised the indiscriminate bombing of Germany's major cities and the deliberate targeting of civilians. On 22 February 1942 Arthur Harris was appointed as the new commander-in-chief of Bomber Command to implement the new directive, which was euphemistically referred to as 'area bombing'. Harris maintained, to the point of obsession, that the 'area bombing' of each major German industrial city would win the war by destroying the factories, the workers' homes and, more controversially, by killing the workforce. A German, whether in overalls or a uniform, was deemed a legitimate target. Churchill set his doubts to one side and endorsed the strategy. The first raids under Harris's leadership delivered mixed results from bomb raids on Billancourt near Paris, Essen, Augsburg, Lübeck and Rostock. The greatest damage was caused in Lübeck and Rostock. Both towns were deliberately selected by Harris because they possessed medieval town centres with largely wooden buildings vulnerable to fire. His judgement proved correct when both historic centres were reduced to ashes by a calculated mix of high explosive and incendiary bombs. In response, Hitler ordered Göring to launch reprisal bombings against key tourist cities in England. The resulting Luftwaffe air raids against Norwich, Exeter, Bath, York and Canterbury in late April were dubbed the Baedeker raids by Goebbels, after the popular German tourist guide. The destruction of tourist centres was not the war-winning strategy promised, and Harris came under pressure to demonstrate results. To silence his critics, and to prove his strategy, Harris visited Churchill at his country home, Chequers, and proposed Operation Millennium, a raid by 1,000 bombers on a single German city. Churchill enthusiastically endorsed the proposal as a propaganda demonstration of Britain's rising military strength and to answer Stalin's frequent complaints of inaction in the west. Cologne was selected as the target and Harris managed to assemble 1,047 bombers by scraping together every available aircraft, including many light bombers, and by pressing pupil pilots and their instructors into operational duty. It was a high-risk strategy because of the serious danger of collision from so many aircraft over one target and from the Luftwaffe night-fighters faced with a feast of targets.

On 30 May the bombers took advantage of bright moonlight glinting off the surface of the river Rhine and followed the river into the heart of Cologne town centre. A total of 898 bombers successfully reached and bombed the city with a mixture of high explosives and incendiary bombs. The resulting fierce fires burnt out over 600 acres of the city. However, only 469 people were killed – a testimony to good civil defence procedures and deep bomb shelters. Bomber Command lost forty-one bombers shot down and a further two in a single collision over the city. At a time of total war and the knowledge of 40,000 deaths resulting from the Luftwaffe Blitz, few moral objections were raised in Britain against the attempt to raze an entire German city. The cinema newsreels were dominated by a grim tit-for-tat satisfaction and in the *London Evening Standard* on 2 June the popular newspaper cartoonist David Low captured the public mood in a cartoon depicting Göring standing amid the rubble of Cologne with the caption: 'Hey Churchill. This was my idea.' Churchill warmly congratulated Harris and referred to the raid as 'the herald of what Germany will receive city by city from now on'.[4] His words were repeated on leaflets widely dropped over Germany in an attempt to sow public fear, and to stir opposition – even open revolt – against Nazi rule. Bomber Command regarded the bombing of Cologne as a significant victory and proof of the new strategy, but within two months the city was functioning again. No vital industries had been destroyed and the public mood was largely defiant, mirroring the stoicism of the British during the Blitz. In the flush of success Churchill overlooked his own words to the British people during the Blitz on 11 September 1940:

> This wicked man [Hitler] . . . has resolved to try and break our famous island race by a process of indiscriminate slaughter and destruction. What he has done is to kindle a fire in British hearts . . . which will burn with a steady and consuming flame until the last vestiges of Nazi tyranny have been burnt out of Europe.[5]

Churchill's reference to 'indiscriminate slaughter' soon found an echo in Germany where the RAF aircrew were referred to as *Terrorflieger*, and some were later lynched. The accusation of terrorism dogged the remainder of the bomber offensive and Churchill later increasingly questioned, and distanced himself, from the strategy.

The second 1,000-bomber air raid was launched against Essen on 2 June, but poor visibility hampered the bombing runs and the central target, the Krupps works, was not even hit despite the loss of thirty-two bombers. Nor was it hit in three follow-up bomb raids. The third and final 1,000-bomber raid was launched against Bremen on 26 June, but again many bombers missed the city and forty-four were lost. In total Bomber Command's losses for one month of operations was 107 bombers. It was an unacceptably high rate and further 1,000-bomber air raids were cancelled. On 17 April Bomber Command suffered a further defeat when seven out of twelve Lancaster bombers were shot down in a daytime raid on a U-boat diesel engine plant in Augsburg to test their ability to precision bomb. The morale of the aircrews was being steadily undermined by the continual losses, because an average loss of 5 per cent for every raid meant that few airmen would survive their tour of thirty missions. The overall statistics were grim. On average out of every hundred airmen, fifty-six were killed, three were injured, twelve were taken prisoner, two were shot down but evaded capture, and twenty-seven survived.

The commencement of operations by the US 8th Air Force on 17 August under of the command of Brigadier-General Ira Eaker with a raid on Rouen promised to deliver an unbearable intensification of the bomber offensive. Eaker dismissed the RAF strategy of 'area bombing' as too blunt an instrument to win the war and advocated precision raids against key industrial targets to destroy Germany's war-making capacity. To achieve the accuracy required Eaker insisted upon daylight raids in order to see the target and to take advantage of the much-vaunted Norden bombsight which, B-17 crews boasted, permitted them to hit a pickle barrel from 30,000 feet. Harris advised against daytime raids, but Eaker was confident that his more heavily armed B-17s flying in close formation could beat off the Luftwaffe fighters. The B-17s were armed with heavy 0.50 calibre machine guns and in theory could maintain a protective bubble of 360 degree fire. At first the losses were tolerable, and the RAF development of a new navigational device named Oboe improved accuracy by projecting a radio beam to act as an electronic highway to the target. Oboe was fitted to Mosquito light bombers and they flew in advance of the heavy bomber force as 'pathfinders' to pinpoint and mark the target with flares and incendiary bombs.

At Casablanca in January 1943, while Allied forces battled for North Africa, Churchill, Roosevelt and their respective military staffs agreed a new bombing strategy and issued the Combined Bombing Offensive (CBO). The CBO established a joint strategy of RAF raids by night and the USAAF by day against common industrial and military targets. The strategy favoured the USAAF focus on precision bombing of key industries, particularly oil, but Portal and Harris successfully lobbied for a continuation of the RAF strategy of city bombing with the addition of the words 'the undermining of the morale of the German people to a point where their capacity for armed resistance is fatally weakened'.[6] For the rest of the war Harris used this loophole to pursue his preferred strategy of area (city) bombing with the aim of 'de-housing' the German workforce and killing an estimated 900,000 German workers. The morality of targeting civilians was clearly sensitive because for the rest of the war the Air Ministry refused to admit openly that such aims existed. When the Labour MP for Ipswich Richard Stoke pressed Air Minister Sir Archibald Sinclair in the House of Commons on the morality of RAF bombing he was assured that Bomber Command was attacking industrial targets and that any civilian loss of life was regretted. Other critics, notably the historian Liddell-Hart and the Bishop of Chichester, George Bell, were equally reassured that Bomber Command was fighting a morally defensible war. This official policy of deceit later destroyed the reputation of Bomber Command and betrayed the brave aircrews who died in pursuit of an unsound military strategy. The CBO was formalised and issued to the USAAF and Bomber Command as Operation Pointblank on 10 June 1943. The 'scatter-gun' of Bomber Command was directed against three principal targets in 1943 and 1944: the Ruhr, Hamburg and Berlin. The exception was the Dam Buster raid of 17 May 1943 when 617 Squadron under the command of Wing Commander Guy Gibson breached the Mohne and Eder dams in the epitome of a precision bombing raid, using a bouncing bomb designed by Barnes Wallis. The raid captured the public imagination for its daring, but the third target – the Sorpe

Dam – escaped damage and eight of the eighteen bombers were shot down. Gibson was awarded the Victoria Cross, but on 19 September 1944 he was shot down and killed over Holland while returning from an air raid on the Ruhr that he had volunteered to join. Churchill, speaking at the Guildhall in London on 30 June, firmly upheld the bomber offensive with the words: 'those who sowed the wind are reaping the whirlwind'. Later in the same speech Churchill promised an intensification of the bomb attacks and 'the utmost application of exterminating force'.[7] However, in private, as quoted at the start of this chapter, Churchill was wrestling with his conscience and harboured personal doubts about the morality of the bomber offensive.

Churchill's 'exterminating force' was soon in evidence. Bomber Command laid waste the Ruhr between March and July 1943 and Hamburg was effectively razed to the ground by thirty-three air raids from July to November 1943. The most damaging of the raids was the 'firestorm' of 27–28 July when a heavy concentration of high explosives tore the buildings asunder and churned their contents into highly combustible fodder for the follow-up incendiary bombs. The resulting conflagration was so intense that it generated a vortex of hurricane-force flames and sucked the oxygen out of the air, asphyxiating many of those taking cover in the bomb shelters. Approximately 42,000 died on this single night in a death toll that exceeded the entire Luftwaffe Blitz on Great Britain from 1940 to 1941. Bomber Command successfully reduced its losses with the first use of 'window' – thousands of small strips of aluminium foil that swamped the German radar with false contacts as they floated to earth. Albert Speer, the German minister for armaments, was shocked by the scale of the destruction and predicted that Germany would be defeated if such raids were maintained, but he later revised his opinion when the people of Hamburg cleared the streets and recreated a functioning city within six weeks. Speer's reorganisation of German war production was so successful that production actually increased in 1943, in denial of one of the major goals of the bomber offensive. Between January and December 1943 the German production of tanks increased from 760 per month to 1,229 per month and aircraft production for the year was 25,094 as against 15,288 for 1942. In total German war production increased threefold during 1942 and 1943. Speer gave ironic thanks to Harris for protecting German military production by bombing cities. Speer's major fear was that Bomber Command would alter its strategy and join the USAAF in targeting war production. A particular concern was ball-bearings. On 17 August the USAAF bombed the ball-bearing plant at Schweinfurt and the Messerschmitt factory at Regensburg – but at a high cost of sixty out of 376 B-17 bombers. Speer remarked that similar sustained attacks would have brought the armaments industry 'to a complete standstill and the war would have been over'.[8] On 14 October 1943 the USAAF returned to Schweinfurt and lost a further sixty bombers in a significant triumph for the Luftwaffe fighters. Eaker was forced to accept that his B-17s could not effectively defend themselves and he suspended further USAAF air raids until long-range fighters were available to escort the bombers to and from their targets.

Harris was undeterred and advised Churchill that a major assault on Berlin would prompt the collapse of Nazi rule for the estimated cost of some 500 bombers. He directed sixteen raids against Berlin from 18 November to 2 March 1944, but despite widespread destruction of the city, including Hitler's Chancellery, there was no crack in the German resolve to continue the war. Only 6,000 Berliners were killed, due to the existence of reinforced concrete shelters that could accommodate thousands of people in safety. However, Bomber Command lost over a thousand bombers – double the number predicted – and morale plummeted when the aircrews absorbed the limited prospect of survival and some openly questioned their mission orders. There was a noticeable increase in the number of bombers 'damaged' and forced to set down in neutral Sweden. A rise in personal breakdowns was insensitively dismissed by the RAF as men lacking in 'moral fibre'. The final blow for the confidence of the aircrews was the disastrous raid on Nuremberg on 30 March 1944 when ninety-four bombers were lost and 545 aircrew killed in return for very minor results. The bravery of the aircrews in risking their lives in such hazardous raids was never sufficiently acknowledged by either Bomber Command or the nation. Harris never developed the personal touch and never visited his airfields or addressed his aircrews.

The Luftwaffe counter-offensive in 1943 successfully arrested the Allied bomber offensive, but by D-Day, 6 June, 1944, the Luftwaffe was a broken force and the bombers were able to range over Germany virtually unchallenged. Allied air supremacy was delivered between February and June 1944 by two significant developments: first, the deployment in February 1944 of the US P-47 Thunderbolt, P-31 Lightning and P-51 Mustang long-range fighters, which not only outperformed the Luftwaffe but had the range to escort the bombers to and from their targets; second, the success of precision bomb raids by the USAAF against oil refineries in Germany and the single oilfield in German hands at Ploesti in Romania. The new fighters, especially the Mustang, knocked the Luftwaffe fighters out of the sky in high numbers. In 'Big Week', which marked the return of the USAAF to the bomber offensive from 20 February 1944, the USAAF conducted thirteen major bomb raids and in the process the US fighter escort shot down an estimated 517 German fighters. The Luftwaffe possessed the potential to regain air supremacy with the successful development of the world's first operational jet fighter, the Me-262, capable of over 500 m.p.h., but modifications demanded by Hitler delayed its entry into service to December 1944. In angry exchanges with Göring in February 1944 he had snapped: 'I want bombers, bombers, bombers.'[9] Hitler was consumed by a desire for revenge bomb raids on London and insisted upon the conversion of the Me-262 into a fighter-bomber. The sustained precision attacks on Germany's twelve synthetic oil refineries by the USAAF, beginning in February 1944, significantly reduced production of aviation fuel. In May 1944 Germany produced 156,000 tons of aviation fuel; by June this had fallen to 52,000 tons; by August it dropped to 17,000 tons; by March 1945 it was zero. Oil production at the Ploesti oilfield in Romania was also significantly reduced to 10,000 tons per month against a minimum military requirement of 160,000 tons, and all production was lost following the Red Army occupation of Romania in September 1944. The Luftwaffe's aircraft, especially the new Me-262, were grounded for want of fuel in a victory for precision rather than area bombing.

The bomber offensive effectively ended in April 1944 when all Allied bombers were tasked with orders to support the D-Day landings by conducting sustained attacks on all German fortifications and road and rail communications across northern France. It was an order Harris had initially rejected and attempted to evade, but the bomb attacks proved to be highly effective in denying the Germans the free movement of reinforcements during and after D-Day. The denouement of the bomber offensive was reached in February 1945 when Harris recommended Operation Thunderclap to aid the Soviet advance by disrupting any eastward movement of German reinforcements. Harris proposed disabling attacks on Berlin, Leipzig and Dresden and hoped to deliver a knock-out blow and truncate the war. Bomber Command, aided by the USAAF, raised a firestorm in the historic town of Dresden on 14 February 1945 and killed 40,000 to 60,000 people. An accurate total will never be known because the city was crowded with civilian refugees fleeing from the Soviet advance. On 28 March 1945 Churchill, in a memo to the chiefs of staff, recommended an end to RAF indiscriminate bombings with the words: 'the question of bombing cities simply for the sake of increasing terror though under other pretexts should be reviewed. I feel the need for more precise concentration upon military objectives.'[10] After protests from Portal over the use of the word 'terror'. Churchill withdrew the memo, but his words reflected mounting public and political unease at the death of an estimated 600,000 German civilians and the serious injury of a further 800,000 for intangible results. Harris was openly unrepentant and on 29 March, in a letter to Sir Norman Bottomly, the deputy chief of Air Staff, he wrote: 'I submit that the strategic bombing of German cities must go on.'[11] Whereas there is no doubt that the RAF bomber offensive assisted the Soviet Union by keeping considerable resources of men and guns in the west, this would have to be equally true if the bomber offensive had been directed against military and industrial targets rather than civilian areas. After the war Prime Minister Attlee refused to award Harris any honour and, more controversially, not to strike a campaign medal for the aircrews of Bomber Command. The latter was an unnecessary injustice because the aircrews had bravely implemented the bomber offensive at the direction of the highest military and political command. Over half of the Bomber Command aircrews were lost in action; the highest losses of any single combat group in the war. Their bravery was beyond question, but they were betrayed by a failure to end the policy of area bombing long after it was shown to be militarily invalid. However, this judgement must be tempered by the 'area' bombing of Hiroshima and Nagasaki in August 1945. The shock of the destruction of both cities by atomic bombs undeniably shortened the war against Japan and resulted in the post-war superpowers embracing the strategic bomber as the major weapon of deterrence and war. It would appear that Douhet's thesis and Harris's strategy were merely awaiting a bomb with the force to erase rather than simply ruin cities.

References

1. Martin Gilbert, *Second World War*, Phoenix, 1989, p. 441.
2. John Terraine, *The Right of the Line: The RAF in European War 1939–45*, Hodder and Stoughton, 1988, p. 275.
3. John Keegan, *The Second World War*, Hutchinson, 1989, p. 421.
4. Martin Gilbert, *Second World War*, Phoenix, 1989, p. 329.
5. Martin Gilbert, *Churchill: A Life*, Heinemann, 1992, p. 676.
6. Martin Gilbert, *Second World War*, Phoenix, 1989, p. 393.
7. Winston Churchill, *Great War Speeches*, Corgi, 1957, p. 258.
8. Joachim Fest, *Speer: The Final Verdict*, Weidenfeld and Nicolson, 2001, p. 166.
9. Roger Manvell and Heinrich Fraenkel, *Göring*, Mentor, 1968, p. 219.
10. Robin Neillands, *The Bomber War: Arthur Harris and the Allied Bomber Offensive 1939–45*, John Murray, p. 372.
11. Max Hastings, *Bomber Command*, Penguin Books, 1992, p. 370.

26 Kriegsmarine repulsed

> The U-boat was fast becoming one long funeral procession for us . . . Unless Headquarters produced dramatic countermeasures, all our proud new U-boats would be turned into a surplus of iron coffins.[1]
>
> U-boat captain Herbert Werner in May 1943, shortly before
> U-boat operations in the Atlantic were suspended

At 10.45 p.m. on 11 February 1942 the Kriegsmarine battlecruisers *Scharnhorst* and *Gneisenau*, and the heavy cruiser *Prinz Eugen*, left the French port of Brest and managed to dash the length of the English Channel to the safety of Wilhelmshaven in the Baltic. Their breakout had been expected, but through a series of false assumptions and blunders the Royal Navy and the RAF failed to detect their departure. It was not until 11.09 a.m. on 12 February that their passage was spotted by a routine Spitfire patrol in the approach to the Dover Straits. An immediate intercept order was issued, but to compound the embarrassment the Royal Navy had no ships in the vicinity except for a squadron of motor torpedo boats (MTBs). They failed to penetrate the strong destroyer and E-boat escort around the cruisers. The RAF hastily ordered all available aircraft into the attack, but lost forty-two, including six Swordfish torpedo dive-bombers of the Fleet Air Arm, in vain attempts to arrest their progress. The Swordfish flight leader Lieutenant-Commander Eugene Esmonde, a veteran of the attack on the *Bismarck*, was posthumously awarded the Victoria Cross for his determined efforts to breach the superior Luftwaffe Me-109 and Fw-190 fighter screen. The only compensation for the RAF was that air-dropped mines laid off the Dutch coast succeeded in damaging the *Gneisenau* and the *Scharnhorst*. The latter was holed and limped into Wilhelmshaven, after shipping 1,000 tons of water, with her port engine and turret gear inoperable. *The Times* leader of 14 February thundered: 'nothing more mortifying to the pride of sea power has happened in Home Waters since the 17th century'.[2] It was a propaganda victory for the tiny Kriegsmarine, but it was a victory of evasion and ultimately underlined the reluctance of the German surface fleet to confront the Royal Navy following the sinking of the *Bismarck* in May 1941. The 'Channel dash' had been ordered by Hitler in an attempt to concentrate his surface fleet in the Baltic and Norwegian waters because he suspected that Churchill was planning landings in Norway to link up with the Soviet Union. Hitler had commenced his naval build-up a month earlier with the movement of Germany's most powerful battleship, the *Tirpitz*, armed with eight 15-inch guns, from the Baltic to the Norwegian port of Trondheim. The relocation gave Hitler a potent counter to any Allied landings. It also raised a threat to convoys in the North Atlantic and forced the Royal Navy to maintain a substantial picket in the North Sea, thereby reducing the ships available for convoy escort duties in the Atlantic.

A victory in the Atlantic was a renewed priority for Hitler following both the failure of Operation Barbarossa from June–December 1941 to defeat the Soviet Union and the entry of the United States of America into the war in December 1941. Hitler was aware that at some point in 1942 or 1943 the US Army would seek to cross the Atlantic in strength, and it was a passage he intended to deny. He was also hopeful that an offensive by the U-boat fleet against the Atlantic convoys would force Britain to surrender for want of food and oil, as well as ending the flow of military aid reaching the Soviet Union. The first Arctic convoy to the Soviet Union, designated PQ1, had reached Archangel on 11 October 1941 and opened up a new and extremely hazardous front for the Royal Navy and the merchant marine. The Arctic conditions proved to be as great a challenge to survival as enemy action.

The year 1941 ended with a marked decline in U-boat successes because the Royal Navy had perfected the escort of convoys and were using Catalina flying boats operating from Northern Ireland, Scotland, Newfoundland and Iceland to spot and attack U-boats.

However, the morale of the Kriegsmarine was restored during January–March 1942 when a U-boat wolfpack despatched by Admiral Donitz to the eastern seaboard of the United States scored considerable successes. The United States Navy (USN) had naively dismissed the need for convoys and failed to black-out its coastline, with the result that merchant ships in coastal waters were silhouetted against the bright shore. By the time the USN corrected its mistakes, the U-boats had sunk 1.34 million tons of shipping between January and March 1942. The total losses for the month of March were the highest total since the commencement of the war, with the loss of 273 ships totalling 834,184 tons. The U-boat losses were tolerable: eleven U-boats out of an operational fleet of 121, and future victory was confidently expected due to improvements in design. The new U-boats entering service had welded hulls giving more protection against the shock of depth charges, and had the ability to dive to greater depths. The U-boats were also provided with crude but effective Metox radar detectors that identified the electronic emissions from an approaching aircraft and gave an early warning of attack. The Metox 'whistle' only provided a very brief warning of attack but it was sufficient for most U-boats to crash dive to safety. In addition, the development of large cargo U-boats, *Milchkuhe*, to transport fuel and spare parts also extended U-boat patrols. As the new battle of the Atlantic developed Donitz also unwittingly restored the U-boat's greatest advantage of stealth by blocking the British code-breakers. On 1 February he re-equipped the U-boats with an upgraded Enigma machine that used four rotor arms for encryption rather than three. The new code – 'Triton' to the Germans and 'Shark' to British naval intelligence – appeared unbreakable because without knowledge of the rotor settings there were too many permutations to calculate manually or by using the first early computers installed at Bletchley Park. The only consolation for Bletchley Park was its continued ability to read dockyard radio traffic and thus log U-boat arrivals and departures. Donitz expanded the U-boat onslaught in the Spring of 1942 with the despatch of U-boats into the south Atlantic and around the Cape of Good Hope where there was no convoy system. He also directed U-boats to operate in the 'black gap' in mid-Atlantic beyond the range of allied air cover. His tactics resulted in high losses for Allied shipping and particularly the prized target of oil tankers. The resulting shortage of petrol pushed up prices in Britain and prompted the *Daily Mirror*, on 19 March, to publish a Zec cartoon of a shipwrecked merchant seaman clinging to a raft with the caption: 'The price of petrol has been increased by one penny – official.' The government regarded it as defeatist, whereas the *Daily Mirror* defended it as an acknowledgement of the hidden human cost of oil supplies.

June 1942 was the worst single month of the Atlantic War for the Allies, with the loss of 173 ships amounting to 834,196 tons. This was followed on 7 July 1942 by the worst single day of the Atlantic War for the Allies, with the loss of twenty-three ships from Arctic convoy PQ-17. It was a victory for a combined German air, surface and U-boat attack codenamed Rosselsprung, or Operation Knight's move. Grand Admiral Raeder directed his principal surface ships *Tirpitz, Admiral Hipper, Admiral*

Scheer and *Lutzow*, plus six escort destroyers, to intercept PQ-17. The First Sea Lord Sir Dudley-Pound responded to intelligence reports of the German fleet putting to sea by ordering PQ-17 to scatter for maximum protection – against the advice of his staff and Admiral John Tovey, who was in command of the convoy. His order proved disastrous because the *Kriegsmarine* surface fleet was recalled to port, without making contact, and the isolated merchant ships were subsequently picked-off by U-boat and dive-bomber attacks. The Royal Navy setbacks continued in October when naval frogmen failed in a mission to attach mines to the *Tirpitz*, but the year ended with two notable British successes. First, the code-breakers of Bletchley Park broke 'Shark' on 13 December following the dramatic seizure of Enigma codebooks from U-559 in the Mediterranean on 30 October. U-559 was successfully forced to the surface and boarded, but as Lieutenant Tony Fasson and Able Seaman Colin Grazier from HMS *Petard* passed the code books from the conning tower to 16-year-old Tommy Brown, U559 suddenly sank taking both men with it. The Shark code was broken by cross-checking the new code against weather reports from U-boats at sea and the Kriegsmarine weather stations that still used the older, less secure Engima machines. The second British victory arose in the Barents Sea on 30 December when Raeder, hoping to repeat his successful attack on convoy PQ-17, ordered the *Admiral Hipper* and *Lutzow* to intercept convoy JW-51B bound for Murmansk. Captain Robert Sherbrooke, on board HMS *Onslow*, directed the escort destroyers into a pre-emptive attack and, although they were heavily outgunned, they successfully sank one German destroyer and forced the withdrawal of the Kriegsmarine. Sherbrooke was awarded the Victoria Cross for his bravery for continuing to direct the counter-attack despite sustaining a serious facial injury that knocked his left eyeball out of its socket. The destroyer HMS *Achates* and the minesweeper *Bramble* were both sunk, but the convoy was successfully protected and proceeded unscathed. Vice-Admiral Kummitz, in command of the *Admiral Hipper*, had not pressed his attack out of a fear of incurring Hitler's wrath following a radioed warning not to take any risks. Kummitz's caution served only to unleash rather than avoid Hitler's wrath. In an emotional tirade, Hitler condemned the Kriegsmarine surface fleet as militarily useless and ordered it to scrapped and melted down and converted into U-boats. Raeder tendered his resignation, and on 30 January 1943 he was replaced as grand admiral by Donitz. In turn Rear-Admiral Godt was appointed to the operational command of the U-boat fleet. The year 1942 was the year of the U-boat: a total of 1,200 Allied ships, or approximately 7 million tons of shipping, were sunk for the loss of ninety-six U-boats. The success of the U-boat fleet was feted across Germany – especially the exploits of the leading U-boat aces such as Wolfgang Luth, the commander of U-181. He returned to the U-boat pen in Bordeaux on 18 January 1943 after 129 days at sea, during which U-181 has sunk twelve ships totalling 57,000 tons. His continued successes in 1943 resulted in the presentation by Hitler of Germany's highest military decoration, the Knight's Cross with oak leaves, swords and diamonds on 9 August 1943. He was the first person in the Kriegsmarine to receive such an award and only the seventh person in the entire Wehrmacht. Luth ended the war with a tally of forty-eight ships sunk, making him the second leading U-boat ace after Otto Kretschmer. He survived the war but, in a bizarre incident late at night on 13 May 1945, he was shot dead by one of his own sentries when he failed to hear, or to answer, a challenge. In a rare mark of respect the British occupation force permitted his funeral to be conducted with full Nazi regalia, including a German military honour guard.

The severe winter weather of January 1943 reduced Allied losses, but in February and March 1943 the U-boats pressed their advantage. Donitz concentrated his expanded U-boat fleet in the mid-Atlantic 'black gap' to overwhelm the convoy escort and to permit the U-boats to target and sink oil tankers. The tactic was successful, and on 9 February thirteen ships from convoy SC-118 were lost. In the first three weeks of March a total of 107 merchant ships were sunk when the U-boats successfully breached the destroyer screens and penetrated the convoys. The Admiralty warned of the real possibility of defeat in the Atlantic if the convoy escorts failed to deter and ward off the U-boat attacks. The battle of the Atlantic was in the balance, but in attacking the heavily defended convoys the U-boats sowed the seeds of their own destruction because they were forced to take greater risks. The graph of U-boat losses demonstrated a remarkable change in fortunes. Whereas in the first half of 1942 the average number of U-boats lost per month was 3.5, this leapt to 6.5 U-boats per month in the second half of the year. A brief lull ensued in January 1943 with the loss of only six U-boats, but the upward trend was renewed in February and March with nineteen and fifteen U-boats sunk respectively. The rising losses rapidly depleted the U-boat fleet of its most experienced crews and captains, and the result was the promotion of officers to command with minimal or in some cases no prior experience of combat. Most did not survive their first operational patrols. By March 1943 the U-boat fleet was losing the war of attrition and after March 1943 it was broken by a highly effective Allied counter-offensive. The genesis of the counter-offensive was the Allied Atlantic Convoy Conference on 1 March, which reviewed convoy operations and established separate operating zones for the United States Navy, the Canadian Navy and the Royal Navy. Admiral Sir Max Horton was given authority to introduce new tactics and, in a matter of weeks, he significantly reversed fortunes in the Atlantic by transforming the U-boats from hunter into quarry. Horton used an increase in the number of destroyers available for escort duties to form hunting patrols to shadow convoys and to attack and pursue any U-boats sighted. Ordinarily the U-boats were safe from sustained attack because the escort destroyers had to maintain pace with the convoys and were restricted to warding off attacks. However, the destroyers of the hunting groups maintained the pursuit for days if need be, until the U-boat was destroyed. The days of hit and run were over. The hunters' task was aided by the development of 'Huff Duff' high frequency direction-finding radar, which detected U-boats on the surface and, combined with ASDIC ('sonar' in the USN), gave the Royal Navy the ability to track U-boats whether on the surface or submerged. Once the quarry was in range, a new bow mounted 'hedgehog' depth-charge launcher was used to fire a spread of twenty-four contact charges forward of the ship. This increased the speed of attack and significantly reduced the evasion time for the U-boat compared to the use of the standard stern-dropped depth charges. However, the greatest new threat to the U-boats was the deployment by RAF Coastal Command of very long range (VLR) aircraft, principally the Liberator B-24 bombers, with the range to patrol the Atlantic 'black gap'. They were fitted with ASV 111 radio location equipment to detect U-boats and could attack with little warning using powerful Mark IV depth charges and the newly developed Mark 24 depth charges. The Mark 24 was not a depth charge but a homing torpedo that followed the cavitations of the U-boat screws, although it was deliberately described as a depth charge to disguise the breakthrough in technology. The U-boats 'Metox' aircraft early warning equipment could not pick up the electronic emissions from the new Allied radar sets and was rendered redundant. Consequently the U-boats were suddenly very exposed to attack and could no longer risk travelling on the surface for fear of sudden aerial attack. The cover of night, which had normally afforded protection, was also removed by the development of the Leigh light. This powerful searchlight, mounted under the noses of the Liberator bombers, spotlighted the U-boats during the attack run to ensure an accurate strike. The bright light was often the only warning the U-boats received of an impending attack. It ended the tradition of loitering on the surface in the cool of the night to recharge batteries and to permit the crew to obtain some fresh air. The nerves of the U-boat crews were stretched to breaking point by the frequent crash dives and the violent shaking delivered by exploding depth charges. The success of the new Allied tactics was measured by a further sharp rise in U-boat losses from fifteen in March to forty-one in May 1943. On 23 May, Donitz accepted defeat and recalled all U-boats from the Atlantic pending refit and the deployment of more advanced U-boats fitted with snorkels to permit underwater cruising. Among the U-boats lost in May 1943 was U-954 with all hands, including 21-year-old Peter Donitz, son of Grand Admiral Donitz. Later, on 13 May 1944, Donitz also lost his second son, Klaus, when the E-boat S147 was sunk in the English Channel. Attempts to relocate operations to the Azores and the Bay of Biscay were largely unsuccessful and by the end of the year the U-boat losses had soared to 237 compared to ninety-six for the year 1942.

The Kriegsmarine surface fleet was equally defeated when the Royal Navy Home Fleet sank the *Scharnhorst* on 26 December 1943. The *Scharnhorst* left the Altenfjord on 23 December with the intention of attacking the Allied arctic convoy JW55B, but her departure was reported by Norwegian agents with the coded message 'grandma just left on her holidays', and was also confirmed by Engima intercepts. The convoy was escorted by some of the most powerful ships of the Royal Navy Home Fleet – namely, *Duke of York, Jamaica, Belfast, Onslow, Orwell, Sheffield* and *Norfolk*. The *Norfolk* was the first to encounter the *Scharnhorst* and after an exchange of fire the *Scharnhorst*, having missed the convoy in the arctic darkness and mountainous seas, turned for port with the Home Fleet in hot pursuit. The *Scharnhorst* outpaced the Home Fleet, but a chance hit knocked out her starboard boiler room and forced a reduction of speed from 33 knots to 28 knots. The superior Home Fleet closed the distance and disabled the *Scharnhorst* with a series of direct hits and multiple torpedo strikes. At a range of only 2,000 yards, HMS *Jamaica* and *Duke of York* opened fire with devastating effect. A huge explosion rent and peeled back the entire foredeck, and the *Scharnhorst* turned over and sank within minutes; 1,932 German sailors were lost. Two days later a further three German destroyers were sunk by the Royal Navy in the Bay of Biscay.

The engagement marked the last significant Kriegsmarine challenge of the war and, although the U-boat fleet continued to attack shipping to the end of the war, the Kriegsmarine could only harry rather than pose a strategic threat to the Allied convoys. In 1944 all Allied convoys enjoyed full air cover from convoy escort carriers and from VLR aircraft. On D-Day, only thirty-six U-boats were available to counter the invasion fleet. They failed to penetrate the strong anti-U-boat air and sea patrols and, in later weeks, only six Allied ships were sunk for the cost of eleven U-boats. The deployment of the new snorkel-equipped U-boats had little impact because the Allies continued to improve their weaponry with the deployment of the forward-firing Squid depth-charge launcher. Squid was a refinement on 'Hedgehog'. It fired a triangular pattern of three powerful depth charges to fall forward and to either side of the U-boat, all primed to explode at the precise depth of the U-boat as reported by ASDIC. The odds were heavily stacked against the U-boat, and by the end of 1944 the U-boat fleet endured its highest annual loss with 241 sinkings.

The attention of the Royal Navy returned to the *Tirpitz*, Germany's most powerful battleship, after it was reported to be repaired and seaworthy following damage sustained in an attack by six midget submarines (X craft) in September 1943. Lieutenants Cameron and Place had been awarded the Victoria Cross for their part in the attack when they detonated four large mines under the *Tirpitz*. The force of the combined explosion was so powerful that it lifted the *Tirpitz* six feet out of the water, causing extensive damage. A strike by carrier-based aircraft on 3 April 1944 caught the *Tirpitz* unawares while raising steam and disabled the ship for a further three months. The RAF followed this success with a series of bomb attacks and managed to cripple the ship in a raid on 15 September. Donitz ordered the *Tirpitz* to be moored off Haakoy Island near Tromso to act as a floating fortress, but here, on 12 November 1944, it finally received a fatal hit from a 'tallboy' 12,000 pound bomb dropped by a Lancaster bomber. The *Tirpitz* turned turtle, trapping over a thousand men inside her hull; of those only eighty-seven were rescued.

The Kriegsmarine's war was effectively over and the much-vaunted XXIII and XXI improved U-boats entered service too late to alter the course of the war. The latter was capable of high underwater speeds of up to 20 knots, as against the normal 4 knots, using an improved Oelfken snorkel. They also operated at twice the depth of conventional U-boats and were armed with six torpedo tubes rather than four, and all loaded by hydraulic rams rather than by hand. In addition the torpedoes could be fired at a depth of 50 metres and home-in on their target independently. The XXI was a potent new weapon, but the first operational patrol by an XXI was conducted only one week before the end of the war.

Following Hitler's suicide Donitz finally admitted defeat, and on 5 May 1945 all U-boats were ordered to hoist a black flag and to enter the nearest Allied port and surrender. During the war the U-boat fleet had sunk 2,882 merchant ships and 175 warships and, at its operational height in the winter of 1942–43, it came close to isolating and defeating Great Britain by cutting off essential supplies. Statistics of U-boat losses vary, but the memoirs of U-boat ace Herbert Werner record 779 U-boats sunk out of 824 launched, and the death of 28,000 men out of 39,000 in the U-boat service. It was an operational loss of 94 per cent, and even when lower figures are accepted the *Unterseebootflotte* suffered the highest losses of any military service in the whole of the Second World War. The high death rate confirmed Werner's despairing judgement, as quoted at the start of this chapter, that the U-boats were little more than, 'iron coffins'.

References

1. Herbert A. Werner, *Iron Coffins: A U-boat Commander's War 1939–45*, Cassell, 1999, p. 134.
2. *The Times*, 14 February 1942.

27 Invasion of Italy

> My dear Duce, it isn't any good any more. Matters are very serious.
> Italy is in ruins ... At this moment you are the most hated man in the country.[1]
> King Vittorio Emmanuel to Mussolini immediately
> prior to placing him under arrest, 25 July 1943

At 4.30 a.m. on 30 April 1943, after a brief service, a body was lowered into the sea off Huelva on the southern coast of Spain from the Royal Navy submarine *Seraph*. It was no ordinary commitment to the deep. The body was the centrepiece of an elaborate deception by British intelligence, codenamed Operation Mincemeat, intended to convince the Germans that the Allies planned to land in Sardinia and Greece rather than the real target of Sicily. The intelligence service MI5 dressed the body in the uniform of the Royal Marines and added him to the active service list as Major William Martin. Before he was dropped into the sea a briefcase was handcuffed to his wrist. It contained top-secret documents addressed to General Alexander in Egypt with references to Allied plans for landings at Kalemata and Cape Araxos on the coast of Greece. The body was retrieved from the sea by Spanish fishermen and, as anticipated, the Spanish authorities read and copied the documents and passed them on to the Germans. Within days the code-breakers at Bletchley Park picked up orders from Hitler for the transfer of the 1st Panzer Division from France to Greece under the direction of Field Marshal Rommel. The deception had worked, and Major Martin was later buried in the Cemetery of Solitude, Huelva. After the war the British government refused to release the real identity of Major Martin, ostensibly out of sensitivity to the next of kin; it is probable, though, that the body was 'enlisted' without the permission of the wider family. In consequence, up until 1996 Major Martin was known only as the 'Man Who Never Was'. The mystery was finally resolved in 1996 when research conducted by the amateur historian Roger Morgan identified the dead man as Glyndwr Michael from Wales. He was a 'down-and-out' who had apparently died from pneumonia after several years of living rough in London. However, in 2003 new research by the authors John and Noreen Steele has indicated that at the last moment Michael's body was replaced by the body of a sailor drowned in the Clyde when HMS *Dasher* exploded and sank with the loss of 379 of the crew. The tragedy presented British Intelligence with a genuine victim of drowning, thereby strengthening the deception in the event of a post mortem. The evidence presented by the Steeles suggests that the 'man who never was' was Lieutenant John McFarlane, one of the crew of the *Dasher*.

The Allied decision to invade Sicily, followed by Italy, was only arrived at after months of protracted and at times ill-tempered argument between the British and US chiefs of staff. The US chiefs of staff had vigorously opposed the campaign in North Africa and were equally opposed to Churchill's proposals for the invasion of Sicily and Italy. The invasion of Sicily was grudgingly accepted as a necessity to secure the sea-lanes for Allied shipping to the Suez Canal, but any further military action in the Mediterranean theatre was firmly resisted. The Americans questioned Churchill's logic of defeating Hitler by taking the long road to Berlin from Egypt through Libya, Tunisia, Sicily, Italy and France, rather than the short road of a direct cross-channel invasion. Churchill's further proposals for landings on the Greek Dodecanese islands, particularly Rhodes, were met with greater American incredulity. Churchill fondly referred to Italy and Greece as the soft underbelly of Axis Europe, and he believed that the collapse of Italy and successful landings in Greece would cause Turkey to declare for the Allies and place the Allies on Hitler's southern border. However, a glance at the map of Italy shows a barren mountainous terrain criss-crossed by fast-flowing rivers and with few good roads. Italy was a defender's paradise, and the battle for Tunisia had amply demonstrated the strong German defensive capabilities. At the Casablanca conference with Roosevelt in January 1943 Churchill overturned US opposition when it was confirmed that the necessary resources to support D-Day could not be assembled until spring 1944, rather than summer 1943 as originally envisaged. This left a dangerous vacuum in Allied military action and raised a concern that Stalin might opt for a peace settlement with Hitler rather than fight on alone. Consequently, at the Washington Conference in May 1943, the decision for an invasion of Italy after Sicily was placed on the table and finally deferred to the military judgement of General Eisenhower. It was all Churchill needed, and he immediately visited Eisenhower's headquarters in North Africa on 29 May to lobby him personally to endorse the invasion of Italy. Eisenhower gave a provisional undertaking, but subject to the primacy of D-Day for men and equipment. The result was a piecemeal invasion plan which at its height pitted at best fourteen Allied divisions (most American divisions were entering battle for the first time) against twenty-four battle-hardened German divisions firmly established in strong defensive positions. The campaign confirmed the worst fears of the Americans and developed into one of the hardest and most costly Allied military operations of the war, rather than the soft underbelly advanced by Churchill.

The first Allied step towards the invasion of Italy was the successful invasion of the tiny island of Pantelleria midway between Tunisia and Sicily on 11 June, followed by the neighbouring islands of Lampedusa and Linosa on 12 and 13 June respectively. Mussolini had boasted that Pantelleria was an impregnable fortress, but, to his embarrassment, the defending Italian troops surrendered without a fight. The lack of resistance confirmed that support for Mussolini and Fascism was on the wane and in June, at Berchtesgaden, Hitler confirmed plans for the German occupation of Italy in the event of an Italian capitulation.

On the night of 9–10 July the Allies launched Operation Husky, and commenced the invasion of Sicily. An armada of 2,500 ships and landing craft, including the first deployment of Landing Ship Tank (LST) and Landing Craft Tank (LCT), closed on the beaches to the east and west of Cape Passero on the south-east coast. The US 7th Army, commanded by General George Patton, landed west of Cape Passero, and the British 8th Army, commanded by General Montgomery, landed east along an invasion front of 85 miles. Patton's objective was to secure the west of the island, while Montgomery was awarded the strategic prize of seizing the port of Messina on the north-eastern tip of Sicily and severing the link with the mainland. The invasion strategy envisaged the 7th Army as the shield and 8th Army as the sword, but to Montgomery's chagrin the strategy disintegrated into an open race to Messina and the victor's crown.

Both sets of landings were virtually unopposed. With Allied landings possible on any shore, General Alfredo Guzzoni, charged with the defence of Sicily, had largely deployed the 230,000-strong Italian 6th Army in the centre of the island. Field Marshal Kesselring, with Hitler's approval, directed the 15th Panzer Grenadiers and the Hermann Göring Panzer Division, composed of Luftwaffe ground troops, to provide motorised and armoured support. In the air the Allied air forces enjoyed an eight to one superiority, but to the immense irritation of the troops on the ground the invasion beaches were regularly bombed and strafed by the Luftwaffe. Allied planes refused to operate in a direct ground support role and stuck to a strategy of destroying the enemy airfields and support facilities. It was eventually effective, but uncomfortable for the troops in the interim. The only significant challenge to the invasion was provided by Tiger tanks of the Herman Göring Division at Piano Lupo and Gela in the US sector on 10 and 11 July. However, this resistance was swiftly crushed by naval gunfire and artillery directed by Patton from a rooftop using one of the first 'walkie-talkie' radio sets employed in the war. Montgomery's 8th Army encountered lighter resistance and occupied Syracuse on the first day, entering Augusta on 13 July.

By 15 July both beachheads were firmly secured and Patton and Montgomery were ranging inland. Montgomery's hopes for a swift advance to Messina evaporated when the 8th Army ran into fierce opposition as it pushed north from Augusta. The direct route to Messina was along a narrow coast road that meandered high up into the rocky slopes of Mount Etna. Each narrow mountain pass and village was defended by well-dug-in German troops, and Montgomery took a unilateral decision to alter his line of attack by ordering the 1st Canadian Division north along Highway 124 in order to loop around Mount Etna to outflank the German positions. It made good strategic sense, but caused considerable friction with generals Patton and Bradley when the US forces allocated to Highway 124 were forced to yield to the British advance. Patton lodged a strong protest with General Alexander and the dispute added a bitter edge to the British and American competition to be the first into Messina. In contrast to the British experience, the US 7th Army advanced across western Sicily largely unopposed and entered Palermo on the north-west coast on 22 July. Kesselring accepted that Sicily was lost and directed a staged withdrawal to the key port of Messina and the mainland.

The success of the Allied landings produced Mussolini's downfall. After defeat in North Africa and the Eastern Front most of Mussolini's Fascist hierarchy and Italian military believed that Axis defeat was inevitable. Mussolini was urged to confront Hitler at Feltre in northern Italy on 19 July with demands for a peace settlement, but he lost his nerve and, coupled with the first Allied bombing of Rome, the king and senior Fascists concluded that Mussolini should resign. On 24 July Mussolini attended a hastily convened meeting of the Fascist Grand Council, the first since 1939, and accepted, without comment, a vote by nineteen to seven to end his dictatorial powers and leadership of the war. Mussolini nevertheless expected to remain in government, but the next day he was shocked when King Emmanuel (as quoted at the start of the chapter) abruptly dismissed him as prime minister and placed him under arrest. Italian Fascism evaporated overnight and it was left to Hitler to plot Mussolini's escape in a vain attempt to resuscitate Fascism in Italy. Aware of this danger, the Italian Army first imprisoned Mussolini on the island of Ponza, followed by the island of Maddalena, before a final transfer to a remote hotel high in the Gran Sasso mountains north of Rome. In secret the new government of Italy, headed by Marshal Pietro Badoglio, opened surrender negotiations with the Allies while simultaneously assuring Hitler of Italy's continued loyalty in an attempt to avoid a German occupation. Their caution was justifiable. Hitler ordered Rommel to be prepared to occupy Italy at the first sign of Italian treachery and for Mussolini to be located and released from imprisonment.

In Sicily, an Allied victory was assured when Montgomery's 8th Army successfully wrapped around Mount Etna and steadily gained ground in a bloody village by village advance. On the northern coast, Patton avoided a similar slow slogging match by using landing craft to leapfrog along the northern coast and entered Messina at 10.15 a.m. on 17 August. A frustrated and weary Montgomery and the 8th Army followed two hours later. Patton's triumph was marred by two serious lapses of judgement during the campaign for Sicily. On 10 August, while touring the Sant' Agata military hospital, he accused two soldiers, one of whom had been admitted for malaria and the other for shell shock, of cowardice. He publicly slapped both men and ordered them out of the hospital and back to the front line under threat of a firing squad. The second incident, which further besmirched his reputation and that of the US 7th Army, was a rare example of an Allied war atrocity when in a fit of anger Sergeant Horace T. West shot dead forty-five Italian and three German prisoners of war. Patton's instinct was to order a cover-up, but General Bradley refused to co-operate and insisted upon a court martial. The supreme commander of Allied Forces, General Eisenhower, admonished Patton and ordered him to make an unprecedented public apology to the entire US 7th Army.

The successful occupation of Sicily was a hollow triumph because, whereas 164,000 Axis troops were either killed or taken prisoner, approximately 102,000 Axis troops successfully conducted an ordered withdrawal across the three-mile Straits of Messina to the mainland, along with all of their vehicles, tanks, and artillery. The Allies lost 5,552 killed and 14,410 wounded. The failure to close the Straits was significant because in the months ahead the Allies were forced to re-engage the same forces in the battle for Italy.

At 4.30 a.m. on 3 September the 8th Army and the 1st Canadian Division, under the command of Field Marshal Montgomery, landed at Reggio di Calabria on the toe of Italy and re-established an Allied presence on the continent of Europe on the fourth anniversary of the war. There was no opposition because General Heinrich von Vietinghoff, in command of German forces in southern Italy, had ordered a phased withdrawal northward. The local population welcomed the Allies ashore and even helped to unload the landing craft. It was the moment the Italian High Command had been waiting for and, in secret, General Giuseppe Castellano, on behalf of the Badoglio government, signed an unconditional surrender document and promised the active support of all Italians to help defeat the Germans.

The surrender was made public on 8 September as two Allied invasion fleets steamed for Italy direct from North Africa. The US 5th Army, under the command of General Mark Clark, headed for the beaches of the Gulf of Salerno south of Naples while a force of 3,600 British paratroopers headed for the port of Taranto on the heel of Italy. The major landing was to be at Salerno to seize the major port of Naples to support a drive north to Rome. The landing at Taranto was a secondary landing to secure the eastern flank of the 8th Army advance from Reggio di Calabria. The news of Italy's surrender was relayed to the 55,000 troops en route to Salerno, and most predicted a triumphant march into Naples. To the dismay of ordinary Italians, King Emmanuel and the new Italian government led by Marshal Badoglio fled to the far south, to Brindisi, to be inside the protective cordon of the 8th Army advancing out of Taranto. In response Hitler activated Operation Achse (Axis) on 10 September, occupied northern Italy and placed Rome under German martial law. Badoglio had issued no orders to the Italian Army to assist the Allied landings. Consequently, apart from some limited fighting in Rome which was easily contained, the majority of Italian soldiers surrendered or simply cast off their uniforms, discarded their weapons and headed for home. Belatedly, on 13 October Badoglio directed the Italian armed forces to fight alongside the Allies to help liberate Italy. Across Italy, Yugoslavia and Greece the Germans disarmed their erstwhile Italian allies and transported most of the 650,000 prisoners to work as forced labourers in Germany. On the Greek island of Cephalonia, approximately 7,000 Italian troops were shot dead for resistance to German orders, and a further 3,000 were drowned when transports taking them into captivity were sunk by the Allies unaware that they were POW ships. The Italian Navy and Air Force were better prepared than the army for surrender and both transferred to Allied territory. The Italian Navy, bar the flagship *Roma*, successfully escaped to Malta. The *Roma* was sunk, with the loss of Admiral Carlo Bergamini and 1,552 of her 2,000 crew, following a direct hit by a glider bomb. Within days, the Germans also imposed the race laws, which had been ignored by the Italians to Hitler's annoyance, and began to identify and list the Jewish population. At the Wannsee Conference in Berlin, January 1942, Adolf Eichmann had identified a population of 58,000 Jews in Italy to be subject to the Final Solution.

At 3.10 a.m. on 9 September the US 5th Army and the British 10th Corps commenced landings at six points along the Gulf of Salerno. Vietinghoff, in command of the German 10th Army, ordered an immediate attack on the Allied beachhead by the 16th Panzer Division and, from the outset, the Allies came under heavy fire. The Germans occupied the high ground and successfully confined the four Allied divisions landed to their beachhead while further reinforcements were rushed forward to press the attack. Many of the inexperienced American troops panicked and in the confusion opened fire on each other, or abandoned their positions and retreated towards the beaches. The Luftwaffe also regularly bombed and strafed the beachhead and targeted the ships of the invasion fleet, launching further glider bombs to deadly effect, sinking the cruiser HMS *Uganda* and four transports. By 12 September the landings were in the balance and Vietinghoff predicted a German victory as his forces advanced towards the beaches.

On the same day Hitler received further good news when a detachment of airborne troops under the command of SS Hauptsturmführer Otto Skorzeny freed Mussolini from captivity. Mussolini had been imprisoned in the Albergo-Rifugio hotel high up in a deserted ski resort in the Gran Sasso mountains north of Rome, but he was unexpectedly left behind when Badoglio and the Italian government abandoned Rome and fled south. The transfer of Mussolini into Allied hands was a condition of the surrender document, but Mussolini was left behind in German-controlled territory. Skorzeny discovered Mussolini's whereabouts from careless radio traffic, and in a daring assault he landed a detachment of troops by glider directly alongside the hotel. There was no resistance from the Italian guards and, within minutes, Mussolini was bundled into a Storch light aircraft and flown to Munich where he was reunited with his family before being taken onward to *Wolfsschanze* to meet with Hitler. The rescue was overly dramatic because the resort was within German-occupied northern Italy, and it was unlikely that the Italian guards would have executed Mussolini to prevent his release. Mussolini thanked Hitler and requested to be allowed to retire, but Hitler insisted that he return to northern Italy to rally support for Fascism and to establish a new Fascist regime. As always, Mussolini proved unequal to Hitler and meekly agreed.

At Salerno, General Mark Clark contemplated defeat when the Germans pressed their counter-attack. The British 8th Army was requested to make all speed to Salerno to assist the beleaguered US 5th Army but, with over 300 miles of narrow mountain roads to negotiate from Reggio di Calabria, there was little prospect of any significant assistance. Whether Montgomery could have made faster progress became a bitter debating point. In his private diary Montgomery complained: 'every operation teed-up by Fifth Army Group heads for disaster and has to be pulled out of the fire by the Eighth Army'.[2] Eisenhower and Alexander refused to countenance a withdrawal from Salerno and ordered the navy and air force to aid the stricken 5th Army with concentrated attacks on the German troop positions in and around Salerno. Over the course of 15 and 16 September the substantial Allied bomber fleet, aided by the battle-ships *Warspite* and *Valiant* plus six escorting destroyers, rushed from Malta and targeted and destroyed all identified German strong-points and panzer formations. Nothing was able to withstand the 15-inch shells fired by the battleships, and the sustained air and sea assault successfully broke the German line. To reinforce the exhausted troops on the ground, the US 82nd Airborne Division, with only 12 hours' notice of action, was dropped directly into the beachhead. All available troops in North Africa were also rushed to Salerno, but some 700 of the British troops refused to join the battle in protest at being integrated into unfamiliar units. All were found guilty of mutiny; they only reluctantly agreed to obey orders when all the privates were threatened with imprisonment and all the sergeants with a firing squad. By the end of 16 September the Allies had regained superiority, with the equivalent of seven divisions safely ashore against four German divisions, and in addition the German flank was under threat by the slow but certain arrival of the 8th Army from the south. Vietinghoff, who for a few days had held victory within his grasp, was forced to withdraw – but he had scored a significant tactical success over the Allies. The Allied advance was severely blunted and the Germans demonstrated that the defection of the Italians not only failed to disrupt their defensive plans but conferred little if any military advantage upon the Allies. Nowhere was this more the case than on the Greek Dodecanese island chain where Churchill, in defiance of American opposition, had authorised an entirely British attempt to seize the major islands of Kos, Leros, Samos, Simi, Salino, Castelrosso and Rhodes from German control. Only Rhodes had a large German garrison, and with the surrender of Italy the Italian garrisons on the other islands were encouraged to welcome the British ashore in late September. It was envisaged as a first step to the invasion of Rhodes, but Hitler ordered immediate counteraction. German troops landed on Kos and Leros in October and November respectively and, with heavy support from the Luftwaffe, defeated the minor British forces and forced Britain to withdraw from the Dodecanese and to abandon all hopes of taking Rhodes. Churchill's stub-bornness and insistence upon mounting the operation without adequate air cover or logistical support had handed Hitler a further victory.

Mussolini was installed in northern Italy on 27 September to direct and rally support for a new Fascist state, the Repubblica Sociale Italiano (the Italian Social Republic). In reality he had simply exchanged captors and rarely left his villa in Gargnano on Lake Garda or received visitors. The headquarters of his new regime were based in nearby Salo, but few were attracted to the revival of Fascism and Mussolini placed most of his energy into tracking down the '25th of July traitors' who had voted him out of office. Five, including his son-in-law Count Ciano, were captured (Ciano had voluntarily rejoined Mussolini); all were executed in January 1944 without mercy. Mussolini's distraught daughter Edda refused to speak to him again.

Vietinghoff and Field Marshal Kesselring had no long-term plans to hold southern Italy. Their plan was to yield territory at maximum cost to the Allies as they slowly withdrew northwards to hold northern Italy along the Gustav or winter line established across the high Apennine mountains south of Rome. The continued slow pace of the 8th Army as it paused to link up with supply columns from Taranto permitted Victinghoff to block the advance of the 5th Army towards Naples. At Taranto the 8th Army detachment found itself in virtual possession of the heel of Italy, entered Brindisi on 11 September and, in the absence of any opposition, travelled a further 60 miles up the coast and occupied the port of Bari. This unexpected success presented the Allies with three large ports on the Adriatic coast, and the opportunity was taken to land reinforcements at Bari on 22 September. In contrast, the advance on Naples was firmly held in check by determined German resistance and it was not until 1 October that the first British advance units entered the city. They entered a wasteland of destruction wrought by German demolition engineers and Allied bombers, but within days the first cargo ships were docked and reinforcements and supplies poured in to support the advance north to Rome. The Allied forces now numbered seven nationalities – American, British, Indian, Canadian, New Zealanders, French Moroccans and Polish – and in an entry in his diary on 27 October Montgomery despaired of the lack of co-ordination and a clear plan of action:

> what we want in Italy is a proper and firm plan for waging the campaign. At present it is haphazard and go-as-you-please. I fight my way forward as I like . . . as far as I know no high authority has ever said what is wanted.[3]

The Germans regrouped north of Naples along the line of the river Volturno and here, in the first heavy autumn rains, they held the Allies for two weeks into mid-October. In Rome on 18 October the first trainload of over a thousand Jews was despatched to a known fate at Auschwitz; despite many pleas for the Pope to speak out and condemn the deportations, he remained steadfastly silent.

Once the Allies, by sheer weight of numbers, threatened to overrun the Volturno Line Vietinghoff withdrew a further 15 miles to a new defensive line along the mouth of the Garigliano river. The terrain was a defender's paradise because the high Apennine mountain chain in the centre of Italy confined the Allied advance to both narrow coastal plains. On the west coast the US 5th Army maintained its advance out of Naples and to the east of the Apennines on the Adriatic coast the British 8th Army maintained a parallel advance. Both advances were reduced to a crawl when the Germans took advantage of a succession of fast-flowing mountain rivers to frustrate Allied progress. Throughout November and December 1943, in driving rain and snow, the Allied troops were forced to charge forward in Great War-style frontal assaults against heavily fortified positions along each river. The cost was high for minimum German effort. Hitler was delighted by the slow progress of the Allies and Kesselring's tactics, and he gave Kesselring full command over the defence of Italy on 21 November, transferring Rommel to take command of the Western Front.

By December the Allies were exhausted, and all hope of a breakthrough and entry into Rome by Christmas was abandoned when they encountered the Gustav Line. The Allies had advanced only 70 miles from Salerno in four months. The Gustav Line was a major chain of German fortified positions stretching across northern Italy from coast to coast. The German and Allied focus was the town of Cassino on the western edge of the Apennine mountains. The main highway to Rome, Route Six, ran through Cassino and here, and on the steep slopes above the town, the Germans were firmly dug-in around the ancient Benedictine monastery of Monte Cassino. It was a formidable defensive line and it left the Allies stranded in the heart of Italy with no clear strategy for victory. At the end of December Montgomery handed command of the 8th Army to Lieutenant-General Oliver Leese in order to return to England to take up command of land forces for D-Day. In a personal letter to Mountbatten, written on Christmas Eve 1943, he summed up the failure to achieve victory in Italy with the words: 'there was no clear policy or planning ahead. The whole thing was ad-hoc.'[4] The Italians and the Germans would probably have agreed with Montgomery because both had questioned why the Allies had chosen to land on the toe of Italy, 600 miles from Rome, rather than landing on the coast near Rome and cutting off all German forces in the south. Belatedly the Allied chiefs of staff pinpointed Anzio, south of Rome, for a major Allied landing to bypass the Gustav Line and to secure the fall of Rome.

References

1. Christopher Hibbert, *Benito Mussolini: The Rise and Fall of Il Duce*, Penguin, 1962, p. 224.
2. Stephen Brooks (ed.), *Montgomery and the Eighth Army*, Bodley Head, 1991, p. 290.
3. Ibid., p. 313.
4. Ibid., p. 349.

28 Pacific reversal

Isn't there someplace where we can strike the United States? . . . After suffering all these defeats why don't you study how not to let the Americans keep saying, We won, We won![1]
Emperor Hirohito admonishing General Sugiyama,
5 August 1943, following a string of US victories in the Solomon Islands

Emperor Hirohito dismissed the naval defeats at the battles of Coral Island (May 1942) and Midway (June 1942) as setbacks rather than decisive engagements and urged the Chief of the naval staff 'to ensure that future operations continue bold and aggressive'.[2] The navy had lost one aircraft carrier in the Coral Sea and a further four carriers at Midway, but the scale of the losses was concealed from the army and the nation to avoid harming morale. The complacency within the Imperial Court reflected the fact that the war in China, rather than that in the Pacific, was regarded as Japan's major war front. Over a million Japanese troops were engaged in China and preparations for a new offensive, codenamed Operation Gogo, were unaffected by the loss of the aircraft carriers. Hirohito was reassured by the regular 'Assessments of the World Situation', prepared by the Japanese general staff, that predicted no significant Allied counteraction in the Pacific until 1943 at the earliest. By then the army was expected to have achieved victory in China and to be able to release troops and aircraft to secure the new Japanese Pacific empire behind an impregnable perimeter of fortified island bases. In the interim, Hirohito's greatest concern was to guard against a surprise attack in Manchuria by the Soviet Union, Japan's oldest adversary and one of the three principal Allied powers. In consequence, Japan maintained a substantial army in Manchuria. However, it was not until 9 August 1945 that the Soviet Union, having secured victory in the west and anxious to win territory in the east, finally crossed the Manchurian border. The US victory in the Coral Sea left the Japanese advance into the south-west Pacific stalled at New Britain in the Solomons. It also ended plans for expansion into the Samoa islands and the Indian Ocean and more ambitious proposals for the invasion of Australia.

Faced with this Allied check on expansion, the Japanese sought to consolidate their position by occupying the whole of New Guinea, the Bismarck Archipelago and the Solomon Islands chain to the north and north-west of Australia. The aim was to deny the Allies any forward bases from where they could mount future incursions into the southern or central Pacific. The islands also offered the Japanese unsinkable aircraft carriers within range of the northern coast of Australia and control over the major sea lanes between the United States and Australia.

In the absence of aircraft carriers to shepherd a major invasion fleet the Japanese planned to achieve their goal with short hops from island to island. The first hop occurred in early June 1942 when an estimated 3,000 Japanese troops crossed from Tulagi Island and commenced the construction of an airfield at Lunga Point on nearby Guadalcanal in the Solomon Islands. On 21 July approximately 2,000 Japanese troops landed at nearby Buna and Gona on the north coast of Papua New Guinea. Their aim was to march across the island to the south coast to seize Port Moresby, the last Allied outpost in the South Pacific. This goal had been denied by the earlier US victory in the Coral Sea. In little over a week the Japanese advanced inland some 50 miles to Kokoda, but the attack stalled in the high Owen Stanley mountain range in what became Australia's front line.

The movement of Japanese troops was monitored and reported by a force of Allied 'coast watchers' from hideouts across the south-west Pacific islands. The majority were Australians who had lived and worked on the islands, and all volunteered to remain behind when the islands were evacuated to act as Australia's 'eyes and ears'. The report by the 'coast watcher' Martin Clemens of the construction of a Japanese airfield on Guadalcanal caused consternation in Washington and Canberra, and pressure for counteraction. Admiral Ernest J. King, the US chief of naval operations, succeeded in persuading President Roosevelt to override the primacy of the European theatre and to permit an immediate US intervention to prevent the Japanese from establishing an operational airbase. The 1st Marine Division, under the command of Major-General Alexander Archer Vandegrift, was tasked with securing Guadalcanal for the Allies. The outcome for Japan was the commencement of a two-front war and their first major reversal in the Pacific.

At dawn on 7 August Martin Clemens's sleep was broken by the roar of naval guns, when the USN cruiser *Quincy* commenced the pre-invasion bombardment of Guadalcanal. From his mountain vantage point he watched as, in his words, a 'fleet majestical' closed on the beaches of Tenaru on the island of Guadalcanal. Within a matter of weeks the local waters were renamed Iron Bottom Sound, given the number of ships that were sunk off Guadalcanal. The Japanese labour battalion building the airfield melted away into the jungle as the Americans landed. In simultaneous action 32 miles to the north-west of Guadalcanal a second US task force landed troops on the islets of Tulagi, Gavutu and Tanambogo off Florida Island. The islands commanded the approaches to Guadalcanal.

Approximately 20,000 marines secured Guadalcanal, but the marine landings on Tulagi, Gavutu and Tanambogo were strongly opposed by a garrison of 800 Japanese combat troops dug into concealed bunkers and deep caves. It took sustained naval gunfire to break the Japanese resistance and close-quarter battles throughout 7 and 8 August to secure the islets.

The commander-in-chief of Japanese forces, Vice-Admiral Gunichi Mikawa, ordered an immediate air attack and took personal command of five heavy and two light cruisers to drive off the US fleet. His rapid counter-attack was highly successful. Twenty-one US fighters were lost defending the US fleet, and on 8 August the destroyer *Jarvis* was sunk by a direct bomb hit. Admiral Frank Fletcher, concerned by the high loss of fighters, withdrew the US aircraft carriers *Enterprise*, *Saratoga* and *Wasp* to re-equip and refuel. His decision was widely criticised as premature because it left the landing fleet and marines without any close air cover. The next night, in the first of four major naval engagements, the Japanese cruisers caught the US fleet by surprise in the Savo Sea. Mikawa used the cover of darkness to slip past the US picket destroyers *Blue* and *Ralph Talbot* and in a surprise attack sunk the US cruisers *Vincennes*, *Quincy* and *Astoria* and the Australian cruiser *Canberra*. The American crews had little or no practice of night-time operations and were defeated by the speed and accuracy of the Japanese attack. Fortunately for the Americans, Mikawa was unaware of the withdrawal of the US carriers and failed to press his attack against the defenceless transports of the landing fleet. The US naval commander, Captain Howard D. Bode, accepted full responsibility for the losses and in an action rare in western military service he shot himself. The only Allied consolation was the sinking of the Japanese cruiser *Kako* by the US submarine S-44 a day later.

With the successful rout of the US fleet, Mikawa and General Harukichi Hyakutake, the commander of the 17th Army based on Rabaul, New Britain, turned their attention to driving the isolated US marines off Guadalcanal. Both expected a quick victory because Japanese intelligence reported the marines' strength at only 2,000. However, with no troops available for immediate action it was not until 18 August that an advance force was landed. The detachment of 815 troops, under the command of Colonel Kiyono Ichiki, was landed under the cover of darkness from destroyers operating out of the major Japanese naval and airbase in Rabaul, New Britain. In the months ahead this supply route was nicknamed the 'Tokyo Express' by the American troops, after Rear-Admiral Raizo Tanaka introduced a regular shuttle run between Guadalcanal and New Britain to evacuate the Japanese wounded and to deliver supplies and reinforcements. The delay in action gave the marines time to complete the airstrip, using construction equipment and plant abandoned by the Japanese, and to prepare a strong defensive line around the airfield perimeter. The airstrip received its first aircraft on 20 August and was named Henderson Field in memory of Major Lofton Henderson, a marine hero of Midway. The pilots adopted the call sign of the 'Cactus Air Force', following the US naval radio code 'cactus' for Guadalcanal. At 1.30 a.m. on 21 August Ichiki, without waiting for the arrival of the main Japanese force, led a charge on the US positions with fixed bayonets. He believed that his highly experienced troops would be capable of defeating the Americans, but the marines had used their time well and were dug-in at the top of a ridge with a clear field of fire. The Japanese attack was halted by accurate fire and canister shot. A further charge also ended in failure. Ichiki realised his mistake and retreated to the cover of the jungle to await reinforcements while keeping the marines under fire. Vandegrift used his superior numbers to keep the Japanese engaged while part of his force infiltrated the jungle and successfully encircled the Japanese troops on 22 August. The trapped Japanese troops refused to surrender and maintained a fanatical resistance despite being heavily outnumbered. Vandegrift pressed the newly formed 'Cactus Air Force' into service to bomb and strafe the Japanese pocket and steadily gained ground aided by Stuart light tanks. The Japanese fought to the death and the tanks were forced to advance over the bodies of the wounded and the dead in horrific scenes that transformed the treads of the tanks, in Vandegrift's words, into 'meat grinders'. It was the first taste of the fanatical resistance that became the hallmark of Japanese defence in the Pacific War. Only seventeen of the 815 Japanese troops were captured alive; thirty-five US marines were killed in the action. To avoid the 'disgrace' of capture Colonel Ichiki shredded and burnt his regimental flag and committed ritual hara-kiri.

The result was stalemate, with the Japanese victorious at sea and the Americans victorious on land. Both sides rushed reinforcements to Guadalcanal to ensure victory in this first major battle of the new Pacific front line. The block to Japanese action was the supremacy of the US Navy, and in particular the carriers *Enterprise*, *Saratoga* and *Wasp*, which checked any significant movement of Japanese troop transports. Admiral Isoroku Yamamoto planned to regain the initiative by drawing the US carriers into a trap. The resulting battle of the East Solomons was a resounding US victory, with seventy out of eighty Japanese planes shot down. The following day the Japanese suffered a second major blow, when dive-bombers of the Cactus Air Force intercepted and sank a Japanese troop transport approaching Guadalcanal. The Japanese bowed to US air supremacy and reverted to the 'Tokyo Express' night runs to transfer reinforcements to Guadalcanal by fast destroyers. By early September they were ready to reopen the land battle with a force of over 5,000 Japanese troops. At 9 p.m. on 12 September Japanese cruisers bombarded the marines' ridge top position, named 'Bloody Ridge'. After two days of fighting approximately 600 dead Japanese troops littered the slope, but the Japanese continued to attack, sustained by the nightly 'Tokyo Express' supply runs. In turn the US line was reinforced on 15 September by the landing of a further 4,000 marines. Hirohito insisted upon victory and gave the recapture of Guadalcanal priority over the campaign on New Guinea. On 9 October the first elements of the Japanese 17th Army were landed and over subsequent nights the 'Tokyo Express' increased Japanese strength to 22,000, supported by medium tanks and artillery. The USN sought to derail the 'Tokyo Express' and sparked the third major naval battle of the campaign on 11 and 12 October when both navies clashed off Cape Esperance west of Savo island. The Japanese convoy cruiser *Furutaka* and three destroyers were sunk but, as the two sides grappled in the dark, misidentification resulted in US ships opening fire on each other and, in the confusion, the Japanese slipped away without further loss. The next morning the US 164th Infantry Division was successfully landed and increased US strength to 23,000 troops. The Japanese seized the initiative and over three successive nights from 13 to 15 October the Japanese Navy bombarded the US positions with an estimated 3,000 shells and churned Henderson Field into a wasteland of mud and deep craters. Only forty-two out of the Cactus Air Force total of ninety planes survived the onslaught, but with the airfield destroyed they were grounded. The eradication of US airpower gave the Japanese troops a significant advantage and Vandegrift angrily denounced the lack of US naval protection. However, after three days of intense fighting the Japanese broke off their attack on 26 October with the loss of 3,500 men for no gain. More US marines were incapacitated by the tropical conditions than by enemy action. Over 3,000 marines were stricken by malaria and thousands more suffered from fungal infections from the constant wet and damp conditions. Swarms of flies, large tropical wasps, leeches and biting ants all added to the misery. At sea, on the same day, an equally ferocious battle for supremacy raged as both fleets sought to protect and support their respective land forces. The US carrier *Hornet* was sunk and the carrier *Enterprise* was badly damaged. The success raised Japanese hopes for victory and Emperor Hirohito urged immediate follow-up action to retake Guadalcanal. He signalled Admiral Yamamoto: 'officers and men exert yourselves to even greater efforts . . . Guadalcanal is the focal point of the war . . . so don't rest on small achievements. Move quickly and recapture it.'[3] Yamamoto obeyed with the despatch of a fleet to renew the bombardment of Henderson Field and a major invasion force escorted by a second fleet. He held a third fleet in reserve to counter any USN intervention. The result was the decisive battle for Guadalcanal between 13 and 15 November and a crushing US victory. In a succession of engagements the USN lost two cruisers and six destroyers, but the Japanese suffered the loss of two battleships, two cruisers and three destroyers. More importantly, seven Japanese troop transports were sunk in transit and a further four were destroyed on their landing beaches by dive-bombers from Henderson Field. The victory all but extinguished the Japanese threat to Guadalcanal.

The weary but undefeated US marines were relieved on 9 December 1942 by the US 14th Army Corps under the command of Major-General Alexander Patch. The Japanese troops cut off from reinforcement or supply were a broken force, and many died of starvation and from untreated wounds. Raids by the desperate Japanese troops on local villages to steal food provoked revenge attacks by the native tribes who killed and displayed the shrunken heads of dead Japanese troops in their long houses. In Tokyo, in the presence of Emperor Hirohito on 31 December 1942, the Imperial Headquarters Conference accepted defeat and recommended a withdrawal from Guadalcanal. Hirohito assented, but on condition that Japan demonstrated that it was unbowed by launching a decisive offensive elsewhere.

After probing attacks on the Japanese lines, General Patch, with 50,000 troops at his disposal, launched an offensive on the marooned Japanese on 17 December 1942. The weight of numbers gradually pressed the Japanese back to the coast at Cape Esperance and from 1 to 7 February 1943 the 'Tokyo Express' worked in reverse and successfully evacuated 11,000 surviving Japanese troops. The battle for Guadalcanal had been a costly failure for Japan, with the loss of 25,000 troops, one aircraft carrier, two battleships, four cruisers, eleven destroyers, six submarines, 892 planes and 1,882 pilots and aircrew. The Allied losses were more bearable, but to hold a single island the Allies (mainly American) had lost 1,598 troops, two aircraft carriers, eight cruisers, seventeen destroyers and four transports. The future was more islands and therefore a demand for more ships and more aircraft, but in a war of production the US economy was bound to win.

In parallel to the defeat on Guadalcanal the Japanese were also defeated on New Guinea. On 24 August 1942 Major-General Tomataro Horii arrived at Kokoda to direct a major two-pronged advance on Port Moresby personally. He planned a new attack on the Australian line on the Kokoda Trail in the mountains north of Port Moresby, while a second force landed on the coast and threatened Port Moresby from the south-west. On 25 August the offensive commenced, with the landing of 2,000 troops on the southern tip of the Papuan peninsula at Milne Bay. Unknown to the

Japanese, two Australian infantry brigades were stationed at Milne Bay to protect the construction of a new airfield, and heavy Australian reinforcements had joined the defence of the Kokoda Trail. The Japanese landing was largely destroyed on the beaches and Horii was halted at the Ioribaiwi Ridge some 30 miles from the goal of Port Moresby. On 24 September 1942 the Japanese High Command accepted defeat and ordered a retreat back to the north coast and the major Japanese supply bases at Buna and Gona. Horii was killed during a stand at the Kumusi river, and by the end of November the Japanese were besieged at Buna and Gona. The Japanese transported reinforcements from New Britain and in return General Douglas MacArthur despatched 15,000 US troops to assist the Australian offensive under the command of General Robert Eichelberger. He was starkly instructed to either take Buna or not to return. After sustained pitched battles Gona fell on 10 December to the Australian 21st Brigade, but the more heavily defended Buna held out to 2 January 1943. Many Japanese troops swam out to sea to drown rather than suffer the indignity of capture, and several officers committed hara-kiri kneeling on the shore. The six-month battle for control of Papua New Guinea finally ended on 23 January 1943 when the last pocket of Japanese resistance in the mangrove swamps at Sanananda, north of Buna, was defeated. The survivors refused to surrender and retreated along the coast to Lae, Salamaua and Finschhafen – they continued to fight and contest the Allied possession of New Guinea to 1945. The reversal on Guadalcanal and Papua New Guinea was a considerable shock to the Japanese High Command and resulted in a flow of reinforcements to the Solomon Islands to close this American door into the southern and central Pacific. However, the defeats continued. On 3 March 1943 a Japanese attempt to land a further 7,000 troops at Lae misfired when the convoy was intercepted in the Bismarck Sea by US and Australian bombers and erased. All eight troop transports were sunk, with the loss of 3,500 troops and four destroyers. In addition 102 Japanese aircraft were shot down. It was a powerful demonstration of Allied air power and illustrated that the Japanese forces were rapidly losing their freedom of movement.

Admiral Yamamoto commenced a tour of the Solomons during April and May 1943 to boost the morale of the beleaguered Japanese troops and to examine defence arrangements with the local commanders. However, his travel plans were monitored by US intelligence and the Cactus Air Force was ordered to intercept his planned visit to Bougainville Island. At 9.35 a.m. on 18 April Yamamoto's flight began its descent to land on Bougainville. It was jumped by a flight of eighteen American P.38 Lightning fighters which had flown 500 miles from Guadalcanal at wave-top height to avoid detection. Yamamoto was travelling in a 'Betty' bomber accompanied by his staff in a second 'Betty' bomber, escorted by six Zero fighters. The escorts were overwhelmed and within minutes both 'Bettys' were shot down and crashed in flames into the jungle, killing Yamamoto and his staff for the loss of a single Lightning. Yamamoto's ashes were returned to Tokyo for burial on 21 May, but the US forces refrained from any comment to protect their ability to read Japanese naval traffic. To protect their own naval traffic against Japanese intelligence intercepts, the US marines recruited Native Americans to generate unbreakable codes using the little-known Navajo language. Battleships were referred to as *lo-tso*, the Navajo word for a whale, while a tank was encoded as *chay-da-gahi* or tortoise. The code was never broken by the Japanese. On 26 July 2001 the military service of the Navajo 'code-talkers' was belatedly recognised in the United States with the award of the Congressional Gold Medal to four of the five survivors out of an original thirty volunteers.

The only Japanese consolation during the reverses in the Pacific between 1942 and 1943 was the failure of a British advance down the Mayu Peninsula in Burma. General Wavell insisted upon pursuing the offensive, against the advice of his own staff. With insufficient troops and limited air support, the offensive was swiftly blocked and contained by the Japanese. In January 1943 a continuous retreat ensued and by May the entire Allied offensive had been rolled back. A more limited but successful 'invasion' of Burma was conducted by Brigadier Orde Wingate, who organised and trained the 77th Indian Brigade to operate behind enemy lines as a guerrilla strike force.

They were designated the 'Long Range Penetration Group', but were popularly known as the 'Chindits', a misheard pronunciation of the mythical Burmese half-lion and half-eagle 'Chinthe'. On 14 February 1943, 3,000 Chindits, operating in two separate columns, crossed into Burma from Imphal and began to wreak havoc behind the Japanese lines by blowing road and railway bridges. On 15 March they crossed the Irrawaddy river and forced the Japanese to deploy two divisions to counter their sabotage attacks. Exhausted and in danger of being captured, the Chindits commenced an orderly withdrawal back to India on 26 March. Wingate lost 800 men, with a further 600 incapacitated by tropical diseases, but he had demonstrated that Allied troops could master jungle warfare and forced the Japanese to guard the entire frontier with India against further incursions.

On 12 May 1943 the Americans suddenly switched their challenge to the Japanese Pacific empire from the South Pacific to the far north Aleutian Island chain when the US 7th Infantry Division was landed on the island of Attu. The Japanese had seized Attu and nearby Kiska as part of the Midway campaign in June 1942, but both island garrisons were very isolated. Only 2,500 Japanese troops defended Attu, but despite the landing of 11,000 American troops they refused to surrender and fought to the death. It was not until 31 May that the last resistance was crushed at a cost of 1,000 American dead. Only twenty-eight Japanese soldiers were taken prisoner. Similar resistance was expected on Kiska island, but when a combined American and Canadian invasion force of over 30,000 troops swept ashore on 15 August 1943 they discovered that the island was deserted. The Japanese had predicted the Allied move and opted to withdraw their forces two weeks earlier. To the embarrassment of the USN, the Japanese had slipped away unseen despite regular surveillance flights and several weeks of preliminary naval and air bombardment.

On 30 September 1943, in the presence of Emperor Hirohito, Prime Minister Tojo and the High Command took stock of the Pacific reversal and identified an 'absolute defence line' in the central Pacific to be held at all costs. It was a commitment to total war regardless of the consequences for the nation.

References

1. Herbert P. Bix, *Hirohito and the Making of Modern Japan*, Duckworth Press, 2000, p. 466.
2. Ibid., p. 450.
3. Ibid., p. 458.

Rout

29 Fall of Rome

> We hoped to land a wildcat that would tear the bowels out of the Boche.
> Instead we have stranded a vast whale with its tail flopping about in the water.[1]
>
> Churchill's verdict on the Anzio landings during
> discussion with his chiefs of staff, 29 January 1944

In January 1944 the Allies were only sixty miles from Rome, but their path was barred by the formidable barrier of the German Gustav Line. The Germans had controlled the Allied advance up the Italian peninsula by forcing the Allies to fight for every river crossing and mountain top. The result was high Allied casualties due to the German tactic of defending each position to the point of being overwhelmed before falling back and reforming further to the north. The time gained by this slow, controlled retreat permitted the Germans to prepare the Gustav defence line across the waist of Italy from Minturno on the west coast to Ortona on the Adriatic coast. The Germans had never intended to hold southern Italy. Their strategy was to deny the Allies possession of northern Italy and the key strategic prize of Rome, and therefore the German defence was concentrated on the western sector of the Gustav Line to block the direct route to Rome along Highway Six. The battlefront was only 18 miles wide from Minturno on the Tyrrhenian Sea to Cassino on the edge of the high Apennine Mountains in the centre of Italy. The terrain significantly favoured the defender. Some 5 miles inland from the coast were the Aurunci Mountains and the heights of Monte Girafano, followed by the natural barrier of the Rapido and Liri rivers and, most formidable of all, the heights of Monte Cassino on the edge of the towering Abruzzi mountains that commanded the town of Cassino and Highway Six to Rome. The summit of Monte Cassino was surmounted by an ancient abbey founded by St Benedict in AD 529. Its strategic importance as a gatehouse to Rome was underscored by the fact that it had been sacked four times in its history: first by the Lombards in 569, followed by the Saracens in 883, the Normans in 1030 and the French in 1799. At first the Allies intended to bypass the abbey, but in 1944 it was bombed and destroyed for the fifth time. Today the restored abbey once again dominates the landscape.

Field Marshal Albert Kesselring in command of the defence of Italy, deployed the Tenth Army commanded by General Heinrich Scheel von Vietinghoff along the Gustav Line and held the 29th and 90th Panzergrenadier Divisions as a mobile reserve, in the vicinity of Rome, to counter any Allied landings north of the Gustav Line. Kesselring and Hitler feared that the Allies would take advantage of their command of the sea to bypass the Gustav Line. In consequence Kesselring prepared detailed counter-attack plans that involved a chain reaction of troop movements from northern Italy, France and Yugoslavia. All were placed on 12 hours' notice of movement to ensure that any Allied landings in northern Italy were rapidly contained and destroyed. Kesselring also considered the danger of sabotage and ordered all key road and rail routes into Italy to be guarded by German troops, and for repair crews to be on standby to repair any damage from Allied bombing. The scale of the advance planning reflected Hitler's anxiety to regain the initiative in the war by decisively defeating any Allied landing in northern Italy on the beaches. Hitler hoped that a significant defeat with heavy casualties would deter the Allies from launching a cross-Channel invasion and grant the Wehrmacht time to turn east in strength to combat the Red Army. To the widespread alarm of all Germans, the Red Army had entered Poland on 6 January 1944 and brought the war uncomfortably close to Germany's borders.

Kesselring and Hitler had correctly predicted Allied strategy. As early as October 1943, General Sir Harold Alexander had recommended amphibious landings in conjunction with a major land assault to break the Gustav Line and seize Rome. However, the plan, codenamed Operation Shingle, was shelved because the slow Allied advance throughout November and December 1943 meant that the 5th Army could not be in position before all landing craft in the Mediterranean were due to be withdrawn to England for D-Day preparations. Churchill, who had lobbied for the invasion of Italy against American opposition, returned to the fray from his sick bed in Tunis at Christmas 1943. He was recovering from pneumonia and suffered a mild heart attack, but in a series of meetings and negotiations by telegram he succeeded in winning the approval of General Eisenhower and President Roosevelt to extend the deadline for the withdrawal of the landing craft to 15 January 1944 and, later, to an absolute deadline of 6 February.

Operation Shingle was revived, and on 2 January 1944 General Alexander issued orders for two Anglo-American divisions to land at Anzio under the command of Major-General John P. Lucas. The strategy was to distract and draw off German forces from the Gustav Line to permit a breakthrough and a rapid advance on Rome. The Allies failed to appreciate the determination of Hitler to defend Rome and his willingness to transfer reinforcements from France and Yugoslavia rather than weaken the Gustav Line. The immediate Allied objective was to destroy the German positions on

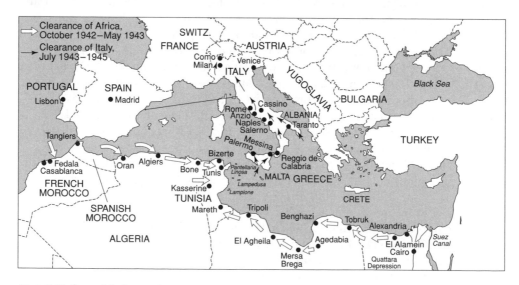

Map 7 Defeat of Italy

Monte Cassino to open the road to Rome. The abbey perched on the summit of Monte Cassino was a well-known treasure house for medieval art, tapestries and sculptures, and home to some 70,000 original parchment scrolls; consequently it was marked on all Allied maps as a protected building. President Roosevelt and General Eisenhower were sensitive to the charge that most of Italy was a 'china shop' and they were keen to rein in the Allied 'bull' to ensure that Allied forces did not despoil Italy's rich cultural heritage. The Germans were equally sensitive to the uniqueness of Monte Cassino and from October to December 1943, with the co-operation of the abbot, gregorio Diamare, had organised an evacuation of all art treasures, as well as most of the monks, to the greater security of Rome. The art treasures included crates of artefacts previously moved out of Naples. The Germans held a press conference in Rome on 8 December 1943 to highlight their concern to protect Italy's cultural heritage. However, officers acting to satiate Hermann Göring's considerable appetite for art diverted some of the paintings and sculptures to his private collection. After the war the 'lost' artworks were found in a salt mine near Alt-Aussee in Austria. Only the Abbot and seventeen monks chose to remain in the abbey, but they were joined by an increasing tide of refugees seeking shelter from the heavily bombed town of Cassino. The Germans fixed a 300-metre exclusion zone around the abbey for their troops and chose not to occupy the abbey. Instead the 1st Parachute Division spread out across the slopes below the abbey and on the adjacent mountain ridges, which gave commanding fire points on Cassino and Highway Six to Rome. Whether any German troops actually entered the abbey has always been a bitter matter of dispute.

On 17th January, after some earlier probing attacks to test the defences, the US 5th Army launched a major frontal assault along the Gustav Line, but with a focus on breaking the German hold on Cassino and Highway Six. The Germans held the Allied advance and in freezing blizzards and heavy snow both sides entered into a determined battle to gain the advantage. The Allied trump card was sea power and five days into the battle on 22 January some 36,000 troops of 6th Corps were landed on the beaches of Anzio under the command of Major-General Lucas. The intention was to sweep behind the Gustav Line and to cut off the German troops from reinforcement and supply. There was no German presence in the immediate area and, in contrast to the experience at Salerno, the landing was unopposed. However, the Allied drubbing at Salerno weighed heavily on the mind and strategy of Major-General Lucas. Rather than rush inland he ordered the troops to dig in to hold off the inevitable German counter-attack. Lucas intended to wait until his main force of a further 60,000 troops, were landed with all their equipment and artillery, before he risked an advance. It was a cautious strategy that in other circumstances might have been wise, but Lucas failed to detect that there were no significant German forces in the area. With hindsight he squandered an opportunity for an uncontested advance to the strategic Alban Hills that dominated the approaches to Rome. His caution provoked Churchill to fury, as quoted at the start of this chapter, and played into Kesselring's hands because, in response to the invasion alert codenamed Case Richard, German reinforcements poured into northern Italy with direct orders from Hitler to push the Allied invaders back into the sea. All Lucas had achieved was to corral his men for German attack and to present the Germans with the advantage of a self-imposed encirclement, referred to by the Germans as a *Kesselschlacht* (cauldron battle). The Germans held the high ground and by 24 January they began to rain artillery shells into the heavy concentration of Allied troops trapped in the *Kesselschlacht*, bringing up two heavy 280 mm siege guns mounted on railway flat cars to add to the bombardment with devastating 250 kg high-explosive shells. The guns operated under cover of darkness and were pulled back into deep railway tunnels in the daytime to deny Allied bombers a target. The Luftwaffe also launched daily air attacks on the beachhead, and in a succession of attacks sank a number of ships including the destroyer *Janus*, the cruiser *Spartan* and the clearly marked hospital ship *St Davids*.

Lucas had little choice but to break the siege conditions or to watch a steady annihilation of his forces. On 25 January he directed an advance towards Cisterna and Campoleone, but it was firmly contained by the Hermann Göring Panzer Division. An attempt to outflank the Germans at Cisterna by US Rangers on 30 January ended with only six survivors out of 767. Campoleone was taken with further heavy losses, but after four days the Allies were forced to withdraw. On 11 February, the Allied attack on the Gustav Line petered out after three weeks of intensive fighting that had cost over 14,000 Allied lives, with the Americans taking the brunt. Allied frustration was expressed by a controversial decision to bomb the abbey on Monte Cassino. The pressure came from Lieutenant-General Bernard Freyberg, commander of the New Zealand 11th Corps, and Major-General Francis Tuker, commander of the Indian Division. Both forces were brought out of reserve to launch a fresh assault on Monte Cassino, but both commanders and hundreds of ordinary Allied troops were convinced that German fire was coming from the abbey and that German artillery spotters had taken up residence. War correspondents picked up the concerns and filed stories that essentially accused Allied commanders of sacrificing Allied lives in order to protect Italy's heritage. A lively correspondence raged in the letters columns of the *The Times* and *New York Times* for and against a decision to bomb the abbey. General Mark Clark was entirely opposed to the bombing, but he finally agreed – more out of concern to raise troop morale than any proven military need. Warning leaflets were showered over Monte Cassino on 14 February from artillery shell canisters to urge Italian civilians and Benedictine monks to evacuate the area. The next day most of the abbey buildings were reduced to a heap of rubble by over 450 tons of Allied bombs. An estimated 230 Italian civilians who had chosen to remain, or where too infirm to move, were killed. However, due to poor Allied planning no Allied attack was timed to take place in the immediate aftermath of the bombing. It took two days for Freyberg to assemble sufficient troops for an assault on the abbey ruins on the night of 17 of February, but the attack by the Indian Division was decisively defeated because the bombing had not touched the German positions. The destruction of the abbey conferred no advantage on the Allies because days later the Germans occupied the ruined abbey in strength and established numerous strong points amid the jumble of tumbled stone and half-standing walls. Instead of destroying a fortress the Allies had merely created one. It was the mistake the Germans had made at Stalingrad, albeit on a larger scale.

The Germans were gaining the upper hand on both fronts and on 16 February they launched a major attack on the Anzio beachhead with four divisions to fulfil Hitler's command to drive the Allies into the sea. The attack would have succeeded except for the decisive intervention of Allied naval and airpower, which inflicted heavy losses and broke the German attack. The Anzio landings, far from assisting the Allies to breach the Gustav Line, had proved to be an embarrassing debacle. In frustration, and in an attempt to gain the initiative, Clark relieved Lucas of his command on 22 February and replaced him with Major-General Lucien K. Truscott. Allied airpower was the key and by 2 March a sustained bombing offensive finally broke the German containment and secured the Allied beachhead.

At Cassino the Allies launched their third major assault on the Gustav Line on 15 March, in the aftermath of an air and artillery bombardment that destroyed every single building in the town. The Allied troops advanced across a moonscape of craters, some so wide and deep that they had to be bridged. The terrain was as much an obstacle as the enemy, and in the heights above the town similar slow progress was made towards the ruined abbey by New Zealand, Indian and Gurkha troops. Casualties were high for very minor territorial gains and German snipers concealed on the mountain slopes took a heavy toll. The exhausted Allied forces accepted defeat on 23 March. On the same day in Rome, Italian partisans detonated a bomb on the Via Rasella, killing thirty-three SS troops in a passing truck. Hitler ordered reprisals and initially demanded the execution of fifty Italians for every German killed, but he was persuaded to reduce the figure to ten per German. In consequence the Gestapo in Rome trucked 330 prisoners to the Ardeatine caves south of Rome. All were forced to kneel and were shot dead with their hands tied behind their backs. Local priests entered the caves on 27 March to confirm the reports of the executions and urged Pope Pius XII to condemn the executions and to demand that the Germans release the bodies for Christian funerals. The Pope ignored the requests and refused to give leadership or comfort to the families involved. He seemed more concerned that the partisans might be communists. Hitler authorised Kesselring to take similar reprisals against any further partisan actions. The decision imported the terror of the east to Italy when in the months ahead many thousands of ordinary Italians were executed on the whim of individual German commanders. The most notorious single atrocity occurred between 29 September and 1 October 1944 when the entire population of the village of Marzabotto, south of Bologna, was executed. An estimated 1,830 men, women and children, including nuns and priests, were murdered. The Pope still remained silent, but Mussolini was moved to protest against the scale of the random murders.

The German strategy of converting northern Italy into a fortress appeared to be working, and after the failure of the landings at Anzio the dominant question was how to break in. The chief of staff of the 15th Army Group, Lieutenant-General John Harding, provided the answer. He proposed to use the Allied preponderance in manpower and airpower to launch an overwhelming assault, codenamed Operation Diadem along the entire 18-mile front from Minturno, on the coast, to Cassino. His logic was that the Germans could not be strong everywhere and that the attack would stretch them to breaking point and open up gaps in the line. The Allies also had the advantage of substantial reinforcements, with the deployment of the Canadian 5th Armoured Division, the Polish 2nd Corps, the South African Armoured Division and the French Expeditionary Corps (FEC) composed of hardy mountain troops from Tunisia, Algeria and Morocco. The battle plan envisaged four major points of attack. The order of attack from west to east was for the US 2nd Corps to advance along the coast, the FEC to infiltrate the steep, rugged Aurunci mountains, the 8th Army to advance across the Liri and Rapido rivers into the Liri valley, and the Polish 2nd Corps to renew the assault on Monte Cassino. In conjunction with the land offensive, Allied airpower was directed to implement Operation Strangle and to destroy all key road and rail junctions across northern Italy to deny the movement of German reinforcements. At 11 p.m. on 11 May the Allied offensive commenced. The US 2nd Corps under the command of Major-General Geoffrey Keyes made slow but determined progress, and by 15 May had reduced the German 94th Division to a third of its strength. The 8th Army, under the command of General Sir Oliver Leese, was ordered to cross and bridge the 60-foot wide river Rapido regardless of the cost. The weight of numbers gave the advantage, and by 16 May they had successfully established a bridgehead and advanced three miles, but at a cost of 4,000 killed. At Monte Cassino the Polish 2nd Corps, led by General Wladislaw Anders, was pinned down by highly accurate German fire and forced to break off the attack on 12 May. A renewed attack on 16 May was equally beaten back with heavy losses. The Allied attack was in danger of being contained but, in the least promising sector of the advance, the FEC succeeded in breaking the German line high up in the Aurunci mountains. It vindicated the strategy of General Alphonse Juin who had earlier identified the mountains as the 'Ardennes' of the German line. Like the Ardennes in 1940, the Aurunci mountains were reputedly impassable but the French breakthrough threatened the German forces in the Liri valley with encirclement. Consequently, on 16 May Kesselring ordered the German troops to abandon the Gustav Line and to fall back on the Hitler Line eight miles to the rear to keep the front line intact. At 10.20 a.m. on 18 May, soldiers of the 12th Podolski Regiment cautiously entered the deserted abbey of Monte Cassino and raised a makeshift Polish flag over the ruins. It had taken six months to achieve. General Anders never forgot the sacrifice of some 4,000 of his men and, when he died in 1970, his last wish to be buried in the Polish cemetery at Monte Cassino was honoured.

The Allies maintained the momentum of the advance and gained the advantage on 23 May when the German cordon around Anzio was finally breached by General Truscott's 6th Corps. The cordon had been weakened by a withdrawal of troops to reinforce the Hitler Line, but on the same day the Canadian 1st Division breached the Hitler Line and forced the Germans into a general retreat. Hitler, to Mussolini's disappointment, declared Rome to be an open city. Mussolini had never forgiven the Romans for their open joy at his arrest and wanted Hitler to order a street-by-street battle to hold the Allied advance. The key concern for the retreating German 10th Army was to avoid encirclement as the 6th Corps moved out from the Anzio beach-head directly east to cut Highway Six at Valmontone. It was the main escape route north for the German 10th Army. Kesselring despatched the Hermann Göring Panzer Division south to Valmontone to hold the road open. The race was on, but in a surprise decision Clark ordered the bulk of the US 6th Corps to swing north to capture Rome. He acted to ensure that American troops rather than the British 8th Army were the first to enter Rome, but his decision resulted in the escape of the 10th Army and marred the success of the breakthrough on the Gustav Line. Clark was known to be a highly ambitious general who regularly courted the press, and he could not resist the lure of a victorious entry into Rome. By accepting the victor's crown before the battle was won, he delivered a hollow victory.

In the early evening of 4 June 1944 the first troops of the US 88th Division entered Rome and parked their jeeps in St Peter's Square. The next day the ambivalent attitude of the Italians to the war was on public display with the flying of the Italian flag alongside the British and American flags from the town hall, and the Romans greeted the Allies with wine and flowers as liberators. The happy scenes were in stark contrast to the later capture of Berlin. The objective of Rome had finally been reached, but in a campaign that revealed a poverty of Allied leadership and at a cost of 105,000 Allied casualties and 80,000 German casualties. Some 20,000 of the latter were incurred at

Monte Cassino defending a hilltop that was never taken in battle. The Germans had dictated every stage of the battle for Italy and still eluded the Allies, because to the north of Rome the veterans of the Gustav Line regrouped along the Gothic Line and prepared to deny the Allies entry into southern Germany. Clark's triumph was short lived: on 6 June world attention switched to Normandy and Operation Overlord, the invasion of Europe.

References

1. Gilbert Martin, *Churchill: A Life*, Heinemann, 1992, p. 767.

30 Rollback on the Eastern Front

> If I settled with Russia today I would only come to blows with her again tomorrow – I just can't help it.[1]
>
> Hitler's rejection of advice from Foreign Minister Ribbentrop
> to negotiate a settlement with Stalin in September 1943

Stalin travelled to the front line on 1 August 1943 to receive, at first hand, reports from his commanders on the Kalinin Front in central Russia. Much was made by Soviet propaganda of his 'morale raising' tour of the front line, including an overnight stay in a simple peasant hut in the village of Khoroshevo, but Stalin kept well back from the front line and never met any ordinary troops or officers. Stalin was a consummate politician and his tour was designed to renew his credentials as a war leader for domestic and Allied consumption rather than any genuine interest in the conditions of the troops. Throughout the war Stalin had never shown the slightest interest in casualty rates or the hardships of the front line. He treated the Soviet people as no more than a dispensable commodity, and whether they died fighting the Germans or fulfilling industrial or agricultural goals was a matter of indifference. On his return to Moscow, Stalin declined an invitation from Roosevelt and Churchill to attend an Allied conference in Quebec, scheduled for 13 to 19 August. He cited the pressing demands of the front line and the need for his close direction. During the Quebec conference Churchill and Roosevelt resolved to give priority to the defeat of Germany over Japan and agreed 1 May 1944 as the provisional date for Operation Overlord. On 31 August Stalin achieved his desired propaganda reward when in a radio broadcast Churchill lamented Stalin's absence from the Quebec talks with the words: 'Marshal Stalin, in direct command of the victorious Russian armies, cannot at the present time leave the battle-fronts upon which he is conducting operations of vital consequence...'[2] Churchill's public flattery of Stalin reflected his anxiety to bind Stalin to Allied plans with a tripartite Allied conference at the earliest opportunity. Churchill feared that Stalin might be swayed by peace overtures from Hitler and opt to renew the Nazi–Soviet Pact of August 1939, leaving Hitler in occupation of western Europe. He was also anxious to reach an agreement with Stalin on the composition and nature of the future post-war governments of eastern Europe. Of most concern was the future of Poland, following the joint Nazi–Soviet invasion of that country in September 1939. Much to the irritation of the Polish government in exile in London, the United States and Britain studiously downplayed Stalin's partnership with Hitler between 1939 and 1941 out of a fear of damaging the Alliance. In April 1943, the Alliance was severely tested when the Germans uncovered the bodies of approximately 11,000 Polish army officers buried in a forest in Katyn, 12 kilometres from Smolensk. All had their hands bound behind their backs and had been shot in the back of the head. A total of 22,000 Polish army officers and intellectuals were taken into Soviet custody during 1939 and 1940, and all were subsequently executed by the NKVD (Soviet secret police). Stalin denied any knowledge of their murder and blamed the Germans following their invasion of the Soviet Union in 1941. Goebbels seized the propaganda initiative and ferried war correspondents and the Red Cross to the site, in the hope of confirming Soviet guilt and promoting a split in the Alliance. Churchill and Roosevelt accepted the Soviet denial and later, at the Nuremberg War Crime Trials in 1946, they offered no challenge to the Soviet 'scientific evidence' of German guilt. It was not until 1989 and the era of glasnost that the Soviet Union finally admitted responsibility for Katyn.

Churchill's fears of a renewal of the Nazi–Soviet Pact were well grounded because both sides had flirted with the possibility of a settlement. After the Soviet victory at Kursk in July 1943, Foreign Minister Joachim von Ribbentrop had urged Hitler to seek a settlement with Stalin. Hitler permitted some informal contacts to be made with an official attached to the Soviet legation in Stockholm, but recoiled when Stalin demanded a return to the 1914 Soviet–German border. To the disappointment of Ribbentrop and the Wehrmacht, Hitler refused to contemplate any compromise and, in a rare burst of honesty, as quoted at the start of this chapter, he ordered Ribbentrop to break off the contact.

Hitler had reached a point of no return and despite the defeat at Kursk, the capitulation of Italy and the downfall of Mussolini he remained fixed on victory. His strategy was to hold the line on the Eastern Front in order to transfer reserves west to destroy the expected Allied invasion of France on the beaches. He assured his generals that the deployment of new 'super' weapons in 1944, especially jet aircraft, rocket bombs and snorkel-enabled U-boats, would not only defeat the Allied landings but knock Britain out of the war. In the interim, Hitler demanded complete faith in victory from his generals and an acceptance that providence was on the German side. Most subsequently failed the test and were sacked, and many others gave active or passive support to the bomb plot of July 1944 in an attempt to assassinate Hitler and end the war.

Hitler's decision to fight a defensive war in the east was welcomed by the Wehrmacht, but disagreements soon emerged when Hitler issued stand-fast orders that defied military logic. Here was the kernel of the crisis between Hitler and his commanders: faith versus reason. Hitler's concept of a defensive war was simply to stand still and to defend every inch of conquered territory, whereas the Wehrmacht argued for a strategic withdrawal to a pre-prepared defensive line – the 'Eastern Rampart' or 'East Wall'. The model was the successful defence of Italy by Field Marshal Kesselring, who had dictated the course of the battle in Italy by falling back to the prepared defences of the Gustav Line. However, in August 1943 the Eastern Rampart was more of a concept than a reality. It was envisaged as a heavily fortified line from the Baltic coast in the north to the Sea of Azov in the south, following the natural defensive lines of the

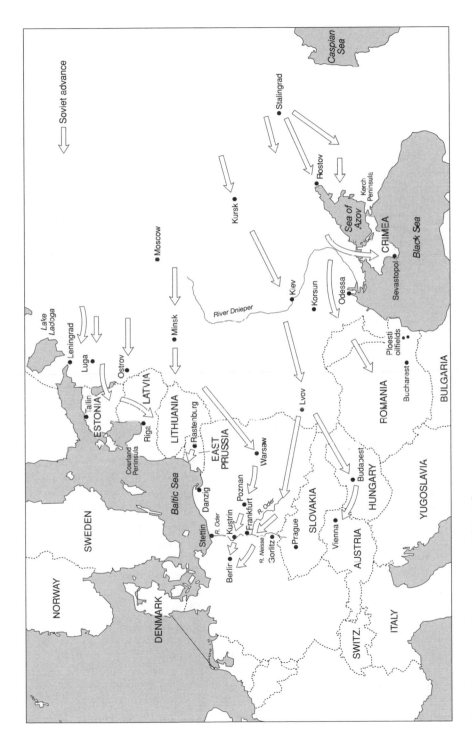

Map 8 German defeat in the east, 1944-45

river Narva (the Panther Line) in the north and the river Dnieper in the south. Once ensconced behind the Eastern Rampart, the Wehrmacht was confident that it could hold the Red Army and gain the necessary breathing space to defeat the Allied landings in the west. However, Hitler rejected all suggestions for a strategic withdrawal to the Eastern Rampart and ordered all three army groups to hold their positions and not to yield territory.

Hitler had seriously underestimated the recovery of the Soviet Union, now reaping the rewards of the transfer of industry to Siberia beyond the reach of the Luftwaffe in 1941 and 1942 and the full mobilisation of the population. In the summer of 1943 the Red Army was able to field 6.5 million troops against 4.5 million German troops and enjoyed a two to one superiority in tanks and aircraft. The Soviet Union was also benefiting from a sharp increase in US Lend-Lease supplies in 1943. US trucks and jeeps substantially underwrote the mobility of the Red Army and eased the transport of supplies. Soviet troops dined on US rations and, in readiness for the winter campaign, all Soviet soldiers were issued with warm felt boots manufactured to Soviet specifications in the United States. Morale in the Red Army had also soared following the German defeats at Stalingrad and Kursk, and in September 1943 the Red Army renewed its advance in the south and centre, with the goal of liberating the Crimea and the cities of Smolensk and Kiev. Manstein appealed to Hitler to permit an immediate withdrawal behind the line of the river Dnieper from the Black Sea to Kiev as the only chance of holding the Soviet advance in check. Hitler responded by flying to Manstein's headquarters at Zaporozhe on 8 September to urge greater effort. It was to be his last time on Soviet soil. On 15 September he finally acceded to Manstein's request, but he refused permission for the 17th Army to withdraw from the Crimea. As the Crimea was a virtual island only connected to the mainland by the narrow Perekop peninsula, Hitler insisted that it be held to deny the Red Army airfields in range of the Ploesti oilfields in Romania. Manstein ordered his retreating forces to dig in along the Dnieper and pressed thousands of Russian peasants into forced labour to try and improve the defences.

In the centre of the front, Smolensk fell on 25 September following a sustained six-week battle. To maintain the momentum of the advance, Stalin promised the Soviet Union's highest military decoration – 'Hero of the Soviet Union' – to the first soldiers to cross the Dnieper and breach the East Wall. In turn Hitler promised his soldiers the Iron Cross and six months' leave to deny the Red Army passage. All along some 400 miles of the Dnieper south of Kiev, the Red Army swam, waded, floated, rowed and bridged the river with the aim of liberating Kiev, the capital of the Ukraine. There was not one crossing point but a multitude because the continuous Soviet offensive denied the Wehrmacht time to complete the fortifications. The much-vaunted barrier of the East Wall was little more than a patchy network of strong points. Defeat in the centre was swiftly followed by defeat in the south, when the Red Army crossed the mouth of the Perekop peninsula on 31 October and trapped an estimated 210,000 German and Romanian soldiers in the Crimea. The prize of Kiev fell on 6 November, on the eve of the annual celebrations of the Bolshevik Revolution, and triggered wild revelry in Moscow. Fifteen German divisions had been smashed trying to hold Kiev and their defeat permitted the Red Army to drive a deep corridor between German army groups Centre and South. No reinforcements were available to plug this yawning gap in the East Wall because, only days before, Hitler had ordered all fresh troops and equipment to reinforce the West Wall. The retreating Germans stripped Kiev of every movable commodity and left the city in ruins: out of a pre-war population of 400,000 only an estimated 80,000 survived. The capture of Kiev exposed Army Group South to encirclement when the Red Army surged forward some 30 miles beyond Kiev to Fastov. South of Kiev, the Dnieper ascribed a sharp semi-circle to the Black Sea; inside the 'bend' the bulk of Army Group South found itself engaged in a desperate battle for survival.

On 8 November Hitler addressed the annual rally of the Nazi Party faithful in Munich and, in the absence of any victories to report, he boasted of victory to come in 1944 with the deployment of Germany's new super weapons. Those present were heartened by his confidence but, away from the set-piece theatre of speech making, all who met Hitler were shaken by his physical decline. Hitler had visibly aged. He walked with a stoop and he regularly fought to control a trembling left arm and dragged his left leg. He was reputedly sustained by a daily assortment of twenty-eight pills from his personal physician Dr Theo Morell, including the poisons strychnine and atropine, in an apparent attempt to jolt his nervous system out of his increasingly dark depressions.

In contrast, on 28 November 1943 the Allied leaders Stalin, Churchill and Roosevelt were in buoyant mood when Churchill finally secured the first tripartite conference of the war in Tehran. Attendance involved Stalin's first and last plane flight. During the short flight from Baku an encounter with air turbulence intensified his fear of flying and ruled out any repeat. The talks were cordial and the D-Day landings were confirmed for 1 May, weather permitting. Stalin also promised to launch a major offensive in the east to force the Wehrmacht to defend both fronts. The future of Poland was also settled when Churchill and Roosevelt agreed to satisfy Stalin's border grievances by moving Poland westwards at the expense of German territory. The decision essentially legitimised the Red Army invasion of eastern Poland in September 1939. Like Czechoslovakia in 1938, Poland was to discover that military power rather than democratic principles was the final arbiter.

Hitler's response to the mounting crisis of the Eastern Front was to order counter-attacks to retake Kiev and to drive the Red Army back. Some checks to the Soviet advance were delivered, but Manstein warned Hitler that all three army groups were in a state of collapse and recommended the retreat of army groups North and South into the centre to bar the Soviet pathway into Poland and Germany. On 4 January 1944 he visited Hitler at *Wolfsschanze* and requested freedom of action, like Kesselring in Italy, to conduct a fighting retreat – but Hitler refused to delegate authority or to lift his 'stand fast' orders.

Two days later, Manstein's worst fears were realised when the Red Army broke the German front line and pushed Army Group Centre back across the Soviet border into Poland, leaving Army Group South trapped against the Black Sea and Army Group North trapped against the Baltic. The Red Army was dictating the course of the battle and could decide where and when to attack. On 14 January the blow fell on the northern front when a total of 375,000 Soviet troops launched a final offensive to relieve Leningrad. The siege had been broken a year earlier with the opening of a narrow road and rail corridor into the city, but the city was still shelled on an almost daily basis. The German line was overrun on 17 January, and ten days later Army Group North was driven 120–170 miles in a retreat to the borders of the Baltic States. Only the Finns to the north still threatened Leningrad, but they were too weak to mount an offensive. In Leningrad a minimum of 632,253 people, and perhaps as many as 1.1 million, had died during the three-year siege from the daily shelling, starvation and hypothermia induced by the long Russian winters. Throughout the siege there had been no distinction between civilians and soldiers. All had been on the front line and their courage was one of the greatest feats of endurance of the entire war.

On the same day as the Soviet triumph Hitler addressed all his senior commanders, and dramatically insisted upon their unconditional loyalty with the injunction: 'I must have as my last line of defence around me the entire officer corps who must stand with drawn swords'.[3] Manstein made the mistake of interrupting Hitler to assure him of the loyalty of the officer corps and received a firm rebuke for his public breach of protocol. On 29 January Hitler's mounting anger with his senior commanders was expressed by the dismissal of Kuchler, the commander of Army Group North, for failure, and his replacement by Field Marshal Walther Model.

The next blow fell in the south when on 24 January the Red Army, under the command of General Ivan Koniev, renewed its offensive and, in a classic pincer attack, encircled 60,000 German troops at Korsun. A mini-Stalingrad ensued when Manstein tried to lift the siege and to resupply the trapped men from the air. Forty-four Junkers Ju-25 transports were shot down in five days in a vain attempt to deliver supplies. A breakout was launched on the night of 17 February, but it turned to disaster when an estimated 52,000 German troops were cut down, many literally, by charging Cossacks on horseback wielding sabres. The architect of the Soviet victories on the southern front, General Nikolai Vatutin, was killed in the fighting and was replaced by Marshal Zhukov. Hitler's reaction to the defeats was to issue Order No. 11 on 8 March forbidding any further retreat and ordering encircled troops to stand their ground. He grandly termed the surrounded pockets of German troops as 'German fortresses' that would stand firm against Soviet attack and provide 'the pivot points and corner posts of the front as well as jumping off bases for counter attacks'.[4] Few accepted Hitler's reasoning that encirclement conferred a strategic advantage, not least Manstein who flew to *Wolfsschanze* to request reinforcements to prevent a complete collapse in the south. Hitler reluctantly conceded and transferred the 2nd Panzer Army from France in an attempt to stabilise the front line. However, only a temporary relief was achieved and greater problems loomed as Hungary and Romania, both Axis allies, became increasingly perturbed by the approach of the Red Army to their borders and contemplated an accommodation with Stalin. German intelligence had recorded tentative contacts with the Allies and Hitler feared a sudden 'Italian-style' defection that would collapse the entire German defence. It was too great a risk to ignore and on 18 March, at a meeting in Klessheim, Hitler browbeat Admiral Nikolaus Horthy, the regent of Hungary, into agreeing to a German occupation of Hungary. Ion Antonescu of Romania was also not trusted, and on 23 March the Germans occupied Romania to secure the vital oilfields at Ploesti. Adolf Eichmann immediately took advantage of the German occupation of Hungary to commence the round-up of Hungary's Jews, who had been almost untouched by the Holocaust. The steady advance of the Red Army in the Ukraine finally undermined Manstein's position, and that of Field Marshal Kleist in command of Army Group A. On 30 March, both were summoned to the Berghof by Hitler and sacked for failure. Hitler reshuffled his commanders and insisted that the Red Army be held in check until the defeat of Allied forces in Normandy released troops for a new offensive on the Eastern Front. It was an impossible task. The Red Army crossed the river Prut into Romania on 2 April, and the key port of Odessa on the Black Sea, which supplied the trapped 17th Army in the Crimea, fell on 8 April.

On the same day the Red Army launched a major offensive to clear the Crimea, and Hitler ordered a fight to the death and refused permission for a retreat across the Black Sea. After three weeks of close-quarter fighting which left the last of the German defenders beaten to the shore at Cape Kherson, west of Sevastopol, Hitler finally authorised a withdrawal from 4–11 May. It was too late. By then an estimated 110,000 troops had been killed or captured, at a time when Hitler needed every division for the looming battle for Poland.

In mid-May 1944 Stalin and Hitler considered their positions. Despite the military setbacks on the Eastern Front, Hitler expected Field Marshal Rommel to drive the Allies back into the sea, and the swift defeat of the western Allies to restore the confidence of both the German people and the Wehrmacht in a final victory. Stalin had more tangible reasons for confidence in a future victory because in the space of a year the Red Army had advanced up to 600 miles and broken the Wehrmacht hold on the Soviet Union. The Red Army was poised along a 2,000-mile front line from the Baltic to the Black Sea to drive the Germans out of the Soviet Union and to enter Greater Germany. At Tehran, Stalin had promised Churchill and Roosevelt that he would launch a major Soviet offensive to coincide with Operation Overlord in the west. On 20 May, after a review of the military options, Stalin agreed plans for Operation Bagration to smash Army Group Centre and to take the most direct route to Germany and Berlin through Poland. The operation was named after Prince Bagration who had died defending Russia during Napoleon's invasion of Russia in 1812. The date selected by Stalin was 22 June 1944, the third anniversary of Hitler's invasion of the Soviet Union.

To disguise the direction of their attack the Red Army created the impression of a pause in their offensive against Army Group Centre for resupply by engaging in defensive works. Numerous dummy encampments were also constructed south of the Pripyat Marshes to convince the Wehrmacht of a build-up that pointed towards Romania and the Ploesti oilfields. The deception succeeded and in response Hitler stripped Army Group Centre of tanks and troops to reinforce the south. Hitler's attention was also distracted by the opening of the second front in Europe (third when Italy is counted) on 6 June 1944, and the subsequent landing of a million Allied troops in Normandy. Operation Bagration opened on 22 June with a minor assault on Army Group Centre to draw the Germans forward and was followed 24 hours later by the shock of a major bombardment and advance. It was the first of five interlinked offensives designed to crush Army Group Centre and to open a direct line of attack to Minsk, followed by Warsaw and eventually Berlin. Army Group Centre was assaulted by an army of 1.2 million men, spearheaded by 4,000 tanks and 6,000 aircraft, and in little over a day the Red Army broke the German line and surged forward towards Minsk. The commander of Army Group Centre, General Ernst von Busch, had only 500,000 men at his disposal, and with few tanks or aircraft his forces were threatened by encirclement when Soviet armoured columns broke through into the German rear. Hitler revived his theory of 'fortress localities', ordering all encircled troops to stand fast and, in a familiar response to adversity, he blamed the commander. Busch was sacked and replaced by Hitler's 'fireman', Model. Chief of General Staff Zeitzler, who was labouring under accusations of defeatism from Hitler, suffered a nervous breakdown on 1 July. His place was taken by Field Marshal Guderian, but he too found himself regularly berated by Hitler who questioned and often countermanded his every decision.

Guderian and Model had no reserves to stem the Soviet advance. The Red Army, unchecked by any significant German counter-attack, enveloped Minsk from the north and south in a classic pincer attack which owed much to earlier German tactics. The fighting core of Army Group Centre was trapped, and to prevent reinforcement from Army Group North, the First Baltic Front, commanded by General Ivan Bagramyan, advanced into the Baltic states of Latvia and Lithuania driving a Soviet corridor between Army Groups Centre and North. The attention of Army Group North had been deliberately distracted away from the centre by a Soviet offensive launched against the Finnish front line north of Leningrad on 10 June. The Finns resisted furiously but eventually sued for peace on 19 September. The collapse of Army Group Centre at Minsk cleared the way for further Soviet advance by the First Ukrainian Front, commanded by Marshal Ivan Koniev, on 13 July, towards the Polish cities of Lvov and Lublin. Overall, the interlinking offensives tore a 250-mile-wide hole in the German line and essentially destroyed and removed Army Group Centre from the battlefield, with the capture or loss of an estimated 400,000 men. It was a stupendous military triumph that opened the road to Warsaw and Berlin.

Hitler left Berchtesgaden on 14 July for the last time and returned to *Wolfsschanze* to personally direct the defence of Germany as the Red Army swept towards Vilnius in Lithuania and threatened East Prussia. In Moscow the defeat of Germany and the liberation of the Soviet Union was celebrated on 17 July by a parade of 57,000 German prisoners, including eighteen generals. There was little public triumph but rather a grim satisfaction that the war was essentially won.

The opposite realisation within the ranks of the Wehrmacht produced a near successful assassination attempt on Hitler on 20 July. There had been active anti-Hitler assassination plots within the Wehrmacht from July 1943, but by luck and by keeping his movements a closely guarded secret Hitler had survived. Himmler disbanded the office of military counter-intelligence, the Abwehr, in February 1944 out of suspicion of disloyalty to Hitler. His suspicion was well placed because the head of the Abwehr, Admiral William Canaris, was a long-standing opponent of Nazism. He had regularly used his position to try and undermine Hitler's military plans and had gathered around him a group of dissidents who actively plotted the assassination of Hitler during 1943 and 1944. They intended to appoint General Beck, who had actively opposed Nazism in 1938, as head of state, and to appoint Field Marshal Rommel commander-in-chief of the Wehrmacht. Count Klaus Schenk von Stauffenberg was on the fringe of the conspiracy, but in July 1944 his appointment to the command of the Reserve Army promoted him to the centre of the conspiracy when his new position gave him a place at Hitler's military conferences in *Wolfsschanze*. At 12.32 p.m. on 20 July Stauffenberg placed a briefcase containing a bomb with a ten-minute fuse at Hitler's feet under the map table in the conference hut of *Wolfsschanze*. He excused himself, ostensibly to take a telephone call, and in the confusion of the subsequent explosion managed to bluff his way out of the compound. Although four of those present were killed, Hitler survived the blast with only slight injuries. His life was saved because General Brandt moved the briefcase to the far side of the thick oak leg of the map table and also because the sides of the wooden hut blew out and dissipated most of the blast. It is highly likely that no one would have survived the blast if the conference had been held in the normal concrete bunker. Later in the day Hitler was fit enough to guide Mussolini around the ruins when the latter arrived for a planned conference. The conspirators, convinced that Hitler must have been killed in the explosion, revealed themselves prematurely and all were swiftly arrested. In Berlin General Fromm ordered the arrest and immediate execution of Stauffenberg, Beck and two other conspirators in the courtyard of the General Staff headquarters. He acted to demonstrate his own loyalty and out of fear that under Gestapo torture they might implicate him in the conspiracy. Himmler was given full powers to root out conspirators across the Wehrmacht and the most prominent were put on trial in a 'People's Court' presided over by the notorious judge Roland Freisler. The verdicts were never in doubt, and the first eight to be found guilty of conspiracy were hanged in Plotzensee prison north-west of Berlin on 8 August. In the absence of a gallows, meat hooks were hastily screwed into a wooden beam in a cellar and all eight were suspended and slowly strangled to death by nooses made from piano wire. Their deaths were filmed for Hitler to watch and, over the months ahead to the end of the war, an estimated 5,000 people, including Admiral Canaris and General Fromm, were arrested and executed for complicity in the assassination attempt.

Operation Bagration had ground to a halt 10 miles from Warsaw on 31 July for resupply and re-equipment after a continuous advance of 450 miles in five weeks. The proximity of the Red Army triggered a rising by the Polish 'Home Army' in Warsaw, both to hasten the defeat of the Wehrmacht and, to Stalin's concern, to assert their independence on behalf of the Polish government in exile in London. The Home Army miscalculated and found itself entirely at the mercy of the Wehrmacht when Stalin not only refused direct military assistance to the Home Army but refused permission for USAAF and RAF supply planes to use Soviet airbases close to Warsaw. Stalin ignored appeals from the Pope, Churchill and Roosevelt to assist the Home Army, and in an unequal battle the Wehrmacht and Luftwaffe razed Warsaw to the ground street by street. The Home Army held out for sixty-three days against the odds, but capitulated on 3 October 1944 with 15,000 dead, along with an estimated 200,000 civilians. While the Germans crushed the Warsaw rising Stalin focused his military efforts on consolidating his hold on Romania, and on 20 August the Red Army crossed the border in strength. In events reminiscent of the collapse of Italy, King Michael ordered the arrest of Ion Antonescu on 23 August and three days later announced that Romania had joined the Allies. The Romanian troops turned against their erstwhile German allies and, with their assistance, the Red Army entered Bucharest on 28 August. Army Group South was annihilated as a fighting force, with over 200,000 killed or wounded. This success permitted the Red Army to occupy the Ploesti oilfields on 2 September and to cut off Germany's only major source of oil. Only a few minor oilfields east of Lake Balaton in Hungary remained in German hands. Over the months ahead, the shortage of petrol quickly grounded the Luftwaffe and halted the panzers.

In the space of only three months, the entire 2,000-mile German front line from north to south had been rolled back out of the Soviet Union. Compared to Operation Overlord, Operation Bagration is virtually unknown in the west, but it was Bagration and the Soviet rollback of German forces on the Eastern Front from 1943–44 that shattered the Wehrmacht and Hitler's Third Reich. In the midst of this conquest, during the early hours of 17 August 1944, Private Alexander Afanasevich Tretyak crossed the river Sheshupe from Lithuania into East Prussia and earned the distinction of being the first Soviet soldier to stand on German soil. With surrender and the assassination of Hitler no longer options for the Wehrmacht, Germany faced nemesis.

Reference

1. Michael Bloch, *Ribbentrop*, Bantam Press, 1992, p. 387.
2. Winston Churchill, *Great War Speeches*, Corgi, 1957, p. 267.
3. Ian Kershaw, *Hitler 1936–45: Nemesis*, Penguin, 2000, p. 619.
4. Bob Carruthers and John Erickson, *The Russian Front 1941–45*, Cassell, 1999, p. 159.

31 Overlord

Make peace, you idiots. What else can you do?[1]
Field Marshal von Rundstedt's reply to
Field Marshal Keitel's request for advice,
1 July 1944, following the success of Overlord

Operation Overlord 6 June 1944, is firmly associated with the defeat of Nazi Germany, but it was only one half of an east–west pincer attack. On the third anniversary of the Nazi invasion of the Soviet Union, 22 June 1944, the Red Army launched Operation Bagration in support of Overlord (see Chapter 30). Whereas in the west the Allies faced sixty German divisions (only fifteen divisions were in the Normandy sector, and one of those was stationed on the Channel Islands), the Red Army in the east confronted and ultimately destroyed 228 German divisions. On the 'forgotten' front of northern Italy, the US 5th and the British 8th armies also aided Overlord by tying down twenty-eight German divisions. Nevertheless, Overlord was one of the most significant Allied triumphs of the war. It not only shortened the war but guaranteed the liberation of western Europe from Nazi rule. If Overlord had failed Stalin might well have been tempted to renew the Nazi–Soviet Pact, leaving Hitler in possession of western Europe. The triumph was a product of detailed Allied planning that left little to chance in the execution of the largest amphibious landing in military history. The outcome, by July 1944, was the safe landing in Normandy of an Allied army of over a million men. After Overlord Hitler's defeat was never in doubt.

The planning for Overlord formally commenced in March 1943 under the direction of Lieutenant-General Frederick Morgan. His task was to examine the landing options and to make recommendations for the approval of the as-yet-unnamed supreme commander. The need for wide shelving beaches and the desire to keep within the umbrella of full Allied air cover reduced the landing options to northern Belgium, Pas de Calais, the Somme estuary, the Seine estuary and Normandy. The Pas de Calais was attractive because it offered the shortest sea crossing and the most direct path into Germany, but those advantages also made it too obvious a choice. Consequently it had the heaviest fortifications of Hitler's Atlantic Wall and was guarded by sixteen divisions. After an exhaustive study of the four other options Morgan finally recommended Normandy. The attractions of Normandy were a good depth of sea, sheltered by the Contenin peninsula, to marshal the invasion fleet; wide shelving beaches to permit a

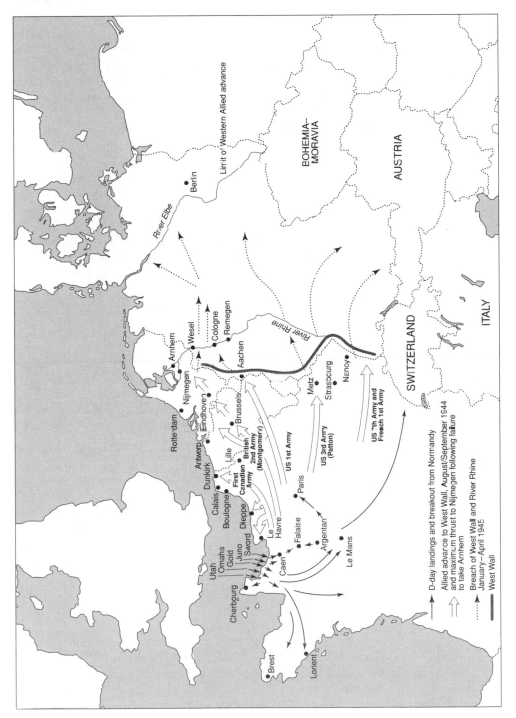

Map 9
German
defeat in
the west,
1944–45

Berlin

River Elbe

Limit of Western Allied advance

BOHEMIA–
MORAVIA

AUSTRIA

Arnhem
Wesel
Cologne
Remegen

River Rhine

Nijmegen

Rotterdam

Eindhoven

Antwerp

Brussels

Aachen

Metz
Strasbourg
Nancy

ITALY

SWITZERLAND

Dunkirk

Lille

Calais
Boulogne
Dieppe

First
Canadian
Army

British
2nd Army
(Montgomery)

US 1st Army

US 3rd Army
(Patton)

US 7th Army and
French 1st Army

Le Havre

Paris

Sword
Juno
Gold
Omaha
Utah

Caen

Falaise

Argentan

Le Mans

Cherbourg

Brest

Lorient

D-day landings and breakout from Normandy

Allied advance to West Wall, August/September 1944
and maximum thrust to Nijmegen following failure
to take Arnhem

Breach of West Wall and River Rhine
January–April 1945

West Wall

rapid build up of troops; and evidence of minimal German defences. The only significant disadvantage lay beyond the beaches. The Normandy countryside, or *bocage*, was a landscape of endless narrow country lanes and a patchwork of small fields all bounded by high earth embankments and tall hedges. The *bocage* protected the numerous orchards of Normandy from stiff Atlantic breezes, but it represented a serious threat to Allied mobility and favoured the less mobile German divisions by offering good defensive positions. To overcome this disadvantage, the seizure of the town of Caen was specified as a D-Day objective because south of Caen the *bocage* gave way to wide rolling plains and a battleground that would play to the Allied strengths in tanks and airpower. The port of Cherbourg was also a key Allied objective in order to gain a major seaport to support the rapid build up of troops and supplies.

Hitler had also identified the Normandy beaches as a likely invasion point, but after discussion with the commander-in-chief of the *Westheer* or western army, Field Marshal Gerd von Runstedt, Hitler concluded that the main Allied landings would be at the Pas de Calais, but with diversionary landings in Normandy or the Seine estuary or even Norway. This conclusion was largely based upon disinformation fed to German intelligence by German agents captured and successfully turned by British intelligence. The Twenty Committee of British intelligence (named from the Roman numerals XX for 'double cross') successfully mounted Operation Fortitude to direct Wehrmacht attention away from Normandy by inventing a fictional US 1st Army Group, under the command of General Patton, based in south-east England, opposite Pas de Calais, and a fictional British 4th Army Group based in Scotland within striking range of Norway. The deception was enhanced by false army encampments covering acres of land, complete with rows of dummy tanks and the generation of regular fake radio traffic. The deception was so successful that it was not until nearly three weeks after D-Day that Hitler finally accepted that no further Allied landings were planned.

On 3 November 1943 Hitler issued Führer Directive 51 and gave the *Westheer* primacy over the *Ostheer* for men and resources to ensure that the Allied landings in the west were rapidly defeated. Three days later, he transferred Field Marshal Rommel from Italy to review and improve the Atlantic Wall defences. Rommel was unnerved to discover that beyond the showcase fortifications at the Pas de Calais, most of the Wall was non-existent. He requested a minimum of 50 million mines to mine the coastline adequately, but received only 6 million, and his request for a minimum of 240 rail carloads of cement per day to construct fortifications was met with only forty-seven carloads. However, he successfully pursued the construction and liberal distribution of inexpensive beach obstacles to deny easy access to the beaches. At low tide he directed the placement of thousands of stout wooden posts angled seaward, each capped with a contact mine. These were interspersed with steel 'hedgehogs' and tetrahydra designed to rip the bottoms out of landing craft. Rommel and Rundstedt bitterly disagreed on the best defensive strategy. Rundstedt favoured holding the six panzer divisions of Panzer Group West as a central reserve near Paris, whereas Rommel insisted that the panzers should be deployed near to the coast to ensure that the landings were swiftly engaged and defeated on the beaches.

The Allied plans for Normandy were confirmed during the Tehran Conference on 29 November 1943, attended by Stalin, Churchill and Roosevelt. Whereas Stalin welcomed confirmation of the plans he questioned the absence of a named commander for Overlord, which renewed his suspicions that Overlord might be a 'paper' plan. Stalin had often expressed doubts about the military commitment of Churchill and

Roosevelt, following the cancellation of earlier plans for landings in France in 1942 and 1943. As an act of good faith Stalin asked for the commander of Overlord to be appointed within a week of the end of the conference. On 7 December 1943 Roosevelt named General Dwight David Eisenhower as commander of Supreme Headquarters of the Allied Expeditionary Force (SHAEF). Eisenhower arrived in London on 16 January 1944 to take up his command in fog so dense that two men had to walk in front of his car. At SHAEF headquarters at Bushy Park, west of London, Eisenhower entered into detailed planning for the invasion with Field Marshal Sir Bernard Montgomery, Air Chief Marshal Sir Trafford Leigh-Mallory and Admiral Sir Bertram Ramsay, the operational commanders-in-chief for land, air and sea respectively. Five invasion beaches were confirmed. From west to east the beaches were codenamed Utah, Omaha, Gold, Juno and Sword. Utah beach was centred at La Madeleine at the base of the Cotentin peninsula, with the aim of sweeping north to seize the port of Cherbourg, supported by the Omaha landings between Vierville and St Honorine. Both beaches were allocated to the US 1st Army Group under the direct command of Lieutenant-General Omar Bradley. Gold, Juno and Sword beaches were allocated to the British 2nd Army, under the direct command of Lieutenant-General Miles Dempsey. His command included the largely Canadian landing at Juno beach. Gold beach ran from Arromanches to La Riviére, and from there Juno beach stretched to St Aubin; after a gap of approximately four miles Sword beach extended from Lion sur-Mer to Ouistreham. The French were included in the landings, with the US-equipped 2nd Armoured Division under the command of Major-General Philippe Leclerc; Polish and Belgian forces were also represented. However, General de Gaulle was rarely consulted because his grand imperious manner alienated Churchill and Roosevelt and prevented a cordial relationship.

At Berchtesgaden, on 19 March 1944, Hitler settled the defence arguments between Rommel and Rundstedt by transferring the 15th and 7th armies to Rommel's direct operational command and by dividing Panzer Group West between Rundstedt and Rommel. It was a compromise that satisfied neither general.

From 1 April 1944 the Allied air forces, including both RAF and USAAF strategic bomber commands, were directed to support Overlord by targeting all road and rail communications across northern France. The RAF and USAAF bomber commands, under the leadership of Air Chief Marshal Arthur Harris and General Carl Spaatz respectively, had initially refused to co-operate. Both men jealously guarded the independence of their bomber fleets and refused to 'abandon' their bombing strategy in favour of fulfilling army goals. Their attitude reflected a deep faith in the ability of strategic bombing to win the war without recourse to the high-risk strategy of a military invasion of occupied Europe. It took an ultimatum and a threat of resignation from Eisenhower before Harris and Spaatz agreed to place their bombers at the disposal of Overlord.

On 23 May Eisenhower set D-Day for 5 June to take advantage of favourable tides and a full moon, but on 1 June the weather in the Channel steadily deteriorated and by 4 June a force 5 gale was blowing. Eisenhower cancelled the D-Day order, and ships already at sea had to be hastily recalled. The weather delighted Rommel. He believed that the invasion would not be attempted until August at the earliest, and on 5 June he left his headquarters for his family home at Ulm, to celebrate his wife Lucia-Maria's birthday, before travelling on to Berchtesgaden to consult with Hitler. It was a fateful decision: earlier that same morning, at 4.15 a.m., Eisenhower had reset D-Day for first light on 6 June. It was a significant risk, but Eisenhower had either to go ahead or to disembark all the soldiers who were already wet, cold, hungry and seasick from being confined to their ships and landing craft in the midst of a gale.

First into action were the parachute and airborne troops who were tasked with guarding the flanks of the invasion beaches and disrupting German communications and the movement of reinforcements. The French Resistance, renamed the French Forces of the Interior (FFI) in May 1944 to identify them as a 'legal' military formation, was given 24 hours' warning of the invasion by a BBC radio broadcast. A single line from the poem 'Chanson d'automne' by Paul Verlaine, 'blessent mon coeur D'une langueur monotone' (wound my heart with a monotonous languor), was the order for action, and across France on the night of 5–6 June approximately 120,000 resistance fighters destroyed road, railway and telephone communications. Their actions were very effective. The FFI destroyed more locomotives than the pre-D-Day bombing and cut off telephone communication across France. In the east 13,000 troops of the US 101st and 82nd Airborne divisions were directed to secure the exits from Utah beach, while in the west the British 6th Airborne Division aimed to secure the exits from Sword beach and, in particular, to seize the Canal de Caen bridge near Benouville to open the road to Caen. The latter were the first Allied troops to land on French soil at 11.55 p.m. on 5th June and succeeded in surprising the few German guards and seizing the bridge intact. It was subsequently renamed Pegasus Bridge in honour of the airborne troops with their Pegasus shoulder flashes. In the east, the US airborne drop was bedevilled by poor pilot navigation that dropped the troops all over the Cotentin peninsula, including into the sea where many drowned under the weight of their equipment. Despite the chaos, sufficient troops were rallied and, by dint of surprise, seized the town of Ste Mere Eglise, which earned the distinction of being the first town in France to be liberated by the Allied invasion.

At 1.50 a.m. on 6 June Admiral Hoffman, still in his dressing gown and slippers, sent urgent invasion alerts to Field Marshal Rundstedt and to Hitler. Neither displayed any sense of urgency given the vague reports of parachute landings, and both were content to monitor the situation before ordering any counteraction. Hitler went to bed at approximately 3 a.m. seemingly untroubled by the news and with apparent satisfaction that the waiting appeared to be over.

In the Channel, Operation Neptune, commanded by Admiral Ramsay, reached its climax during the early hours of 6 June with the assembly, 8 miles south-east of the Isle of Wight, of the largest invasion fleet in military history. An estimated 800 warships and 6,000 transports formed up into five task forces, one for each invasion beach, and slowly approached the Normandy coast, preceded by a flotilla of minesweepers. The landings were all timed to coincide with sunrise and ranged west–east from 6.30 at Utah to 7.25 at Sword. Any German doubts that the invasion had arrived were removed by a sustained naval bombardment of the Normandy coast and continuous bombing raids by an Allied air force that could muster 11,000 aircraft. First in were the Underwater Demolition Teams (UDT) to clear pathways to the beaches, followed by a range of specially equipped and adapted tanks to give fire support to the infantry. Known as 'funnies', six different versions were extensively tested and perfected by Major-General Percy Hobart to assist the breakout from the beaches. The most significant was the Duplex Drive (DD) tank which could independently motor to the beach and drive straight out of the sea to give fire support. Its secret was the attachment of a canvas buoyancy skirt and propellers.

At Utah beach, the troops discovered few beach fortifications or Germans, and only twelve soldiers were killed during the landings from shellfire. Higher casualties were experienced at Gold, Juno and Sword beaches due to fierce German resistance and a higher than expected tide that concealed many of the beach obstacles, with the result that several landing craft were blown out of the water by mines. However, Hobart's 'funnies' broke the German defences and permitted the troops to move off the beaches. Only at Omaha beach was there near disaster and a heavy loss of life. The US troops had the misfortune to encounter the 352nd Infantry Division, who were all battle-hardened troops from the Eastern Front, and to land on a beach that was enclosed by cliffs with steep shingle rises and few exits. The preliminary bombing and naval bombardment had failed to dislodge the well-dug-in Germans and, when the landing craft approached, the US troops were raked by machine gun, mortar and artillery fire. Hundreds died as soon as the protective ramps were dropped, and hundreds more drowned in the heavy surf under the weight of their equipment. Fire support from DD tanks might have made the difference, but only five of the thirty-two DD tanks of the 741st Tank Regiment reached Omaha beach. The mystery of why they floundered was finally resolved in 2002 by an underwater examination of the position of the tanks on the seabed. It would appear that the commander of the 741st Tank Regiment, in order to correct a drift away from his aiming point of the Colleville church steeple, ordered the tanks to change their course. In doing so, the tanks presented their broadsides to the rougher than expected seas. The thin canvas skirt that kept the tanks afloat was immediately flattened and the tanks were swamped by the sudden inrush of water. The Omaha beach was only finally secured by close-in support from eight destroyers which poured shells into the German pillboxes, and by the bravery of ordinary troops, many of whom were inspired by Colonel George Taylor to charge forward despite the intense German fire. They successfully overwhelmed the German positions by sheer weight of numbers. The US mischance on Omaha was compounded by the wasted effort of the US 2nd Ranger Battalion which, under heavy fire, scaled the cliffs of Point de Hoc 2 miles west of Omaha beach only to discover that the German battery they intended to assault had been withdrawn. The German naval and air response to Overlord was almost non-existent. Only eighty Luftwaffe fighters were operational, compared to 6,000 Allied fighters, and their impact was minimal. At sea mines rather than naval action proved to be the greatest danger to Allied shipping and continued to claim ships for days after the initial landings.

Rommel arrived back at his headquarters at 5 p.m. to discover that the Allies were safely ashore on all five beaches and was dismayed to discover that little counteraction had been ordered by Rundstedt and Hitler. Rommel recommended the immediate commitment of the panzer reserve from around Paris and the transfer of reinforcements from the Pas de Calais. However, Hitler and Rundstedt were adamant that Normandy was a feint to draw attention away from the Pas de Calais. It was a major triumph for Allied deception, and in particular the fiction of the uncommitted US 1st Army at Dover. In addition, throughout the night of 5–6 June the movement of large naval and air forces in the Dover Straits was simulated by dropping copious amounts of radar-reflective 'window' to mimic the approach of a large air armada. Similarly, in the Channel a flotilla of small ships towing radar reflective balloons gave the appearance of large troop transports on German radar. The deception was enhanced by real planes disgorging thousands of paratroopers over the Pas de Calais, but all were quarter-sized dummies collectively named Rupert.

The only serious counter to the invasion came in the late afternoon at 4 p.m. when the 21st Panzer Division, under standing orders to counter-attack any Allied landings, successfully barred the road to Caen. However, by nightfall on 6 June the Allies had successfully landed 130,000 troops and established firm beachheads at four of the five beaches. The exception was Omaha where, because of the determined German resistance, the US troops had penetrated only a mile inland; but by 10 June Omaha was secure and all five beachheads were linked. Churchill, who had gloomily predicted 20,000 Allied deaths to secure the beaches on D-Day, was relieved to discover that only 2,500 had died. It was a very light death rate against a defended shore, but 1,100 of those who died had been killed on the narrow stretch of Omaha beach. A panzer counter-attack was the dominant Allied concern but, in a further victory for the code-breakers at Bletchley Park on 8 June, the headquarters of Panzer Group West at La Caine was successfully pinpointed from intercepted signals traffic. A subsequent airstrike killed seventeen of the staff officers and caused serious disruption to the command of the panzer divisions. Rommel directed his slender forces to hold Caen and diverted the few reinforcements under his command to the Cotentin peninsula. Rommel and Rundstedt believed that the immediate Allied target was Cherbourg in order to gain a port to reinforce their bridgehead. However, off the Normandy coast the first units of two artificial Mulberry harbours were slowly towed into position. No one on the German side had suspected that the Allies would bring prefabricated ports with them. Despite spending months poring over pictures of the construction of the huge steel and concrete cassions at building yards around Britain German intelligence had never guessed their purpose. Success for both sides depended upon who could win the military build-up. It was a race won by the Allies, aided by a vast reserve of men and resources sitting across the Channel ready for transport and an unhindered 24-hour shuttle of ships. Rommel's fear of Allied airpower was well founded because the Germans discovered that movement by day was impossible, and that roads and railways were destroyed as quickly as they were repaired. All bridges across the Seine into Normandy were down. The SS 9th and 10th Panzer divisions, transferred from Poland to Normandy, took two weeks to arrive because of the block on movement. However, they arrived in time to hold the German line at Caen on 1 July against a determined Allied offensive. The added sabotage by the FFI further frustrated German troop movements and triggered extreme reprisals from the SS. On 9 June SS Das Reich hanged a hundred men at random in the village of Tullen and the following day, at the village of Oradour-Sur-Glane, the SS rounded up the entire population and shot 642 villagers, including 190 schoolchildren. Only two of the population escaped. Today the ruined village remains untouched as a permanent memorial to the dead.

Montgomery's advance west stalled against the panzer restriction at Caen, and in the east the US advances on St Lo and north along the Cotentin peninsula to seize Cherbourg were also stalled by a tenacious German defence that took advantage of the Normandy *bocage* to transform every field into a fortress.

On 12 June Churchill, who was only prevented from accompanying the Overlord invasion fleet by the direct intervention of King George VI, arrived by destroyer in Normandy and visited Montgomery's headquarters at Cruelly 3 miles from the front line. On his return to England on board HMS *Cossack* he invited Captain Vian to 'have a plug at them ourselves before we go home'.[2] Vian duly opened fire with all *Cossack*'s guns on the German front line. Two days later General de Gaulle stepped back onto French soil for the first time since 1940 and visited the front line at Bayeux.

The separate visits indicated the extent of the strained relationship between the two leaders.

The failure of the Allies to break out of the beachhead encouraged Hitler. On 13 June he gained further hope by the long-awaited deployment of the *Vergeltungswaffen* (V1) self-propelled bomb. However, the OKW were disappointed to discover that the guidance system was not accurate enough to target the Allied beachhead. The first V1 launch on 13 June was unimpressive. Of ten launched only four reached the vicinity of London, but on 15 June seventy-three out of 224 V1s did hit London and by the end of the first week 526 people had been killed. The bombardment returned London to the days of the Blitz and generated considerable fear, because at first the V1 appeared to be unstoppable. The V1 flew at 400 miles per hour, which was faster than most fighter aircraft, and the distinctive throb of its engine resulted in the public nickname 'doodlebug' or 'buzz bomb'. The V1 carried a one-ton warhead and fell to earth when its fuel ran out with sufficient explosive impact to destroy whole streets. The rising death toll sparked a new evacuation of London; by mid-July 500,000 women and children had evacuated London and by September more than a million. Churchill was so alarmed by the threat that he considered the use of mustard gas to retaliate against the German civilian population. However, the V1 was slowly countered by lining the identified flight corridor with barrage balloons and artillery, and the RAF pilots soon perfected a series of successful 'shoot-down' and 'knock-down' techniques that included flying alongside and using a gentle nudge to tip them over before they reached London.

Hitler travelled to a forward military bunker at Margival, near Soissons, on 17 June to confer with Rundstedt and Rommel. He was pensive and subdued but fixed his strategy on containing the Allied beachhead while the V1 and the planned V2 rocket offensive bombed Britain into submission. He refused to risk the transfer of troops from northern France because he still feared an Allied landing at the Pas de Calais, or even a surprise invasion of Denmark. His strategy was containment, and he issued his familiar order of no retreat and ordered General von Schlieben in Cherbourg to fight to the last round. Rommel openly expressed his pessimism and urged Hitler to negotiate an end to the war, but Hitler curtly told him to mind his own front line and not to worry about the future course of the war. The exchange was an indication of Rommel's mounting disillusionment with Hitler's leadership and reflected his passive support for the anti-Hitler conspirators within the Wehrmacht. That same day in London thirty-seven people were killed by flying bombs, and Hitler narrowly missed becoming a victim of his own weapon when a flying bomb misfired and fell close to the command bunker in Margival. From 19–21 June the Allied build-up of men and supplies was unexpectedly hit hard when a sudden gale in the Channel destroyed the US Mulberry harbour and badly damaged the British harbour. It raised a more urgent need for the seizure of Cherbourg to provide port facilities.

Cherbourg was heavily bombed on 21 June and, to further aid the Allied ground assault, three battleships and four cruisers shelled the city on 25 June. The next day Schlieben surrendered Cherbourg, and on 30 June the final pockets of German resistance north of the city at Cap de la Hague also surrendered. The loss of Cherbourg darkened Hitler's mood and, following Runstedt's pessimistic report at a conference at Bertesgaden on 29 June and his outburst to Field Marshal Keitel, as quoted at the start of this chapter, Hitler relieved him of his command. On 3 July Hitler appointed Field Marshal Gunther von Kluge in his place and also took the opportunity to replace

Schweppenburg and Field Marshal Hugo Sperrle, who had commanded air defence in the west. The pattern of defeat and dismissals, familiar on the Eastern Front, was now repeated by Hitler on the Western Front as he sought in vain to find a commander who could conjure up a victory.

Rommel, who had been present at Bertesgaden and who had concurred with Rundstedt's report, also expected dismissal for defeatism, but on 17 July his war ended in a more dramatic fashion. Rommel was seriously injured when an RAF fighter strafed his staff car near Caen, and three days later the attempted assassination of Hitler at *Wolfsschanze* (see Chapter 30) eventually ensnared him when the Gestapo investigation uncovered evidence of his knowledge and apparent approval of the conspiracy. To maintain the propaganda that those involved in the assassination plot were minor figures, Rommel was offered poison on 14 October 1944, which he gladly took to protect his family. He was reported to have died from complications arising from his head injuries and three days later received a full state funeral in Ulm.

The day after Rommel's hospitalisation, the US forces broke the German encirclement at St Lo after two weeks of pitched battles and at a high cost of 10,000 casualties. The victory was immediately exploited by the launch of Operation Cobra on 25 July. Cobra smashed the German line at Avranches on 31 July and opened the road west to Brittany and east to undercut the entire German front holding the British forces in check at Caen. At Caen there was disappointment when the third major offensive, directed by Montgomery between 18 and 20 July and codenamed Operation Goodwood, petered out without achieving a breakthrough. In response to the mounting criticism Montgomery insisted that his aim was to engage and grind down (or 'write down' to use Montgomery's terminology) the panzer opposition. Montgomery was facing six panzer divisions at Caen, compared to two at Avranches, and he argued with some justification that his offensives were steadily engaging and destroying the bulk of the panzer opposition in France. The dispute was never satisfactorily resolved, but clearly Montgomery would have preferred a breakthrough to a standstill.

US General Patton was returned to operational command, following his disgrace in Sicily, and subsequent command of the fictional US 1st Army, with command of the newly formed US 3rd Army. He quickly revived his reputation for decisive action by directing a powerful armoured thrust through the Avranches gap deep behind the German lines. He directed a rapid advance across Brittany, and by the end of the first week in August he had set siege to the German garrisons of the major ports of St Malo, Brest, Lorient and St Nazaire, aided by some 20,000 members of the FFI. The German garrisons of Lorient and St Nazaire defied all attempts to take the ports and held out until the end of the war. In the air over the invasion beaches the first operational Messerschmitt Me-262 jet fighter took reconnaissance photographs on 2 August, but it was only one of a squadron of nine. They were too few and too late to have any impact on the battle, and by the time more were deployed in the autumn of 1944 they were grounded by the acute shortage of aviation fuel. The key battle for France was east, and on 8 August Patton executed a deep sweep south-east to Le Mans and successfully undercut the bulk of the German forces still stubbornly blocking Montgomery at Caen. The move threatened the German 7th Army with encirclement and placed Patton on the road to Paris. The battle for Normandy was essentially over and opinion within the Wehrmacht favoured an orderly retreat behind the line of the Seine to regroup. However, it was not an opinion Kluge dared share with Hitler. His caution was judicious because Hitler's reaction to the defeat was to order a deep counter-offensive to try and retake Avranches and to split the Allied front. It resulted in the destruction of Hitler's last reserve of panzers by US Thunderbolts and RAF Typhoons from 6–8 August and forced the Wehrmacht into retreat. At Caen a fresh offensive by the 2nd Canadian Division and the 51st Highland Division, codenamed Operation Totaliser, finally broke the German line and permitted an advance south towards Falaise. It presented an opportunity to encircle the retreating Wehrmacht at Falaise by linking with elements of Patton's 3rd Army pushing north. In the far south, the immense superiority of Allied manpower and resources was further demonstrated by the launch of Operation Dragoon, the invasion of southern France. On 15 August a joint US and French force over 400,000 strong swept ashore between Cannes and St Tropez against minimal German resistance. They advanced inland, driving the Germans before them, and by the time they linked with the 3rd Army in northern France in September 1944 they had taken 79,000 prisoners and liberated the whole of southern France.

Kluge was highly concerned by the danger of encirclement at Falaise and personally inspected the front line on 15 August. His tour was truncated by an Allied artillery bombardment that forced his car off the road and compelled him to take cover in a ditch for the best part of 12 hours. On his return to his headquarters he was summarily sacked by Hitler who suspected him of entering into surrender negotiations with the Allies when his staff had been unable to confirm his whereabouts. There was no truth in the accusation, but Kluge had been tainted by the 20 July conspiracy and Hitler strongly suspected his loyalty. He was directed to return to Germany. In his place Hitler transferred his 'fireman', General Model, from the Eastern Front. Model arrived too late to alter the course of the battle – not least because he had no fresh reinforcements to make a difference.

On 20 August some 50,000 German troops were successfully trapped in the Falaise pocket, but to Patton's immense frustration conflicting aims and orders had permitted the escape of 30,000 troops. Allied fighters relentlessly strafed the fleeing German columns and littered the roads with lines of burning vehicles, dead and injured horses and men. The defeat marked the end of effective German resistance. Beyond the river Seine, Model could only muster 120 panzers and four divisions out of the fifteen divisions that had originally confronted the Allies in Normandy. The casualties on both sides were high. The Germans had lost an estimated 400,000 killed or wounded since D-Day, the Americans 124,000, the British 64,000 and the Canadians 16,000.

On 19 August Patton's 15th Corps crossed the Seine at Mantes Gassicourt 40 miles north of Paris. Within the city the FFI and the communist resistance ordered a general rising to liberate Paris. On the same day Kluge ordered his driver to stop by the road side on his way to Germany and swallowed a cyanide pill. In a personal letter to Hitler he beseeched him to think of the German people and to end the war. His death was explained as a heart attack to avoid any spread of defeatism.

The rising in Paris placed considerable pressure upon Eisenhower to intervene when his preferred strategy was to bypass Paris and to let the German garrison atrophy. Paris was garrisoned by 22,000 troops with fifty panzers under the command of General Dietrich von Choltitz, and Hitler had ordered Choltitz to defend the city street by street and to reduce it to ruins. General de Gaulle urged permission for the 2nd French Armoured Division to enter Paris, following a decision by the FFI and the communist resistance to engage the German garrison. Leclerc, encouraged by de Gaulle, had already disobeyed orders, moved his division to the outskirts of Paris and was apparently ready to enter Paris regardless of orders to the contrary. Eisenhower relented and at 10.30 p.m. on the evening of 24 August the first French soldiers entered Paris and seized the Hotel de Ville. Sporadic fighting erupted across Paris on 24 and 25 August, but the feared destruction of the city never occurred because Choltitz quietly ignored Hitler's orders to demolish Paris and surrendered his garrison at 2.30 p.m. on 25 August. An estimated 1,483 resistance fighters had died in the fighting, together with 300 soldiers of the French 2nd Armoured Division and 2,788 Germans.

General de Gaulle, who had urged his countrymen to resist Fascism and not to surrender in June 1940, was vindicated and on 26 August he led a victory march down the Champs Elysées studiously ignoring German snipers who took pot shots at him and his entourage. Paris was free and the tricolour was triumphantly raised above the Eiffel Tower in place of the swastika. Within a week the whole of France was successfully liberated as the Allies pressed forward towards the German border.

References

1. Anthony Read and David Fisher, *The Fall of Berlin*, Hutchinson, 1992, p. 176.
2. Martin Gilbert, *Churchill: A Life*, Heinemann, 1992, p. 778.

32 Islands

This war is essentially for our self defence and very self existence. So whether Germany wins or is beaten we have to fight on to the end . . .[1]

Prime Minister Tojo addressing senior commanders at Imperial Headquarters in the presence of the emperor, 30 September 1943

By August 1943 US forces had established a firm presence in the Solomon Islands in the south-west Pacific and forced open a door into Japan's Pacific empire. The next steps in the campaign were discussed between Churchill, Roosevelt and the prime minister of Canada, Mackenzie King, at the Quadrant conference in Quebec between 19 and 24 August 1943. The primacy of 'Europe first', confirmed at the earlier Casablanca Conference in January 1943, was upheld, but approval was also given for an intensification of the war in the Pacific. Vice-Admiral Louis Mountbatten was appointed commander-in-chief of the Allied South East Asia Command (SEAC) and his deputy was confirmed as General Joseph Stilwell, the American chief of staff to Jiang Jieshi's nationalist army in China. Their task was to press the Japanese in Burma with the aim of reopening the Burma road supply route into China, and to increase the airlift capacity over the Himalayas, referred to as the 'hump' by the Allied aircrews, to support an eventual ground and air offensive by the Chinese nationalists. At the same time the US army and navy confirmed plans to exploit the breakthrough in the Solomon Islands with a twin thrust into the heart of the Japanese Pacific empire, codenamed Operation Cartwheel. In conditions of top secrecy, Churchill and Roosevelt alone reviewed the progress of the atomic bomb development programme and signed an undertaking for joint control over the bomb.

Operation Cartwheel set a strategy of driving two parallel pathways from east to west across the Pacific to the Philippines with projected extensions to Formosa (Taiwan) or mainland China. The primary aim was to cleave the Japanese Pacific empire in two, thereby ending the free movement of Japanese reinforcements south and the flow of resources north to Japan. Japanese industry was dependent upon its southern empire for a host of raw materials vital to the war effort, primarily oil, rubber and iron ore. Little consideration had been given by the Japanese military to the loss of these supplies or the husbanding of resources to sustain a war of attrition because they had expected to fight a short war. The merchant marine sailed unprotected and increasingly fell victim to US submarines, and whereas the US had twenty-two carriers under construction from 1943 to 1944 the Japanese had three. The US strategy was to isolate the southern half of the Japanese empire, aided by the British and Indian forces on the Burmese border, the Chinese in South East Asia and the Australians in the South Pacific. Inside this Allied perimeter, the intention was to leave most of the Japanese-held islands and territories to 'wither on the vine', cut off from all reinforcement and

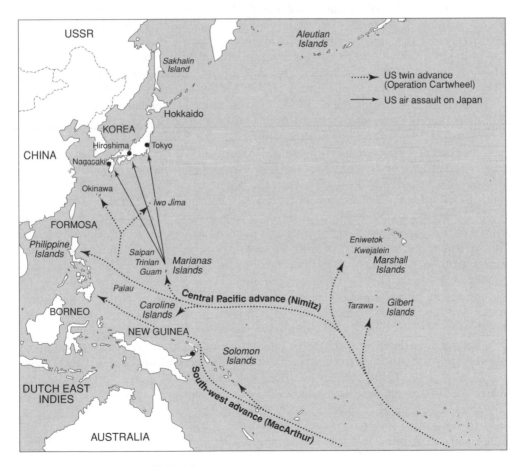

Map 10 Defeat of Japan 1944–45

supply. Once the south was contained the US intended to establish airbases on mainland China or on islands in the North Pacific within striking range of the Japanese home islands by B-29 Superfortresses. Essentially, Churchill and Roosevelt intended to harry and weaken Japan in a war of attrition until the defeat of Nazi Germany permitted the release of sufficient Allied troops to invade the home islands and to confront the Japanese Army in China. To assist with the latter both were keen to secure a Soviet entry into the Pacific war once Germany was defeated.

The south-west pathway to the Philippines was anchored in the Solomons and entrusted to General Douglas MacArthur, who had famously stated 'I will return' after he was forced to flee the Philippines on 11 March 1942. MacArthur's goal was to secure the upper Solomon Islands and from there to advance along the northern coast of New Guinea to the Philippines. The parallel advance across the central Pacific was placed under the command of Admiral Chester Nimitz. His plan was for an island by island advance through the Gilbert Islands, the Marshall Islands, the Caroline Islands and the Mariana Islands before converging on the Philippines, although Nimitz also favoured an invasion of Formosa. The emergence of two separate commands represented the failure of Roosevelt and the US Chief of Staff General George Marshall to settle the rivalry between the US navy and army for primacy in the Pacific. Nimitz had no confidence in MacArthur and consistently refused to subordinate naval strategy to his command, whereas MacArthur perversely ignored the fact that the Pacific consisted more of water than of land, and insisted upon a dual command. However, the inter-service rivalry, far from weakening the US effort, ultimately delivered a death blow to the Japanese Pacific empire because the simultaneous advances stretched the slender resources of the Japanese navy and air force to breaking point

Between June and September 1943 the US Army consolidated its hold on the Solomon Islands by ranging outward from Guadalcanal to land on New Guinea and New Georgia. MacArthur's aim was to isolate the major Japanese naval base and airbase at Rabaul on the island of New Britain and to wear down the garrison gradually with regular naval and air bombardments. On 1 November he took his first major step westwards with landings on Bougainville, the largest island in the Solomons, with the aim of establishing a forward airbase in easy striking range of Rabaul.

On 20 November Nimitz opened the campaign in the central Pacific with landings at Makin and Tarawa atolls, approximately a hundred miles apart in the Gilbert Islands. Makin had a minor garrison of 800 Japanese troops and they fought to the death rather than surrender. The battle for the tiny island of Betio within Tawara atoll produced a greater shock, particularly because it was the first Pacific battle to be photographed by war correspondents. Fierce Japanese resistance left the shallow blue water and white sands of the idyllic palm-fringed atoll littered with the bodies of hundreds of US marines. The pictures provoked a storm of controversy and resulted in a 35 per cent slump in recruitment for the marines. Thereafter strict censorship of photographs from the war front was introduced. By the end of the battle for Tarawa on 23 November, 1,000 marines had been killed and 2,000 injured, and of the estimated 4,850 Japanese defenders only seventeen were captured, along with 129 Korean labourers. The level of fanaticism displayed by the Japanese troops, and their willingness to die rather than to surrender, forced the marines to kill men at point-blank range and to use flame-throwers and hand grenades to take every bunker and pillbox. It was a savage conflict that took its toll on men's nerve, leaving the island strewn with the grotesque sight of thousands of smashed and mangled torsos – and all to take a remote island only 3 miles long. The exposure to such horror, coupled with the endemic anti-Japanese racism prevalent in the US media and armed forces, was blamed for the regular mutilation of Japanese corpses as the Pacific war unfolded. It became commonplace for US marines to collect 'war trophies' of severed heads and strings of severed ears, and to post home 'souvenirs' of skulls, necklaces made from Japanese teeth and even letter openers carved from the thigh bones of the Japanese dead. Many US marines also routinely inspected the teeth of Japanese corpses for gold fillings and pulled them out in grisly competitions for the highest personal gain.

The pressure placed on Japan increased on all fronts from December 1943 to January 1944, with Allied advances in China, New Guinea, Burma, and New Britain in the Solomons. The focus of action returned to the central Pacific when Nimitz directed landings at Kwejalein in the Marshall Islands on 31 January. Nimitz applied the lessons of Tawara, and the US marines were supported by a more sustained naval bombardment, the deployment of 'landing tractors' specially adapted to transport the troops across the coral lagoons, numerous amphibious tanks and liberal quantities of flame-throwers and explosive charges to destroy bunkers. The tactics were a significant success and the Japanese garrison of 8,000, devoid of naval or air support, were rapidly over-whelmed by an invasion force of 40,000 marines supported by over 1,100 aircraft. The Japanese refused to surrender and resorted to suicidal charges with fixed bayo-nets. The battle ended with only 130 Japanese captured for the loss of 372 US marines and infantry. Similar resistance on the adjacent islands of Roi and Namur produced 3,742 Japanese and 190 American deaths.

In an attempt to regain the initiative, Japan sought the endorsement of the nations within the Japanese Co-Prosperity Sphere as a welcome liberator from European impe-rialism. Sovereign status was offered to Burma, Malaya, Thailand and Indo-China, and this proved attractive because few wanted a return to British or French colonial rule. Both Britain and France had steadfastly refused to withdraw from empire in the east. In India, many ordinary Indians were attracted by the possibility of an end to British colonial rule, and in Burma an Indian army recruited from POWs under the command of Subhas Chandra Bose fought on the Japanese side. Prime Minister Tojo hoped to stir American opposition against fighting a war on behalf of European imperialism and to demonstrate that Japan was engaged in a war of liberation rather than empire expan-sion. However, Japan's diplomatic offensive was largely negated by the widespread murder and mistreatment of civilians and Allied POWs across Asia and the Pacific by the Japanese Army. On 28 January 1944 a formal denunciation of Japanese war crimes was released in Washington and London with a commitment to post-war prosecution for those responsible. The Allied successes in the Pacific left Japan with few military options other than to stand firm and to fight to the death island by island, but in Burma and China the existence of strong, well-equipped forces gave the option of an offensive. Like Hitler in Germany, Prime Minister Tojo and Emperor Hirohito hoped to inflict such heavy casualties on the Allies that they would sue for peace and leave Japan in possession of most of her conquered territory.

In Burma, to stem increasing advances from India, General Kawabe planned two linked offensives. Operation Ha-go was designed to defeat and roll back the British advance into Arakan and to distract the Allies, while Operation U-go launched a major cross-border offensive into India from central Burma to occupy Imphal. Kawabe was also prepared to exploit any breakthrough at Imphal by an immediate advance on Delhi, with the aim of ending British rule in India and installing a pro-Japanese government under the leadership of Subhas Chandra Bose. Ha-go was launched on 4 February and successfully broke the British and Indian line at the Ngakyedauk Pass (Okeydoke Pass to the British troops), but the Japanese force proved to be too weak to exploit the breakthrough and was forced to withdraw on 24 February.

Nimitz meanwhile, encouraged by the success of US tactics on Kwejalein, targeted Eniwetok on the extreme north-western edge of the Marshall Islands and Truk in the adjacent Caroline Islands – the main anchorage of the Japanese Combined Fleet. US air power was the decisive weapon and over the course of two days, 17 and 18 February, Japanese air and naval forces on Truk were erased by a sustained air blitz that destroyed an estimated 260 planes and sank nine warships and twenty-four merchant ships. The bulk of the Japanese Combined Fleet, including the carriers, escaped destruction because Admiral Kogo had prudently ordered their withdrawal a week earlier, having anticipated the US attack. In a simultaneous action Nimitz directed landings on Eniwetok and its outlying islands. Most of the Japanese garrison was killed on the first day by the intense naval bombardment and continuous strafing from carrier planes, and by 21 February the last opposition was crushed. Of 2,741 defenders only sixty-four were taken prisoner, while the Americans lost 258 killed.

On the night of 7 March 1944, 100,000 Japanese troops of the 15th Army crossed the Chindwin river into India and opened Operation U-go, but by mid-April the Allied ability to fly in fresh reinforcements turned the course of the battle. During the fighting on 24 March Churchill's protégé Major-General Charles Orde Wingate was killed when his plane crashed into the Bishenpur hills near Imphal in a tropical rainstorm. His 'Chindit' raiding force was eventually absorbed into the infantry, but Wingate's controversial tactic of deep penetration strikes into the Japanese rear was carried forward by 'Merrill's Marauders', a US jungle infiltration unit formed by Colonel Frank Merrill.

The Japanese resistance on New Guinea was equally tenacious, but MacArthur was able to employ the well-practised and honed tactic of naval bombardments and landings to bypass Japanese strongpoints and leapfrog along the coast. On 22 April 1944 the capital of Dutch New Guinea, Hollandia, was seized and the Japanese garrison routed. The only Japanese success was an advance in southern China during April and June 1944 to overrun US airbases within range of the home islands. MacArthur followed up the successful seizure of Hollandia with a series of further hops along the New Guinea coast, and by 30 July he had secured the whole of the northern coast of New Guinea with landings on the Vogelkop peninsula. The Japanese retreated into the interior where they continued to resist until the end of the war.

The Japanese hoped to defend the Philippines and stem the US advance by luring the US carriers into the range of land-based planes. The opportunity arose in the first week in June 1944 when Task Force 58, under the command of Admiral Raymond Spruance, approached the Marianas Islands and landed marines on Saipan. However, there was no surprise because the US capability to read all Japanese signals traffic had laid the plan bare and gave Spruance a considerable advantage. The USN air and ship crews were also all highly experienced, whereas following heavy losses the Japanese were reliant on inexperienced and trainee pilots. The resulting air battle on 19 June was dubbed the 'Marianas turkey shoot' by the US pilots and ended with 242 Japanese planes shot down for the loss of only twenty-nine US planes. The next day the Japanese lost a further 238 planes and, of greater significance, two carriers for the loss of an additional 101 US planes. The majority of the latter were lost because they were forced to engage the Japanese Navy at extreme range and at night, and on the return leg most ran out of fuel and had to ditch in the sea. On Saipan the Japanese displayed a complete disregard for their own lives and launched regular suicidal *banzai* charges on the marine positions. The battle ended on 7 July, with all but 2,000 of the original 32,000 Japanese garrison wiped out. A desperate attempt to counter-attack the US forces on Saipan with plague-carrying fleas developed by the secret biological warfare unit of the Japanese Army Unit 731 was defeated when the transport ship was sunk en route by a US submarine oblivious to its deadly cargo. The commander of Japanese forces on Saipan, General Saito, committed ritual hara-kiri and Admiral Nagumo, who had commanded the air strike on Pearl Harbor, shot himself. An estimated 8,000 Japanese civilians, convinced by Saito that the Americans would torture and kill them, leapt to their deaths into the sea from the Morubi Bluffs. Many of the dead included children held in their parents' arms or thrown to their deaths.

Emperor Hirohito at first refused to accept the loss of the Saipan, and insisted that the navy present plans for its recapture, but at an imperial conference on 25 June he reluctantly accepted that it was militarily impossible. Defeat was also accepted in India and on 8 July 1944 a general retreat was ordered from Imphal and the remnants of the Japanese 15th Army fell back into Burma broken and defeated. They had fought a gruelling battle and lost over 30,000 killed, compared to 2,700 British and Indian troops killed.

The string of defeats raised open criticisms of Prime Minister Tojo and on 18 July 1944 he resigned, along with his entire cabinet. Hirohito regretted his resignation and warmly congratulated Tojo for his hard work and service. The virtually unknown General Kuniaki Koiso was appointed in his stead. The change of government did not presage a search for peace but an intensification of the war effort. Hirohito endorsed Koiso's proposals for total war and declared his own intention to fight to the death. The US campaign in the Marianas ended with the successful invasion and capture of the islands of Tinian on 1 August and Guam on 10 August 1944. In both cases there were similar scenes to those encountered on Saipan with forlorn *banzai* charges and civilian suicides. On Tinian the entire garrison of 9,000 troops was killed for the loss of 394 US marines, while on Guam 18,250 Japanese were killed and 1,250 taken prisoner for the loss of 1,744 Americans killed. The extreme fanaticism of the Japanese defenders was illustrated in 1960 when two soldiers finally emerged out of the jungle in Guam and surrendered. They were unaware that Japan had lost the war *fifteen years before*.

Hirohito remained fixed on a victory in the Pacific. In an address to the Eighty-Fifth Imperial Diet on 7 September 1944 he urged greater effort, and stated: 'you who are the leaders of our people must now renew your tenacity and uniting in your resolve, smash our enemies' evil purposes, thereby furthering forever our imperial destiny'.[2] The initiative lay with the Allies, and on 12 September 1944 Churchill returned to Quebec for the Octagon talks with Roosevelt to discuss the next steps in the European and Pacific wars. Earlier in July at Pearl Harbor Roosevelt had authorised landings in the Philippines by General MacArthur and for Nimitz to bypass Formosa in favour of landings on the northern islands of Iwo Jima and Okinawa. The aim was to destroy Japanese fighter bases on Iwo Jima and Okinawa because they posed a threat to the B.29 Superfortresses flying out of the newly established US airbases on Tinian and Saipan. On 14 September, while the talks were in session, US forces invaded the Palau Islands as a stepping stone to the Philippines. The Palau Islands were thought to be lightly defended, but in grim scenes, reminiscent of Tarawa, a larger than expected garrison tenaciously defended the main island of Peleliu and cost the United States their heaviest casualties of the Pacific War. An estimated 9,171 US troops and 10,500 Japanese were killed on Peleliu. MacArthur brought forward his plans for the invasion of the Philippines by two months when air raids on the Philippines in September encountered little opposition. At 12 noon on 20 October 1944, two hours after the first US troops had landed, MacArthur stepped ashore on the island of Leyte in the central Philippines, accompanied by president-in-exile Sergio Osmena. There was little opposition from the minor Japanese garrison of 21,500 and by nightfall approximately 100,000 US troops were landed. The commander-in-chief of the Japanese forces on the Philippines was General Yamashita, who had famously routed the British Army in Malaya and Singapore in 1942. He had only taken up his new command on 9 October 1944, but with 225,000 troops under his command across the scattered Philippine islands he was prepared to fight a long war of attrition. At sea over two days, 24 to 26 October, the Japanese Combined Fleet was vanquished in a series of haphazard and scattered encounters with the US Navy in and around the Leyte Gulf. The Japanese lost the element of surprise when their approach to the Philippines was shadowed and reported by two US submarines, and thereafter a running battle commenced. Whereas the US Navy lost one light carrier and five other ships the Japanese lost four carriers, three battleships, six heavy cruisers, three light cruisers and eight destroyers. The defeat removed the capability of the Japanese Navy to challenge or to prevent the US Navy from advancing on the home islands. This stark realisation drove the Japanese to the extreme measure of launching kamikaze air attacks because it was the only viable weapon left. Hundreds of young men volunteered for rudimentary training in flying with the goal of crashing their planes, laden with explosives, into American ships. On 25 October 1944 the US escort carrier *Saint Lo* was sunk and five other US ships were damaged by the first kamikaze attacks of the war.

In Burma, in mid-October 1944, British and Indian forces launched Operation Capital to occupy central Burma, reopen the Burma Road to China, and ultimately to liberate the whole of Burma. The advance was supported by US and Chinese troops, who crossed the Chinese border into northern Burma, and in Arakan on the coast British and Indian troops also renewed their offensive. Following the defeat at Imphal, General Kawabe had been sacked; his replacement, Lieutenant-General Hyotaro Kimura, conducted a slow fighting retreat. The fighting in thick jungle and deep mud, and the constant assault by leeches and mosquitoes, made for a difficult and costly campaign. The Allies successfully reduced the danger of malaria by an inoculation programme, but more Japanese fell victim to malaria than to Allied attack. Kimura withdrew his forces behind the formidable natural barrier of the river Irrawaddy, in places 1.5 miles wide, and hoped to hold the Allied advance. However, on the night of 13 February 1945 the river was successfully crossed and thereafter the liberation of Burma was only a matter of time.

The battle for Leyte was effectively ended in December 1944 when US forces were increased to 180,000 troops, giving them a three-to-one advantage. MacArthur next directed landings on Mindoro on 15 December to gain airstrips to support the invasion of the main island of Luzon. The tiny garrison of only 1,000 Japanese troops was quickly overwhelmed, but offshore one US carrier and two destroyers were disabled by kamikaze attacks. On 10 January 1945 US troops poured ashore at Lingayen Gulf, Luzon, on the same beaches crossed by the Japanese three years earlier. Yamashita had withdrawn his men inland into the mountains, away from the firepower of the US fleet, in an attempt to command the centre of Luzon and to deny the control of the airfields, particularly the extensive Clark Field airbase. The battle for the Philippines lasted to the end of the war, but any hopes of protecting the home islands from attack were removed by US airpower. On 10 February 1945 eighty-four B-29 bombers, based on Saipan, bombed an aircraft plant at Ota near Tokyo. Five days later aircraft from an awesome US fleet of twenty carriers protected by ninety warships raided Honshu Island.

Meanwhile, at Yalta in the Crimea between 5 and 11 February 1945, the 'big three' – Roosevelt, Churchill and Stalin – were meeting for their second tripartite conference of the war. Most of their discussions centred on the future of Poland and Germany as the war in Europe entered its final phase. The war against Japan was not the immediate priority because it was widely expected to stretch into 1946. However, Stalin reconfirmed that the Soviet forces would enter the war against Japan three months after the defeat of Nazi Germany, and he laid claim to southern Sakhalin and the Kurile Islands to recover territory lost to Japan in the defeats of 1895 and 1905. At the Los Alamos laboratories at Alamogordo in New Mexico, scientists working under the direction of Robert Oppenheimer were in the closing stages of perfecting the atomic bomb. The end of the war with Japan was closer than even Churchill or Roosevelt anticipated.

References

1. Herbert P. Bix, *Hirohito and the Making of Modern Japan*, Duckworth Press, 2000, p. 469.
2. Ibid., p. 481.

33 Stalemate on the West Wall

I live only for the purpose of leading this fight, because I know if there is not an iron will behind it this battle cannot be won. I accuse the General Staff of weakening combat officers who join its ranks, instead of exuding this iron will, and of speading pessimism . . . if necessary we will fight on the Rhine.[1]

Hitler speaking to his generals on 31 August 1944

Following the successful Allied breakout from Normandy in August 1944 there was considerable optimism within Allied circles for an overall victory by Christmas 1944. By September 1944 the Wehrmacht had fallen back across the borders of Belgium and Luxembourg after a chaotic retreat across northern France. The Allies' only significant problem was keeping pace with the rapid German retreat. Prior to Overlord the supreme commander of Allied forces, General Dwight D. Eisenhower, had predicted a slow, heavily contested step-by-step advance against fierce German resistance. Therefore the Allied strategy was for a broad advance to press the Wehrmacht back into Germany gradually. Faced with the unexpected German collapse, General Montgomery proposed a radical rethink of Allied strategy and recommended the abandonment of the broad-front advance in favour of a single powerful Allied drive into the heart of Germany by approximately forty divisions. There were three major possibilities. A northern advance through Belgium and Holland into the Ruhr, a central advance through the Ardennes and Luxembourg into the Saarland, or a southern advance through the Moselle to Frankfurt. Of the three, Montgomery urged the northern route under his leadership, ostensibly on strategic grounds because it would permit the occupation of the Ruhr, Germany's industrial powerhouse, and offered the shortest route to Berlin. Eisenhower reacted with caution. He was more politician than general and he was wary of offering Montgomery the lead – and, potentially, the glittering prize of Berlin – over the US generals Bradley, Hodge and Patton. Montgomery's stock was low with the US general staff and the US press, because of his reputation for excessive caution in Normandy and his condescending and arrogant manner. In contrast, General George Patton had won considerable praise for his rapid clearance of Brittany and it was his drive across central France that was widely regarded as having routed the Wehrmacht in Normandy. Patton personified action and the best American 'can do' spirit, whereas Montgomery embodied caution and the worst English superiority. Consequently, Eisenhower was not prepared to subordinate US forces to Montgomery's leadership and he rejected his narrow front proposal in favour of maintaining a broad-front advance to the Rhine by six Allied armies. Nearest to the Channel coast, the 1st Canadian Army were charged with opening the ports of Boulogne, Calais, Dieppe and Dunkirk. On their flank, the 2nd British Army advanced towards western Belgium, and in parallel the US 1st Army, commanded by Hodge, advanced towards eastern Belgium and Luxembourg. Further east the 3rd US Army under the command of Patton targeted the fortress city of Metz and the Moselle region. Finally, skirting the border with Switzerland, the US 7th Army and the French 1st Army closed on Belfort.

Hitler reacted to the defeat in Normandy, and to the bomb plot of July 1944, as a failure of will on the part of the Wehrmacht, and he roundly castigated the General Staff as unworthy of his leadership. Pressed from east and west, Hitler vowed to win the war by drawing on the spirit of National Socialism to launch a total war, and to maintain a total war, until 'one of our enemies gets too tired to fight anymore'.[2] Goebbels encouraged Hitler to rely upon the loyalty of the people and Nazi Party over the Wehrmacht. On 25 July, after much prompting, Hitler appointed Goebbels Reich plenipotentiary for total war, with sweeping powers to direct the war effort and to prepare the population to fight to the death to defend Germany against invasion. To defend the Reich, Goebbels commenced a drive to release as many able-bodied men as possible from business and government service for military service. To whip up nationalist fervour he commissioned the action film *Kolberg*, filmed with the assistance of 187,000 soldiers drafted in as extras. The film depicted the heroic resistance of the ordinary people of the Baltic town of Kolberg against the armies of Napoleon more than a century before.

The propaganda of total resistance was Germany's only major weapon, given the absence of any reserves to stem the Allied advance. In total 2 million Allied troops were on the move across northern France, and by late August the major Allied difficulty was keeping them on the move. Cherbourg was the only French port in Allied hands and, with the railroad network across France knocked-out by pre-D-Day bombing, all supplies of food, ammunition and petrol had to be trucked 250–300 miles to the front line. A one-way road loop from Cherbourg to the front was reserved entirely for a constant flow of US heavy trucks, nicknamed the 'Red Ball Express' by the US troops after a fast-freight service. British forces were similarly supplied by 'Red Lion' truck convoys, but the British Leyland trucks proved prone to break-downs and their failure increased the reliance on the Red Ball Express. Further supplies were airlifted, but petrol in particular was in short supply across the front. Hitler was alert to the Allied predicament and ordered the besieged garrisons of Dieppe, Le Havre, Boulogne, Calais and Dunkirk to fight to the last round to deny the Allies further ports. Dieppe was the first to fall on 1 September, but Le Havre held out to 12 September, Boulogne to 22 September and Calais to 30 September. In each case the port facilities had all been expertly demolished prior to surrender. The final Channel port in German hands, Dunkirk, held out to the end of the war.

On 1 September 1944 General Eisenhower took command of all land forces from Montgomery in a planned reshuffle of the Allied command and established his head-quarters at the seaside resort of Granville at the foot of the Cotentin peninsula. Montgomery, who had been promoted to Field Marshal on 31 August, was given command of the 21st Army Group comprising the 1st Canadian Army and the 2nd British Army, while General Omar Bradley was given command of the 12th Army Group comprising the US 1st, 3rd and 7th armies. The acute shortage of petrol forced Eisenhower to suspend the broad front advance and to give priority to the capture of ports to shorten supply lines. Consequently, the US 3rd Army was ordered to pause to conserve fuel, while priority of supply was given to Montgomery's 2nd Army to support a drive north to secure the major Belgian port of Antwerp. Patton was furious and ordered his tanks to advance to the last drop of petrol, and once exhausted, for the crews to walk. He had no confidence in Montgomery, but in the space of a week the 2nd British Army advanced 250 miles from the Seine and liberated Brussels on 3 September in a rapid advance referred to as the 'Great Swan'; this contributed to a widespread belief that the war would be over by Christmas. On 4 September the port of Antwerp was captured intact, but the port effectively remained in German hands because it lay at the end of the heavily mined 75-mile-long Schelde estuary. Both banks were controlled by the German 15th Army, and the addition of a strong garrison on Walcheren Island at the mouth of the estuary denied passage to Allied shipping. Montgomery argued against turning his troops westwards to secure the Schelde estuary. Instead, having encountered negligible opposition, he urged Eisenhower to approve an immediate dash north into Holland to occupy the German Ruhr followed by an advance on Berlin. Montgomery proposed to leave the clearance of the Schelde estuary to the 1st Canadian Army and to maintain the momentum of his advance north aided by a spearhead of airborne troops. Eisenhower suspected that Montgomery was trying to bounce him into approving a narrow-front advance and, by default, handing him the prize of Berlin. His preferred strategy was for the six Allied armies to wrap around the Rhine from the Swiss border to Holland and secure their lines of supply before launching a drive to Berlin across the weakest identified sector. Discussion was hampered by poor communication. Eisenhower had made no attempt to keep pace with the Allied advance and his headquarters at Granville was now 400 miles behind the front line. It underlined Eisenhower's reputation as a 'desk' commander and, to make matters worse, there was no telephone link. All orders by telegram or by letter took a minimum of 24 hours to arrive – and often twice as long – whereas Hitler maintained direct teleprinter links with all his commanders. In Belgium the 2nd British Army as swept up into victory fever by the jubilant Belgian population. The troops were pressed with food, wine and a comfortable bed for the night. After enduring an exhausting battle for France and a restrained, to the point of hostile, welcome by French civilians, the British troops relaxed and many convenient vehicle 'breakdowns' and 'shortages of petrol' were overlooked as the troops entered into a prolonged victory celebration.

Patton had managed to maintain his advance by 'requisitioning' petrol and by the fortuitous and undeclared capture of 110,000 gallons of German petrol. His tanks reached the river Moselle on 5 September, while on the central front the US 1st Army rapidly crossed Luxembourg and discovered a largely undefended German border.

Montgomery's strategy for a northern advance belied his reputation for caution and attracted the criticism of Patton and Bradley for being too radical and unlikely to succeed because of the need to secure passage over five canals and three rivers. However, it contained the attraction of bypassing the German West Wall ('Siegfried Line' to the Allies) which ended at the Dutch border, and involved a plan to cross the lower Rhine at Arnhem in Holland. In contrast, Patton offered not so much a strategy but his reputation as a human bulldozer to smash a pathway through the West Wall and across the Rhine. Both the West Wall and the river Rhine were formidable barriers to the Allied penetration of Germany. The West Wall ran for approximately 350 miles along the German frontier from Switzerland to the Dutch border. Some 50 miles deeper into Germany the broad river Rhine coursed across western Germany and through Holland to the North Sea. However, in September 1944 most of the pillboxes of the West Wall contained nothing more deadly than chickens and stores of root vegetables belonging to local peasants. The defences had been abandoned in 1940 following the German conquest of France in favour of the Atlantic Wall: the new edge of the German Reich.

Beneath the undergrowth, however, a formidable barrier of tank-stopping 'dragon's teeth' (pyramids of reinforced concrete), barbed wire, anti-tank ditches and reinforced concrete pillboxes remained intact and offered a major obstacle to the Allied advance. All that was lacking was the men. The collapse of the Wehrmacht in France had left the Germany bereft of troops, and into late September 1944 most of the West Wall was unmanned. The opportunity for an uncontested breach of the West Wall existed, but Eisenhower refused to sanction a major advance into Germany on any front until the port of Antwerp was opened to ensure a reliable flow of supplies, especially petrol. Montgomery insisted that the opportunity merited the risk and argued that the ports of Boulogne, Dunkirk, Calais and Le Havre would soon be in Allied hands and would be more than sufficient to underwrite an offensive. At an ill-tempered meeting on board Eisenhower's aircraft at Brussels airport on 10 September, Montgomery berated Eisenhower for his caution to the point the Eisenhower was forced to state: 'Steady Monty. You cannot talk to me like this. I am your boss.'[3] Eisenhower eventually succumbed to Montgomery's pressure – but only in part. He approved the release of the airborne reserve in England to support Operation Market Garden: an advance by Montgomery to Arnhem and the Ruhr. However, thereafter he insisted that the British 2nd Army turn west to clear the Schelde estuary and to open the port of Antwerp to Allied shipping. Only then was Eisenhower prepared to commit the Allies to an advance on Berlin. Montgomery agreed, but he later issued orders for the Canadian 1st Army to clear the Schelde estuary in his rear. It would appear that Montgomery had no intention of turning west away from Berlin and acting as a 'harbourmaster' to support an advance by Patton and the US 3rd Army.

Montgomery's case for an immediate advance into Holland was aided by the first V2 attack of the war on 8 September. The rocket was estimated to have been fired from near the Hague on the Dutch coast and hit Staveley Road in Chiswick, London. Only three people were killed, but the one-ton amatol warhead gouged a crater 30 feet across and 10 feet deep and destroyed most of the street. Flying at 3,600 m.p.h., the V2 was unstoppable and in order not to spark a panic Churchill ordered a cover-up, with the explosion being subsequently explained as the unfortunate result of a leaking gas main. It was not until 10 November 1944 that Churchill finally admitted the truth – long after Londoners had stoically logged a hundred 'flying gas mains'. The V2 was primarily a terror weapon, but it was never launched in sufficient numbers to fulfil Hitler's promise to blast Great Britain into submission. Churchill urged the rapid clearance of Holland to overrun the V2 launching sites and therefore gave his full support to Market Garden.

Without any fanfare, troops of the 85th Reconnaissance Squadron attached to US 1st Army in Luxembourg quietly became the first Allied troops to set foot in Germany. At 6.05 p.m. on 11 September three US soldiers and a French interpreter, led by Sergeant Warner Holzinger, crossed the border from the Luxembourg hamlet of Stolzembourg to the deserted German hamlet of Gmuend. The border was also crossed at many other points, sparking rival claims to be the first across, but all discovered deserted pillboxes.

In the space of only six days Montgomery confirmed the operational plans for Market Garden. The 'Market' element of the plan was for the seizure of the key canal and river bridges across Holland and was assigned to the Allied airborne reserve, comprising the US 82nd and 101st Airborne divisions, the British 1st Airborne Division and the Polish 1st Airborne Brigade. The 'Garden' element of the plan was for a rapid drive north by an armoured spearhead, entrusted to 30th Corps under the command of Lieutenant-General Brian Horrocks. When the overall plan was first revealed to the assembled officers of 30th Corps on 16 September in a cinema in the Belgium town of Bourg Leopold, there was considerable private unease. Six days was a very brief time to prepare for a major advance and few believed that the plan was feasible because the tight timetable permitted no margin for delay. However, the widely held view that the Germans were beaten suppressed any negative comment. Montgomery was convinced that the 64-mile dash to Arnhem was more than feasible when the same forces had advanced 250 miles from the Seine into Belgium in a week

At 2.15 p.m. on 17 September Lieutenant General Horrocks watched from a factory roof at the start line of Neerpelt as some 350 guns opened fire in support of Garden, the armoured advance to Arnhem. At 2.35 p.m. he gave the order to advance and the lead tanks of the Irish Guards rolled forward. Overhead the artillery kept pace with a rolling barrage, and waves of Typhoons, operating in a cab-rank formation, engaged any German positions. After only 3 miles German infantry equipped with anti-tank guns knocked out the lead tanks, but they were swiftly silenced by overwhelming fire from tanks and Typhoons. Further opposition at Valkenswaard slowed the advance and after an advance of only 7 miles 30th Corps stopped for the night. It was an ill omen as ahead lightly armed airborne divisions battled to secure the key bridges at Eindhoven,

Nijmegen and Arnhem. Furthest north at Arnhem the 2nd Parachute Battalion of the British 1st Airborne Division, under the command of Colonel John Frost, staked a precarious claim to the northern end of the road bridge at 8.45 p.m. under accurate fire from SS troops at the southern end. The nearby railway bridge was destroyed on their approach. They had lost the element of surprise, and ultimately the bridge itself, by being dropped 6–8 miles west of the town rather than directly alongside the bridge. The RAF had advised against flying over Arnhem due to the presence of heavy flak batteries that would take a heavy toll of the slow-flying transports. It meant a two-hour march to Arnhem and gave the Germans time to counter-attack. Most of the 1st Airborne Division got no closer to the bridge than the suburb of Oosterbeck, where their advance was held in check by SS troops. The presence of SS troops in the area was known prior to the attack. They were the battered remnants of the 9th and 10th Panzer divisions moved to the quiet of Arnhem to recover and re-equip following a severe battering in Normandy. The defeat in Normandy had reduced their number from 3,600 troops to 700 and panzers from 300 to twenty. However, against lightly armed airborne troops they remained a formidable threat. The danger was highlighted by the chief intelligence officer for the 1st Airborne Division, Major Brian Urquhart, following warnings from Dutch intelligence and confirmation from a Spitfire reconnaissance flight. However, his warnings were discounted to the extent that he was ordered to go on sick leave, or face a court martial, to silence his doubts. To add to the mounting catalogue of difficulties, the commanding officer of the 1st Airborne Division, Major-General Robert Urquhart, never returned from a scouting mission across Arnhem to find and achieve a link-up between his scattered battalions. He was presumed dead, but was in fact cut off by a sudden influx of German reinforcements into Arnhem and forced into hiding. He was trapped for two nights and ended up in the attic of a terraced house before being able to cross the German lines and rejoin his men battling in Oosterbeck.

The German counter-attack was co-ordinated by Field Marshal Model, who was eating lunch at his headquarters in the Harstein Hotel, Oosterbeck, at 12.40 p.m. on 17 September when the first parachutists landed only 2.5 miles away. At first he assumed it was a commando raid aimed at his capture, because no Allied action was expected in Holland.

At Arnhem the Allied situation deteriorated further on the morning of 18 September when a German soldier discovered a full copy of the campaign maps and schedule of further landings in a crashed glider. The later Allied drops were met by heavy German fire. On the northern end of the road bridge a tiny force of at best 740 troops of the 2nd Parachute Battalion, led by Colonel John Frost, held their positions under strong and determined attacks by tanks and armoured cars. The remainder of the 1st Airborne Division were equally under siege in Oosterbeck and were unable to reach the bridge. Their physical isolation was aggravated by the failure of their radios. Without radios they could not call-up RAF strikes on the German tanks and troop concentrations. At Oosterbeck the troops had the additional frustration of watching much-needed supplies of food and ammunition fall into German hands because the pre-planned drop zones had been overrun, and without radio communication there was no means to redirect the supply drops. This continued over the days ahead, with the RAF pilots enduring heavy flak and many losses in their wasted efforts to get supplies to Allied troops.

By late morning on 19 September, the 30 Corps entered Nijmegen having covered 30 miles north, but a tenacious German defence held the road bridge over the Waal. In an act of considerable bravery, the US 504th Parachute Regiment, under the command of Brigadier-General Gavin, crossed the fast-flowing river in canvas boats under heavy fire. Thirteen of the first twenty-six boats were blasted out of the water, but sufficient troops gained the north bank to establish a bridgehead and by 5 p.m the bridge was in American hands. Arnhem was only 10 miles to the north and the jubilant American troops urged an all-out drive by the 30th Corps to relieve the beleaguered British 1st Airborne Division. In a controversial decision, Captain Lord Carrington (later British Foreign Secretary), in command of the lead tanks, refused American entreaties to advance. The British forces insisted on waiting to daylight because the road ahead was narrow and the German strength was unknown.

At Arnhem the 1st Airborne Divison had fought without respite from the afternoon of 17 September. By the morning of 21 September Tiger tanks, impervious to the paratroopers' light weapons, crossed Arnhem bridge and at point-blank range began systematically to destroy every building held by Frost's battalion. Out of an original defending force of 740 troops only 150 were uninjured and able to return fire, and, with the situation hopeless, Frost surrendered the bridge at 9 a.m. The Tigers immediately rolled on to Elst 4 miles south of Arnhem and successfully blocked the path of the advancing 30th Corps. At 3.30 p.m. on 21 September, after delays caused by poor weather, the Polish Parachute Brigade was dropped at Driel on the south bank of the Neder Rijn opposite Oosterbeek where the remnants of the 1st Airborne Division were trapped with their backs to the river. However, they were too few and too ill-equipped to make a difference: a mere fifty-two managed to cross the river in small boats. The more powerful spearhead of 30th Corps reached Driel by nightfall on 22 September, but the barrier of the river prevented any relief for 1st Airborne. On 24 September Horrocks made a personal assessment of the situation from the church tower at Driel and attempted to retrieve the situation by pushing the 43rd Dorset Infantry across the river. A shortage of boats, and, more frustratingly, the arrival of boats without paddles, resulted in fewer than 400 troops reaching the north bank in the early hours of 25 September. With strong German counter-attacks at Elst and a build-up of German troops to the east there was a danger of encirclement; consequently, Horrocks reluctantly accepted that the battle for Arnhem was lost. During the night of 25–26 September the weary survivors of 1st Airborne were evacuated under heavy German fire. Out of an original force of 8,905 committed to Arnhem only 2,163 escaped. Prior to the attack General Browning had predicted that Arnhem 'might be a bridge too far'. Thirtieth Corps retreated to Nijmegen and stabilised the front line along the river Waal while Montgomery absorbed the sting of failure. The operational failures were many, but the strategic failure – and in particular the failure to commit full resources to Montgomery's drive north for the Ruhr – belonged to Eisenhower, Patton and Bradley. Too late, Eisenhower held a military conference at his new headquarters in Versailles on 22 September to review strategy. Montgomery did not attend, largely because he did not trust himself to remain diplomatic and sanguine in public. His decision revealed his own failure. Whereas his strategy was sound it was lost because of his open contempt for those he considered less experienced, raising opposition rather than co-operation.

The Allied failure to cross the Rhine at Arnhem gave Hitler the necessary breathing space to reorganise the defences of Germany and to pour men into the West Wall.

On 25 September 1944 Hitler signed an order to create the *Volkswehr* (people's defence) and raised fresh divisions from all men aged 16–18 and 50–60 previously untouched by conscription. They were fashioned into *Volksgrenadier* (people's infantry divisions) and, after at best six weeks' basic training, were transported to the front line. Goebbels also scoured the medical records for those deemed unfit for military service due to duodenal ulcers, rheumatism, hearing difficulties, gallstones and other 'minor' complaints, gathering them into 'stomach and ear' divisions. Most had only rudimentary military skills, but behind the reinforced concrete walls of the West Wall they were able to deny the Allies progress. Nor was Hitler simply relying upon holding a defensive line. As early as mid-August he had contemplated a new offensive in the west, and on 15 September 1944 he informed his startled general staff of his decision to build a reserve powerful enough to destroy the Allies armies in December. Himmler, with responsibility for the *Volksgrenadier,* selected the best to serve in the new offensive around a core of SS panzer units, while the standard working week was raised to 60 hours to ensure the generation of sufficient new panzers and aircraft. Thousands of women were also drafted into industry to release men for military service, as were children aged 12–14 for light work. It was a public admission of failure from a Nazi regime that had promoted family life and the importance of motherhood. Goebbels and Himmler had little doubt about the final outcome, and both sought to end the war. In mid-September Goebbels attempted to interest Hitler in opening negotiations with Stalin against the west via the intermediary of the Japanese ambassador to Germany, but Hitler refused to consider any deal. Later in October, Himmler authorised secret informal contacts with the western powers via the Italian industrialist Franco Marinotti, and sought to interest the western Allies in a settlement in the west to allow the Wehrmacht to stop the advance of the Red Army into Europe. The Allies insisted upon unconditional surrender, and whereas Goebbels was prepared to share Hitler's fate Himmler made increasingly frantic attempts to strike a deal with the west to preserve his Aryan Germany.

The first German town to fall into Allied hands was Aachen across the Luxembourg border, but it was only taken after a prolonged battle from 2–21 October with high casualties. South-east of Aachen, in the forest of Hurtgen, four US divisions suffered 10,000 casualties in failed attempts to breach the West Wall. The onset of winter in late October brought freezing temperatures and snow; Allied morale plummeted and was expressed in high desertion rates and illness. Thousands were discharged due to trench foot from weeks spent in waterlogged trenches, and thousands more contracted genito-urinary disease during leave. The only significant Allied success was the clearance of the Schelde estuary on 31 October and the successful invasion of Walcheren Island on 8 November, to permit the opening of the port of Antwerp. However, it had taken nine weeks and 27,635 Allied casualties. Beyond the front line the V2 rockets continued to claim lives in London. On 25 November a branch of Woolworths at New Cross in London received a direct hit, killing 160 shoppers and passers-by.

The stationary Allied Army presented ideal conditions for Hitler's planned counter-offensive, codenamed Operation Wacht am Rhein (Watch on the Rhine). On 20 November he left *Wolfsschanze* in East Prussia for the last time and after a brief spell in Berlin travelled to a new forward headquarters, *Adlerhorst* (Eagle's Eyrie), at Ziegenberg near Frankfurt on 10 December to direct the offensive personally. Hitler planned to repeat the triumphant German blitzkrieg of May 1940 by sweeping through the Ardennes and carving a corridor across Belgium to Antwerp. His intention was to split the Allied front in two and to force a new Dunkirk upon the Allied forces trapped north of the line, thereby winning time to defeat the Red Army in the east. He also set subsidiary plans for advances in northern Holland, Lower Roer and northern Alsace to take advantage of the distraction and anticipated transfer of US reinforcements to the Ardennes. Few in the Wehrmacht believed in the plan, and Rundstedt urged Hitler to consider a less ambitious advance, but Hitler insisted that his orders were to be obeyed to the last detail and wrote 'not to be altered' across the operational orders. After the war Runstedt commented: 'it was a nonsensical operation and the most stupid part was setting Antwerp as the target. If we had reached the Meuse we should have got down on our knees and thanked God.'[4]

At 5.30 a.m. on 16 December 1944, on the Ardennes front, the troops of the US 99th Division, the 28th Infantry Division and the 106th Division (which had only entered the line six days earlier) were subjected to an intense artillery bombardment, followed by the sudden appearance of massed panzers. Along an 85-mile front from Monchau in the north to Echternach in the south, a German army of 250,000 men of the 7th Army, largely comprised of *Volksgrenadiers* and the 5th and 6th Panzerarmees comprising 950 panzers, broke through the lightly defended US front line and commenced what the Americans termed the Battle of the Bulge. On the same day in Antwerp a V2 rocket hit a cinema crowded with British servicemen and killed a total of 567 soldiers and civilians – the largest number killed in a single strike. The ability of Hitler to repeat the surprise attack of 1940 has raised suspicions that Eisenhower deliberately ignored intelligence warnings of a German build-up in the Ardennes in order to lure the Germans out from behind the shield of the West Wall and thus permit superior allied tank and air power to finally break the Wehrmacht in the west. However, it would appear that Eisenhower discounted the warnings due to the widely held judgement that the Germans were a beaten force incapable of mounting a major offensive. The German advance was aided by a force of some 150 English-speaking commandos with American accents under the command of SS Lieutenant-Colonel Otto Skorzeny, who were infiltrated behind the American lines. Dressed in US uniforms and driving captured US jeeps, they misdirected reinforcements, cut telephone lines, destroyed ammunition dumps and acted as a scout force for the main attack. Within 24 hours the lead panzer division, Leibstandarte Adolf Hitler, under the command of SS Lieutenant-Colonel Joachim Peiper, had advanced 25 miles and intensified rather than weakened US resistance by shooting captured US soldiers at Honsfel, Bullingen and the Malmedy crossroads. As the German advance threatened to split the Allied front Montgomery, to his unconcealed delight, was invited by Eisenhower on 20 December to take command of all Allied forces north of the German bulge. Earlier, on 30 November, Eisenhower had tactfully ignored an abrupt letter from Montgomery that condemned his poor strategic leadership and effectively invited him to stand down as commander of land forces. Montgomery positioned the armoured divisions of 30th Corps along the Meuse between Liege and Namur to block the pathway to Antwerp and, to the immense irritation of Bradley and Hodges, he entered Hodges' headquarters, in the words of his own staff, like 'Christ come to cleanse the temple'. He contemptuously refused to consult the US operations map in favour of his own and, in grand manner, instructed Hodges on how best to deploy his forces. Having delivered his instructions, he declined Hodges' invitation to join him for lunch and dined alone with his own thermos flask and box of sandwiches. The 5th Panzerarmee swept through the US lines towards Dinant on the Meuse. In the path of the German advance was the strategic crossroads town of

Bastogne, but, despite facing superior firepower from the 47th Panzer Corps, General Anthony McAuliffe refused to surrender the town. In answer to the demand for his surrender, McAuliffe gave the celebrated reply 'nuts' and directed a tenacious defence of the town by the 101st Airborne Division and elements of the 10th and 28th Infantry divisions. The siege was lifted on 26 December by tanks of Patton's 3rd Army. With the bulge contained by Patton's 3rd Army in the south and Hodges' 1st Army in the north, the westward advance of the 5th Panzerarmee was blocked at Celles, 4 miles from Dinant, by combined British and US armour commanded by US Major-General 'Lightning Joe' Collins. The low cloud cover that had prevented the intervention of Allied air support (and curtailed Luftwaffe operations) briefly lifted and fighter bombers added their considerable firepower to the Allied counter-attack. The panzers, low on fuel and cut off by the advance of Patton's 3rd Army in their rear, ground to a halt some 60 miles deep into the Allied lines but about 4 miles short of the river Meuse, their first major objective. Rundstedt's judgement was vindicated but, to his surprise, Hitler refused to acknowledge defeat and ordered the commencement of Operation Nordwind (Northwind) in Alsace to the south, to take advantage of the distraction provided by the Ardennes offensive, and a fresh advance on Bastogne on 3 and 4 January to try and hold the gains made. However, on 8 January Hitler finally authorised a fighting withdrawal, and by 28 January 1945 the bulge in the line was entirely pressed back to its starting point. The failure in the Ardennes cost the Germans 120,000 casualties and an estimated 800 panzers and 1,000 aircraft. The Allied casualties were approximately 81,000 US troops and 1,400 British and a similar number of tanks, but whereas the Allies could restore their losses within weeks the Germans had exhausted their last reserves. The tension between Montgomery and his American counterparts was sharply renewed on 7 January 1945 when, at a press conference, Montgomery clumsily and arrogantly boasted that his intervention had been decisive in turning the battle. Eisenhower was so incensed that he offered to resign, along with generals Patton and Bradley. It was a remark too far. Churchill, alert to the deterioration in Allied relations, condemned Montgomery's comments at a meeting with the chiefs of staff on 12 January, and in the House of Commons on 18 January he paid fulsome tribute to the American fighting spirit. Montgomery was sufficiently chastened to issue an apology, but only in terms of a misunderstanding.

The unexpected Ardennes battle delayed Allied plans for a major offensive in January 1945, but with the Germans in full retreat Eisenhower set 8 February 1945 for a drive to the Rhine and the occupation of the Ruhr. His decision vindicated Montgomery's Market Garden strategy, but the disagreements over strategy and the failure to fully resource the drive north had cost the Allies six months and considerable casualties. It might also be argued that the resulting stalemate along the West Wall cost the western Allies Berlin and the possibility of a different post-war future for Germany.

References

1. Alan Bullock, *Hitler and Stalin: Parallel Lives*, HarperCollins, 1991, p. 954.
2. Ibid., p. 955.
3. Anthony Read and David Fisher, *The Fall of Berlin*, Hutchinson, 1992, p. 180.
4. George Forty, *The Road To Berlin: The Allied Drive From Normandy*, Cassell, 2000, p. 134.

34 The Holocaust

The war will not end as the Jews imagine it will, namely with the uprooting of the Aryans, but the result of this war will be the complete annihilation of the Jews. Now for the first time they will not bleed other people to death, but for the first time the old Jewish law of an eye for an eye, a tooth for a tooth, will be applied . . . the hour will come when the most evil universal enemy of all time will be finished, at least for a thousand years.[1]

Hitler, speaking to the German people at the
Sportpalast on 30 January 1942

On 7 December 1941, 700 Jews were rounded-up in the Lodz ghetto, Poland, and transported 40 miles to the first purpose-built death camp at Chelmno. All had been promised better conditions at an agricultural work camp to the east, and many volunteered to go in order to escape the chronic overcrowding and hunger in the ghetto. On the morning of the 8 December they were all directed to take a shower. Naked and in groups of sixty at a time they were herded and beaten down a corridor and directed up a short ramp into the back of a plain-grey enclosed truck. The doors were bolted and the driver, dressed in an SS Totenkopf or Death's Head uniform, drove the truck a short distance into the surrounding forest. The truck parked at the edge of a pre-prepared burial pit and as the driver stepped down from the cab he flicked a switch to divert the exhaust gases into the back of the hermetically sealed truck. Frantic banging on the sides of the truck ensued as the exhaust gases were pumped into the truck down two perforated tubes laid in parallel along the floor. The tubes were protected by a raised wooden grating and concealed from view by a covering of loose straw mats. After approximately fifteen minutes all had been asphyxiated, and a waiting detachment of Jewish slave labourers were beaten into action with whips and clubs and ordered to drag the bodies from the truck. Gold teeth were pulled out with pliers and orifices were searched for hidden valuables, especially diamonds, before the bodies were flung into the burial pit. All 700 were gassed. Over the next four days a further 1,000 Jews per day were transported from the Lodz ghetto and murdered in the same way. This was the first act of the 'mechanised' Holocaust, as opposed to the random and chaotic shootings conducted by the Einsatzgruppen across the Baltic States and the occupied Soviet Union. The term 'Holocaust', from the Greek *Holos* (whole) and *caustos* (burn), is used in the western world to denote the period of the death camps between 1942 and 1944 when the majority of Europe's Jews were systematically rounded-up and gassed. In Hebrew the preferred term is '*Shoah*', meaning a devastating storm. Chelmno was the first death camp to enter service and it provided an easily disguised and faster means of mass murder than the continuing Einsatzgruppen actions of mass shootings in the Soviet Union, following the decision for the Final Solution (see Chapter 17). Himmler turned to Christian Wirth for advice and guidance on how to replicate Chelmno on a larger scale. Wirth was one of the key 'experts' associated with the *Sonderbehandlung* or special treatment programme for those deemed unfit for work in the concentration camps. The prisoners were gassed by carbon monoxide gas in small chambers, within the camps, often disguised as shower rooms. Wirth dismissed the operation at Chelmno as too clumsy and slow, and he proposed the construction of *Vernichtungslager*, or annihilation camps, with large, static gas chambers capable of gassing 1,000 people at a time and to dispose of the bodies in crematoria. Himmler approved an immediate expansion of the *Vernichtungslager* with a capacity not only to empty the ghettos of Poland of 'unproductive' or sick Jews but to gas the entire Jewish population of occupied Europe. With the death camps under construction, Himmler delegated the practical arrangements for the transport of the Jews of Europe to their deaths to Reinhard Heydrich, the head of the Reich Security Main Office. Heydrich chaired a meeting of the fifteen key administrators of occupied Europe in Berlin on 20 January 1942. The conference was held in a luxury villa on the shores of the Wannsee, which was Heydrich's intended home after the war. The meeting had been originally scheduled for 9 December 1941, but was postponed following the unexpected Japanese attack on Pearl Harbor on 7 December. The meeting only lasted ninety minutes, and the minutes record that Heydrich listed the estimated number of Jews in each European country and confirmed that all were to be subject to the Final Solution. The stated total was 11 million, ranging from 5 million Jews in the Soviet Union to only 200 in tiny Albania. The list of Jews included 8,000 living in neutral Sweden and 330,000 living in undefeated Great Britain. The detailed arrangements for the transports were left to Adolf Eichmann, who had been promoted to SS Lieutenant-Colonel in November 1941. In the months and years ahead he was to become the chief administrator of the Final Solution. Heydrich specified a death sentence for all European Jews:

> The Jews are to be utilised for work in the East in an expedient manner in the course of Final Solution. In large (labour) columns, with the sexes separated, Jews capable of work will be moved into those areas as they build roads, during which a large proportion will no doubt drop out through natural reduction. The remnant that eventually remains will require suitable treatment . . . the evacuated Jews will first be taken, group by group to so-called transit ghettos to be transported further east from there.[2]

No direct mention was made of death camps or gassing but the so-called 'transit ghettos' envisaged screening the transports for those fit for hard labour and those for immediate gassing. The end result for those who survived hard labour was also death or, in Heydrich's words, 'suitable treatment'. Against this background of the preparation of death camps and transport schedules Hitler addressed the crowds at the Sportspalast in Berlin (as quoted at the start of this chapter) and firmly restated his promise of January 1939 that the war would result in the complete annihilation of the Jews.

A total of six *Vernichtungslager* were established in eastern Poland: Chelmno, Sobibor, Belzec, Treblinka, Majdanek and Auschwitz-Birkenau. Only Chelmno and Sobibor were purpose-built death camps. The other four camps were originally constructed as concentration or labour camps, but during 1942 all were transformed into *Vernichtungslager* by the addition of large gas chambers. After Chelmno the first camp to commence mass gassings was Belzec on 17 March 1942, closely followed by Majdanek and Sobibor in April 1942. Treblinka received its first major transport on 23 July 1942. Auschwitz-Birkenau had first been opened on 26 May 1940 on the outskirts of the village of Oswiecim, in Upper Silesia as a slave labour camp for Polish prisoners. In March 1941 the camp was substantially extended with the addition of a subsidiary camp at Birkenau, 2 kilometres from the main camp, to house Russian prisoners of war. It was this second camp that was identified by Himmler, during the summer of 1941, as a key transit camp for the Final Solution because of its excellent rail communication links.

In most of the camps, only a handful of the able-bodied were retained to maintain the camp labour force. However, in Auschwitz-Birkenau and Majdanek all the able-bodied were selected to work as slave labourers in adjacent industrial plants. Some of Germany's best-known industrialists opened factories alongside the death camps, and alongside other concentration camps across Germany, to take advantage of the slave labour. They included Bayer, BMW, Daimler-Benz, I.G. Farben, Siemens, Krupp and Volkswagen.

In four of the six death camps those selected for death were gassed by carbon monoxide from a dismounted diesel truck engine, but in Auschwitz-Birkenau and Majdanek the faster-acting Zyklon B prussic acid gas was used. Zyklon B was originally supplied to the camps as rat poison in pellet form but once exposed to the air it rapidly vaporised and killed people within minutes of exposure. A typical transport of 1,200 people was ordinarily 'processed' and reduced to ashes inside two hours. Their belongings created huge mounds of booty for the SS. In camp warehouses (known as 'Kanada' in Auschwitz), the suitcases were opened and possessions were sorted into piles for onward transport to the Reich for disposal. All manner of clothes and personal goods were stockpiled, including pens, watches, wallets, razors, cufflinks, glasses, jewellery and even artificial limbs. The dental gold was melted down and converted into bars, and along with cash and precious stones was all credited by the SS to the fictional account of Max Heiliger in the Reich Bank in Berlin. The bank soon ran out of storage space and flooded the jewellery market in Germany, Austria and Switzerland with gems and valuables at knock-down prices. The market was saturated and after the war stockpiles of jewellery were discovered stored in a salt mines. This was only the tip of the wholesale robbery of the Jewish citizens of Europe. Homes and businesses were appropriated, and even the money deposited in banks in neutral Switzerland by German Jews for safe keeping was far from safe. After the war most of the banks failed to reveal the existence of the accounts to the next of kin and millions that might have helped destitute relatives released from the camps enriched the banks. All 'confiscated' Jewish goods were designated state property, but Hoess noted in his memoirs that it was impossible to prevent the spread of corruption. Most of those involved in the death camps, from train drivers to SS officers, enriched themselves by smuggling out money, gold and precious stones. Himmler issued death sentences to SS officers found guilty of theft and, more bizarrely, for the 'illegal' killing of prisoners. Despite the fact that thousands of prisoners were being murdered on a daily basis in the camps, Himmler was anxious to press the distinction between state-sanctioned murder and an individual whim. Himmler was insistent that the SS were not common murderers or thieves but were obeying state orders for the greater good of the nation.

Heydrich did not live to see the full implementation of his Wannsee Directive. On 27 May 1942 he was ambushed by Czech agents trained in Britain, and fatally injured on his way to his headquarters in central Prague. Hitler gave Heydrich a state funeral and as a reprisal for his death the entire population of the Czech village of Lidice, 6 miles north-west of Prague, was executed and the village was razed to the ground and removed from German maps. The daily gassing of the Jews from the Polish ghettos was named Operation Reinhard in his memory.

On 19 July 1942, two days after a tour of inspection of Auschwitz-Birkenau, Himmler issued an order for all remaining Jews in Poland to be gassed by 31 December 1942. The largest number were held in the Warsaw ghetto, and virtually all were murdered in Treblinka. Starting from 22 July 1942, the leader of the Jewish Council of Warsaw, Adam Czerniakow, was ordered to identify 6,000 people per day, regardless of age or sex, for transport to the east. This total was later raised to 10,000 per day, and by the end of the transports in early October 1942 an estimated 310,322 had been transported and gassed. The Nazis pressed the Jewish councils, under threat of execution of their families, to implement increasingly repressive policies, including the round up of fellow Jews. Some Jewish leaders like Adam Czerniakow committed suicide rather than select others for death, but most co-operated and in many ghettos it was Jewish policemen who beat their fellow Jews onto the transports. Co-operation was the only certain means of survival, and also resulted in some Jewish prisoners accepting work as *Sonderkommandos* and helping to gas and cremate their fellow Jews. Some were prepared to fight, and on 28 July 1942, in Warsaw, the Jewish Fighting Organisation ZOB (Zydowska Organizacja Bojowa) urged all young, fit Jews to arm themselves to resist the transports.

To fulfil Himmler's target, four new gas chambers capable of gassing and cremating 12,000 a day were built at Auschwitz-Birkenau, with adjacent crematorium facilities. By December 1942 approximately three-quarters of the Jews in Poland had been gassed, leaving only an estimated 700,000 still alive in the ghettos. Beyond the death camps, the Einsatzgruppen continued to scour the villages and towns of the occupied Soviet Union, and shot and buried in mass graves all the Jews they captured. On 31 December 1942 Himmler presented Hitler with Report No. 51 on the large print 'Führer type-writer' that reported the shooting of 363,211 Jews in the Soviet Union between 1 September and 1 December 1942. The scale of the murders provoked protests from the Wehrmacht and industrialists who regarded Jewish labour as indispensable to the war effort. Himmler overrode all protests and issued a direct order for the removal of reserved occupation status from all Jews and for their immediate transport to the death camps.

The brutal round-ups of Jews across Europe could not be disguised, but the Nazi claim that the Jews were merely being transferred to work camps was at first hard to disprove. Model camps like Theresienstadt, with a range of employment opportunities, were used to demonstrate to the Red Cross and foreign representatives the existence of basic but humane living and working conditions for the Jews. Few believed that the Nazis would actually murder so many people, and simple devices like directing new arrivals to write postcards confirming that they were safe and well helped to maintain an illusion of the existence of Jewish agricultural settlements in the east. A typical dictated postcard read: 'The food is good, with hot lunches, cheese and jam sandwiches in the evenings . . . we have central heating . . . there are magnificent shower arrangements with hot and cold water.'[3] The truth of what was happening to the Jews who were transported east was first comprehensively revealed by a collation of eyewitness reports sent to the Allies in May 1942 by the underground Jewish Socialist Party in Poland, the Bund. The Bund report described the gassings at Chelmno and made headline news across the western world, with demands for Allied action. However, with Europe under firm Nazi occupation no military intervention was deemed possible. In September 1942 President Roosevelt urged Pope Pius XII to use his moral authority to condemn the Holocaust, but he refused to speak out and cited the unreliability of the evidence. However, the evidence was not doubted by the Allied governments, and on 17 December 1942 they issued a common statement of condemnation of the 'bestial Nazi policy of cold blooded murder'. All at war with Nazi Germany signed the Declaration, but the Pope again refused openly to condemn the mass murder of Jews or to forbid Catholics in Europe from co-operating with the Holocaust. Whether the Pope was personally anti-Semitic or restrained from acting openly, by as yet unspecified reasons, remains one of the most controversial aspects of the Holocaust. However, it is notable that in July 2001 the Vatican ended its co-operation with a commission of Catholic and Jewish historians investigating the inaction of the Pope by refusing to open its sealed wartime archives.

By the end of 1942, the remaining Jews in the Warsaw ghetto were aware of what awaited them in the east; this produced a flow of recruits into ZOB under the command of 23-year-old Mordechai Anielewicz. A few guns and explosives were smuggled into the ghetto, but weapons were largely improvised. Armed resistance commenced on 18 January 1943, and after three days of fighting the SS were forced to withdraw, leaving fifty dead. Himmler ordered SS Brigadier-General Stroop to erase the ghetto and on 19 April 1943 the SS entered in force. Stroop used tanks and heavy artillery to destroy the ghetto methodically, block by block. The last resistance around the headquarters of ZOB on Mila Street was finally defeated on 16 May 1943 and Anielewicz committed suicide rather than be taken alive. Approximately 7,000 Jews were killed in the fighting and some 48,000 were subsequently gassed in Treblinka and Majdanek. Only a few hundred Jews escaped the ghetto or remained undetected in walled-up cellars. Stroop was awarded the Iron Cross First Class by Hitler and was inordinately proud of his 'achievement' – to the extent that he published a leather-bound report of the action. A year later, in August 1944, it is notable that the Pope publicly urged the Allies to act to save the Polish people of Warsaw during the Warsaw rising, whereas he had offered no similar plea to save the Jews in the Warsaw ghetto.

After March 1943 most Jews were killed in Auschwitz-Birkenau in the newly completed gas chambers and crematorium. By the summer of 1943 most of Poland's Jews had perished and the expanded capacity of Auschwitz-Birkenau meant it was capable of 'processing' all further transports. Consequently, Himmler ordered the other death camps to be closed and for all traces of their existence to be destroyed. Commando 1005, commanded by SS Colonel Paul Blobel, was ordered to open all mass graves across the occupied Soviet Union and in the death camps and to burn the bodies. On 2 August 1942 the end of the transports to Treblinka sparked an armed rebellion by the *Sonderkommando* once they realised that they were destined to die. They successfully burnt down a large part of the camp, and an estimated 800 prisoners charged the wire and the guards. Most were shot down, but approximately a hundred escaped. There were similar scenes at Sobibor on 14 October 1943, and here most of the SS officers were killed before the revolt was overcome. Both camps were demolished, and the land was ploughed over and transformed into working farms run by ex-guards. By December 1943, little or no trace of either camp remained. Belzec was also restored to farmland during January and February 1943, after Commando 1005 had disinterred and burned all the bodies. Chelmno was closed and largely demolished in March 1943, but briefly reactivated from April to July 1944 to assist with the liquidation of Jews from the Lodz ghetto; it was finally obliterated in January 1945. Majdanek continued to operate to July 1944 and, in a hurried evacuation, was only partially destroyed. The league table of death in the 'secondary' death camps is estimated as follows: Treblinka 800,000, Belzec 600,000, Majdanek 500,000, Chelmno 360,000 and Sobibor 250,000.

Auschwitz-Birkenau was left in operation as the primary death camp, and throughout 1943 and 1944 Eichmann supervised the round-up and transport of as many Jews as possible from across occupied Europe to their deaths in Auschwitz-Birkenau. There was a considerable variation in the levels of co-operation, both from the Wehrmacht and the local police and officials. Less than half of Belgium's 52,000 Jews were rounded up, and in Bulgaria and Italy the round-ups were openly opposed. The Italian Army actively blocked deportations from southern France and managed to save 80 per cent of the Jewish population. One of the more surprising interventions on behalf of the Jews was in Denmark, in September 1943, when the SS plenipotentiary Dr Werner Best personally warned the Jewish community of the proposed date of the round-ups and the Danish people either hid the Jews in their homes or used a flotilla of small boats to ferry them across the Kattegat to the safety of Sweden. Only 477 Jews out of 6,500 Danish Jews were subsequently captured, and Werner even managed to redirect their transports to the Theresinstadt work camp where most survived the war.

The last major Jewish community in Europe to be targeted by Eichmann for transportation to their deaths was in Hungary. The pre-war population numbered 700,000, but wartime refugees had swollen the population to 800,000. The first were transported to Auschwitz-Birkenau on 23 April, and by July 1944 some 435,000 Hungarian Jews had been transported and gassed. The Allies were pressed by Jewish representatives to bomb the gas chambers and the railway lines to save Jewish lives, but despite the fact that bomb raids were being made on the industrial plants surrounding Auschwitz-Birkenau RAF Bomber Command refused. It remains an uncomfortable example of the ambivalent Allied reaction to the Holocaust. Hoess noted in his memoirs that at the height of the operation Auschwitz-Birkenau recorded it largest single murder rate with 9,000 Hungarian Jews gassed and cremated in a single day. By late 1944 Germany was in a state of military collapse and to Eichmann's dismay Himmler began to seek ways of using the Jews as bargaining chips in an attempt to open negotiations with the western Allies. Himmler had apparently no wish to join Hitler in a glorious last stand but hoped to interest the Allies in an anti-communist pact that would permit the survival of Nazi Germany under his leadership. With the Red Army closing on eastern Poland, the last transports to Auschwitz-Birkenau were received on 28 October 1944. Two days later the SS commenced the burning of all camp records and the destruction of the gas chambers and the crematorium. On 2 November Himmler ordered the end of the extermination programme, but many thousands of prisoners, including Jews from Hungary, were marched west to work as slave labourers in the continuing war effort. Those who could not maintain the pace were shot dead, or died from exposure when sleeping in the open in snow and ice. The mass evacuation of prisoners from Auschwitz-Birkenau commenced on 18 January, a day after the final camp roll-call logged a camp population of 54,651. The majority of those were housed as slave labourers in Camp Three. The symbolic end of the Holocaust arrived on 27 January 1945 when the Red Army liberated Auschwitz-Birkenau and discovered only 2,800 prisoners still alive. The evidence of mass murder that the SS had hoped to erase was found in the ruins of the gas chambers. The chemical signature of hydrocyanic acid (HCN) from the Zyklon B crystals could not be erased. In addition, not all storage buildings were destroyed and the Red Army discovered vast heaps of clothing, shoes, spectacles and seven tons of neatly baled human hair. The number killed at Auschwitz-Birkenau is variously estimated from a low of 1.5 million to a high of 2.5 million. In his memoirs, Hoess dismissed the latter as being beyond even Auschwitz-Birkenau's destructive capacity, and 2 million is perhaps the upper limit. Gilbert provides the most detailed survey of the total numbered killed in the Holocaust and has estimated that a minimum of 5.75 million Jews were murdered between 1939 and 1945. This total does not include those not registered for transport, the babies who were born and died in captivity, and the millions of others like homosexuals, gypsies and Russian POWs who were also routinely murdered in the camps. The mechanised holocaust ended January 1945, but thousands of Jews continued to be worked to death and were shot in random executions across Germany to the end of the war. The post-war world was also unsafe, and in Poland in particular Jews who attempted to return to their villages and towns were shunned and often murdered. Across Europe those who had profited from the acquisition of a Jewish home or business more often than not rejected the claims of survivors or the next of kin. The Holocaust was the passive and active work of the many, not the few.

References

1. Martin Gilbert, *The Holocaust: The Jewish Tragedy*, Fontana, 1986, p. 285.
2. Ronnie S. Landau, *Studying the Holocaust: Issues, Readings and Documents*, Routledge, 1998, p. 73.
3. Martin Gilbert, *The Holocaust: The Jewish Tragedy*, Fontana, 1986, p. 506.

Nemesis

35 Mussolini's last stand

> I am finished. My star has set. I still work but I know that everything is a farce. I await the end of the tragedy strangely detached from it all.[1]
>
> Mussolini's words during an interview with the journalist
> Madeleine Mollier in December 1944

Mussolini met with Hitler at *Wolfsschanze* on the afternoon of 20 July 1944, only hours after Hitler had survived the bomb blast that was meant to end his leadership and the war. Hitler personally conducted him on a tour of the still-smoking ruins of the map room and declared that he had been spared by Providence. Later over tea, Hitler lapsed in a brooding silence and largely ignored Mussolini but, following a passing reference to the Rohm purge of 1934, he leapt to his feet and launched into a hysterical thirty-minute denouncement of all traitors. Mussolini was shaken by Hitler's loss of control and he returned to his isolated villa at Lake Garda disillusioned and with his faith in Hitler finally broken. With Rome occupied, the Allies firmly ashore in Normandy and the Red Army threatening East Prussia, Mussolini had few illusions about the outcome of the war. He no longer made military decisions but was reduced to the position of a spectator and was rarely consulted by the commander-in-chief of German forces in northern Italy, Field Marshal Albert Kesselring, or his own Fascist hierarchy. The latter spent most of their time enforcing their own fiefdoms and enriching themselves through drug running and control over the black market. Mussolini spent most of his days in melancholy silence, reading and appeasing his wife Rachele who objected to the installation of his mistress Claretta Petacci in a neighbouring villa. Kesselring shared Mussolini's overall assessment that the war was lost, but he was determined to fulfil his duty and to prevent any Allied breakthrough into southern Germany. He was aided by an Allied strategy that gave priority to the liberation of France before defeating the Wehrmacht in northern Italy. The decision left the Allies and Wehrmacht in Italy with a rough balance of manpower, although the Allies enjoyed a marked superiority in aircraft, tanks and artillery and also benefited from a rising tide of Italian partisan activity behind the German lines. Kesselring could not match Allied firepower. Consequently he renewed the defensive strategy that had frustrated the Allies throughout the Italian campaign by taking advantage of the mountainous terrain and numerous fast-flowing rivers to construct the Gothic defensive line. It snaked across Italy for 200 miles from La Spezia on the west coast across the jagged heights of the central Apennine mountain chain to Pesaro on the Adriatic coast. Every mountain top, pass and river crossing was heavily defended with pillboxes, artillery and minefields, and behind the line Kesselring had the benefit of Highway 9 – the ancient Emilian Way – that ran in parallel to the front for the rapid movement of men and supplies. Kesselring intended to repeat the success of the Gustav Line which had sapped

Allied morale and cost high Allied casualties in the earlier battle for Rome (see Chapter 29). In the short term his strategy was to prove highly successful.

On 4 August General Sir Oliver Leese, in command of the British 8th Army, proposed a major offensive, codenamed Olive, along the narrow Adriatic coastal plain to breach the Gothic Line before Kesselring had time to consolidate his defences. He planned to overwhelm the German defence by secretly concentrating the weight of the 8th Army on the Adriatic front to gain local superiority and, once the Wehrmacht was fully engaged, for the US 5th Army, commanded by General Mark Clark, to strike in the centre of the line towards Bologna. The attack commenced on 25 August, watched by General Alexander and Churchill from a hilltop olive grove. Churchill remarked that 'the Germans were firing with rifles and machine guns from thick scrub . . . this was the nearest I got to the enemy and the time I heard the most bullets in the Second World War'.[2] Earlier, as part of a tour of the Mediterranean front on 15 August, Churchill had joined the Operation Dragoon invasion fleet off the southern coast of France to monitor the Allied landings in person. The attack was initially successful, but Kesselring countered the advance by rapidly moving reinforcements along Highway 9, including the experienced 16th Panzer Division. The Allied advance was further hindered in early September by the onset of torrential rain, which converted the river plains into muddy swamps and slowed the Allies to a crawl. Rimini was taken on 21 September, aided by landings on the Adriatic coast, but Vietinghoff fell back on the line of the river Uso (the historic Rubicon) and continued his stubborn defence. After a month of sustained pressure the US 5th Army breached the Gothic Line and came within 5 miles of Bologna, but the advance was contained. The Allied advantage in aircraft and tanks was checked by the poor weather and mountainous terrain, and on 27 October the Allied advance faltered and ground to a halt. In contrast, across the Adriatic in the Balkans and Greece the Wehrmacht was forced to yield control. On 14 October Greek partisans, with British assistance, liberated Athens, and on 20 October Tito's partisan army in Yugoslavia drove the Wehrmacht out of the capital, Belgrade, and cut off all German road and rail links across the country. The defeats marooned some 30,000 German troops on the Greek islands and, combined with the Red Army advances into Romania, Bulgaria and Hungary, successfully liberated the whole of the Balkans from German rule. In November 1944 the rain in northern Italy turned to freezing sleet and snow and reduced Allied morale to the point of widespread desertion. After a final unsuccessful attempt to occupy Bologna in December 1944, General Alexander ordered a halt to the offensive as the troops were too few and too exhausted to achieve a decisive breakthrough. He planned to wait for reinforcements and to allow a period of rest before renewing the offensive in the spring.

In the interim the failure of Hitler's Ardennes offensive (January 1945) to stem the Allied advance into Germany made the war in Italy inconsequential and significantly reduced the morale of the Wehrmacht in Italy. Their mission of guarding southern Germany was meaningless when little stood between the Allies and Berlin. The defeatist mood was deepened when Hitler rejected the advice of Kesselring and General Vietinghoff for a strategic withdrawal to the Alps. A hotel at Zurs had been requisitioned to serve as Mussolini's headquarters, with a last stand planned for Valtelline on the Swiss border. However, Hitler insisted upon no withdrawals from the Gothic front and for all troops to fight to the death. During February 1945, General Karl Wolff, the commander of all SS forces in Italy and Himmler's adjutant, opened secret surrender negotiations with the Allies. It would appear that Wolff was not acting independently but with Himmler's full knowledge and approval. There is also some evidence that Hitler was aware of the contacts and was willing to explore a deal in the west. Mussolini also signalled his readiness for a peace settlement. Contacts were established via the office of Cardinal Idelfonso Schuster, the archbishop of Milan, and Wolff was also placed into contact with Allen Dulles, head of the US Office of Strategic Services in Switzerland (the forerunner of the Central Intelligence Agency). Wolff attempted to interest the Allies in an anti-communist pact that would include the survival of Nazi Germany. The contacts produced face-to-face negotiations between Wolff and Dulles, first in Zurich and then at Ascona on the Swiss border on 19 March, but the Allies maintained their insistence upon unconditional surrender. In secret, Himmler pursued further contacts with the west via Sweden in a vain attempt to interest the Allies in a peace settlement, with him as the head of a new German government.

On 9 April 1945 the Allies opened their long-awaited spring offensive on the Gothic front. The British 8th and US 5th Armies had gained significant reinforcement over the winter and enjoyed superiority in troops, tanks and artillery, as well as complete command of the air. The advance was preceded by a devastating demonstration of Allied firepower from an air fleet of 234 medium bombers, 825 heavy bombers, 740 fighter-bombers and 1,500 guns. General Vietinghoff, who was appointed commander-in-chief of the Wehrmacht in Italy following the transfer of Kesselring to the Western Front, renewed the request for a strategic retreat to the Alps but was ordered to hold his line by Hitler. Despite the inevitability of defeat, with the Red Army already in possession of Austria and engaged in the battle for Berlin, Vietinghoff obeyed and the Wehrmacht strongly resisted the Allied advance. However, within a week the German line buckled under the relentless Allied pressure and on 19 April a full breakthrough was achieved. On the same day Mussolini evacuated his headquarters at Lake Garda and travelled to Milan accompanied by Claretta Petacci and a small German escort commanded by Lieutenant Birzer. His wife Rachele stayed behind having refused Mussolini's entreaties to fly to Spain. The end was signalled by the bloodless Allied occupation of Bologna on 21 April when the Germans agreed to withdraw without a fight. Most of the ordinary German troops simply wanted to return to their families, and were aware that behind them the partisans controlled all road and rail links into Germany and that they were essentially encircled. Hitler still refused permission to surrender, but both Vietinghoff and Wolff were professional soldiers, who saw little point in needless sacrifice when not just the battle but the entire war was lost. On 23 April both agreed to disregard Hitler's orders and to reopen surrender negotiations. The partisans ordered a general anti-Fascist rising for 25 April. From the outset their main interest lay in the capture and execution of Mussolini and all senior Fascists, who were regarded as having betrayed the Italian people. To this end they offered the Wehrmacht safe passage out of Italy in return for non-interference in Italian affairs, which included the arrest of all Italian Fascists.

Mussolini met with the archbishop of Milan on 25 April to request his support as an intermediary with the Allies, and was appalled to discover that Vietinghoff had already entered into a deal for the safe passage of Germans and that the partisans in Milan had orders for his arrest and summary execution. In a state of high dudgeon, Mussolini ordered an immediate drive north to Como near the Swiss border where he was informed that a band of 3,000 Fascist Blackshirts, commanded by one of his most loyal followers Alessandro Pavolini, were preparing to make a last stand. At Como there was no sign of Pavolini or any Blackshirt force and, after some hesitation, Mussolini drove deeper into the mountains to Menaggio and commandeered the Miravalle Hotel as a temporary headquarters. Over the next two days he waited for the Blackshirts to assemble, but most of his entourage deserted him and attempted to find routes over the Alps into the safety of Switzerland. On 27 April Pavolini finally appeared. In answer to Mussolini's urgent enquiry as to how many Blackshirts accompanied him he was forced to reply that only twelve had volunteered to join him. With insufficient men to force a passage through the partisan forces guarding the road to Switzerland, Mussolini accepted a suggestion from Birzer that he join a retreating German convoy. The convoy set off with Mussolini persuaded to ride inside an armoured car, but only 6 miles north of Menaggio it was stopped on the shores of Lake Como by a partisan roadblock of felled trees. After a brief exchange of gunfire, the partisans approached under a white flag and offered safe passage across the border for all Germans, but demanded to search the convoy and to arrest any Italians. A standoff ensued for some six hours before the partisan terms were accepted and the convoy was escorted to the village of Dongo to be searched for any escaping Italians. Birzer pressed Mussolini to wear the greatcoat and helmet of a corporal in a Luftwaffe anti-aircraft unit and placed him in the back of one of the German trucks. At Dongo a partisan climbed into the truck and was suspicious of the soldier who never looked up. He asked if he was an Italian and, in a personal decision to end the charade, Mussolini immediately answered 'yes'. He was arrested and temporarily imprisoned in the mayor's office, where Claretta Petacci insisted on joining him. Out of fears of a rescue mission, he and Claretta were moved several times and were finally taken to spend the night of 27 April in a tiny farmhouse. In Como a US force was already searching for him with an Allied arrest warrant, but on the morning of 28 April 1945 a group of partisans from Milan, under the leadership of Walter Audisio arrived, ostensibly to escort Mussolini to Milan and into captivity. Mussolini and Petacci were bundled into the back of a car but they had only travelled approximately two miles before the small convoy stopped outside the high brick wall of the Villa Belmonte near Mezzegra. Both were ordered to stand by the wall and were shot dead by Audisio without ceremony. Fifteen other leading Fascists who had travelled with Mussolini were also captured and executed, including Pavolini and Claretta's brother Marcello. Their bodies were all taken back to Milan in the back of a furniture van and tipped out in the Piazzale Loreto at dawn on 29 April. A crowd soon gathered and the bodies were all kicked and mutilated. One woman fired five shots into Mussolini's body in a stated act of revenge for the death of five of her sons. To permit the large crowd to see the bodies, four of them, including those of Mussolini and Claretta Petacci, were hoisted up by the feet to hang upside down from the girders of a half-completed garage. On the same day General Vietinghoff signed an unconditional surrender, and on 2 May victory in Italy was proclaimed six days before the end of war in Germany. In his Berlin bunker Hitler received the news of Mussolini's death without comment, but he privately resolved not to meet a similar ignominious end.

References

1. Christopher Hibbert, *Benito Mussolini: The Rise and Fall of Il Duce*, Penguin, 1962, p. 316.
2. Martin Gilbert, *Churchill: A Life*, Heinemann, 1992, p. 790.

36 *Götterdämmerung*

> Not a stalk of wheat is to feed the enemy, not a German mouth to give him information, not a German hand to offer him help. He is to find every footbridge destroyed, every road blocked. Nothing but death, annihilation and hatred will confront him.[1]
>
> The *Volkischer Beobachter*, reporting Hitler's orders for a
> scorched earth policy on 7 September 1944

After the failure of the Ardennes offensive to deliver a decisive victory in the west, Hitler returned to Berlin on 16 January 1945 and took up residence in the Führer bunker buried 15 metres deep behind the Reich Chancellery building. The bunker was an extension of the original Chancellery air raid shelter completed in 1936 and hastily added to during the autumn of 1944. The bunker consisted of two floors connected by a spiral staircase. On the upper floor were the kitchens and staff accommodation. In April, four of the rooms were cleared to accommodate the Goebbels family. On the lower floor was Hitler's living quarters, with an adjacent room for Eva Braun, a conference room, switchboard, surgery and a tiny office for Martin Bormann, secretary of the Nazi Party and Hitler's intermediary with the outside world. The bunker was painted throughout in battleship grey and was reported by all who entered it to be a damp, dismal and depressing place. Hitler had rejected the offer of more comfortable living accommodation in the Wehrmacht headquarters bunker at Zossen or the Luftwaffe bunker at Wannsee. After the assassination attempt of 20 July 1944 he refused to trust the Wehrmacht, only feeling safe in the confines of his own bunker surrounded by his personal SS guards who rigorously screened and searched every person who entered his presence. A warren of adjacent bunkers housed Bormann's staff and other essential Chancellery personnel. Above ground, few buildings in Berlin were left undamaged owing to the nightly attentions of RAF Bomber Command. The old Imperial Chancellery was largely in ruins, but the new Chancellery standing alongside was comparatively undamaged. Here Hitler still maintained his operations room and directed his daily *Führerlage*, or military briefings, attended by Chief of the General Staff Heinz Guderian and other senior staff.

The *Füehrerlage* rapidly degenerated into a daily conflict between Guderian and Hitler, the former attempting to salvage a future for Germany whereas Hitler appeared to be set upon *Götterdämmerung* and the complete destruction of the entire German nation. Hitler had remarked to his Luftwaffe adjutant, Captain Nicholas von Below, 'We'll not capitulate. Never. We can go down. But we'll take a world with us.'[2] Guderian's recommended strategy was to transfer all available divisions to the Eastern Front to bar the pathway of the Red Army to Berlin while negotiations were opened with the western powers for a peace settlement. He advised stripping Norway, Denmark, Italy and the Western Front of divisions to reinforce the Eastern Front. In particular, he pressed Hitler to permit the withdrawal across the Baltic Sea of an estimated 200,000 troops of Army Group North who were trapped in the Courland Peninsula in Latvia. Hitler refused to yield any territory and on 9 January 1945, when Guderian warned of an imminent Soviet offensive, he exploded with rage and denounced the Wehrmacht intelligence reports for crediting the Red Army with resources beyond their capabilities. He refused to believe that the Soviet Union was capable of fielding the major forces reported after the heavy losses inflicted during three years of fighting from 1941 to 1944. However, only three days later at dawn on 12 January 1945 the First Ukrainian Front, commanded by Marshal Ivan Koniev, opened the drive in western Poland with a massive artillery barrage that smashed the German line. The advance was spearheaded by newly deployed 'Stalin' or JS-3 tanks with 122 mm guns – the most powerful tanks of the war that could both outrange and outgun the panzers. Two days later the First Belorussian Front, under the command of Marshal Georgi Zhukov, also broke through the German line with an armoured wedge of some 1,000 tanks. The firepower was overwhelming and confirmed Guderian's most pessimistic assessment. The Red Army had attacked with 163 divisions, 6,500 tanks and 4,700 aircraft, whereas the Germans fielded at best seventy-one divisions, 1,800 tanks and 800 aircraft. The Red Army troops were battle-hardened veterans of Stalingrad, whereas many of the German troops were Hitler Youth and 'stomach and ear' conscripts and *Volksgenadiers* – essentially civilians pressed into military service with little or no military training. By 16 January, Warsaw was enveloped from north and south and the retreating Germans sacked the city in an orgy of destruction. The city fell the next day and Hitler, who had issued a 'fortress' order (a euphemism for a fight to the death), subjected the defeated Wehrmacht commanders to hours of interrogation by the Gestapo to uncover any signs of treachery. Hitler's futile offensive in the Ardennes had squandered the Wehrmacht's last major reserves of manpower, tanks and aircraft, and Guderian could only watch as the Red Army swept virtually unchallenged across Poland, enveloped Pozan and turned northwards towards Elbing and Danzig on the Baltic coast. The unexpected advance north severed eastern Prussia from the Reich on 20 January and resulted in the encirclement of some 500,000 troops and widespread civilian panic. Most had heard reports of the routine rape and murder of civilians by Soviet troops in revenge for Hitler's war of annihilation in the east. Consequently, hundreds of thousands of German civilians pressed into the Baltic ports and attempted to find passage on any ship to escape. Off shore, Russian submarines patrolled the coast waiting to intercept and sink all ships leaving port. The worst single loss occurred on 31 January when the liner *Wilhelm Gustloff* was torpedoed and went down with an estimated 7,000 civilians crammed on board. On 21 January, at Tannenburg, the scene of the German victory over Tsarist Russia in 1914, the remains of Field Marshal von Hindenburg and his wife were disinterred and trucked to the safety of Berlin and his tomb and monument were blown up. That same day in Berlin Isle Braun visited her sister Eva and found her entirely devoid of any understanding of the scale of the unfolding military catastrophe. She firmly rebuked her sister with the words: 'your Fuhrer is a fiend. He's dragging you into the abyss with him and all of us along with you.'[3]

Hitler reacted to the military collapse by issuing an order that no divisions, or even individual units, were to be moved without his personal authorisation. He accused the Wehrmacht of defeatism and on 24 January appointed Heinrich Himmler to command the newly formed Army Group Vistula in order to inject true National Socialist ardour and fighting spirit into the Wehrmacht. Himmler had little experience of military strategy or field command and had few illusions about his ability to make a difference. On 30 January 1945, the twelfth anniversary of his accession to power, Hitler made his last defiant radio broadcast to the German people. He declared Goebbels to be the 'Defender of Berlin' and demanded total faith in victory, although earlier that day he had been warned by Albert Speer that Germany's last stocks of oil, ammunition and food would soon be exhausted. By the end of January the Red Army had reached the river Oder, the last natural barrier before Berlin. The Oder entered the Baltic at Stettin (later the starting point of the 'Iron Curtain') and stretched directly south to the Czech frontier. Along its length the towns of Zehden, Kustrin, Frankfurt-am-Oder, Furstenberg and Gorlitz were all designated by Hitler as fortress towns, to be held to the last man in order to defend Berlin. Hitler's instinct was to return to the offensive as the best means of defence. To Guderian's fury, Hitler ordered the transfer of two panzer divisions from the Oder front and the 6th Panzer Division from the west to launch an offensive in Hungary. Hitler insisted that his fortress towns would hold the Red Army on the Oder while his new offensive reclaimed the initiative on the Eastern Front. Following Speer's warning, his primary interest was oil. On 18 January the Red Army had entered Budapest and threatened to overrun the oilfields east of Lake Balaton, the last in German hands. Hitler also convinced himself that a German offensive in Hungary would force the Red Army to switch its resources away from the Oder front and thereby reduce the threat to Berlin. Guderian could not contain his anger at Hitler's entirely unrealistic grasp of the strength of the Red Army arrayed along the Oder, and during the *Führerlage* on 13 February he directly questioned Hitler's judgement and openly challenged Himmler's competence as a military commander. According to Guderian, Hitler approached him, 'his fists raised, his cheeks flushed with rage, his whole body trembling, the man stood there in front of me, beside himself with fury and having lost all self control'.[4] Hitler unexpectedly gave way and accepted Guderian's suggestion for General Walther Wenck to direct a counter-attack rather than Himmler, but he insisted on maintaining his strategy of holding the Red Army on the Oder while the SS secured the Balaton oilfields. He hoped to win time for cracks to appear in the Alliance. On 27 January he had speculated, in the company of Göring and Field Marshal Jodl, that Churchill would welcome a settlement to avoid any further Soviet advance into Europe; Göring encouraged the notion with the remark that 'they should expect a wire from Churchill within a few days'.[5] This optimism was shattered by the Allied press conference that ended the second major Allied conference of the war at Yalta in the Crimea from 4 to 11 February 1945. Roosevelt, Churchill and Stalin had conferred in the Livadia Palace on the edge of the Black Sea and, to Hitler's disappointment, their press release renewed the demand for the unconditional surrender of Germany.

Any lingering hopes for a cease-fire on the Western Front were ended on 8 February 1945 by the opening of Operation Veritable. A total of eighty-five US, Canadian and British divisions, backed by overwhelming air and artillery support, commenced a drive to the Rhine. Only twenty-six German divisions were stationed along the Rhine, but the broad river presented a formidable barrier. Hitler ordered all bridges to be destroyed and for the Rhine to be held at all costs. The main weight of the attack was entrusted to Field Marshal Montgomery's 21st Army Group positioned along the northern extreme of the Allied front line at Nijmegen. It was here that the front line had stabilised in September 1944, following the failure of Operation Market Garden to cross the lower Rhine at Arnhem. Further south, in the Moselle region east of Luxembourg, General Bradley's US 12th Army Group, comprising the US 1st Army commanded by General Hodges and the US 3rd Army commanded by General Patton, also advanced towards the Rhine on a broad front between Cologne and Mannheim. The rivalry between Patton and Montgomery was unabated and, although the 12th Army Group was meant to act in support of Montgomery's offensive, Patton was determined to seize any opportunity to promote a greater role for the US 3rd Army. On the Eastern Front the Red Army launched an unexpected thrust north into Silesia and Pomerania towards the Baltic. Stalin's strategy was to secure his northern flank, regain possession of the Baltic States and to wipe out the fortress pockets along the Oder before advancing on Berlin. Poznan fell on 20 February and the ancient fortress city of Kustrin, only 48 miles from Berlin, was surrounded and placed under siege. On the Western Front the US 1st Army entered Cologne on 6 March. The next day, advance units of the US 9th Armoured Division, moving south along the line of the river, seized the Ludendorff railway bridge at Remagen following the failure of the demolition charges to destroy the bridge. Within hours Hodges had upstaged Montgomery by pushing three divisions across the bridge to form the first Allied bridgehead on the east bank of the Rhine. US sergeant Joe Delisio earned the distinction of being the first Allied soldier to cross the Rhine. Hitler was enraged by the failure of the officers in charge to blow the bridge and four were subsequently executed. Hitler also sacked the commander-in-chief of the Wehrmacht in the west, Field Marshal Gerd von Rundstedt, and withdrew Field Marshal Albert Kesselring from Italy to take his place. Ultimately the bridge proved to be of little value to the Allied advance. It was further weakened by near misses from Luftwaffe air attack and by artillery bombardments and collapsed after only ten days under the weight of the continuous Allied traffic. On 15 March, Hitler finally ended his close relationship with Himmler and the SS by giving Himmler, in his own words, an 'extraordinarily severe dressing down' for military failure.[6] Four days later Hitler met with Albert Speer and ordered the complete destruction of Germany's infrastructure in the face of the advancing Allies. When Speer strongly protested that basic services had to be maintained to feed and support the population, Hitler answered:

> If the war is to be lost, the nation will also perish . . . the nation has proved itself weak and the future belongs solely to the stronger eastern nation. Besides those who remain after the battle are of little value; for the good have fallen.[7]

Speer was appalled by Hitler's disregard for the survival of the German people and quietly ignored his orders. On 20 March Guderian approached Hitler and managed, without too much persuasion, to gain Hitler's approval for Himmler's replacement by the highly experienced Colonel-General Gotthard Heinrici to improve the front-line defences. The next day Guderian made the mistake of confiding in Himmler his belief that the war was lost and inviting him to support an approach to Hitler to negotiate for peace. The mistake ended his command. Himmler saw an opportunity to restore his battered reputation and immediately reported the discussion to Hitler. After the conclusion of the military briefing on 21 March, Hitler invited Guderian to take immediate sick leave. Guderian accepted but agreed to remain in post until his nominated successor as chief of the General Staff, General Hans Krebs, was fit enough to return to duty following injuries sustained in a car crash. Himmler was entirely duplicitous. While denouncing Guderian for defeatism, in secret he had opened peace negotiations with the west via the Red Cross in Switzerland and Count Folke Bernadotte of the Swedish Red Cross. He had also used his SS chief of staff in Italy, Karl Wolff, as an intermediary to open discussions with Allen Dulles of the US Office of Strategic Services based in Geneva. All the talks were aimed at breaking the western alliance with the Soviet Union and establishing a separate peace in the west, but Himmler was frustrated by the continued Allied insistence upon unconditional surrender.

On the Western Front, the successful crossing of the Rhine at Remagen emboldened Patton and, in a surprise move, he directed a further crossing of the Rhine at Oppenheim on 22 March. Montgomery studiously ignored both US advances. The US crossings were minor rather than strategic and at 9 p.m. on 23 March Montgomery launched Operation Plunder, the planned Allied advance across the Rhine. First across were advance units of the 51st Highland Division in Buffalo amphibious troop carriers. They met little opposition. Two weeks of preliminary air and artillery bombardment had smashed the German defences and, if anything, the destruction of roads and towns hindered rather than assisted the Allied advance. The next morning 40,000 paratroopers from the British 6th and US 17th Airborne divisions were dropped to protect the bridgehead, and on 25 March the first major objective, the town of Wesel, was taken. Churchill, who delighted in visiting the major battle fronts, flew the length of the British line on 24 March in Montgomery's light Messenger aircraft, and the following day, in defiance of Eisenhower's orders, he crossed the Rhine with Montgomery in a US launch. On 27 March the last V2 rocket of the war hit a block of flats in Stepney, East London, and killed 137 people. That same day British armour advanced virtually unchallenged across the north German plain and Montgomery, with Churchill's encouragement, announced his intention to continue the advance to Berlin. Eisenhower firmly objected and rebuked Montgomery for trying to impose his strategy on the Allied campaign, ordering him to stop at the River Elbe. Eisenhower regarded Berlin as a political objective, whereas the military imperative was to neutralise the strong German forces in the Ruhr and to occupy southern Germany to forestall any last minute flight by Hitler and the Nazi hierarchy from Berlin. Rumours were rife of a 'National Redoubt' being prepared in the Bavarian Alps for Hitler's last stand. Consequently, Eisenhower ordered Montgomery and Bradley to converge on the Ruhr and under no circumstances to cross the Elbe. To reinforce his decision, and to reassure Stalin that the Allies were not planning to negotiate with Hitler, he sent Stalin a telegram on 28 March which confirmed his orders and Allied objectives. Stalin was aware of Himmler's contacts with the West and was highly suspicious that an anti-communist pact might be agreed. That same day, Hitler burst into a torrent of abuse against the entire Wehrmacht for military incompetence, following Guderian's report of the fall of Kustrin, the last major town before Berlin. It came after news of the collapse of the SS bid to hold the Balaton oilfields in Hungary and shattered Hitler's hopes of winning a respite on the Eastern Front and time to achieve a settlement in the west. His disappointment was expressed in a bitter denunciation of the SS for failure; he ordered Himmler to travel to Hungary and to personally strip the SS 6 Panzer Division, and their commander Sepp Dietrich, of their insignia and military decorations. Guderian, in turn, openly lost his temper and bluntly listed Hitler's military mistakes to the point that Hitler 'slumped further down into his chair all the colour draining from his face'.[8] Those present feared for Guderian's immediate arrest and execution, but in private Hitler calmly ordered him to implement his sick leave immediately. Guderian retired, but survived the war and was found not guilty of war crimes charges, dying in 1954 aged 65. Across Berlin, in the Beethoven Hall, the Berlin Philharmonic Orchestra played their last concert. They had only narrowly escaped the *Volksturm* draft by the personal intervention of their patron, Speer. He attended the concert and requested that the programme should open with Wagner's *Die Götterdämmerung*, an opera depicting the 'Twilight of the Gods' when the home of the Gods, Valhalla, was razed to the ground.

Stalin was uncertain whether to trust Eisenhower's telegram. He still harboured a suspicion that the Allies might try to snatch Berlin and he was determined that after four years of unremitting struggle the prize of Berlin should go to the Soviet Union. Consequently, in his reply to Eisenhower on 1 April, he dismissed Berlin as merely a secondary objective of little importance but in secret he ordered Zhukov and Koniev to bring the date for the Soviet advance on Berlin forward by two weeks.

On the same day the US 1st and 9th armies linked up at Paderborn and encircled the whole of Wehrmacht Army Group B in the Ruhr. Some twenty-one divisions under the command of Field Marshal Model, amounting to 325,000 men, were trapped. Over the next two weeks they were gradually pressed into isolated pockets and left with little choice but to surrender. It marked the collapse of Wehrmacht resistance in the west and permitted advance units of the 9th Army to reach the Elbe on 11 April, only 50 miles from Berlin. The success renewed British pressure on Eisenhower to permit a dash to Berlin, but he refused to risk a split in the Alliance. On a more practical level he was also conscious that street fighting in a city the size of Berlin would inflict very high casualties of at least 100,000. Consequently, with German resistance along the Elbe stiffening following the arrival of the newly formed 12th Army commanded by General Walter Wenck, Eisenhower restated a firm Allied halt order on the Elbe. The possibility of an Allied dispute over territory and a split in the Alliance was the final hope that sustained Hitler. In his sitting room in the bunker he spent much time in silent contemplation, gazing at Anton Graff's portrait of Frederick the Great of Prussia. Hitler had purchased the portrait in 1934 in Munich, and thereafter it had travelled with him to every headquarters and was his talisman. On the night of 5 April, after a further acrimonious *Führerlage*, Goebbels, seated alone with Hitler, read aloud a passage from Carlyle's *History of Frederick the Great*. The passage described how, when Frederick was facing defeat and contemplating suicide in the Seven Years War (1756–63), he was unexpectedly saved from defeat by the sudden breakdown of the enemy alliance ranged against him. Goebbels recorded that Hitler was moved to tears and his faith in victory was restored. Exactly a week later President Roosevelt died in office and within hours Vice-President Harry Truman was sworn in as president of the United States. An ecstatic Goebbels telephoned Hitler and hailed Roosevelt's death as the fulfilment of Hitler's destiny and a precursor for the imminent collapse of the Alliance and a German victory. Triumphant leaflets were rushed to all fronts with a prediction of an imminent momentous political change and final victory for Germany.

Little else could save Berlin. The defence plan for the city involved eight concentric defensive rings, but each ring only consisted of street barricades made from rubble and overturned trams, and manned by young boys of the Hitler Youth aged between 14 and 16 and the older men of the *Volkssturm*. The rest of the male population had mostly perished or been taken prisoner. The inner ring, codenamed Zitadelle, was drawn around the Tiergarten, Reichstag and government quarter, including Hitler's Chancellery and bunker. Directly facing the massive Soviet build-up on the Oder east of Berlin were the 3rd Panzer Army, the 9th Army Group and remnants of Army Group Vistula commanded by Heinrici. To the north was General Felix Steiner and a ragtag collection of displaced units and SS police raised to the status of the 11th Army Group; to the south was the 4th Panzer Army and scattered units of Army Group South commanded by Field Marshal Ferdinand Schorner. In the west, guarding against any sudden US thrust, was Wenck and the 12th Army, and in reserve a further six divisions under the command of

General Karl Weidling. In total they numbered approximately a million men, but they lacked tanks, aircraft, guns and ammunition. In contrast, the Soviet Army formed a colossal phalanx along the line of the Oder comprising some 2.5 million men and with an awesome array of artillery, rocket launchers, tanks and aircraft. An estimated 7,500 Soviet aircraft faced 300 Luftwaffe fighters, 41,600 Soviet guns to 500, and 6,250 Soviet tanks and self-propelled guns confronted 850.

At 3 a.m. on 16 April, the final Soviet advance on Berlin commenced when Zhukov ordered the Soviet artillery to open fire, but in an unexpected reversal Heinrici successfully disrupted and temporarily broke the Soviet advance. Heinrici had established a strong defensive line along the horseshoe-shaped ridge of the Seelow Heights and carefully ranged his limited artillery on the Soviet crossing and line of advance. Zhukov was forced to commit his main reserves to overcome the unexpected resistance, whereas in the south Koniev's simultaneous advance had proceeded in a textbook manner and entered the outer suburbs of Berlin. On 19 April, in a forest clearing near Dusseldorf, Field Marshal Model, who had once enjoyed a reputation as 'Hitler's fireman' because of his reputation for being able to turn around impossible military situations, shot himself.

By 20 April, the day of Hitler's 56th birthday, the forces commanded by Zhukov and Koniev had wrapped around Berlin from the east and south respectively and were probing the outer defensive lines. Within the Zitadelle, a line of Hitler Youth were assembled amid the rubble of the Chancellery gardens to greet Hitler and to receive decorations for personal bravery. It was Hitler's last trip above ground and his last public appearance. He shuffled along the line and awarded Iron Crosses to the young boys. Earlier, General Weidling had angrily rejected the deployment of Hitler Youth as a needless sacrifice. Hitler showed no similar compunction, and as they returned to battle he went back underground to receive birthday greetings from the assembled Nazi hierarchy. Bormann, Göring, Himmler, Ribbentrop, Speer and Goebbels all awaited him, but none bar Goebbels and Bormann had any intention of remaining in the bunker to share Hitler's fate. That morning, Göring had personally depressed the plunger to demolish his beloved mansion, Karinhal, and filled twenty-four trucks with art treasures to accompany him south once the *Führerlage* was over. After a briefing that indicated that Berlin would soon be entirely encircled, all present beseeched Hitler to abandon Berlin and to make a last stand in the Bavarian Alps; he refused. Five days earlier Eva Braun had joined Hitler in the bunker and her arrival confirmed to all that he had no intention of leaving. Outside, at approximately 2 p.m., the first Soviet artillery shells fired by troops of the 79th Rifle Corps fell in the city centre and killed many Berliners who were standing in queues to receive the extra food rations that had been released in honour of Hitler's birthday. The bombardment galvanised Hitler into action and, invigorated by cocaine drops supplied by Dr Morell, he pored over the situation maps. His eyes fixed on a marker for SS General Steiner on the northern flank of the Soviet advance and he ordered Steiner to launch a counter-attack to cut-off the Soviet spearhead threatening Berlin. Steiner had few troops to command, but Hitler overrode his attempted protests and ordered all available reserves to be placed at Steiner's command and for him to break the Soviet advance immediately. The newly designated 'Army Group Steiner' existed only on paper, but Hitler declared: 'the Russians are about to suffer the bloodiest defeat of their history at the gates of Berlin'.[9] On 22 April Hitler's euphoria was punctured when he was informed during the last formal military briefing of the war that Steiner had insufficient forces to sustain an advance. The news was apparently too much for Hitler to bear, and those present reported that he turned 'deathly pale and purple in the face, shaking in every limb. His voice cracked and he screamed about disloyalty, cowardice, treachery and insub-ordination.'[10] It was clearly a cathartic release because thereafter his mood mellowed and he encouraged all to escape Berlin as best they could, though stating that his own intention was to remain to the end and then shoot himself. He directed Admiral Donitz to take command of all German forces in the north of Germany and Field Marshal Kesselring to do likewise in the south, and the next day he listened calmly when Speer confessed that he had not fulfilled his scorched earth policy. Instead of ordering his arrest and execution for treachery, Hitler simply wished him well. He was less forgiving of Göring who, on the evening of 23 April, sent him a telegram from the Obersalzberg in Bavaria proposing to take over the leadership of the Reich, unless otherwise directed, in fulfilment of his position as Hitler's deputy. Göring planned to enter into peace negotiations with Eisenhower and to establish a new government. Bormann condemned the telegram as an insulting usurpation of power and encour-aged Hitler to issue an order for Göring's arrest and dismissal. That same night, in Lübeck, Himmler invited the Swedish diplomat Count Bernadotte to convey an offer of surrender to the western powers. He too was planning to succeed Hitler, and to lead the new Reich under the banner of the Nationale Sammlungspartei (Party of National Concentration). Hitler was as yet unaware of Himmler's disloyalty and occu-pied himself with finding a replacement for Göring as commander-in-chief of the Luftwaffe. He promoted Colonel-General Ritter von Greim as Göring's successor, but instead of simply conferring the promotion by a written order he ordered Greim to fly to Berlin from Munich. Greim completed the trip under heavy fire in a Fieseler Storch flown by his mistress, a young test pilot, Hanna Reitsch, and during the final approach to Berlin suffered a severe shrapnel wound to his foot. Thus the new commander-in-chief of the Luftwaffe was both wounded and confined to the bunker.

By 25 April the Soviet forces had battled through the suburbs of Berlin and were poised to assault the Zitadelle. Hitler pinned his final hopes for survival on a last-minute advance from the south-west by Wenck's 12th Army. Zhukov advanced, levelling every city block with heavy artillery, while below ground the Soviet troops advanced through the cellars of the large tenement buildings and the tunnels of the U-Bahn and, notori-ously, raped most women in their path. A minimum of 90,000 women were brutally raped in Berlin, and many more across eastern Germany. Hundreds committed suicide following the daily experience of multiple rape by Soviet soldiers, who regularly searched homes commanding, 'Frau Komm'. To block their path Hitler ordered the subway flooded, but he only succeeded in drowning hundreds of injured Berliners who were sheltering from the fighting and were unable to escape the rising water. The remnants of the SS, including the few surviving members of the French SS Charlemagne Battalion, aided by fanatical members of the Hitler Youth, manned the street barricades and refused to surrender, while SS execution squads roamed the streets and hanged from lamp-posts any able-bodied men found without rifles. On the afternoon of 26 April a member of the Hitler Youth was presented to Hitler in the bunker to be rewarded with an Iron Cross for his single-handed destruction of a Soviet tank with a *panzerfurst*. He was duly congratulated by Hitler and returned without hesitation to the front line less than a mile distant. All that remained of the Third Reich was a narrow east–west strip just 1–3 miles broad and approximately 10 miles long.

On 27 April, a potent symbol of Allied victory was celebrated on the banks of the Elbe at Torgau when troops of the US 69th Infantry Division met up and shook hands with troops of the Soviet 58th Guards Division. The east–west pincer attack on Germany that had commenced in the west with Operation Overlord on 6 June 1944, and the Soviet Operation Bagration on 22 June 1944, was finally complete.

At 10 p.m. on 28 April news reached the bunker that Himmler had assumed power and was trying to negotiate surrender with the western powers. Hitler denounced it as 'the most shameful betrayal in human history',[11] and issued orders for his imme-diate arrest and execution for treason. He also ordered the arrest of Himmler's representative in Berlin, General Hermann Fegelein, on suspicion of collusion. Fegelein was married to Eva Braun's youngest sister, Gretl, but he was nevertheless dragged from his bed by the SS and executed in the courtyard of the Chancellery. Hitler was roused to action and he ordered Greim and Reitsch to risk an escape from Berlin by plane to deliver personally Himmler's arrest and execution order to Admiral Donitz. Under heavy fire shortly after midnight on 28 April, they succeeded in taking off unscathed from the broad east–west highway Unter den Linden in a small Arado 96 training plane. The Soviet troops watching the small plane disappear overhead feared that Hitler had made his escape. Hitler turned to settling his personal affairs and visibly appeared to relax. In the early hours of 29 April, between 1 a.m. and 3 a.m. while Soviet troops closed on the Reichstag and Chancellery, Hitler married Eva Braun. The ceremony was conducted by a minor official of the Propaganda Ministry, Walter Wagner, who had been plucked from a *Volkstruum* unit manning the front line near the bunker. Less than an hour later he was killed on duty. After the marriage service, Hitler dictated his last will and testament to one of his personal secretaries, Traudl Junge. He named Admiral Donitz as his successor as Reich president, Goebbels as Reich chancellor and Bormann to continue in his familiar role as party secretary. Hitler blamed the entire war on the Jews and directed the new government to 'scrupulous observance of the laws of race and to merciless opposition to the universal poisoner of all peoples, universal Jewry'.[12] Later in the day Hitler supervised the poisoning of his beloved Alsatian Blondi and her pups, and ordered the despatch of three emis-saries to deliver copies of his last will and testament to Donitz. He received the news of the death and mutilation of Mussolini without comment, and at 11 p.m. that night he wired Field Marshal Jodl for any news of an advance by General Wenck. There was none, and by the afternoon of Monday 30 April Hitler accepted that there was to be no relief. At approximately 3.20 p.m., while Soviet troops were storming the nearby Reichstag, Hitler, accompanied by his new wife, bade farewell to his staff and retreated to the privacy of his sitting room. Here some ten minutes later Eva and Hitler swallowed cyanide capsules and Hitler also shot himself in the head. Without ceremony their bodies were wrapped in blankets, carried up to the Chancellery gardens and cremated in a shell crater using some forty gallons of petrol. Less than half a mile from the bunker, it took Soviet troops all day to secure the Reichstag, but at 10.50 p.m. sergeants Yegorov and Kantariya reached the roof and raised the Red Banner above the bronze statue of Germania and her horse. With Hitler dead, Bormann and Goebbels despatched the chief of the General Staff, Krebs, during the early hours of 1 May to try and open cease-fire negotiations with General Chuikov, whose forces were besieging the Chancellery. It was an entirely unrealistic prospect, and when Stalin insisted upon unconditional surrender Josef and Magda Goebbels decided to commit suicide rather than be captured. In the Chancellery garden, at approximately 8.15 p.m. on 1 May, both took cyanide, an SS orderly ensuring that they were dead by firing single bullets into the backs of their heads. Earlier that evening Magda had personally used the drug

Finodin to sedate her six children, ranging in age from twelve to three, and then assisted Hitler's personal surgeon Dr Stumpfegger to kill each child by crushing a cyanide capsule into their mouths. Bormann's last act was to transmit the news of Hitler's death and his last will and testament to Admiral Donitz.

At 10.20 p.m. Donitz announced Hitler's death to the German people on the radio and disguised the truth by stating that he had died a hero's death fighting at the head of his troops against Bolshevism. Donitz immediately pledged to save Germany from Bolshevism and ordered all Germans to transfer their allegiance to him as the new Führer. That same night, under the cover of darkness, Bormann, accompanied by the last of Hitler's personal staff, struck out from the bunker to try and escape capture. Hitler's secretaries, including Junge, successfully made it through the Soviet lines to the west, but Bormann disappeared and was never seen again. For many years it was assumed that he had successfully escaped from Berlin, but in 1972 his remains and those of Stumpfegger were discovered by workmen digging foundations. Glass fragments from cyanide ampoules were found in both jaw bones. At 6 a.m. on 2 May the German forces in Berlin unconditionally surrendered after General Weidling released them from their pledge to defend Hitler to the death following his suicide. Stalin instituted a vigorous search by the NKVD in the rubble of the Chancellery gardens for proof of Hitler's demise. No recognisable bodies were found, apart from the partially burned remains of Josef and Magda Goebbels and the bodies of their six children left in their bunk beds. However, on 3 May, Private Ivan Churakov unearthed some fully charred remains, including parts of skull, jaw bone and teeth. They were at first ignored but were exhumed two days later for closer examination by NKVD colonel Ivan Kilmenko. Hitler's dental technician, Fritz Echtmann, and a dental assistant, Katchen Heuser, were tracked down by Colonel Vasily Gorbushin and interpreter Elena Rzhevskaya. The latter carried the teeth and jaw bone in a red cigar box. When it was opened Echtmann and Heuser both immediately recognised Hitler's and Eva Braun's teeth from the bridgework and the gold crowns. Dental records confirmed their identification and the remains were secretly transported back to Moscow. The other remains, including those of the Goebbels family, were secretly buried in the grounds of a Soviet army base at Magdeburg in East Germany. Echtmann and Heuser were sent to Siberia to ensure their silence and all involved were ordered never to reveal the truth. During the post-war Sovietisation of eastern Europe it was useful for Stalin to maintain the fear that Hitler had escaped and was perhaps being sheltered in the West. Zhukov was not even trusted with the information by Stalin and it was not until 1965 that he was told the truth. In April 1970 the remains of Hitler and the Goebbels were secretly exhumed, ground to a fine powder, and flushed down the sewage system.

Few mourned the passing of Hitler and Nazism. One of the few was the prime minister of the Irish Republic, Eamon de Valera, who called into the Germany embassy in Dublin on 3 May 1945 to register his sorrow at the news of Hitler's death. The following day, in a tent on the barren windswept Luneburg Heath, Montgomery received a German delegation led by Admiral Hans Georg von Friedeburg and accepted the formal surrender of all German forces in the west. Attempts to establish a separate peace with the West were brushed aside by Montgomery, and on 7 May Field Marshal Jodl met with British, Soviet, US and French representatives in Rheims and signed a comprehensive unconditional surrender document that applied to all fronts. In an attempt to distance himself from the Nazi regime, and to be accepted by the Allies as the new leader of Germany, Donitz condemned the excesses of the concentration camps and ordered all involved to be arrested. However, in secret he met with Himmler and aided him to escape arrest, disguised as Heinrich Hitzinger, a sergeant in the Geheime Feldpolizei, and also permitted the commandant of Auschwitz, Rudolf Hoess, to adopt a new identity as Franz Lang, a bosun's mate in the Kriegsmarine. He decided not to act on Hitler's arrest and execution order, faithfully relayed to him by Greim, because he shared Himmler's aim of trying to achieve a negotiated settlement with the West. Stalin was enraged by the lack of discussion concerning the surrender arrangements and he insisted that the capital city, Berlin, was the place for the Wehrmacht to surrender. Consequently, just before midnight on 8 May at Karlshorst in eastern Berlin, Field Marshall Wilhlem Keitel was directed to sign a further surrender document in the presence of representatives of all four major Allied powers. The war in Europe was finally officially over, although it was not until the end of 9 May that Nazi resistance in Prague was fully crushed. The news sparked Victory in Europe (VE Day) celebrations in London, Paris, New York and Moscow and across liberated Europe on 8 May. On 23 May Donitz's hopes of acceptance by the Allies as the post-war leader of Germany were ended when he was finally arrested, along with all other members of the German High Command. That night Heinrich Himmler, the man most associated with the worst excesses of the racial war and the aims of a 1,000-year Reich, bit into a cyanide capsule concealed in his mouth and died within minutes in his prison cell at 11.04 p.m. He had been arrested two days earlier for questioning by British soldiers manning a checkpoint near Bremervorde, and volunteered his true identity once he was confined to a British interrogation unit based at Barfeld near Luneburg. Earlier, at the height of the war on 9 June 1942, he had addressed SS Gruppenfuhrers in Berlin following the assassination and state funeral of his deputy Reinhard Heydrich and stated: 'I have the conviction now . . . that in the final analysis the others will die sooner than us . . . the whole S.S. will march on with beating drums and helmets donned. And if another blow strikes us, we will march on.'[13] On 25 May, Himmler's body was trussed up in camouflage netting, tied with telephone wire and buried at an unmarked location somewhere in Luneburg Heath by Sergeant-Major Austin. Only three years after Himmler's speech there was no one left to march. The Nazi Reich that Hitler had boasted would last for a thousand years had lasted for a mere twelve.

References

1. Anthony Read and David Fisher, *The Fall of Berlin*, Hutchinson, 1992, p. 187.
2. Ian Kershaw, *Hitler 1936–45: Nemesis*, Penguin, 2000, p. 747.
3. Anthony Read and David Fisher, *The Fall of Berlin*, Hutchinson, 1992, p. 213.
4. Ibid., p. 242.
5. Peter Padfield, *Himmler: Reichsfuhrer SS*, Papermac, 1991, p. 560.
6. Ibid., p. 569.
7. Alan Bullock, *Hitler: A Study in Tyranny*, Penguin, 1962, p. 775.
8. Gerhard Boldt, *Hitler's Last Days: An Eyewitness Account*, Sphere, 1973, p. 98.
9. Anthony Read and David Fisher, *The Fall of Berlin*, Hutchinson, 1992, p. 354.
10. Gerhard Boldt, *Hitler's Last Days: An Eyewitness Account*, Sphere, 1973, p. 122.
11. Ian Kershaw, *Hitler 1936–45: Nemesis*, Penguin, 2000, p. 819.
12. Alan Bullock, *Hitler: A Study in Tyranny*, Penguin, 1962, p. 795.
13. Peter Padfield, *Himmler: Reichsfuhrer SS*, Papermac, 1991, p. 383.

37 The bomb

The time has come when we must bear the unbearable.[1]
Emperor Hirohito announcing his decision to surrender to the
Supreme War Council at 11.30 p.m. on 9 August 1945

The US naval victory at the Battle of Leyte Gulf in October 1944 was a major turning point in the Pacific War. The victory confirmed US naval supremacy, and the subsequent US invasion of the Philippines cleaved the Japanese empire in two and established a broad US corridor running east–west across the central Pacific. South of the US corridor the Japanese armies fighting in Indo-China, New Guinea, the Philippines, Burma and the scattered islands of the Pacific were forced to be self-sufficient and to continue the war without hope of reinforcement or resupply. North of the corridor the home islands were isolated and cut off from all essential supplies, especially oil and food. Japan was essentially defeated, but the Imperial Court refused to contemplate surrender and rejected the renewed Allied demand for unconditional surrender within the Yalta declaration of February 1945. For the Japanese military and many ordinary Japanese it was unthinkable that Japan should be occupied by foreign powers or that the emperor should be forced to face trial and possible imprisonment as a war criminal. The fanaticism of the Japanese military was illustrated in February 1945 by the refusal of 16,000 Japanese marines besieged in Manila, the capital of the Philippines, to surrender. Despite a hopeless military situation, they embarked on a killing spree that lacked both military honour and any sense of humanity. The Japanese marines rampaged through the streets of Manila subjecting women of all ages to gang rapes, and bayoneting or beheading thousands of Filipino civilians at random in some of the most barbaric scenes of the war. The city finally fell to the US troops on 17 February, but for the Filipino people the liberation was tinged with immense sadness because not only was their city almost entirely destroyed but amid the ruins lay the corpses of an estimated 100,000 civilians.

The strategy adopted by the US Joint Chiefs of Staff was to end the war by the most direct means: an invasion of the home islands of Kyushu and Honshu. The islands of Iwo Jima and Okinawa were identified as essential staging posts for the build-up of an invasion force of 700,000 mainly US troops and, more urgently, for airbases to permit an intensification of the bombing raids on Japan. Sustained air raids on Japan had commenced in November 1944 by B-29 Superfortresses based on the islands of Tinian and Guam in the Marianas Islands chain, but the losses were high primarily because the 2,800-mile round trip precluded fighter escorts. Iwo Jima and Okinawa, 350 and 250 miles from Tokyo respectively, offered the USAAF the prize of airbases within fighter range of the whole of the home islands. The former was the first target for invasion. Iwo Jima was not a Pacific idyll, but the raw projection of a dormant volcano of jagged lava and black ash. Frequent sulphur emissions also wreathed the island in a 'bad egg' smell and gave the island its name of Iwo Jima – literally 'sulphur island'. Although the island (shaped like a pork chop) was only five miles long and 2.5 miles broad at its widest point, it had a major garrison of 26,000 Japanese troops under the command of Lieutenant-General Tadamichi Kuribayashi. After the bloody experience of Tarawa and Palaus, the US forces subjected Iwo Jima to months of bomb raids and naval bombardments to destroy all defensive positions. In the three days prior to the invasion over 40,000 naval shells were poured into an area of only 8 square miles. The chief target was the 550-foot-high volcanic cone of Mount Suribachi which commanded the sea approaches and the central plateau of the island.

On the morning of 19 February 1945, US Task Force 52, comprising 450 warships and transports, landed the first US troops on Iwo Jima. There was no resistance and at first it was assumed that the naval bombardment had successfully crushed the Japanese defence. However, in anticipation of the US tactics Kuribayashi had sheltered his men in a network of caves and tunnels that criss-crossed the island interior. Within the caves the Japanese troops were protected from all but a direct hit and once the invasion beaches were packed with men and equipment they opened fire. It was the start of the bloodiest single engagement in US Marine Corps history, largely due to the absence of a conventional front line. The marines were forced to storm an endless series of concealed pillboxes that, once cleared, were reoccupied in the US rear by Japanese soldiers using the tunnel network. By the end of the first day the marines had suffered 2,450 casualties, but by sheer weight of numbers they pushed across the island and isolated Mount Suribachi. It took a further three days of heavy fighting, often hand to hand, aided by continuous naval shelling, to end Japanese opposition on Suribachi. At 10.20 a.m. on 23 February the Stars and Stripes was triumphantly raised, using a drainpipe as a makeshift flagpole. The action was repeated, an hour later, for the camera of Associated Press photographer Joe Rosenthal. It became one of the most celebrated photographs of the war, to rank alongside the photograph of the Red Banner flying over the Reichstag in defeated Berlin. Roosevelt ordered the six soldiers in the photograph to be returned home, but by the time his order was received three had been killed in the subsequent fighting.

After four weeks of pitched battles the island was finally declared secure on 25 March 1945, following the failure of a last desperate suicidal banzai charge conducted by 300 men led by Kuribayashi. To secure the 8 square miles of Iwo Jima, 6,821 marines were killed and over 20,000 were injured, and of the Japanese garrison of 26,000 little more than a thousand were ever taken alive. The refusal to surrender raised deep concerns within the US military about the projected number of US casualties that would arise from an invasion of the home islands. The minimum estimate was 220,000 US dead, and some predicted a casualty rate as high as a million. The casualty toll of Japanese civilians and troops fighting to defend their own cities was expected to run into several millions. This fear of a bloody street-by-street invasion of Japan contributed to the later decision to drop the atomic bomb. The possibility of the US Strategic Bomber Force bombing Japan into submission was an attractive alternative to invasion. It was an option that General Curtis LeMay vigorously promoted, following his appointment on 20 January 1945 to command the USAAF 21st Bomber Command based on the Marianas Islands. The destructive capacity of the USAAF was demonstrated on the night of 9 March, with a major bomb raid on Tokyo by 325 B-29 bombers each loaded with 6–8 tons of incendiaries. A high number of buildings were of traditional wooden construction and the resulting multiple fires erupted into a firestorm greater than that at Dresden, burning out 16 square miles of the city and killing somewhere from 80,000 to 130,000 people. The actual death toll will never be known because the fire reached temperatures of 1,800 degrees Fahrenheit and reduced bodies to ash. Two nights later Nagoya was similarly bombed, followed within a further week by Osaka and Kobe. The emperor toured the ruins of Tokyo on 18 March and raised speculation that he might announce surrender. Instead Hirohito ordered his forces to defeat the anticipated US invasion of Okinawa and thereby force the US to consider a peace settlement to avoid further high casualties.

At first his hopes appeared to be well placed. On the same day as he toured Tokyo, US Task Force 58 was severely mauled by Japanese air attack off the coast of Kyushu, with four carriers sustaining heavy damage. At 8.30 a.m. on 1 April 1945 US troops commenced landings on Okinawa without incident, and by nightfall approximately 60,000 marines were safely ashore. However, the commander of the Japanese defence force, General Mitsuru Ushijima, repeated the tactics of Iwo Jima and opted not to expose his men to the superior US firepower. Ushijima concentrated his troops around the thirteenth-century castle in Shuri, in the south of the island, and on the steep, heavily wooded slopes of the Yaetake and Katsu mountains on the Motobu Peninsula. Here the terrain suited defence, and the Japanese troops sheltered deep inside fortified caves and forced the US marines to battle for every cave and connecting tunnel. On 5 April Hirohito dismissed Prime Minister Koiso for failure and appointed in his place the 78-year-old retired admiral Kantaro Suzuki. The change of government did not signal a search for peace by Hirohito, but rather an intensification of the war effort. The entire population was ordered to mobilise for war; this included all children aged seven or over who were drafted into the munitions and defence industries. All able-bodied men drilled with bamboo spears and were instructed to defend their homeland to the death. Future victory was vested in the formation of 'Special Attack Unit', a euphemism for kamikaze or suicide missions. To defeat the US fleet off Okinawa, Operation Tenichi (literally 'Heaven 1') ordered attacks by kamikaze aircraft and motor boats filled with high explosives. On 7 April, a mass attack by 700 kamikaze planes sank six ships and damaged twenty-four others. That same day the most ambitious kamikaze assault on the US fleet was attempted by the most powerful battleship of the war, the *Yamato*. The *Yamato*, the light cruiser *Yahagi* and eight destroyers were all that was left of the Japanese Combined Fleet following the decisive defeat in the Leyte Gulf. Without sufficient fuel for a round trip, the *Yamoto* was ordered to engage the US invasion fleet off Okinawa with its powerful main armament of nine 18.1 inch guns and, once its shells were exhausted, to beach itself and act as a fortress to smash the US landings. The entire attack plan was intercepted by the US signals intelligence on Hawaii, and at 12.41 p.m. on 7 April US carrier planes commenced the first of a succession of torpedo and bomb attacks, scoring multiple hits. At 2 p.m. a massive explosion in the ship's magazine tore the ship asunder and sent the *Yamoto* to the bottom, along with 3,063 of her crew. The *Yahagi* and two of the escorting destroyers were also sunk. It was the end of Japanese sea power and a potent reminder that the age of the battleship was over. In contrast, the US Navy had grown between 1941 and 1945 to be the most powerful naval force in world history, with fifty aircraft carriers at its disposal.

On 12 April, while sitting for a portrait at his home in Warm Springs, Georgia, President Roosevelt suffered a fatal cerebral haemorrhage and was succeeded by Vice-President Harry Truman. There was celebration in both Berlin and Tokyo in expectation of a change in US policy, but Truman reiterated Roosevelt's commitment to unconditional surrender.

On 3 May the capital of Burma, Rangoon, fell to British and Indian forces after a long, bitter war and signalled the end of the Japanese occupation of Burma. On

19 May, Japanese forces also accepted defeat in southern China. The capital of Okinawa, Naha, fell on 27 May and two days later US troops entered the ancient capital of Shuri. However, it took to 21 June to overcome the final pockets of Japanese resistance around Mabuni. Generals Ushijima and Sho committed ritual hara-kiri rather than surrender and hundreds of their men leapt to their deaths from cliff tops into the sea. The battle realised every American fear of high casualties. A total of 15,500 marines were killed and 51,000 injured, against an estimated 127,000 Japanese casualties – mainly dead. In addition, a minimum of 80,000 and as many as 150,000 Japanese civilians were killed across the devastated island. At sea 36 US Navy ships were sunk supporting the invasion, with the loss of 4,907 crew. Twenty-seven of the ships were lost to kamikaze attacks – a testimony to the effectiveness of suicide missions. However, the fall of Okinawa and defeats in Burma and China confirmed that the overall defeat of Japan was only a matter of time. In private, Hirohito's personal political adviser, Koichi, recommended opening negotiations for a peace settlement to ward off a US invasion of the home islands. Ex-Prime Minister Konoye went further and proposed that Hirohito abdicate in favour of Crown Prince Akihito, and devote the rest of his life to prayer and atonement in a religious retreat. President Truman approved Operation Olympic, the invasion of Kyushu, for 1 November 1945, and Operation Coronet, the invasion of Honshu, for 1 March 1946. In parallel to the invasion preparations, the physicists working on the Manhattan Project, under the scientific leadership of Robert Oppenheimer and overall direction of General Leslie Groves, met four times in May 1945 to discuss the use of the atomic bomb. The final meeting in the Pentagon on 31 May focused on the morality of dropping the bomb on a Japanese city and debated whether or not to demonstrate the power of the bomb in an unpopulated area. Oppenheimer concluded that such a demonstration was impracticable and stated on behalf of the scientific team that there were no acceptable alternatives to direct military use. Truman concurred, and welcomed a weapon that might induce surrender and avoid the need for Operation Olympic with its much greater projected loss of life. He also decided not to reveal details of the atomic research to Stalin, unaware that Stalin was being kept fully appraised of the development of the bomb by Klaus Fuchs, a member of the scientific team.

By June 1945 US 21st Bomber Command ranged at will over Japan, and at sea US submarines intercepted and sank all supply ships approaching Japan. By late 1944 the US submarines struggled to find targets as two-thirds of Japan's merchant marine had been sunk. Consequently, little food or fuel reached Japan and by early 1945 the population was growing vegetables on every spare patch of land to stave off hunger. The power to end the war lay with Hirohito, and on 12 July US signals intelligence decoded the first stirrings of peace prospects. On the eve of the Allied Potsdam Conference, Hirohito invited Stalin to intercede with the United States and Great Britain on Japan's behalf to secure a peace treaty. However, the transmission warned that Japan would 'be forced to fight to the bitter end'[2] if the Allies maintained their insistence upon unconditional surrender. Hirohito was seeking a guarantee of the continuation of the Chrysanthemum Throne and his immunity from prosecution. Future Allied policy was discussed at the third and final wartime Allied conference, held in Potsdam between 16 July and 2 August 1945, attended by Stalin, Truman and Churchill. The latter was replaced by Prime Minister Clement Attlee in the closing stages of the conference following Churchill's defeat in the British General Election.

At 5.30 a.m. on 16 July, in the Alamogordo Desert, New Mexico the world's first atomic bomb was detonated in a test explosion codenamed Operation Trinity, watched by Oppenheimer, Groves and the major scientists attached to the Manhattan Project. While Oppenheimer watched the rising fireball turn night into day he silently muttered the words of Krishna in the sacred Hindu text *Bhagavad Gita*: 'I am become death, the shatterer of worlds.'[3] The next day Truman and Churchill were informed of the successful test with the words 'babies satisfactorily born', and on 24 July Truman obliquely informed Stalin of the successful development of a new weapon of extraordinary power. Stalin needed no further explanation and that night he ordered an acceleration of the Soviet atomic bomb programme. On 26 July the major Allied leaders at war with Japan – the United States, Great Britain and China – issued the Potsdam Declaration:

> we call upon the Government of Japan to proclaim now the unconditional surrender of all the Japanese armed forces and to provide proper and adequate assurances of their good faith in such action. The alternative for Japan is prompt and utter destruction.[4]

The declaration was qualified by demands for the removal of Japan's 'militaristic advisers', but crucially it dropped earlier demands for the abdication of the emperor. It was a major concession at a time when a Gallup poll of US public opinion revealed that one-third of those polled wanted Hirohito executed as a war criminal; only 7 per cent believed that he should remain as emperor. The Potsdam Declaration essentially invited Hirohito to declare a constitutional monarchy, but the offer was unexpectedly rejected by Prime Minister Suzuki. Suzuki believed that there was 'no need to rush', and he treated the Potsdam Declaration as the opening round in negotiations rather than an ultimatum. A clumsy translation of his words was reported in Washington as an abrupt dismissal of the Potsdam Declaration. Therefore on 24 July Truman authorised the use of the atomic bomb on or after 3 August, dependent upon the weather conditions. Four cities were identified as targets: Kokura, Niigata, Hiroshima and Nagasaki. That same day the uranium core, encased in lead, arrived at Tinian Island on board the US cruiser *Indianapolis* to be assembled into the bomb. On the return trip tragedy overtook the *Indianapolis* when on 30 July it was torpedoed and sunk by a Japanese submarine. Approximately 300 crewmen went down with the ship, but approximately 900 were left in the water clinging to debris and a few life rafts. Many were injured and the blood in the water attracted sharks. Over the period of four days relentless shark attacks left only 317 survivors.

At 8.16 a.m. on 6 August the B-29 *Enola Gay* dropped 'Little Boy' on Hiroshima. The bomb detonated approximately 1,900 feet above ground and in one massive explosion scooped up the entire city centre and churned it into dust and rubble. Most of the population were instantly vaporised in temperatures as high as 5,000 degrees Celsius. Thousands of others on the periphery of the blast suffered intense burns and subsequently died, and many others who thought they had survived absorbed lethal doses of radiation. Overall an estimated 80,000 were killed, but a further 50,000 died in the days, weeks, months and years afterwards, according to the degree of exposure to radiation. It was this deadly after-effect that was to earn the bomb its controversial place in history. However, in Tokyo alone conventional bombing had already killed more Japanese civilians and caused greater destruction. Likewise on Okinawa, where the death toll was higher than the combined effect of *both* atomic bombs. More civilians were deliberately shot, bayoneted and burnt to death in the city of Manila by Japanese marines than died in Hiroshima. In China, the Japanese army of occupation had deliberately murdered an estimated 20 million Chinese civilians between 1937 and 1945 in a barely reported holocaust. Most suffered slow painful deaths following the deliberate manufacture and release of cholera, dysentery, typhoid, plague and anthrax into the water and food supply across northern China. Their deaths have been largely forgotten and obscured by the emotional shadow cast by the bomb. In comparison, the total number of Japanese civilians who died during the war, mostly from strategic bombing and on Okinawa, is estimated at 953,000. President Truman was informed of the bombing of Hiroshima while on board the SS *Augusta* off Newfoundland as he returned to the United States from Potsdam. On 7 August he made the nature of the bomb attack public and warned the Japanese to surrender or face 'a rain of ruin from the air, the like of which has never been seen on this earth'.[5] There was consternation within Japan, but the immediate focus was to calm public fears and to seek reports of the extent of the bomb damage. Before any firm assessment of the destruction had been made Nagasaki was destroyed by the second atomic bomb, 'Fat Man', carried by the B-29 bomber *Bock's Car* at 11.01 a.m. on 9 August 1945. The city was only bombed after the selected target city of Kokura was discovered to be shrouded in cloud. The death toll and damage was less than Hiroshima due to the hilly terrain that shielded the southern half of the city from the worst of the blast, but an estimated 70,000 still died. On the same day Japan also received news from Moscow of a Soviet declaration of war. The twin blows of the atomic bomb and the opening of an immediate Soviet offensive in Manchuria were hotly debated by the Japanese Supreme War Council throughout 9 August and into the early hours of 10 August. Despite the scale of the suffering and the inevitability of defeat the Council remained divided, with three for continuing the war and three for surrender. Hirohito expressed his opinion, as quoted at the start of this chapter, that Japan must bear the unbearable and surrender. However, all were agreed that Japan would fight on if the Allies attempted to force the abdication of the emperor or order his arrest as a war criminal. Hirohito personally re-emphasised this point and stated that he would refuse to accept 'any demand which prejudices the prerogatives of His Majesty as a Sovereign Ruler'.[6] No firm guarantees on the post-war position of the emperor were issued by US Secretary of State James Byrnes, but neither was he cited as a war criminal. Consequently, on 12 August Hirohito decided to surrender formally. News of the surrender was received by President Truman at 4.05 p.m. on 14 August, and announced to the nation and the world from a press conference in the White House at 7 p.m. That same night in Tokyo, the decision to surrender sparked a revolt by some army officers, led by Major Kenji Hatanaka, who were determined to continue the war. However, they received no support and were quickly surrounded and trapped in the palace. Hatanaka shot himself and most of his followers committed hara-kiri. The war minister, General Korechika Anami, also committed ritual hara-kiri. He was the first of many Japanese officials and army officers to do so. Over the following year, 1945–46, the police recorded 27,048 suicides.

At noon on 15 August Emperor Hirohito's announcement of the end of the war was broadcast on radio. It was the first time the Japanese people had heard the emperor speak, but few fully understood his stilted court language and heavily qualified statement. The Japanese people were informed that the war was over, but the word 'surrender' was not used – nor was any remorse expressed for the conduct of the war. In Tokyo crowds gathered to weep and to beseech the emperor's forgiveness for failure, whereas in the capitals of the main Allied nations, VJ day (Victory in Japan day) was wildly celebrated. In Manchuria, the war continued for a further week when Stalin urged his troops forward to consolidate the Pacific boundaries of his new vastly expanded Soviet Union. Finally, at 8.30 a.m. on 2 September 1945, Foreign Minister Mamoru Shigemitsu led an eleven-man Japanese delegation on board the US battleship *Missouri*, moored in Tokyo Bay. The formal surrender document was signed by Shigemitsu and the chief of staff of the Japanese armed forces, General Yoshijiro Umezu, in front of the assembled world press, and accepted by General Douglas MacArthur of the US and representatives of the nine Allied powers at war with Japan. After six years of warfare the Second World War was finally over.

References

1. Stephen S. Large, *Emperor Hirohito and Showa Japan*, Routledge, 1992, p. 176.
2. Charles L. Mee Jr, *Meeting At Potsdam*, André Deutsch, 1975, p. 23.
3. Ronald W. Clark, *The Greatest Power on Earth: The Story of Nuclear Fission*, Sidgwick and Jackson, 1980, p. 199.
4. Charles L. Mee Jr, *Meeting At Potsdam*, André Deutsch, 1975, p. 315.
5. Ibid., p. 286.
6. Herbert P. Bix, *Hirohito and the Making of Modern Japan*, Duckworth Press, 2000, p. 504.

Reconstruction

38 Ideals and post-war realities

> After the final destruction of the Nazi tyranny, they hope to see established a peace which will afford to all nations the means of dwelling in safety within their own boundaries and which will afford assurance that all the men in all the lands may live out their lives in freedom, from fear and want.[1]
>
> Article Six of the Atlantic Charter agreed between Churchill and
> Roosevelt on board the battleship *Prince of Wales*,
> 14 August 1941, off Newfoundland

The celebration of VJ or Victory in Japan day on 15 August 1945 brought the Second World War to a formal close eighteen weeks after Hitler's suicide and the defeat of Nazi Germany. The third Axis power, Italy, had surrendered earlier in September 1943 and the new Italian government had not only placed Mussolini under arrest but elected to join the Alliance. Thus Italy ended the war as an Allied nation at war with Nazi Germany.

The declaration of final victory over Japan prompted wild revelry in the United States, Great Britain and Australia, the principal Allied nations at war with Japan. An estimated 2 million New Yorkers choked the streets around Times Square, and in Washington and London enthusiastic congas were danced around the White House and Trafalgar Square respectively. In France the defeat of Nazi Germany was marked on 18 June 1945 by a military parade. It was the same day as the victory parade of 1919 that celebrated the defeat of Imperial Germany in the First World War. De Gaulle made the occasion a French affair to the extent that he reputedly reacted with anger when ambulances belonging to an Anglo-French medical unit, flying the Union Jack alongside the tricolour, received prolonged applause from wounded French servicemen lining the route. After the parade he ordered the unit to be disbanded. His irritation reflected a desire to remove reminders of the division of war and the French reliance on British and American arms. Whereas the war had significantly deepened the bond between Britain and the United States, and united the British and American people in a common drive for victory, the opposite had been true in France. The defeat of 1940 and the extent of French collaboration with the Nazis had left the French nation spiritually and politically broken. De Gaulle feared future subservience to British and American leadership and was anxious to restore France's authority as a Great Power and to wrest European decision-making away from Britain and the United States.

In the Soviet Union the defeat of Nazi Germany was officially celebrated on 24 June 1945. Stalin watched from Lenin's mausoleum as Marshal Zhukov, mounted on a white charger, led a military march past. In driving rain over 200 Nazi regimental banners, captured in battle, were heaped at the base of the mausoleum. Among them was the standard of the 1st SS Panzer Adolf Hitler Division, once Hitler's personal bodyguard. Across Europe and Asia the victory celebrations were tinged with immense sadness for the many millions who had died on the battlefields or on the home fronts, and for those who had been disabled or badly injured. Many more suffered in silence from the horrors they had witnessed on the battlefield, in an age when psychological trauma received scant recognition. The returning soldiers were simply expected to cast off their uniforms and re-enter civilian life. Some 60 million people were homeless, and many millions were also stateless and crammed the roads of Europe carrying their few possessions and seeking shelter and a new beginning. The war left few people, whether from an Allied or an Axis nation, untouched. The conservative estimate of the number who died is 55 million, but as more detailed estimates of the death toll emerge from the Soviet Union, China and countries like the Philippines it is likely that over 60 million perished. In comparison approximately 8 million died in the First World War. In the league table of suffering five countries stand out: the Soviet Union, China, Poland, Germany and Japan. The combined death toll in all five countries was more than two-thirds of the total number killed in the war. The Soviet Union and China each lost a minimum of 21 million killed. Poland suffered the highest percentage death rate of any country in the war with the 18 per cent of the population killed (6 million people), compared to 10 per cent of the Soviet population, the second highest figure. However, 3 million of the 6 million who perished were Polish Jews, often with the connivance of their countrymen. After the war sporadic outbreaks of anti-Semitism continued. On 4 July 1946 forty-two Jews, many of them survivors of Auschwitz, were beaten to death in Kielce in Poland when they attempted to return to their pre-war homes. When the Jewish people are considered as a single nation they emerge as the greatest victims of the war with 6 out of 11 million Jews in Europe murdered, representing a death toll of 55 per cent.

In Germany and Japan the high death tolls of 5.5 million and 3.5 million respectively were largely a product of the fanatical refusals of Hitler and Hirohito to surrender, despite the inevitability of defeat after 1943. However, the Allied insistence upon unconditional surrender also contributed to the high death toll on all sides by encouraging total national resistance. An Allied declaration to negotiate if both Axis leaderships were deposed may have prompted internal rebellions and thereby shortened the war and saved many lives. This more flexible approach was successfully pursued in relation to Italy and resulted in Mussolini's removal from power, a rejection of Fascism and the installation of a pro-Allied government. Some flexibility was also extended to Japan in the closing months of the war with the dilution of demands for the abdication and arrest of Hirohito. A shorter war in Europe may also have kept the Red Army within its borders and avoided the post-war division of Europe and the exchange of one dictatorship for another.

Freedom was the unifying aim of the Allied nations, as first expressed by the Atlantic Charter signed by Churchill and Roosevelt on 14 August 1941 on board HMS *Prince of Wales* off Newfoundland. Article Six of the Charter, as quoted at the start of this chapter, made the goal of freedom explicit. The Charter had eight articles in total and they collectively promised a new world of equal nations and human rights. It was a liberal manifesto for a world of free, independent democratic nations and essentially repeated the core statements of President Wilson's Fourteen Point Peace Plan of January 1918. Following the Japanese attack on Pearl Harbor in December 1941 the Charter commitments were extended to any country who joined the war against the Axis powers. Twenty-six countries signed the Charter in 1942, and in November 1943 the four principal Allied nations – the United States, the Soviet Union, China and Great Britain – issued the 'Moscow Declaration' which proposed a new international body, the United Nations, to replace the discredited League of Nations as the hub of future international co-operation. Whereas the League of Nations had failed to contain the aggression of the Axis powers it was widely praised for its humanitarian work in the fields of science, agriculture, health and education. The underpinning ambition was for all nations to commit their future energy and the expertise of their scientific communities to humanitarian rather than military advances. The Soviet Union was one of the early signatories, but Stalin's commitment was a pragmatic decision at a time when victory remained uncertain without continued western support. The conflict between the Charter ideals and the reality of communist rule was never satisfactorily resolved. Equally, the post-war intentions of Great Britain, France and Holland to reimpose their colonial empires was not questioned, despite the clear Charter commitment to 'free and independent nations'. Churchill demonstrated his early willingness to ignore the Charter principles when, during a wartime meeting with Stalin on 9 October 1944, he proposed a deal which offered Stalin control over most of eastern Europe in return for non-interference in Greece.

The task facing the Allies in 1945 was one of reconstruction and retribution. This was first accomplished with relative speed and ease in Italy. Fascism in Italy amounted to little more than a superficial adherence to the ambition of empire expansion and great power status, bound together by Mussolini's charismatic leadership. The alliance with Germany had never been popular and once Mussolini was arrested Fascism melted away. The Italian people conducted their own retribution with the capture and execution of all leading Fascists, including Mussolini in 1945, and reformed their own political system with the instituting of a constituent assembly in June 1946. A new constitution was agreed and a republic was declared when 54 per cent of the people rejected the monarchy because of its association with Mussolini and Fascism and forced the royal family into exile. The Pope and Church escaped censure and the new republic upheld the Lateran Accords, agreed by Mussolini in 1929, and reconfirmed the Vatican as a sovereign state. The Allies stripped Italy of her remaining vestiges of empire, and conducted border revisions in favour of France and Yugoslavia and restored independence to Albania. Reparations were fixed at 360 million dollars; they were never enforced and were dwarfed by an agreed 2 billion dollar aid package to rebuild Italy. Italy may have lost the war but substantially won the peace.

In Germany the Allied task was more forbidding, given the greater depth of support and involvement in Fascism at all levels of society. An estimated 8 million Germans had joined the Nazi Party, and many more across industry and the army were committed Nazis. An early decision was taken to skim the surface of German society and remove the immediate leadership – those directly involved in war crimes and those industrialists who were significant beneficiaries of Nazism. In the eastern half of Germany, Stalin adopted a more root-and-branch approach and ordered the summary execution of all Nazi officials. The Nazi leadership were tried at Nuremberg between November 1945 and September 1946. Out of twenty-two indictments for war crimes twelve leading Nazis were sentenced to death, three were given life imprisonment, four were imprisoned for terms ranging from ten to twenty years and three were acquitted. Those sentenced to death were hanged, except for Göring, who cheated the gallows by taking poison in his prison cell, and Martin Bormann, who was sentenced *in absentia* and believed to be in hiding. The mystery of his disappearance was finally settled in 1972 when his remains were found in Berlin not far from Hitler's bunker. He had apparently taken poison in the last hours of the war after failing to escape through the Russian lines. The bodies of those executed were cremated in the crematorium ovens of Dachau concentration camp and their ashes were scattered in a river near Munich. Himmler had committed suicide before the commencement of the trials. Further trials and executions of leading Nazi officials, industrialists and scientists continued to 1949, and in occupied countries many thousands of Nazi collaborators were also tried and executed.

In France Pierre Laval, the foreign minister of the Vichy regime, was shot by firing squad on 15 October 1945. Marshal Petain was also given a death sentence, but because of his advanced years his sentence was commuted to life imprisonment by President de Gaulle. He was released from prison in 1951 due to failing health, shortly after his 95th birthday, and died a few months later. A total of 120,000 French citizens were found guilty of collaboration, but out of 4,785 death sentences only 2,000 were carried out.

In Norway Vidkun Quisling was shot by firing squad on 24 October 1945, and in Britain William Joyce, or Lord Haw Haw, who had broadcast propaganda for the Nazis, was hanged on 3 January 1946.

The most notable escapee from justice was Adolf Eichmann who had co-ordinated and directed the implementation of the Holocaust. At the end of the war he was helped to escape to Brazil by a sympathetic Roman Catholic priest. He was tracked down by Israeli agents in 1960, snatched off the street, and returned to Israel where he was tried and executed on 31 May 1962.

The task of rebuilding Germany was formidable because most German cities were in ruins and there was a shortage of men to undertake reconstruction work. The onset of the Cold War also solidified the temporary Allied division of Germany into a permanent East–West division. In this charged political climate the purging of Nazi party members from positions of responsibility or industry was ended. Their anti-communist credentials made them a valuable asset, and Nazi intelligence officers were frequently recruited to work for British or US intelligence. One of the most notorious examples was the American shielding from arrest of Klaus Barbie, the notorious 'Butcher of Lyon', who had tortured and murdered many members of the French resistance. He was spirited away to a new life in Bolivia with the assistance of the US intelligence service. Alfred Krupps, the main manufacturer of arms in Germany, served only three years of a twelve-year sentence imposed for the extensive use of slave labour and returned to run his business. Dr Wernher von Braun, who had perfected the V2 rocket, was transported to the United States, along with 457 members of his scientific team, and all were given immunity from prosecution in return for developing the US postwar missile technology. This relaxation of the pursuit and prosecution of Nazi beneficiaries and war criminals came only months after the Potsdam Declaration of July 1945 promised to bring all war criminals to justice. It reflected the primacy accorded to western security over retribution at a time when a war with the Soviet Union seemed to be a major possibility. Germany and the rest of western Europe and Britain were only finally reconstructed by the commencement of the Marshall Plan in June 1947: a generous injection of US financial aid proposed by US Secretary of State George Marshall and more formally known as the European Recovery Programme. However, it was not until the end of the Cold War in 1989 that the reunification of Germany was finally made possible. On 12 September 1990 the four powers that had occupied Germany in 1945 – the Soviet Union, France, Britain and the United States – finally agreed to German reunification.

On 17 September 1945, fifteen days after the formal surrender of Japan, General Douglas MacArthur, Supreme Commander Allied Powers (SCAP), established his headquarters in the Dai Ichi life insurance offices directly opposite the imperial palace in central Tokyo. Initial fears of a hostile reception to the largely American occupation force were dispelled by a mainly passive response from the Japanese public. MacArthur attributed the Japanese co-operation to the Allied decision not to insist upon the abdication of Emperor Hirohito as part of the surrender terms. He concluded that Allied interests would be best served by keeping Hirohito in power in case his arrest as a war criminal sparked resistance to the occupation forces and a renewal of fighting in China, and in the other occupied Pacific territories where the Japanese were still not fully disarmed. He therefore downplayed any evidence of Hirohito's involvement in the direction of the war and found himself in alliance with the Imperial Court, who were anxious to preserve the Japanese monarchy by distancing Hirohito from any responsibility for the war. Therefore, although Hirohito was the head of state he was not required to attend the formal surrender ceremony on board the *Missouri* in Tokyo Bay on 2 September 1945. On 25 September, in a written answer to questions submitted by American journalists, Hirohito denied any involvement in the decision to bomb Pearl Harbor or any direction of the war. The Imperial Court fostered an image of a runaway military leadership led by General Hideki Tojo, who was prime minister between October 1941 and July 1944. This judgement was accepted by General MacArthur without a full investigation into Hirohito's role, and ultimately, under his recommendation, by the governments of the United States and Great Britain. Only the governments of Australia and New Zealand attempted to have Hirohito deposed and indicted as a war criminal. MacArthur met with Hirohito on 29 September and caused a sensation when they were photographed together leaving his headquarters. MacArthur, dressed casually in an open-necked shirt, towered over Hirohito who was dressed in a formal morning coat and striped trousers. The picture came to symbolise the subservience of Japan to US direction, but Hirohito made no public statement of contrition or regret for the war. Two weeks after the meeting the Japanese navy and war ministries were dissolved and the entire command staff that had directed the war disbanded. All armaments plants were closed and Shinto was abolished as the state religion.

MacArthur focused the blame for the war on the army, and in May 1946 twenty-eight prominent military and government leaders were indicted for war crimes. Tojo, who had botched an attempt at hara-kiri on 11 September 1945, happily accepted his role as a military dictator acting beyond Hirohito's control. He was coached in his answers to the War Crimes Tribunal and his testimony accepted full blame for the conduct of the war, even though he had left office a full year before its end. He was convicted of war crimes and hanged in Sugamo prison on 23 December 1946, along with six others. It was his last duty to his emperor and nation and one that he happily accepted if it would help to preserve the emperor and avoid foreign occupation of Japan. Across Asia a further 1,100 Japanese military commanders were tried and executed for war crimes, but the majority of those accused received prison sentences. As was the case in Europe, US intelligence officers protected those who could assist future military developments. Consequently the key Japanese scientists involved in the development of bacteriological warfare agents in Manchuria were offered immunity from prosecution in return for access to their research data and continued co-operation. The data had been compiled from the results of tests of bacteriological agents on prisoners of war, and the extensive use of bacteriological warfare in northern China which had resulted in the deaths of millions of Chinese civilians. In parallel to the War Crimes trials a new democratic constitution for Japan was written which recast Hirohito as a constitutional monarch rather than a divine ruler. The new constitution was approved in May 1947, Article Nine of which included a ban on the development of any offensive military capability and a rejection of warfare.

The emergence of the Cold War rapidly transformed an enemy into an ally. Japan joined with the United States in opposing Soviet expansion into South Korea and the northern Pacific and approved the building of US naval bases to contain the Soviet Union. In Indo-China, Britain and France also sought Japanese help to stem the rise of communism following the declaration of independence by Ho Chi Minh. Some Japanese POWs were issued with weapons to assist French and British troops to reim-pose French colonial rule. The denial of independence and belief that Ho Chi Minh was a Soviet puppet was to result in the bitter Vietnam War that lasted to 1975 and embroiled the ordinary Vietnamese people in a costly and destructive war that lasted six times longer than the Second World War. Japan was finally granted full indepen-dence as a sovereign, democratic nation on 28 April 1952.

Hirohito's lasting success before his death in 1989 was to help transform post-war Japan into a leading liberal and economic power. However, his mistakes were not to apologise for the war or to compensate the countless victims of the war, including the kidnapping and forced prostitution of countless Korean 'comfort' women, or to expunge the extant core of extreme nationalist and xenophobic opinion within the Japanese polity.

The Second World War arose out of the unfettered ambitions of a minority for terri-tory and dominance and provided the most extreme example of the consequences of the promotion of racial hatred. The majority failed to question and confront the Axis leaderships. Within Japan, Italy and Germany dictatorships were accommodated rather than rejected, and an unrelenting diet of exaggerated national grievances were trans-lated into national goals. Externally the international community upheld national sovereignty over individual human rights and ignored internal oppression and open breaches of international law. The passage of the Atlantic Charter in 1941 and the establishment of the United Nations in 1945 promised a new post-war era of fairness and justice for all. However, despite the lesson of the most destructive war in world history the freedoms that so many valiantly fought and died for remain elusive. The liberal agenda was lost amid the exigencies of the Cold War conflict and today, with the rise of militant theocracy, there is perhaps a need for the world to revisit and reaf-firm the values of the Atlantic Charter.

Reference

1. Henry Steele Commanger, *Documents of American History, Volume 2: Since 1898* (9th edn), Prentice-Hall, 1973, p. 496.

Chronology

PART 1: AMBITION

Japan

July 1919 The Treaty of Versailles provokes outrage among Japanese nationalists when colonial expansion in China and the Pacific is denied.

November 1921 PM Hara Takashi is assassinated by nationalists.

February 1922 Japan signs the Nine Power agreement, settles territorial claims in China, and enters into a naval agreement with GB and the USA.

25 December 1925 Death of Emperor Taisho and accession to the throne of Emperor Hirohito.

14 November 1930 PM Hamaguchi Yuko assassinated by nationalists campaigning for colonial expansion in Manchuria.

18 September 1931 Japanese army in Manchuria commences military takeover.

March 1932 Japan renames Manchuria, 'Manchuko' and declares it to be a Japanese protectorate.

March 1933 League of Nations censures Japan but takes no other action.

February 1936 Nationalist Japanese army officers attempt a coup.

November 1936 Japan signs Anti-Comintern Pact and enters into an anti-Soviet alliance with Germany.

7 July 1937 Outbreak of full-scale war and invasion of China by Japan.

12 December 1937 Rape of Nanking when Japanese troops murder some 340,000 Chinese civilians.

3 November 1938 PM Konoye refers to a 'new order' in the east and establishment of a Japanese empire.

May 1939 Japan decides not to join the Pact of Steel military alliance signed between Italy and Germany.

May–August 1939 Japanese and Soviet troops clash along Mongolian border.

August 1939 PM Hiranuma resigns in 'bafflement' at news of the signing of the Nazi–Soviet Non-Aggression Pact.

Germany

11 February 1919 Ebert appointed first president of a new democratic German republic formulated at Weimar.

7 May 1919 German delegation protests at the terms of the Treaty of Versailles.

28 June 1919 Under threat of occupation the new Weimar Republic signs, but does not accept, the Treaty of Versailles.

21 June 1919 German imperial fleet scuttled at Scapa Flow.

September 1919 Hitler leaves army and joins German Workers' Party.

April 1921 Germany presented with reparations bill of £6.6 billion.

January 1923 French and Belgian troops occupy the Ruhr to enforce reparation payments.

November 1923 Hyperinflation and economic collapse.

8–9 November 1923 Nazi *putsch* defeated.

1924 Hitler serves nine months of a five-year prison sentence for leading the *putsch*.

1924–29 Weimar Republic is stabilised and establishes co-operative relations with the western powers.

October 1929 Wall Street Crash collapses German economy and creates widespread unemployment

30 January 1933 Hitler appointed Chancellor after Nazi rise to position of the biggest political party from 1930–33.

23 March 1933 Passage of the Enabling Act gives Hitler dictatorial powers.

October 1933 Germany withdraws from the international disarmament conference and League of Nations.

2 August 1934 Following death of President Hindenburg Hitler declares himself Führer, or leader.

January 1935 Saarland votes to unite with Germany.

March 1935 Hitler openly declares existence of Luftwaffe and expansion of army in defiance of Treaty of Versailles restrictions.

7 March 1936 Germany reoccupies the Rhineland in defiance of the Treaty of Versailles.

27 April 1937 Luftwaffe 'Condor' legion destroys Guernica in German contribution to Spanish Civil War.

5 November 1937 Hitler outlines his plans for future expansion of Germany to his general staff.

11–12 March 1938 *Anschluss* with Austria.

May 1938 Czech army mobilises in face of threat of German invasion of the Sudetenland border territory.

15 September 1938 PM Chamberlain in negotiation with Hitler at Berchtesgaden.

22 September 1938 PM Chamberlain in negotiation with Hitler at Godesburg.

29–30 September 1938 At Munich PM Chamberlain, PM Daladier, Mussolini and Hitler agree the transfer of the Sudetenland to Germany.

14–16 March 1939 Hitler invades whole of Czechoslovakia.

31 March 1939 PM Chamberlain condemns Hitler and offers guarantee of Poland's borders.

23 August 1939 Nazi–Soviet Non-Aggression Pact.

Italy

20 April 1919 PM Orlando leaves the Treaty of Versailles talks in protest at the denial of Italian empire expansion in the Balkans and North Africa.

23 March 1919 Benito Mussolini forms the nationalist political party Fascii di Combattimentio to campaign for empire.

12 September 1919 The nationalist leader d'Annunzio seizes disputed port of Fiume.

May 1921 Mussolini's 'Fascists' gain thirty-five seats in Parliament and commence a violent street campaign for power. Within months most of northern Italy under Fascist control.

28 October 1922 In order to prevent a threatened Fascist March on Rome King Victor Emmanuel appoints Mussolini PM.

30 October 1922 Mussolini declares Italy Fascist.

1922–32 Mussolini aligns himself with Britain and France and seeks support for empire expansion.

25 July 1934 Mussolini defends Austrian independence following attempted Nazi *putsch*.

December 1934 Clash between Italian and Abyssinian troops at Wal Wal.

2 October 1935 Italy invades Abyssinia.

May 1936 Italian troops enter capital Addis Ababa and declare victory.

July 1936 Mussolini commits Italian troops to aid General Franco in the Spanish Civil War.

1 November 1936 Mussolini enters into the 'Axis' alliance with Hitler.

November 1937 Italy joins the Anti-Comintern Pact with Japan and Germany.

28–30 September 1938 Mussolini acts as the impartial negotiator at Munich between Hitler and Britain and France over the future of Czechoslovakia, but colludes with Hitler.

7 April 1939 Italy invades Albania.

22 May 1939 Mussolini enters into Pact of Steel military alliance with Hitler.

25 August 1939 Mussolini declares Italian Army is not ready for a major war and refuses to join Hitler's invasion of Poland.

PART 2: OUTBREAK

Japan

1939–41 Japanese troops engage in continuous warfare in China against the Chinese nationalist forces led by Jiang Jieshi and Chinese communist forces led by Mao Zedong.

Germany

1 September 1939 Germany invades Poland.

3 September 1939 Britain and France declare war on Germany.

3–6 September 1939 Australia, New Zealand, South Africa and Canada declare war on Germany. USA declares neutrality.

17 September 1939 Red Army invades Poland from the east in fulfilment of secret protocol in Nazi–Soviet Non-Aggression Pact.

27 September 1939 Warsaw falls and Poland surrenders.

6 October 1939 Hitler offers a peace treaty to France and Britain.

November 1939 Hitler postpones attack in the west due to bad weather.

January 1940 British capture of attack plans and heavy snowfalls across Europe cause Hitler to postpone attack in the west, planned for 17 January, to the spring.

Italy

1939–40 Italy remains in alliance with Germany but does not immediately enter the war.

PART 3: ADVANCE

Japan

20 June 1940 Japan takes advantage of defeat of France by landing troops in French Indo-China to aid its war effort in China.

16 July 1940 Konoye appointed PM and appoints Tojo war minister.

18 July 1940 Britain agrees to Japanese demand to close the Burma road to isolate China from supplies.

22 September 1940 Japanese troops occupy northern sector of French Indo-China.

27 September 1940 Japan signs the Tripartite Pact of mutual assistance with Germany and Italy.

Germany

20 February 1940 Hitler sets plans for invasion of Norway to guard his northern flank.

28 March 1940 Britain and France plan to land troops in Norway unaware of German plans.

9 April 1940 German troops invade Denmark and Norway.

10 April 1940 Royal Navy inflicts heavy losses on Germany Navy at Narvik.

1 May 1940 British forces fail to retake central Norway and withdraw.

9 May 1940   German troops invade Holland and Belgium and Allies respond by moving bulk of troops into northern Belgium.

12 May 1940   Bulk of German Army emerges from Ardennes and sweeps west across northern France.

15 May 1940   Holland surrenders.

20 May 1940   Panzers reach Channel coast and trap Allies in Belgium.

26 May 1940   Belgium surrenders and Britain commences evacuation from Dunkirk.

28 May 1940   Allies capture Narvik in Norway.

5 June 1940   Germans turn south towards Paris.

7 June 1940   Allies withdraw from Norway to focus on defence of France and Britain.

10 June 1940   Norway surrenders.

14 June 1940   German troops enter Paris.

16 June 1940   French government resigns and new pro-German government under Marshal Petain sues for peace.

22 June 1940   France surrenders.

1 July 1940   Royal Navy attacks French Navy at Oran after it was deemed hostile.

10 July 1940   Luftwaffe commences regular air attacks against the Channel ports and shipping.

19 July 1940   Hitler offers Britain a peace settlement.

July–October 1940   U-boats score significant successes in the Atlantic against British shipping.

13 August 1940   Luftwaffe commence the Battle of Britain by attacking RAF airfields.

7 September 1940   After enduring heavy losses Luftwaffe switches tactics to bomb London and other major cities. German troops enter Romania to secure Ploesti oilfields.

17 September 1940   Hitler accepts defeat in the air war and cancels invasion plans.

27 September 1940   Tripartite Pact of mutual assistance signed with Japan and Italy.

23 October 1940   Hitler fails to persuade Franco to join the war and support an invasion of Gibraltar.

6 December 1940   Hitler approves first draft of plan for invasion of USSR scheduled for May 1941.

Italy

10 June 1940   With France all but defeated Mussolini declares war on France and Britain.

11 June 1940   Italian Air Force bombs Malta.

4 July 1940   Italians attack British Sudan.

5 August 1940   Italian troops invade British Somaliland.

13 September 1940   Italian troops commence invasion of British Egypt.

27 September 1940   Tripartite Pact of mutual assistance signed with Japan and Germany.

28 October 1940   Italy invades Greece.

3 November 1940   RAF helps to defend Greece against Italian invasion.

6–10 November 1940   Greek Army inflicts significant defeats on the Italians.

11 November 1940   Royal Navy Swordfish sink three Italian battleships at anchor in Taranto.

22 November 1940   Italian 9th Army surrenders at Koritas and Italians withdraw from Greece.

9 December 1940   British forces in Egypt defeat Italians at Sidi Barrani.

PART 4: EXPANSION

Japan

16 October 1941   Tojo new Japanese prime minister following resignation of Koyone.

7 December 1941   The Japanese attack the US Pacific Fleet at Pearl Harbor and the US Pacific command headquarters on the Philippines.

8 December 1941   The Japanese commence the invasion of British Malaya and Burma and attack the US islands of Guam, Wake and Midway. In addition Japanese forces in China cross the border into Hong Kong.

10 December 1941 British forces in Malaya fall into full retreat. Royal Navy battleships *Repulse* and *Prince of Wales* both sunk off Malaya by Japanese dive-bombers.

22 December 1941 Japanese troops invade Luzon in the Philippines.

25 December 1941 The British garrison in Hong Kong surrenders.

26 December 1941 US forces on Luzon retreat into the Bataan peninsula and nearby Corrigedor island.

31 January 1942 British forces in Malaya retreat onto the island of Singapore and blow up the causeway.

8 February 1942 Japanese troops commence an invasion of Singapore.

15 February 1942 British forces on Singapore surrender.

20 February 1942 Darwin in Australia is bombed by the Japanese.

25 February 1942 A Japanese naval task force commences the seizure of Java and the Dutch East Indies.

7 March 1942 British forces in Burma abandon the capital Rangoon and begin a fighting retreat into India.

6–9 April 1942 A Japanese carrier force enters the Indian Ocean and bombs Ceylon.

9 April 1942 The US troops surrounded on the Bataan peninsula in the Philippines surrender.

16 April 1942 A flight of B-25 bombers commanded by General Doolittle lift off from the carrier *Hornet* and bomb Tokyo.

4 May 1942 The US carriers *Yorktown* and *Lexington* prevent Japanese troops landing on New Guinea, but the Lexington sunk.

6 May 1942 The last surviving Allied force in the Pacific on Corrigedor island in the Philippines surrenders.

Germany

1 January 1941 The Luftwaffe 10th Fliegerkorps arrives on Sicily to aid Italy.

11 January 1941 Hitler issues orders for a military offensive in the Balkans and North Africa to secure the southern front.

6 February 1941 Hitler directs Rommel to command the Afrika Korps to deny Britain victory in North Africa.

17 March 1941 Yugoslavia surrenders.

24 March 1941 The Afrika Korps defeats British forces at El Agheila

25 March 1941 An anti-Nazi coup in Yugoslavia ends Hitlers plans for an alliance.

31 March 1941 Rommel gains Mersa Brega, the gateway to Cyrenaica.

April 1941 U-boats in the Atlantic sink 488,124 tons of British merchant shipping, the highest loss for a single month.

4 April 1941 Rommel retakes Benghazi.

6 April The Wehrmacht commences the invasion of Greece and Yugoslavia.

11 April 1941 Rommel places Tobruk under siege and retakes whole of Cyrenaica.

27 April 1941 The Germans take Athens and force the surrender of Greece.

10 May 1941 Rudolf Hess, Hitler's deputy, parachutes into Scotland to try and negotiate a peace settlement.

11 May 1941 The Luftwaffe destroys large tracts of central London, including the House of Commons.

20 May 1941 German parachutists commence the invasion of Crete.

24 May 1941 HMS *Hood* sunk with loss of 1,397 crew in engagement with the *Bismarck*.

27 May 1941 The Royal Navy sinks the *Bismarck*.

31 May 1941 British forces defeated and evacuated from Crete.

17 June 1941 A British counter-attack in North Africa, Operation Battleaxe, fails to dislodge Rommel.

22 June 1941 Hitler launches Operation Barbarossa, the invasion of the Soviet Union.

23 June 1941   Hitler takes up residence in his eastern headquarters at Rastenburg to monitor the invasion.

26 June 1941   Finland joins the Nazi invasion to liberate her country following defeat by the Soviet Union in the Winter War of 1940–41.

31 July 1941   The Final Solution order is issued and across the occupied Soviet Union mass executions of Jews begins.

1 September 1941   German Army sets siege to Leningrad.

19 September 1941   Kiev, the capital of the Ukraine, taken.

4 October 1941   With the German Army poised to attack Moscow Hitler announces victory.

19 October 1941   Stalin cancels plans to evacuate Moscow and states that the city will be held to the last.

25 October 1941   Heavy snow falls across the Eastern Front and hampers the movement of the Germany Army.

4 December 1941   A German patrol comes within 12 miles of the Kremlin.

5 December 1941   The Red Army launches a major counter-attack and forces the Germans into retreat.

7 December 1941   Seven hundred Jews from Lodz ghetto gassed in the first purpose-built death camp at Chelmno, marking the commencement of the Holocaust.

10 December 1941   A British counter-attack from Egypt lifts the siege of Tobruk and forces the Afrika Korps into retreat.

11 December 1941   Hitler declares war on the United States.

20 January 1942   Heydrich chairs the Wannsee Conference in Berlin and plans the round up and execution of all Jews in Europe.

21 January 1942   Rommel renews the German offensive in North Africa and occupies El Agheila.

Italy

15 January 1941   Britain enters Abyssinia and rallies opposition to Italian rule with the support of Emperor Haile Selassie.

22 January 1941   Tobruk captured by Australian forces.

7 February 1941   British troops take Benghazi and liberate whole of Cyrenaica from Italian rule.

1941–43   The Italian Army, although nominally independent, in reality comes under German direction for the rest of the war in North Africa.

PART 5: CONTAINMENT

Japan

14 May 1942   US signals intelligence breaks Japanese military traffic and confirms that Japan intends to invade Midway island.

20 May 1942   The last British and Indian troops retreat from Burma into India.

3 June 1942   Japan lands troops on the islands of Kiska and Attu in the Aleutians to draw US attention away from Midway.

June 1942   Japanese troops commence construction of an airfield on Guadalcanal.

4 June 1942   Japanese carrier planes launch air attack on Midway. The waiting US force strikes and sinks four Japanese carriers for the loss of one US carrier.

21 July 1942   Japanese troops land at Buna and Gona in New Guinea.

7 August 1942   A US naval task force lands marines on Guadalcanal.

8 August 1942   Japanese planes sink the US destroyer *Jarvis* and force the retreat of the main US carrier force.

9 August 1942   The Japanese Navy, in a surprise night-time attack, sink three US and one Australian cruiser.

18 August 1942 Japanese troops land on Guadalacanal.

21 August 1942 Japanese troops attack the US positions, but only seventeen out of 815 survive.

24 August 1942 US carrier planes shoot down 70 out of 80 Japanese planes in battle of East Solomons.

25 August 1942 Japanese open an offensive at Milne Bay on New Guinea with aim of advancing on Port Moresby but are swiftly defeated by superior Australian forces.

12 September 1942 With the support of a naval task force 5,000 Japanese troops attempt to retake Guadalcanal.

24 September 1942 Japanese troops advancing on Port Moresby on New Guinea along the Kokoda Trail defeated and forced into retreat.

9 October 1942 Japanese troop numbers on Guadalcanal increased to 22,000 in determined bid to defeat US marines, now equally reinforced.

26 October 1942 In naval battle off Santa Cruz islands US carrier *Hornet* lost, but Japanese lose a further seventy planes.

13–15 November 1942 Decisive naval engagement for Guadalcanal. Japanese forced to withdraw after heavy losses, including two battleships and seven troop carriers conveying reinforcements.

9 December 1942 US Marine Corps on Guadalcanal relieved by arrival of US 14th Army Corps.

10 December 1942 Japanese forces at Gona on New Guinea defeated.

19 December 1942 In Burma British and Indian troops commence an advance down the Mayu peninsula.

31 December 1942 Japanese accept defeat and commence withdrawal from Guadalcanal.

January 1943 British and Indian troops in Burma forced into retreat.

2 January 1943 Japanese troops holding Buna on New Guinea defeated.

23 January 1943 Last Japanese strongholds on Papua New Guinea peninsula defeated. Surviving Japanese troops flee into jungle and commence a guerrilla campaign.

7 February 1943 Last surviving Japanese troops withdraw from Guadalcanal.

14 February 1943 An Allied guerrilla army, the 'Chindits', under the command of Orde Wingate, cross the Indian border into Burma and successfully attack Japanese positions and force the Japanese to divert troops.

3 March 1943 The US Navy intercepts and sinks eight Japanese troop transports bound for New Guinea and four destroyers.

18 April 1943 US fighters intercept and shoot down a transport plane killing Admiral Yamamoto, the architect of the Japanese attack on Pearl Harbor.

12 May 1943 US marines engage Japanese on the island of Attu in the Aleutians.

31 May 1942 Last Japanese resistance on Attu defeated, but only twenty-eight out of 2,500 Japanese troops taken prisoner.

15 August 1943 The island of Kiska in the Aleutians taken without contest when the Japanese secretly withdraw in advance of the US landings.

30 September 1943 Emperor Hirohito agrees to the establishment of an 'absolute defence line' in the central Pacific to prevent a US advance on the home islands.

Germany

27 May 1942 Heydrich is mortally wounded in Prague by Czech agents trained in Britain. He dies from his wounds on 4 June 1942.

30 May 1942 RAF launches first 1,000-bomber raid on Cologne and generates a 'firestorm' which destroys most of the city.

2 June 1942 RAF destroys Essen in a second 1,000-bomber raid.

21 June 1942 Rommel captures Tobruk after a six-month offensive that rolled the Allies back into Egypt.

23 June 1942 Rommel's combined German and Italian forces cross the border into Egypt.

28 June 1942 Front line stabilises at El Alamein only 200 miles from Cairo.

7 July 1942 Twenty-three ships of Arctic Convoy PQ-17 are sunk by U-boats.

16 July 1942 Hitler moves to new forward headquarters at Vinnista in the Ukraine to monitor new German summer offensive.

19 July 1942 Himmler sets a target of 31 December 1942 for all Jews in Poland to be gassed. He nominates Auschwitz as the principal death camp.

23 July 1942 Germans occupy Rostov and Hitler orders his forces to divide and take Stalingrad to the east and secure the Caucasus to the south.

8 August 1942 General Bernard Law Montgomery appointed to launch an offensive to drive Germans out of Egypt.

22 August 1942 German 6th Army reaches Stalingrad.

31 August 1942 Rommel attacks the British line but is too short of supplies to sustain the attack.

13 September 1942 Germans enter into street fighting in Stalingrad.

30 September 1942 Hitler gives the German people a public commitment of victory at Stalingrad.

23 October 1942 Allies commence offensive at El Alamein.

2 November 1942 German line breaks and Allies achieve a full breakthrough.

3–4 November 1942 Axis forces defeated and fall into a 60-mile retreat to Fuka.

8 November 1942 Combined US and British army lands on coasts of Morocco and Algeria (Operation Torch) and commence advance towards German-held Tunisia.

19 November 1942 Red Army launches a major counter-offensive against the 6th Army at Stalingrad.

21 November 1942 The 6th Army is entirely encircled and trapped in Stalingrad.

12 December 1942 German counter-attack fails to break the Soviet encirclement at Stalingrad.

13–14 December 1942 Rommel abandons Mersa Brega and El Agheila and retreats towards Tripoli.

30 December 1942 Royal Navy wins battle of Barents Sea and forces German Navy back to port.

13 January 1943 Red Army breaks the German siege of Leningrad and opens a supply corridor into the city.

PART 6: CONTRACTION

Germany

18 January 1943 The Jews of Warsaw rise in armed resistance to Nazi rule.

23 January 1943 Rommel withdraws from Tripoli. His depleted force too small to resist advance by British 8th Army.

31 January 1943 Field Marshal Paulus surrenders the 6th Army at Stalingrad and is the first German field marshal to be captured.

1 February 1943 Germans complete a fighting retreat from the Caucasus.

20–25 February 1943 Rommel defeats US advance at Kassarine Pass in Tunisia.

13 March 1943 Disaffected officers on the Eastern Front plant a bomb on Hitler's plane but it fails to explode.

28 March 1943 British 8th Army breaks through German defensive line at Mareth into Tunisia.

15 April 1943 Hitler issues orders for a major offensive at Kursk, Operation Zitadelle, to restore German fortunes on the Eastern Front.

7 May 1943 Allies enter Tunis.

13 May 1943 Axis forces in North Africa defeated.

16 May 1943 The final Jewish resistance in Warsaw is crushed and all surviving Jews are transported to be gassed.

23 May 1943 Admiral Donitz orders all U-boats to return to port in an admission of defeat in the Atlantic.

5 July 1943 Operation Zitadelle commences with a major pincer attack towards Kursk.

12 July 1943 The biggest tank battle in world history, near Kursk, ends with a victory for the Red Army.

27–28 July 1943 42,000 are killed in Hamburg by an RAF 'firestorm' raid.

28 August 1943 Red army retakes Kharkov after continuous advance.

16 September 1943 Last German soldiers in the Caucasus cross into the Crimea.

25 September 1943 Germans defeated at Smolensk.

31 October 1943 Red Army traps Germans in Crimea.

Italy

11 June 1943 Allies defeat Italian forces on island of Pantelleri in the Mediterranean.

12 June 1943 Allies land on Italian island of Lampedusa in the Mediterranean.

13 June 1943 Allies land on Italian island of Linosa in the Mediterranean.

9–10 July 1943 Allies launch invasion of Sicily (Operation Husky).

15 July 1943 Allies race towards Messina in Sicily having secured the landing beaches.

24 July 1943 Mussolini is deposed by the Fascist Grand Council.

25 July 1943 Mussolini is placed under arrest and imprisoned in a hotel in the Gran Sasso mountains.

17 August 1943 Sicily falls into Allied hands when General Patton wins the Allied race to Messina with General Montgomery two hours behind.

3 September 1943 British forces under Field Marshal Montgomery land at Reggio di Calabria on the toe of Italy.

8 September 1943 The new Italian government under Marshal Badoglio surrenders and declares for the Allies.

9 September 1943 Allies land in the Gulf of Salerno, south of Naples.

10 September 1943 The Germans implement Operation Axis and take over control of northern Italy.

12 September 1943 Mussolini is released from imprisonment by a daring glider raid by German commandos led by Otto Skorzeny.

15–16 September 1943 Allied warships shell German positions in the Gulf of Salerno to prevent German victory.

27 September 1943 Mussolini installed under German protection at Gargnano on Lake Garda to be the figure head of the defence of Italy against the Allied invasion.

December 1943 The Allied advance bogged down in bad weather and stops for the winter to give time for resupply.

PART 7: ROUT

Japan

1 November 1943 US troops land on Bougainville in the Solomon Islands.

20 November 1943 US marines land on Makin and Tarawa atolls in the Gilbert Islands and secure both after three days of hand-to-hand combat.

2 January 1944 US reinforcements land at Saidor in New Guinea.

9 January 1944 British and Indian forces in Burma occupy Maungdaw.

31 January 1944 US marines land on Kwejalein in the Marshall Islands.

4 February 1944 Japanese launch an offensive in Burma to regain the initiative.

17–18 February 1944 US Air Force destroys Japanese naval and airbase at Truk.

21 February 1944 US marines seize island of Eniwetok.

7–8 March 1944 Japanese troops in Burma launch a major offensive across the Indian border to Impal.

22 April 1944 Hollandia in New Guinea liberated.

19 June 1944 Marianas 'turkey shoot' when US carrier planes shoot down 242 Japanese planes for only twenty-nine US losses.

7 July 1944   Japanese forces on Saipan defeated, with only 2,000 survivors out of original garrison of 32,000.

8 July 1944   Japanese forces at Impal defeated, with over 30,000 killed, and retreat back into Burma.

18 July 1944   PM Tojo resigns and replaced by Kuniaki Koiso.

30 July 1944   Entire northern coast of New Guinea in Allied hands.

1 August 1944   US marines land on island of Tinian.

10 August 1944   US forces land on island of Guam.

14 September 1944   US marines fight fierce battle for control of Palau Islands as a stepping stone to the Philippines.

13–14 October 1944   British and Indian troops cross the river Irrawaddy in Burma and commence major offensive.

20 October 1944   General MacArthur steps ashore on the island of Leyte in the Philippines with 100,000 US marines.

24–26 October 1944   Japanese fleet all but destroyed in Battle of Leyte Gulf.

25 October 1944   First kamikaze attacks of the war on US warships.

15 December 1944   US marines land on Mindoro in the Philippines.

10 January 1945   US troops storm ashore on the island of Luzon.

31 January 1945   Clark Field airbase on Luzon falls to US forces.

Germany

6 November 1943   Germans defeated at Kiev and retreat to the 'bend' of the Dnieper in a bid to hold the Soviet offensive.

26 December 1943   Royal Navy sinks the *Scharnhorst.*

14 January 1944   A major Soviet offensive to lift the siege of Leningrad commences.

17 January 1944   German Army forced into retreat from Leningrad and fall back 120 miles.

24 January 1944   60,000 German troops encircled at Korsun.

23 March 1944   German troops occupy Romania to secure the Ploesti oilfields.

11 May 1944   Last German troops in Crimea defeated in battle for Sevastopol.

6 June 1944   The Allies land in Normandy and open a second front in the west.

13 June 1944   First V1 rockets fired at London.

19–21 June 1944   Fierce storms in the Channel destroy the US artificial Mulberry harbour and slow the Allied build up.

22 June 1944   The Red Army launches Operation Bagration to drive the Germans out of the Soviet Union and back into Poland.

1 July 1944   German reinforcements hold Caen and prevent major Allied breakout from the Normandy coast.

17 July 1944   57,000 German POWs paraded though Moscow as Red Army scores significant victories on the Eastern Front and enters East Prussia.

18–20 July 1944   Allies fail to break German lines at Caen.

20 July 1944   Hitler survives an assassination attempt at his headquarters.

25 July 1944   Goebbels appointed Reich plenipotentiary for total war with sweeping powers to direct the population into war work.

31 July 1944   Red Army stops some ten miles from Warsaw for resupply.

8 August 1944   General Patton directs a bold sweep south-west from Brittany behind the German lines at Caen and achieves the Allied break-out from Normandy.

15 August 1944   400,000 Allied troops land on the beaches of southern France without contest.

20 August 1944   German forces retreating from Normandy escape through the Falaise gap, but with heavy losses. However, 50,000 are trapped by an Allied pincer attack. Red Army enters Romania and Romania declares for the Allies.

24 August 1944   Troops of the Free French forces enter Paris and accept the surrender of the German garrison.

3 September 1944   Brussels is liberated.

4 September 1944   Antwerp is liberated but Germans still control the Schelde estuary sea approach to the port.

5 September 1944   The Allies wrap around the German border from Switzerland to Holland.

8 September 1944   First V2 rocket falls on Chiswick in London.

11 September 1944   First Allied soldiers cross German border from Luxembourg and find it undefended.

17 September 1944   Operation Market Garden commences. Montgomery launches parachute drops to seize bridges across Holland in order to permit the Allies a rapid advance into Germany at Arnhem.

25–26 September 1944   Allies fail to secure Arnhem and surviving parachutists withdrawn.

14 October 1944   Rommel takes poison to protect his family after discovery of his involvement in the bomb plot against Hitler.

28 October 1944   The last transports of Jews received in Auschwitz prior to closing the camp in the face of the advancing Red Army.

31 October 1944   Allies secure the Schelde estuary and open the port of Antwerp.

16 December 1944   Hitler launches a surprise attack and breaks the Allied line in the Ardennes.

18 January 1945   Auschwitz is partly destroyed and evacuated. The surviving Jews are marched into Germany to act as slave labourers.

28 January 1945   The German offensive is entirely defeated at a cost of most of Germany's reserves of panzers, aircraft and troops.

Italy

17 January 1944   Allied forces commence offensive against the Gustav Line across central Italy which bars the road to Rome.

22 January 1944   US 6th Corps lands at Anzio north of the Gustav Line.

25 January 1944   The Germans contain the US beachhead at Anzio.

11 February 1944   Allied attack on the Gustav Line ends with heavy losses and no breakthrough.

16 February 1944   Germans launch a major counter-offensive against the Anzio beachhead.

2 March 1944   Allied naval and air power finally defeats the German forces at Anzio and secures a significant beachhead.

15 March 1944   Allies launch a further major offensive on the Gustav Line centred on Anzio and the hilltop abbey of Monte Cassino.

23 March 1944   Allied offensive at Cassino defeated.

11 May 1944   The Allies launch an offensive along the entire western sector of the Gustav Line and French troops achieve a breakthrough.

16 May 1944   Germans abandon the Gustav Line, and the abbey of Monte Cassino falls to Polish troops.

23 May 1944   Allied forces advance from Anzio in an attempt to intercept the German columns retreating north from the Gustav Line.

4 June 1944   US troops enter Rome which had been declared an open city.

25 August 1944   Allies commence a new offensive in northern Italy along the German 'Gothic Line'.

December 1944   Allies pause to regroup after a succession of failed attempts to breach the Gothic Line.

PART 8: NEMESIS

Japan

17 February 1945   The capital of the Philippines falls to US troops, but only after Japanese troops murder thousands of the civilian population.

19 February 1945   US forces land on Iwo Jima and enter into an intense battle for the tiny island.

23 February 1945   The Stars and Stripes raised on Mount Suribachi, Iwo Jima, and later repeated for the camera.

9–10 March 1945   Most of central Tokyo destroyed in a 'firestorm' following a raid by B-29 bombers.

18 March 1945   US carrier *Franklin* sunk off Kyushu with 724 killed or missing.

25 March 1945   Japanese forces on Iwo Jima defeated, with only 1,000 survivors out of a garrison of 26,000.

1 April 1945   US forces land on Okinawa.

5 April 1945   PM Koiso dismissed for failure and replaced by retired Admiral Kantaro Suzuki.

7 April 1945   Commencement of mass kamikaze attacks on US fleet off Okinawa by 700 planes and the battleship *Yamato*. Most planes are shot down and the *Yamato* is sunk by US submarines.

12 April 1945   President Roosevelt dies and is succeeded by Vice-President Harry Truman.

3 May 1945   The capital of Burma, Rangoon, falls to Indian and British troops.

31 May 1945   At a top-secret meeting in the White House agreement is reached to drop the atomic bomb on Japan.

21 June 1945   US troops defeat final Japanese resistance on Okinawa.

16 July 1945   World's first atomic bomb is detonated in the Alamogordo desert, New Mexico, in a test explosion.

26 July 1945   The Allies meet at Potsdam following the defeat of Germany and urge Japan to surrender.

29 July 1945   The cruiser *Indianapolis* is sunk by a Japanese submarine. Several hundred survivors fall victim to shark attacks.

6 August 1945   The B-29 *Enola Gay* drops the atomic bomb, codenamed 'Little Boy', on Hiroshima.

8 August 1945   The Soviet Union declares war on Japan and advances into Japanese-held Manchuria.

9 August 1945   The B-29 *Bock's Car* drops the atomic bomb, codenamed 'Fat Man' on Nagasaki.

14 August 1945   Japan announces surrender.

14–15 August 1945   A group of Japanese officers attempt to storm the Imperial Palace to prevent surrender.

15 August 1945   In his first ever radio broadcast to the Japanese people Emperor Hirohito announces not surrender but the end of the war.

2 September 1945   On board the US battleship *Missouri*, moored in Tokyo Bay, the Japanese High Command sign surrender documents and formally end the war.

Germany

12 January 1945   The Red Army ends its standstill before Warsaw and commences a major drive into western Poland.

16 January 1945   Hitler takes up residence in the Führer bunker beneath the Reich Chancellery in central Berlin.

17 January 1945   Warsaw falls to the advancing Red Army.

24 January 1945   Himmler appointed to command the Vistula Front with orders to stem the Soviet advance.

31 January 1945   7,000 civilians drown in the Baltic when the liner *Wilhelm Gustloff* is sunk.

8 February 1945   In the west Montgomery launches a major US and British advance into Germany.

20 February 1945   Pozan falls to the Red Army.

6 March 1945   Advance units of the US 9th Armoured Division capture the bridge over the Rhine at Remagen intact.

23 March 1945   Montgomery directs the major Allied crossing of the Rhine at Wesel.

27 March 1945   The last V2 rocket of the war kills 137 people in Stepney, London.

11 April 1945   US forces reach the river Elbe only 50 miles from Berlin.

16 April 1945   The Red Army launches its advance on Berlin.

20 April 1945   Berlin is surrounded by the Red Army, and in Hitler's bunker his 56th birthday is marked by a brief celebration.

23 April 1945   Hitler denounces Göring for treachery following a telegram from him that appears to declare his assumption of power.

25 April 1945   The Red Army closes on the centre of Berlin.

27 April 1945   US and Soviet troops meet and shake hands on the designated demarcation line of the river Elbe at Torgau.

28 April 1945   Hitler orders the arrest and execution of Himmler after reports of his attempts to enter into surrender negotiations.

29 April 1945   During the early hours Hitler marries Eva Braun and dictates his last will and testament.

30 April 1945   At approximately 3.20 p.m. Hitler and Eva Braun commit suicide.

1 May 1945   Josef and Magda Goebbels both commit suicide having first giving poison to their six children.

2 May 1945   German troops in Berlin surrender.

3 May 1945   Hitler's remains unearthed and taken in secret to Moscow.

7 May 1945   The Wehrmacht surrender on all fronts.

8 May 1945   Victory in Europe declared.

23 May 1945   Admiral Donitz, named by Hitler as his successor, is arrested and the last vestiges of Nazi rule in Germany are ended.

Italy

9 April 1945   The Allies open a major new offensive along the Gothic Line in northern Italy.

19 April 1945   The Allies achieve a full breakthrough. Most Germans, aware that the war is lost, have little wish to continue fighting.

23 April 1945   In defiance of orders from Hitler General Vietinghoff opens surrender negotiations.

25 April 1945   Mussolini, with a small band of supporters, flees from Milan north towards Como.

27 April 1945   Mussolini is captured by partisans when trying to escape across the border into Switzerland in a German convoy disguised as a German soldier.

28 April 1945   Mussolini and his mistress Claretta Petacci are both summarily executed at the roadside near Mezzegra.

29 April 1945   The bodies of Mussolini and Claretta Petacci, and four executed senior Fascists, are strung up in the centre of Milan.

2 May 1945   Victory is declared in Italy.

Index

eBooks – at www.eBookstore.tandf.co.uk

A library at your fingertips!

eBooks are electronic versions of printed books. You can store them on your PC/laptop or browse them online.

They have advantages for anyone needing rapid access to a wide variety of published, copyright information.

eBooks can help your research by enabling you to bookmark chapters, annotate text and use instant searches to find specific words or phrases. Several eBook files would fit on even a small laptop or PDA.

NEW: Save money by eSubscribing: cheap, online access to any eBook for as long as you need it.

Annual subscription packages

We now offer special low-cost bulk subscriptions to packages of eBooks in certain subject areas. These are available to libraries or to individuals.

For more information please contact webmaster.ebooks@tandf.co.uk

We're continually developing the eBook concept, so keep up to date by visiting the website.

www.eBookstore.tandf.co.uk